The
LAND *of*
BLOOD *and*
HONEY

The
LAND *of*
BLOOD *and*
HONEY

THE RISE OF MODERN ISRAEL

Martin van Creveld

Thomas Dunne Books   St. Martin's Press   New York

THOMAS DUNNE BOOKS.
An imprint of St. Martin's Press.

www.thomasdunnebooks.com
www.stmartins.com

Text design: Meryl Sussman Levavi

Library of Congress Cataloging-in-Publication Data

Van Creveld, Martin, 1946–
    The land of blood and honey: the rise of modern Israel / Martin van Creveld.—
1st ed.
        p.   cm.
    Includes bibliographical references and index.
    ISBN 978-0-312-59678-1 (alk. paper)
  1. Israel—History.   2. Jews—Israel—History.   I. Title.
    DS126.5.V324   2010
    956.9405—dc22

                                                                      2009047574

First Edition: August 2010

10 9 8 7 6 5 4 3 2 1

For Orr

To be a free people

in our own land,

the land of Zion

and Jerusalem

CONTENTS

Prologue   xi

1. Forged in Fury (1897–1949)   1

2. Full Steam Ahead (1949–1967)   68

3. The Nightmare Years (1967–1980)   133

4. New Challenges (1981–1995)   194

5. Tragedy, Triumph, and Struggle (1995–Present)   254

    Epilogue: "No More War"?   314

    Glossary of Hebrew Terms   321

    Time Line of Events   325

    Notes   329

    Acknowledgments   339

    Index   341

PROLOGUE

Why and What For

Ever since the time when the idea of building a sovereign Jewish state—the first in almost two thousand years—was floated during the last years of the nineteenth century, it has been surrounded by controversy. Consider, for example, the following passage by the well-known Jewish-Austrian writer Stefan Zweig (1881–1942):

> I was still in the Gymnasium when this short pamphlet [Theodor Herzl's *Der Judenstaat* (The Jewish State), 1896] was published . . . but I can still remember the general astonishment and annoyance of the middle class Jewish elements of Vienna. What has happened, they said angrily, to this otherwise intelligent, witty, and cultivated writer? What foolishness is this that he has thought up and written about? Why should we go to Palestine? Our language is German and not Hebrew, and beautiful Austria is our homeland. Are we not well off under our good Emperor Franz Josef? Do we not make an adequate living, and is our position not secure? Why does he, who speaks as a Jew and who wishes to help Judaism, place arguments in the hands of our worst enemies and attempts to separate us, when every day brings us more closely and intimately into the German world?

Since those faraway days, hardly a year has passed when doubts have not been cast both on the feasibility of the idea and on its desirability. Even today, countless people, especially but by no means exclusively in the Islamic world, continue to question Israel's right to exist; more remarkably still, this even applies to some of the state's own citizens. Some of them, from Iranian president Mahmoud Ahmadinejad to Hezbollah leader Hassan Nasrallah, engage in wishful thinking that they may, one day, do away with it.

This book will attempt to provide a brief but comprehensive outline of the rise of Israel, from its Zionist beginnings at the end of the nineteenth century to the present day. I want to explain its military, political, economic, social, and cultural development as well as the complicated ways in which these various "pillars" interact; also, to give readers who are neither Israelis nor experts a feel for what life is like in a country where almost everybody is a soldier on eleven months' annual leave. Above all, in the face of the endless and often highly unfair criticism that is directed against Israel from all over the world, I want to show it for what it really is: namely, a country that, while coping with every imaginable obstacle, in many ways is perhaps the greatest success story in the entire twentieth century. It is also one whose progress in terms of maintaining and developing its democracy, economic growth, artistic creativity, academic excellence, and, last but not least, military might has eclipsed that of virtually all the rest, to the point where it is now able to field one of the most powerful armed forces on Earth.

The outline of the volume is as follows. Chapter 1, "Forged in Fury," presents a short narrative of the origins of the state from the time of the First Zionist Congress (1897) to the 1948–1949 War of Independence, with special emphasis on the armed struggle against the British and the Arabs. Chapter 2, "Full Steam Ahead," focuses on the period of very successful nation building that started in 1949 and, proceeding amid countless armed clashes with neighboring countries, culminated in the great victory of June 1967. Chapter 3, "The Nightmare Years," deals with the difficult period from 1967 to 1980. In addition to two major wars (the 1969–1970 War of Attrition and the 1973 Yom Kippur War), this period saw the country confront formidable economic and social problems, leading to a real spiritual crisis but ending on a more optimistic note.

Chapter 4, "New Challenges," takes the story from the peace with Egypt through the Lebanese War, the first Palestinian uprising and the first Gulf War, to the assassination of Prime Minister Yitzhak Rabin. Last, chapter 5, "Tragedy, Triumph, and Struggle," focuses on the vast cultural, social, and economic transformation that, starting in the mid-1980s, did much to turn Israel into a first-world country without, unfortunately, solving the problems between Arabs and Israelis or bringing about a situation where swords may finally be turned into plowshares.

Since the period covered here extends over almost a century, the amount of available source material was so vast that I could use only an extremely small part of it. Since my purpose was neither to shatter any "myths" nor to reveal any "secrets," I decided to rely entirely on publicly available sources while dispensing with archival research. Most of the sources are in Hebrew and will mean nothing to foreign readers; hence, I have limited my references mainly to direct quotes. I hope I have succeeded in providing a reasonably coherent picture of where Israel came from; how it developed its unique character; and to what factors it owes its truly amazing, if not unblemished, success both on the battlefield and in other spheres. If so, then I will have achieved my purpose.

The
LAND *of*
BLOOD *and*
HONEY

1

FORGED IN FURY (1897–1949)

"A Terrible Land"

During the nineteenth century, the land roughly known as Palestine was a remote and badly neglected province of the Ottoman Empire, of which it was a part of from 1517 on. Reflecting the undeveloped nature of the area, even its borders had not yet been properly defined. In 1917, the year when the London *Geographical Journal* published an article about its "resources and suitability for colonization," the discussion included considerable parts of what today are Lebanon, Syria, and especially Jordan. The photographs that accompanied the text showed sites as far away as Baalbek and Amman.

The country known since Biblical times as *Eretz Israel,* the Land of Israel (or simply "the Land," as Jews and Israelis say), was considered part of Greater Syria, an arrangement that goes back to Hellenistic times. As if to deny it any political unity, it was divided into three districts. The northern one reached from Acre in the west to the Jordan River in the east and was governed from Beirut, which itself was ruled from Damascus. Farther south the district of Nablus was also governed from Beirut; however, it reached from the Mediterranean across the Jordan into the area known as Hauran, in southwestern Syria. Finally, Jerusalem was an autonomous province that came directly under Damascus.

Until the last decades before 1900 most cities were walled, gated, and locked at night. Outside them, the Ottoman government was unable to assert itself on anything like a permanent basis. The normal method of governance was to send out a party of troops twice a year, billet them on the fellaheen (peasants), levy the sums that the tax farmer claimed were his due, and withdraw until the next time. Partly because the government could not assert itself, and partly because so many landlords were absentees who lived in places as far away as Beirut, Damascus, and even Tehran, day-to-day affairs were left to the *mukhtars* (elders) and sheiks of villages and tribes. In the Negev, a desert area that later formed about half the territory of the State of Israel, Ottoman power hardly penetrated at all.

The country's native population is estimated to have been six hundred thousand, although, in truth, nobody knows what it was exactly. In truth, too, strictly speaking, not all of the people were native. One well-informed contemporary source claimed that they were "best described as Syrians, a mixed race in which much Arab blood [i.e., originating in the Arabian Peninsula] has intermingled with that of the descendants of Canaanites, Hebrews, Greeks, Egyptians, and perhaps even the Crusaders";[1] not to mention a small Circassian community whose members had been driven from their Caucasian home in the nineteenth century and received the Ottoman Porte's permission to settle. Some cities also contained recently arrived immigrants from Syria, Egypt, and Morocco. According to the available guesstimates, about 80 percent of the total were Muslim, mainly Sunnis, though in northern Galilee there were also a few Shiite villages. Christian Arabs, most of whom lived in and around Jerusalem, Ramallah, Bethlehem, Jaffa, and Nazareth, formed perhaps 10 percent of the population. The Jewish community may have accounted for 7 or 8 percent, whereas Mount Carmel was home to a small Druze minority.

About 70 percent of the population lived in the countryside, scattered among some seven hundred villages. However, settlement was anything but even. Contrary to the common pattern in "civilized" countries, the most densely inhabited areas were not the plains. Instead they were the mountains of Judea, Samaria, and Galilee as well as the southern and more salubrious part of the coastal plain. By contrast, the northern coastal plain—the Biblical "Valley of Sharon"—was essentially a desert, green in winter, baking hot (many areas were covered with sand dunes) in summer. Although it did not have dunes, the same applied to the equally celebrated Valley of Esdraelon, with its extensions to the west and to the east. In both areas the lack of settlement was due to malaria, which the local populations, without modern science and technology, were unable to eradicate. It made the areas unsuitable for permanent settlement so that they were mostly left to Bedouin tribes. Other common diseases associated with unhygienic living close to stale water were trachoma (which can lead to blindness), cholera, dysentery, and typhus. Worst of all was leprosy, for which there was no known cure and whose victims were treated as outcasts. To be sure, the government did recognize these problems. However, an English doctor described the steps it took to deal with them as "worse than useless."[2]

Still, comparing the country to "civilized" ones, perhaps the factor that would have surprised the visitor most was its primitive system of transportation. There was not a single deep-water port. Ships simply cast anchor at sea, without any protection from the waves, and embarked or disembarked their passengers and cargo by means of open boats. At the quay they were received by porters, either Arab or Jewish, who were famous for their burliness, strong language, and often kind hearts. Wheeled transport, too, was scarce. The absence of paved roads on one hand, and the rapacity of the government on the other, obstructed the use of vehicles; inside the towns, narrow streets, marked by numerous steps, did the same. As a result, the very first one, appropriately nicknamed "Pharaoh's chariot," was not introduced until 1869. Even so, at the end of the century the journey from Jaffa to the Jewish colony of Hadera farther north, a distance of just over forty miles, took nine hours to accomplish by cart. In winter, when rain transformed much of the terrain into a swamp, it might be impossible; as traffic came to a halt rural settlements were cut off, sometimes for days on end.

Though the distance was similar, the journey from Jaffa to Jerusalem took even longer. There were five different post-coach systems, one operated by the Ottomans and the rest by foreign concession holders as part of the so-called capitulations, the arrangement by which foreign residents were not subject to Ottoman law and were judged by their own consuls. Having made their choice, people would leave in the early afternoon. Like many other parts of the country, the foothills of the Judean Mountains were still inhabited by roving Bedouin, who made it unsafe to travel at night. It was therefore necessary to halt at a caravansary at Shaar Hagai (The Gate of the Valley) some thirty miles away. The next morning the travelers would proceed. They would struggle up and down the winding road, repair a broken wheel if need be, defend themselves against robbers (usually they were accompanied by at least one armed guard), or bribe those they could not fend off before finally reaching their destination, Jaffa Gate, around noon. Even after French engineers in 1892 built a railroad linking the two towns, the journey still took four hours. This was because the curves only allowed the train to travel slowly, so that there were stretches where it could be overtaken by a galloping horse.

As late as 1913, there was only a single motor vehicle in the entire country—this at a time when Ford in Detroit was turning them out by the thousands each day. Communications, too, were few and far between. Influenced by the Koranic experts, or ulema, the Ottomans had been notoriously slow to adopt the art of printing. Only in 1727, almost three centuries after Gutenberg, was the first press established at Constantinople. Still, widespread illiteracy meant that the written word was slow to penetrate, so that the first regular mail service was only established in 1840. As the Ottoman Empire joined the international Post and Telegraph Union, the first telegraph line, which linked Constantinople with Beirut and from there on with Jaffa via Haifa, was inaugurated in 1865. A year later, it was extended to Jerusalem. Just which other towns were hooked up is not completely known, though it has been documented that in 1919, the occupying British military operated a network that included, besides the above, Ramle, Afula (which at that time consisted of houses made of mud, but was the site of a German air base they had taken over), Hebron, Gaza, Tul Karem, Acre, Nazareth, and Tiberias. As for telephones, at the outbreak of World War I there were none.

Then, as today, Palestine was hardly one of the world's great breadbaskets. The climate is semiarid. For seven months a year it practically does not rain at all; "hot and dry" is all the weatherman has to say.

The average annual rainfall is about twenty inches, somewhat more in the north, much less in the south. Generally the farther south one goes, the more limited the water supply, until, in the Negev, year-round sources are limited to a few wells hidden in otherwise dry riverbeds. To the north of Beer Sheba, provided that the supply is carefully conserved and systematically managed, there is enough water to permit a fair level of agricultural activity. The climate is excellent for subtropical crops such as wheat, melons, olives, figs, grapes, dates, almonds, pomegranates, apricots, and the like, all of which have grown since time immemorial.

During the second half of the nineteenth century citrus trees were introduced. Oranges, grapefruit, and lemons soon turned into the country's main export commodities, joining older products such as olive oil and soap. Draft and pack animals such as asses, mules, and camels were available, but horses, which require artificial fodder, tended to be expensive and few and far between. Livestock consisted of rather poor-quality cattle such as was able to survive more or less on its own without need for permanent shelter. In addition, there were a few pigs (raised exclusively by the Arab Christian population), poultry, sheep, and goats. All these were popular because they could feed almost anywhere.

Concerning the goats, another word needs to be said. Most modern scholars agree that, once upon a time, the land was more heavily wooded, was richer in resources, and supported a larger population than was the case around 1900, let alone 1800, when the population only stood at two hundred thousand or so. The arrival of black goats, that came along with the Arabs during the seventh century A.D., changed this situation. The goats, which in some areas may be seen even today, are astonishing animals. Not only do they graze at ground level but they also climb many of the small trees characteristic of much of Palestine. Once they do so they eat and eat, leaving nothing in their way. Visitors to the area were surprised to learn that, in the entire country, there was not a single forest. Especially in the mountains of Judea and Samaria, whole districts that were once cultivated—as is proved by the presence of ancient, half-ruined terraces—were turned into bare limestone rocks capable of supporting almost nothing. With the cultivated areas went the human settlement. Probably no other country has so many place names starting with *Hirbet,* Arabic for "ruins of"; their number is said to be 457.[3] Conversely, the first prerequisite for making an area fruitful again was, and is even today, to fence it so as to keep the goats out.

Other factors, such as periodic droughts, the sudden appearance of swarms of locusts, and the incapacity and rapacity of government, also helped keep agricultural activity—and with it the standard of living—at a very low level. Yet another problem was the ancient system of communal land ownership. Under its terms, each cultivator received a different plot to work each year, and in any given year one-third of the total area was left fallow. Consequently there was little incentive for investment; even dung, though in plentiful supply, was not often used. The great mass of fellaheen dressed in tatters and went bare-footed. Their horizons were limited to their own villages or districts, which they hardly ever left. Come a solar or lunar eclipse, the entire ragged community would form a procession and use whatever primitive musical instruments they could muster to drive the demons away; their children were happy if, by begging, they could obtain a slice of bread smeared with jam. Town dwellers were slightly better off. One contemporary Jewish source describes them as

> proud, wicked, and sly rascals. They feel no mercy for their brothers and co-religionists, skinning them as much as they can. There is no believing in them even if they swear to God, since they readily take false oaths, not considering doing so a great sin. Those who are better to do engage in trade. Either they lend money to the *fellaheen* at horrific rates of interest . . . or else they lease out their estates and chicane and oppress their tenants who have nobody to defend them.[4]

That these sad circumstances were by no means due exclusively to the nature of the country, but rather to the prevailing social conditions among the Muslim population in particular, is proved by the sharply different experience of two groups, the Christian "Syrians" and the German Templers. Following the end of the Crimean War, foreign activity in the Land of Israel, motivated partly by religious impulses and partly by the hopes of the various powers to take over parts of the crumbling Ottoman Empire, increased very sharply; the opening of the Suez Canal further increased its geopolitical importance. This foreign presence benefited local Christians who saw the prohibitions on the open exercise of their religion lifted. They were granted—at least on paper—equal rights as citizens. Some were even given foreign "protection"; with it came far-reaching immunity from the corrupt system of Ottoman law and government. This in turn made possible the erection of numerous new churches, hospitals, inns where pilgrims could stay, and the like. Considered as prestige objects, they tended to be large and very well constructed. During the 1948 War of Independence they were often used as fortresses; those that escaped destruction grace the cities and the landscape to the present day.

Thus assisted, the Christians, hitherto an oppressed minority, began drawing ahead. According to the same contemporary Jewish source, by the early years of the twentieth century

> Galilee in particular has some villages whose inhabitants engage in agriculture. Their labor is better ordered than that of their Muslim brethren, and their way of life and education are also superior. And this is because they are subject to constant spiritual guidance from abroad and come under the supervision of their numerous and well organized priests. The latter well understand what they are about and do what they can to inspire their flocks with feelings of unity, love of work, and unity, and good government. . . . They have good schools in each town and village . . . and specially designed textbooks for teaching in them . . . in brief, they are completely different from us [Jews].[5]

The Templer movement provided even more convincing proof that good government, good social organization, and good education were capable of rapidly improving the condition of the country. The movement originated in Württemberg, Germany, in 1858. A Lutheran priest by the name of Christoph Hoffman, citing certain passages in the Bible, persuaded his followers that they should settle in Palestine so as to hasten the coming of the Day of Judgment. The first five pioneers arrived in 1860. Nine years later, the earliest settlement was established outside the walls of Haifa. Following this, additional ones were established in Bethlehem and Waldheim (near Nazareth), Sarona and Beer Salem (around Jaffa), Refaim (near Jerusalem) and Wilhelma (near Lydda).

As the inscription above the entrance of their first schoolhouse—"If I forget thee Jerusalem, let me forget my right arm"—showed, the Templers were deeply religious in outlook. Professionally, though, most of them were either farmers or craftsmen. They brought with them modern technology, including not only agricultural tools and methods but steam engines for pumps, olive oil and wine presses, and the like. Another important innovation was indoor plumbing; previously water had been carried either in jars on the heads of women (in the countryside) or in leather bags on the backs of donkeys (in the towns). One result was that, as late as the 1970s, Jewish plumbers used German terminology when talking about their profession even though many of them, being of Oriental—Asian or African—origin, had no idea where the words came from or what their real meanings were.

Though the number of German settlers never exceeded two thousand, their colonies prospered. They served as examples of what hard work, thrift, and proper communal organization could achieve even in an out-of-the-way, poor, and fairly inhospitable country; as time went on, their economic success tended to overshadow their religious fervor. A small amount of German diplomatic support, as well as an occasional visit by a German warship, helped. In the words of one German naval officer, the visits "impressed the Turks and Arabs who, like all Orientals, only understand the kind of power they can see with their own eyes."[6] This situation lasted until the beginning of World War II, when the British authorities evacuated the Templers; many eventually settled in Australia.

In this volume, the ethnic group that interests us most is the Jews. Their numbers were small, probably around fifty thousand in all. Still, there had never been a period when Palestine was altogether without them. One village, Peqiin in Galilee, is said to have had a Jewish community going back, without a break, to the days of antiquity. At all times, but especially from 1800 on, there was a trickle of Jewish immigrants; they came to pray, study, or be buried in the Land, which, according to their belief, God had granted their fathers. As in most countries, Jews had long been prohibited from purchasing land in Palestine. Partly for that reason, partly because the Jewish religion is a communal one that requires a minimum number of (adult male) persons to be present so that various ceremonies may be performed, and partly because of the need to find Jewish partners to marry, almost all the Palestinean Jews lived in the towns, where they were able to rent or lease apartments. The most important communities were located in the four holy towns. These were Jerusalem (where, from the 1860s on, they formed the largest single religious group), Hebron, Safed, and Tiberias. During the last decades of the century, congregations also started establishing themselves in other towns such as Jaffa, Haifa, and Gaza.

Originally almost all the Jews in the Land of Israel were Sephardis, meaning that they were descended from those who had been expelled from Spain back in 1492. The language they spoke was Ladino, a variation of medieval Spanish. "In everything concerning home and family," a contemporary tourist guide noted, "they behave just like the country's [Arab] inhabitants."[7] During the nineteenth century they were joined by growing numbers of Ashkenazis, people whose countries of origin were mostly in Eastern Europe and whose language, Yiddish, is a variation of medieval German mixed with Hebrew words. Further divisions existed between groups of immigrants originating in different countries, Ottoman citizens and those carrying foreign passports, not to mention Hassidim and their "learned" opponents (Mitnagdim), conservatives and those who were comparatively liberal in their approach to religion, and so on.

Traditionally the official who represented the Jews in their dealings with the Ottoman authorities, and vice versa, was called Rishon Lezion (Zion's First), a rabbi whose residence was in Jerusalem. He himself was a Sephardi, but the authorities held him responsible for all the Jews; only during the last years before 1914 was the existence of a separate Ashkenazi community recognized. His power—and later that of his Askhenazi counterpart, too—rested largely on the fact that he was authorized, indeed obliged, to gather taxes for the government. He also taught the Torah, certified kosher food, ran the burial society, and presided over the courts that settled the affairs of the Jews among themselves; his wife looked after the *mikveh,* or ritual bath, that Jewish women are commanded to use after menstruation as a condition for having sex with their husbands. All of these were lucrative activities, enabling him to support himself and those who acted in his name.

A great many Ashkenazis depended on alms from abroad—originally Europe, and later, as the nineteenth century progressed, the United States as well—for a living. A system for the collection and distribution (*haluka,* in Hebrew) of those alms was developed, putting great power into the hands of the rabbis who pulled the strings. Concerning that system, one rabbi wrote as follows:

> The [Jewish] inhabitants of the Land of Israel, and even less so those among them who study the Torah, are under no obligation to their benefactors even to the extent of saying, "thank you." And those who argue to the contrary are only trying to dominate us, as if we were slaves, and for this . . . they will be called to account.[8]

Simply living in the Land of Israel was regarded as a cardinal religious commandment. Hence, clearly those who fulfilled that commandment were entitled to subsist at the expense of those who did not do so but still wanted their share in the blessings it bestowed.

Reflecting the growth of world Jewry and its increasing wealth, the sums generated in contributions had been rising throughout the nineteenth century. In 1900 they probably amounted to three million French francs (approximately six hundred thousand U.S. dollars) a year; given Ottoman financial mismanagement and the fact that much money originated from the French baron Edmond de Rothschild (1845–1934), francs were commonly used as a ghost currency in which all calculations were made. The number of recipients was almost twenty-nine thousand, which translated into about a hundred francs per person per year on average. However, the payments were very unequal. The collection of funds was decentralized, so that there was nothing to prevent each community or group that felt like doing so from trying their luck and sending out its own "emissary" to beg for money. The money was distributed without even a semblance of transparency; those in charge were not always above helping themselves first. Among the criteria used to decide what to do with the rest was spiritual attainment—rabbis and Torah students got more than their share—and family size. As far as may be determined, those best provided for got around 180 francs per year, whereas those at the bottom of the scale had to content themselves with 10 to 40.

Whether the system conferred any of the spiritual benefits it promised will not be discussed here. However, some contemporaries and later scholars agree that economically speaking, it was a disaster. It accounted, or helped to account, for a large class of people who had no incentive to engage in productive work of any kind and another with every interest in keeping them in a state of strict dependency. Some accepted their poverty and the often almost intolerable hardship it involved. Others, to the contrary, were driven to look for supplementary sources of income. This was especially true of Sephardis. Coming from countries that were as poor as their adopted fatherland, they got less than their share in the *haluka*. On the other hand, they were more familiar with the country, its language, and its culture. Hence, some of them were active as woodworkers, bookbinders, printers, plumbers, watch- and clockmakers, tailors, cobblers, and tinkers. Others worked as bricklayers, carriage drivers, and porters, whereas among recent arrivals it was possible to find a few doctors, teachers, and the like. There were, however, strict limits on what they—as well as their non-Jewish, mainly Christian, colleagues—could do. Most of the population lived in the countryside. To a large extent, they supplied their own needs for clothing (homespun), tools (such as primitive wooden plows), building materials, and transport. Given the inability and unwillingness of the fellaheen to buy, town-based craftsmen could operate only on a very small scale, not comparable to anything found in contemporary developed countries.

The point where Jews stood at the greatest advantage in comparison with their neighbors, especially the Muslims, was education. Partly because they lived in towns and engaged in urban occupations and partly because their religion honored those who were able to read sacred texts in public, almost all Jewish males had received a smattering of education. Though standards were not always high, very few of them were completely illiterate. By the middle of the nineteenth century, especially among Sephardi Jews in the Land of Israel, this applied to girls, too; boys and girls were often instructed in adjacent rooms of a house by a husband-and-wife team. The traditional curriculum included reading and writing. Once those skills had been mastered, lessons focused almost exclusively on religious studies. The great majority of students left school at age nine or, at the very oldest, thirteen. Higher study, which was likewise exclusively religious, was reserved for a handful of students, all male. Females did not get far in studying Torah, let alone the Talmud. Some, indeed, might be taught to read but not to write.

During the period that concerns us here, two other types of schools made an impact. One was set up by Diaspora Jews, particularly French ones, who had been influenced by the Enlightenment. Like many minorities the world over, these Jews put an enormous emphasis on education as the highway to success. Some of them saw a need to reach out to their "brethren in the East" so as to pull them out of their "Oriental ignorance." Catering to girls as well as boys—a great innovation, and one for which they often came under attack—schools of this kind could be found mainly in Jerusalem, which contained the largest Jewish community of all. Side by side with the usual religious studies, which were considered indispensable, their curricula included foreign languages. The principal languages taught were Turkish, French, and Italian; in fact, a corrupt form of Italian had served as the lingua franca of the eastern Mediterranean ever since the high point of Venetian and Genoese power in the Middle Ages. These schools also offered arithmetic and some smattering of the natural science of their day.

The other kind of school was set up by the Christian missions, of which there were a great many, each one representing a different faith and all fiercely competing with each other for money, students, and influence. Almost all were located in the towns. This, once again, meant that the Jews, almost all of whom lived in those towns, were more exposed to their influence than were the rest of the population. In addition, whereas Muslim custom prohibited attempts to proselytize among them, doing the same among Jews was allowed. Compared to the very small amounts of capital available in the country itself, the sums the missions were able to command and spend were fabulous—as much as three hundred thousand francs for a single building in the center of Jerusalem. True, their success in converting Jews was always extremely limited. But what they did do, and still do, was offer their students modern, often very high quality, curricula. Both the missionary schools and the Jewish schools (called Hebrew schools) had in common that they supplemented the theoretical subjects with practical ones such as carpentry, leatherwork, tailoring, printing, and, for girls, sewing. Both also rejected the control of the rabbis, who increasingly came to stand for backwardness and obscurantism.

The relatively high level of education encouraged the growth of a vibrant press. As already explained, before 1900, when slow change finally got under way, nearly the entire Muslim population outside the towns was illiterate. What instruction they received was given at the local mosque and consisted almost entirely of learning parts of the Koran by heart. When a written message arrived, it was necessary to turn to the Koranic expert, who was the only person who could read it. By contrast, the first Jewish press was established in Jerusalem in 1841, and the first news-carrying paper was published there in 1863. Competition was fierce from the beginning; soon there were several newspapers in the city. The original purpose was to provide Jewish communities in the Diaspora with news concerning events in the Land of Israel and, by so doing, attract both visitors and funding. Soon, however, the papers also found a growing reading public within the country itself.

For decades on end, the two most important Hebrew-language papers were *Halevanon* (Lebanon) and *Hahavatzelet* (The Lily). Both were published by enterprising Ashkenazi owners of printing shops. Both reflected the divisions within the community to which their owners belonged, especially as to how *haluka* money should be administered and distributed. On more than one occasion the authorities took offense and forced them to close down; there was even a time when *Halevanon* and its publisher were forced to move to Paris. However, in this and other matters Ottoman policy was anything but consistent. Often an appeal to a foreign consul or a well-placed bribe could be used to reverse a decision and allow a paper to reopen. Other less important papers, some of them printed in Ladino and Yiddish, appeared and disappeared. By 1914, six or seven may have been published at any one time; though most only reached a limited readership and did not last long, others took their place. In Jaffa, in Haifa, and a few other places, there were even a handful of Arabic language papers, although their number, per head of the population, was far below that of Jewish ones.

These were clearly signs of progress and boded well for the future. As shown by the fact that the port of Jaffa, for all its shortcomings, was by far the largest on the eastern Mediterranean shore, compared with the neighboring countries, the Land of Israel was already drawing ahead. It even attracted immigrants from these countries. It also paid more than its share of taxes into the Ottoman treasury. A young Dutch visitor, Abraham Mossel, who had actually walked all the way from his homeland to the Middle East, described what it felt like: "Whereas other countries appeared settled in their ways, here everything was starting to grow and nobody could know what the future might bring."[9] Nevertheless, poverty was extreme. The country had neither industry, nor industrial workers, nor capital to speak of. The cities were filthy, crowded, and swarming with an ill-clad, barefooted, *Lumpenproletariat* trying to live hand to mouth while constantly pressing foreigners, all of whom were considered wealthy, for baksheesh (alms).

Some villages had barely changed since Biblical times, consisting mostly of one- or two-room hovels made of mud bricks dried in the sun and packed closely together to provide for mutual defense. Inside these dwellings, it was normal for three generations to live together on a raised platform; farther down, the dirt floor was occupied by chickens and goats. Normally the villages' sole link to the world consisted of a mule path. While merchandise was carried on the backs of camels, mules, and asses, people were used to covering distances of fifteen to twenty-five miles on foot to visit friends. Arthur Ruppin (1876–1946), a German-born lawyer, economist, and scholar who for decades was in charge of acquiring land on behalf of the World Zionist Organization, estimated per capita income at seventy-five French francs a year.[10] This was less than one-half of the Japanese figure—Japan was the poorest among the Great Powers—and only 4 percent of the American one.

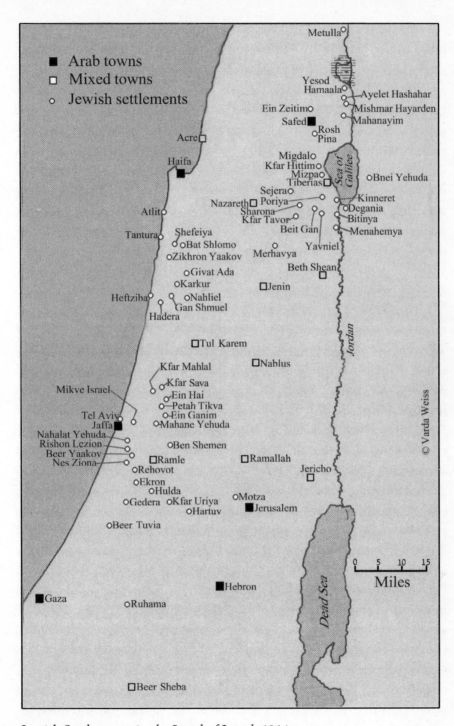

■ Arab towns
□ Mixed towns
○ Jewish settlements

Metulla○

Yesod
Hamaala○
Ayelet Hashahar
Ein Zeitim○
Safed■
Rosh
Pina○
Mishmar Hayarden○
Mahanayim

Acre□

Haifa■

Migdal○
Kfar Hittim○
Mizpa○
Tiberias□
Sejera○
Nazareth□ Poriya○
Sharona○
Kfar Tavor○
Beit Gan
Yavniel○

Bnei Yehuda○
Kinneret○
Degania○
Bitinya○
Menahemya○

Atlit○

Tantura○

Shefeiya○
Bat Shlomo○
Zikhron Yaakov○

Givat Ada○
Karkur○

Merhavya○

Beth Shean□

Heftziba○
Nahliel○
Gan Shmuel○
Hadera○

Jenin□

Tul Karem□

Kfar Mahlal○
Kfar Sava○
Ein Hai○
Petah Tikva○
Ein Ganim○
Mahane Yehuda○

Nablus□

Mikve Israel

Tel Aviv
Jaffa■
Nahalat Yehuda
Rishon Lezion
Beer Yaakov
Nes Ziona○

Ben Shemen○

Ramle□

Ramallah□

Jericho□

Rehovot○
Ekron○
Hulda○
Gedera○ Kfar Uriya○
Hartuv○

Motza○
Jerusalem■

Beer Tuvia○

0   5   10   15

Miles

■Hebron

■Gaza
Ruhama○

Beer Sheba□

© Varda Weiss

Sea of Galilee

Jordan

Dead Sea

Jewish Settlements in the Land of Israel, 1914

Of course, prices for almost everything except imports were much lower in the Land of Israel than in the countries in question. However, then as now, this fact itself was a sign of backwardness. Working as an agricultural laborer, Mossel, the young Dutchman mentioned earlier, rarely ate meat. He went barefoot most of the time, made himself a cape out of sackcloth with three holes in it, and was happy if he could share a whitewashed room with a stone floor, a table, a chair, and a couple of straw-filled sacks to sleep on. His Arab fellow workers made do with far less still, feeding on bread and onions and sleeping wherever they could. Perhaps we should leave the final word to Emperor William II, who visited in 1898. "A terrible country," he noted in his diary, "without water and without shade."

"If You Will, This Is No Dream"

The Jewish religion has always put a strong emphasis on the Land of Israel as the place where the Jewish people was formed, lived, and created the only independent states it had ever possessed. In the Jewish liturgy, almost all of which dates to the two millennia of exile, that Land is often mentioned as an object for longing—"next year [we'll celebrate] in rebuilt Jerusalem," as the Passover Eve prayer puts it. From the sixteenth century on this led to a trickle of immigrants who came to study, worship, die, and be buried on holy soil. As mentioned earlier, this trickle grew somewhat from about 1850 on.

The term "Zionism" appears to have been coined in 1890. By 1911 it was sufficiently well known to merit an article in the *Encyclopaedia Britannica,* written by Lucien Wolf of the Jewish Historical Society of England. He assured readers that the most fundamental Zionist premise, namely that anti-Semitism was "unconquerable," was erroneous; since "nationalities [were] daily losing more of their racial character," the entire movement was "artificial."[11] In fact, Zionism owed its origins to two historical processes that were in some ways contradictory. On one hand was the movement of Jews out of the ghettoes that started around the time of the French Revolution and gathered steam throughout the nineteenth century; on the other, the rise, from about 1860 on, of modern, race-based, anti-Semitism. The first encouraged Jews to integrate themselves into the surrounding gentile society, which they were assisted in doing by the widespread tendency toward civil emancipation in the West. The second frustrated their efforts and often made a mockery of them; the harder they tried, the less accepted they were.

Things were especially bad in Russia-ruled Eastern Europe, where millions were squeezed into the Pale of Settlement. They suffered from every sort of discrimination, lived in dire poverty, and were always waiting for the horrible sound of church bells that called on their gentile neighbors to drop their work, take up cudgels, and start a pogrom. In the words of Leon Pinsker, an Odessa physician whose pamphlet *Auto-Emancipation* was published in Berlin in 1882 and quickly became one of the best-known early Zionist writings: "Against prejudice the gods themselves fight in vain."[12]

Both processes took place against the background of sweeping demographic change that caused the total number of Jews in the world to grow from perhaps two and a half million in 1800 to about six times as many a hundred years later. As various nations in the Balkans, Italy, and Germany created their own states, and as people belonging to many other nations tried to do the same, the idea that the Jews also constituted not just a religious group but a nation (both Jews and others often used the term "race") was not a far stretch. If they were a nation, then logically they, too, should live in a country of their own. At various points proposals to settle them in other places, such as North America and Argentina, were raised; however, all ended up being rejected.

Nor were Jews the only ones who thought in these terms. Especially in Britain, throughout the nineteenth century numerous gentiles came up with their own schemes for solving what was increasingly known as "the Jewish question." Some, like Laurence Oliphant (1829–1888), an author, traveler, and mystic, were motivated by religion. They hoped to bring about the old prophecy concerning the Jews' eventual return to their country as a first step toward the world's redemption. Others, including at one point British Prime Minister Lord Palmerston (served 1855–1858, 1859–1865), had realpolitik in mind. Either they wished to strengthen the Ottoman Empire—"the Sick Man of Europe," as it was known—so it could serve as a bulwark against Russian expansion, or else they hoped to hasten its disintegration and, if possible, inherit its place.

The Zionists themselves did not agree on the kind of community they were to form. Some wanted it to be religious, others secular. Some wanted an independent Jewish state; others, such as Theodor Herzl's rival Ahad Haam ("one of the people," a pseudonym), wanted merely some sort of spiritual center. For all the noisy propaganda conducted by the early Zionists, most Jews did not embrace the idea at all. Hundreds of thousands tried to solve their predicament by emigration, especially to the United States, Canada, Argentina, South Africa, and Australia. Liberals hoped to integrate themselves into existing society; to them, the Zionist claim that Jews were a separate people represented the opposite of everything they were trying to achieve. Socialists, themselves divided into many different groups, preferred to devote their energy to bringing about a revolution, after which all men would become brothers and live together happily ever after. Finally there were the ultra-Orthodox. Claiming to live according to the will of God as expressed in the Old Testament and the Talmud, they clung to their existing way of life as best they could, fearing their gentile neighbors while at the same time deeply contemptuous of them. Many saw the very idea of a Jewish state as apostasy, as they still do. In Russia, where Zionist activity was at best semilegal, ultra-Orthodox believers sometimes called in the tsar's police to break up their rivals' meetings, confiscate documents, and the like.

Dreaming, writing, and lecturing is one thing; an organized movement is something else. The man whose name will forever be associated with the creation of the Zionist movement was Theodor (Benjamin Zeev) Herzl. Born to a middle-class family in Budapest in 1860, Herzl, an only child, was a mother's boy with burning ambition, dark good looks, and a strong sense for the theatrical. He studied law in Vienna, where, among other manifestations of anti-Semitism, he experienced the humiliation of not being permitted to defend his honor by dueling with a fellow student. Later he worked as a journalist, writing witty and amusing (if not very profound) feuilletons about contemporary affairs and trips to various European capitals. Among them was Paris, where he covered the Dreyfus Affair; the howling mobs that accompanied the trial in which Captain Alfred Dreyfus, a Jewish-French officer, was accused of treason, convicted, publicly humiliated, and imprisoned made a deep impression on him. As a thoroughly assimilated Jew, previously he had played with various solutions to what was known as "the Jewish question," including that of mass conversion to Christianity. Now he concluded that it would only be solved by means of the establishment of a Jewish state, and that he himself was the man Providence had chosen to lead the movement toward such a state.

Two years of intense effort—corresponding, speechifying, organizing, fund-raising—passed before Herzl was able to assemble the First Zionist Congress in Basel, Switzerland, in 1897. Some two hundred delegates from all over the world attended; for Herzl personally it was a great triumph. He gave the opening speech, in which he proclaimed that things for the Jews were going from bad to worse—almost universally hated and despised, in many places they were suffering from discrimination and persecution as well—and that a people could only be saved by its own efforts. His reward was a standing ovation that lasted fully fifteen minutes. Not long after, a Zionist Executive, with Herzl itself at its head, was established, as was a Jewish Colonial Trust (around this time colonialism was reaching its peak, so the word "colonial" carried almost exclusively positive connotations). Awestruck by the magnitude of his self-imposed historical mission, Herzl confided to his diary, which he kept religiously: "In Basel I founded the Jewish State."[13] As it turned out, his estimate that fifty years would be needed to accomplish the task was off by only a few months.

During the six years he still had to live, Herzl engaged in prodigious labors, helping to organize six more Zionist Congresses. His own idea, which the First Congress had adopted, was to start from the top, using diplomatic means in order to "secure for the Jewish people a publicly recognized, legally secured, home in Palestine."[14] With this objective in mind he traveled to many capitals, meeting rulers and attempting to convince them that the Jews (whom he pretended to represent to a much greater extent than was actually the case) had something to offer. On the whole he was not very successful. The sultan—of the Ottoman Empire of which Palestine was a part—with whom he had two conversations and whom he described as a "weak, craven, but thoroughly good natured man,"[15] ended up promising nothing. The German kaiser, whom he also met twice and who he hoped would put pressure on his ally the Porte, did the same. Herzl received what was perhaps the most favorable welcome in London, where he talked to the colonial secretary, Joseph Chamberlain. However, the British Empire at the time did not own the Land of Israel. Cyprus, the Sinai Peninsula, and Uganda were also mentioned as possible locations for a Jewish national home, but those discussions came to nothing, either because Britain's representatives objected on the spot or because the Zionists themselves had second thoughts.

In between organizing and traveling Herzl managed to write a novel, *Old-New Land*. As a literary creation it is sallow, full of characters modeled on his Viennese acquaintances whom he used as mouthpieces for his ideas. However, it did set forth his vision of what a Jewish-Zionist community in the Land of Israel might look like in 1923. There was to be a "mutualist" (fearing controversy, he shied away from the word "socialist") society; based on modern trade and industry, it would maintain good relations with the local Arabs who had benefited greatly from rising land prices. The most famous sentence attributed to him, "If you will, this is no dream" appeared as a motto.

At the time he died in 1904, Herzl was convinced that the Zionist enterprise had run into the sand. The paper for which he worked, the *Neue Freie Presse,* refused to acknowledge its existence. Discouraged, he bought a vault for himself and his family in the same Vienna cemetery where his father had been buried. His epitaph, he once wrote, should be "He had too good an opinion of the Jews."[16] Little did he know that thousands would attend his funeral. Most were not members of the assimilated middle class, to which he himself belonged, but the so-called Ostjuden, eastern European Jews, who had recently arrived in the Austrian capital and were desperately trying to make their way in it.

In fact, "the programmatic encouragement of the settlement in Palestine with Jewish agricultural workers, laborers, and those pursuing other trades" (a resolution adopted by the First Zionist Congress) had started twenty years earlier. The signal was given by the Russian pogroms of 1881–1883, which in turn were sparked off by the assassination of Tsar Alexander III. With Pinsker taking the lead, committees were formed in Warsaw (which was then part of the Russian Empire), Odessa, and a few other cities. They carried names such as Hovevei

Zion (Lovers of Zion) and Bet Yaakov Lehu Venelha (Let's Go to the House of Jacob); later they joined the Zionist mainstream. The objective was to raise money, purchase property in the Land of Israel, and send settlers who, building their homes there, would prepare the ground for others to follow.

In any event, the appeal was not very successful. The number of those who, during the 1880s and 1890s, formed the so-called First Migration was limited to a few thousand at most. Most were young, single—as with all emigrant groups, there were more men than women—and well educated by the standards of the day. They were also decidedly, even militantly, secular minded. They neither prayed, nor kept the Sabbath, nor fasted on the appointed days, nor even dressed as Jews had always done. Their objective was to strike root in their new land. However, nobody knew what their ancestors, the original Hebrews, had looked like; hence, often they donned Arab garb complete with headdress, or *keffiye*. These facts explain why they were often far from enthusiastically received by the rabbis of the existing Jewish communities, who saw them as a threat to their own authority. Besides, the newcomers were regarded, with good reason, as competitors in the all-important business of attracting alms.

The first settlement, Rishon Lezion, southeast of Jaffa, was established in 1882. By 1900 there were about twenty other settlements, scattered throughout the country from Metula in the extreme north to Gedera in the south. Contrary to the traditional pattern, most were located not in the mountains but in less densely inhabited plains. None had a population of more than a few hundred souls. Most were much smaller; the total number of residents in all the settlements may have been around forty-five hundred. Though conditions varied greatly, on the whole life, initially in tents and then in wooden shacks with outdoor privies and paraffin lamps for light, was desperately hard. Malaria claimed its victims and could only be eradicated slowly by draining marshes and planting eucalyptus trees. Almost every inch of the land, about which a Jewish joke says that God mistakenly gave it far more than its share of rocks, had to be cleared by hand before cultivation could even begin. The settlers had little experience with outdoor work—then and later, people spoke of "feeble Jewish bodies"—and no knowledge of suitable agricultural methods. Scant wonder quite a few gave up, either returning to their countries of origins or trying their luck overseas.

To these problems was added that of defense. Attacks by Bedouin raiders, who for centuries were accustomed to preying on villages, were common. To survive, each new settlement had to prove its mettle first; either that, or life would be turned into a misery if, indeed, it was possible at all. Divided into numerous tribes and clans with little solidarity among them, the Bedouin were motivated more by their extreme poverty than by nationalist feeling. Among the fellaheen, resentment stemmed from the fact that they might suddenly wake up to see the land on which they had lived for centuries sold from under their feet.

Whatever the source of danger, the outcome was a steady trickle of losses in life and property. A field might be burned, trees uprooted. The head of a coachman might be broken with a club, his gun, wagon, and horses stolen. Women were unable to travel on their own but had to be escorted; a few, such as the wife of future president Yitzhak Ben Zvi, showed their courage by dressing up like men. People were so used to shots being fired at night that they did not regard them as a reason for getting up. The Ottoman authorities did little to keep order. Partly because communications were bad, and partly because they could not care less, their method was to appear on the scene only after everything was over. They would make an arrest or two, confiscate what weapons they could find, negotiate some kind of truce, and return to the town whence they had come.

If most of the settlements managed to survive, then this was due, in large measure, to outside financial support. The most important source was Baron Edmond de Rothschild, bon vivant—unlike most family members, he never entered the banking business—art collector, and philanthropist. His exact motives remain somewhat obscure. Evil tongues claimed that what he really wanted was to prevent more *Ostjuden* from arriving in France, where their poverty and strange ways might cause anti-Semitism to increase. In all he may have spent about $5 million on the enterprise, a fabulous sum for the day (it would have bought a first-rate contemporary battleship), made even more so by the country's relative poverty. However, there was a price to pay. The subsidies originating in Paris enabled the settlements to survive, but they also discouraged healthy economic development.

Furthermore, Rothschild, feeling—no doubt correctly—that his protégés were unable to look after themselves, appointed his own officials to run the settlements. By so doing he invited endless conflicts between the two groups whose members were constantly complaining about one another to him.

Had things gone on in this way, the entire Zionist enterprise would probably have come to naught. The smaller settlements—remote, often located on difficult terrain, and surrounded by hostile neighbors—would assuredly have collapsed. Some of the larger and more successful ones, especially in the Judean Plain, might have survived. However, their relevance to the cause was marginal. By this time they were already beginning to turn into colonial-type plantations, complete with Jewish kulaks who relied on cheap Arab labor and exported their produce, such as wheat, citrus fruit, and watermelons, through the nearby port of Jaffa. That things took a different course was due above all to the members of the so-called Second Aliyah, the next wave of immigration, that started arriving around 1904 and continued doing so until the outbreak of World War I ten years later.

Once again, what sparked the movement were pogroms, which this time around were occasioned by the disastrous Russo-Japanese War. In the pogroms, hundreds of Jews were killed, thousands injured, and entire city neighborhoods wrecked. To spread the news of what had happened, the Jewish Committee in Odessa employed the services of the poet Haim Nahman Bialik (1873–1934). At the time he was just thirty years old, but already recognized as an incomparable master of the Hebrew language. The chief result of his labors was a poem, "In the City of Slaughter," referring to events that had taken place in the city of Kishinev in Moldova. It began by giving a graphic account of how people were killed by having nails driven into their heads; it ended by demanding that, if there was justice in this world, it should appear "immediately." For decades on end, the poem was taught in every Zionist classroom both in the Land of Israel and abroad.

As in 1881–1900, only a small percentage of the Jews who left Russia at this time went to the Land of Israel. Also as in 1881–1900, those who went to the Land of Israel tended to be young, single, and comparatively well educated. Where they differed from their predecessors was in that many were committed socialists, albeit of various kinds. For example, Dvora Zatulovsky (1890–1956), mother of Moshe Dayan, had been born to a well-to-do family in Ukraine. She studied at the University of St. Petersburg, tried her hand as a social worker in an attempt to uplift the Russian masses, and was among the thousands who followed Lev Tolstoy's coffin when he was buried in 1910. By contrast, a British police officer once described the earlier-mentioned Yitzhak Ben Zvi as "a perfect Bolshevik." In the Land of Israel, as in some other countries, communist ideology existed long before there was capital, or industry, or an industrial proletariat to speak of.

When these young people arrived in the port of Jaffa, typically they would spend a few nights at one of the flea-ridden hostels, the only ones they could afford. Next they would set out—normally, on foot—to look for work in one of the existing settlements; David Ben Gurion was exceptional in that he was able to rent a donkey. Others did not come as individuals but formed small groups based on friendships formed in the towns where they originated. They would settle on land bought for them by the World Zionist Federation, usually in some area that had been left uncultivated owing to malaria or bandits, and hence was cheap. The organization also lent them money for tools, seed, and living expenses to last until they could bring in the first harvest and repay their debt; some did so, though others remained dependent for years on end. The fact that they did not own the land they worked all but compelled the settlers to adopt some kind of communal life. Other factors pushing in the same direction were small numbers that militated against a division of labor, extreme poverty (communal living was cheaper), the need for self-defense, and socialist ideology, including, in particular, the works of such nineteenth-century luminaries as Henri de Saint-Simon, Robert Owen, and Lev Tolstoy.

In 1909, seven young people—six men, one woman—set up Degania, on the southwestern shore of Lake Galilee. Thus a beginning was made with what for many decades was seen as the most original Jewish-Zionist creation of all: the kibbutz, best translated as "gathering." Though not all kibbutzim were exactly the same, all did away with individual ownership as it applied to major belongings (in some cases "major" belongings even included clothing, which was provided by the communal magazine). In all of them, work was carried out in common and the resulting products or income were distributed among all. Members took their meals in common—the inauguration of the first proper dining hall was always a cause for celebration—and raised their children not at home but in dormitories. Some went further still, seeking to abolish marriage itself. In practice, though formal weddings may have been dispensed with, men and women continued to form more or less steady alliances. Government was exercised by the general assembly of all members. Not only did this assembly make all the major decisions, but it also elected the *mazkir,* or secretary who was responsible for day-to-day administration.

The radical nature of their social life made the kibbutzim the most famous form of communal settlement by far. They were, however, not the only type: there were others, particularly the moshavim (plural of moshav). The critical difference was that, in moshavim, no attempt was made to do away with the family. People did not live in "rooms," as in the kibbutzim, but in their own houses, however humble, where they raised their own offspring. In some moshavim the land was owned in common, the work carried out on a collective basis, and the product divided equally. In others it was divided into plots and worked by individuals; however, they could neither sell the plots nor subdivide them among their children. Instead one of the sons, normally but by no means always the oldest, would be designated as the "successor"; given the backbreaking nature of work on the farm, moshavniks who fathered only daughters had reason to worry.

Including various hybrid types, the Zionist enterprise gave rise to many different, more or less original, forms of settlement. However, the scale on which it operated was initially very modest indeed. In 1914 there were only forty agricultural settlements in all. Their combined population is estimated at twelve thousand; of those, no more than one thousand or so lived in ten kibbutzim.

By that time, the total number of Jews in the country had gone up to about eighty-five thousand. Clearly most immigrants did not choose agricultural labor at all but settled in the cities of Jerusalem, Tel Aviv, and Haifa. Though the numbers were very small, they already included a sprinkling of professionals such as bankers, doctors, teachers, printers, publishers, photographers, and even artists; Bezalel, the first art school, opened its gates in Jerusalem in 1906. Many people were highly educated, and almost all were secular minded. Their reason for emigrating was to escape the ghetto, not to build a new one. Accordingly they refused to submit to the authority of the rabbis, whom they saw as backward, obscurantist, and interested only in their own power. It was the need to escape that authority, as well as the hostility of urban-living Arabs and the generally unattractive character of the existing Oriental towns, that led to the establishment of the first Jewish city, Tel Aviv, in 1909.

Built on sand—the land was covered with dunes, hence uncultivated and cheap—Tel Aviv was intended as a garden suburb of Jaffa. Accordingly the first streets formed a gridiron pattern typical of such suburbs and were lined with modest one-story buildings. To the south, separated from Tel Aviv by citrus groves, lay Jaffa, which after the 1948 War of Independence became part of its former suburb. To the north lay the fields of the Templer colony of Sarona as well as endless dunes that became famous as a refuge for lovers; to the east were more citrus groves. Many of these lands were later acquired by developers, offering room for expansion. The rest became available in 1948 as a result of the War of Independence. For a long time, the largest building was the Herzliya Hebrew High School, which opened its gates in 1910 and continued to operate until 1961, when it was demolished to make room for Israel's first skyscraper. Other distinguishing features were running water as well as municipal sewage and garbage-removal services—the first, and for some time the only, services of their kind in the country.

Closely associated with schools and education was the question of language. Even before the Jews went into exile during the first centuries A.D., Hebrew had been losing its status in favor of Aramaic (the original language of the New Testament and also parts of the Old Testament and the Talmud). Much later, Jews came to use their own languages, such as the above-mentioned Yiddish and Ladino. Both in Europe and on other continents, many also tended to adopt the languages spoken by their gentile neighbors. Hebrew, though never quite forgotten, came to be used almost exclusively during the daily prayers as well as in the synagogue; apart from that, it only served a handful of literati who wrote for each other. From about 1860 on, rising nationalist aspirations helped a Hebrew press and a modern Hebrew literature to develop, but still the language was hardly ever spoken. All these facts were reflected in Hebrew's limited vocabulary, which lacked words for countless modern ideas, devices, and inventions.

Once the first schools started operating in the Land of Israel, the question as to which language they should use could no longer be evaded. "The Baron," as Baron de Rothschild was popularly known, favored French. In fact, it became common for some of the more successful settlers' daughters, who played the piano and chattered in French, to go to France to complete their education (often, never to return). Others preferred German as the language of both technology and culture. A tug-of-war developed between the old and the young who, having arrived from a great variety of countries, needed Hebrew to communicate among themselves. As so often, the young won, not least by means of a student strike that enforced the use of Hebrew at the Institute of Technology in Haifa in 1913.

By the end of World War I Hebrew had become the public language even though many people did not use it at home. As one story has it, when Bialik came to settle in 1924 he tried to pinch a youth and was satisfied when the response came in perfect, though somewhat uncouth, Hebrew; in one of his lighter moments Ben Gurion himself said that Zionism would have attained its aims when the first Hebrew-speaking policeman arrested the first Hebrew-speaking prostitute. Much of this spread of Hebrew was due to the single-minded efforts of one man, Eliezer Ben Yehuda (1858–1922). Lithuanian born and Paris educated, Ben Yehuda knew Russian, German, and French in addition to his native Yiddish and acquired Hebrew. In 1881 he settled in Jerusalem, establishing a newspaper and starting a propaganda campaign to make people change their habits; whenever a family promised to speak Hebrew exclusively, his wife would bake them a cake. He also invented countless words, from *haidak* (bacteria, literally "small form of life") to *matzneah* (parachute, from the root *tzanah,* to drop) and included them in the dictionary that still bears his name. As immigrants continued to arrive, the Land of Israel became a country where the young taught their elders how to speak the language instead of the other way around. All too often, this has remained the case to the present day.

Looking back, the development of the Jewish community appears even more impressive because it was by no means well received by the Ottoman authorities. Throughout the nineteenth century the Porte, worried that Jewish settlement might result in the Land of Israel being lost to the Empire, resisted it. Things became much worse in 1893. A series of new laws were issued requiring those who entered the country to leave a deposit, ordering them to surrender their passports for custody, and prohibiting the acquisition of land as well as the construction of new housing. Meeting with Theodor Herzl in 1901, all Sultan Abdul Hamid II was prepared to talk about was the consolidation (at Jewish expense) of his Empire's debt. Fortunately for the Zionists a large distance separated Constantinople from their chosen country. Inside the country itself, Ottoman power tended to be rather thin on the ground. Foreign consuls could be called upon to help, local officials circumvented or bribed. Regulations could be evaded by registering land in the name of foreigners; in particular, the chief rabbi of Berlin was a great favorite. Another method, which was used in Degania among other places, was to first construct quarters for animals and then make changes so as to enable people to live in them. All this remained true even after a coup d'état brought the Young Turks to power in 1908. Whereas government remained as brutal as usual, it hardly grew more efficient.

The outbreak of World War I brought these comparatively favorable conditions to an abrupt end. At the time the governor in Damascus was Jamal Pasha (1872–1922). Simultaneously serving as commander of the Fourth Army and as minister of the navy, his powers were practically unlimited. The way he saw things, the time had come for what the Porte, due to both external and internal problems, had never been able to do: namely, put an end to Jewish attempts to set up a state within a state. No sooner did the Empire enter the war in October 1914 than he abolished the capitulations, the system of extraterritorial rights that had grown up over several centuries and to which the Zionist enterprise in the Land of Israel owed much. There followed a sustained campaign that included the closure of Hebrew-language newspapers; removal of Hebrew-language signs; the disbandment of the first Jewish self-defense organization, Hashomer (The Watchman); the prosecution of community leaders on all kinds of excuses; and the expulsion from the country of thousands of Jews who were Russian (i.e., enemy) citizens.

In the numerous meetings he had with the local Jewish leadership, Jamal always denied being an anti-Semite. Certainly he was as hard on his Arab subjects, who by this time were beginning to develop national aspirations of their own, as on the Jewish ones; not for nothing did they call him the Butcher. Be that as it may, as time went on things went from bad to worse. Commanded by a German officer, Field Marshal Colmar von der Goltz, and assisted by some German troops, early in 1915 the Ottomans invaded the Sinai in an attempt to reach the Suez Canal. However, they were repulsed, and in the winter of 1916–1917 the Land of Israel in turn was in imminent danger of being invaded by the armies of General Archibald Murray coming from Egypt. As part of his defense, Jamal ordered evacuations of the Jews in the southern half of the country, including both Jaffa and Tel Aviv, which at the time had thirty-five hundred inhabitants. Jerusalem, too, was supposed to be emptied, but this was prevented at the last moment. Jamal's declared reason was the need to protect the Jews from being massacred by their Arab neighbors. The real one was that he had doubts concerning Jewish loyalty to the Empire.

Those doubts in turn were confirmed by the discovery, later in the same year, of a Jewish espionage ring named Nili, an acronym for a Biblical phrase meaning, roughly, "Israel Will Last Forever." The leader of the ring was Aaron Aaronsohn, a famous agronomical expert based at Atlit, south of Haifa. He was given his opportunity to engage in espionage when a devastating plague of locusts struck in 1915, after which he received special permission to travel all over the country. In October 1917, after a messenger pigeon was intercepted (rumor has it that the Aaronsohn family fell victim to their neighbors' envy), the authorities broke up Nili. Aaronsohn himself was out of the country. His sister Sarah was captured and tortured; when she was allowed to wash herself, she pulled a gun and put a bullet through her head. Yet by then the conspirators had succeeded in providing the new British commander in Egypt, General Edmund Allenby, with an accurate description of the Ottoman order of battle. More vital still was information concerning the location of wells his cavalry could use while making a dash across the arid country between Gaza and Beer Sheba. In November–December, that information helped him capture the entire southern part of the country, including both Tel Aviv and Jerusalem.

In 1914 Menahem Sheinkin (1871–1925), one of Tel Aviv's founding fathers, expressed the general view that "[the war], being waged not by one kingdom against another but among all, could not last for long."[17] Still, it was expected that hostilities, by disrupting foreign trade and cutting off the flow of tourists and pilgrims, would lead to economic hardship. Consequently Meir Dizengoff (1861–1936), the mayor of Tel Aviv, took the initiative in setting up a central committee to represent the entire Jewish community in the Land of Israel and to try to prevent the worst; this was the first time anything of the kind had been attempted. In any case, the committee was torn apart by quarrels among its members, especially those representing the "old" and the "new" communities, and soon fell apart. Still, its segments continued to function. Throughout the war they found themselves begging foreign representatives both in the Land and in Constantinople for assistance, receiving some, and trying to distribute it among their people as fairly as possible.

Most of the assistance came from Germany, which sought to keep on the Zionists' good side and, being allied with the Ottomans, was able to bring pressure to bear on them. Until April 1917 aid also came from the United States, whose Jewish community was rapidly growing in power and influence. Their diplomats tried to intervene; when over seven thousand citizens of enemy countries were expelled from Ottoman Palestine, it was American warships that took them to Alexandria. Other assistance came from Jewish organizations abroad—both Zionist ones and, increasingly, those that were not Zionist but were aware of the deteriorating situation—and took the form of money, medical supplies, and food. All of this was extremely welcome but insufficient to prevent an economic catastrophe from overtaking the community. Things were made worse by the Ottoman army. Not only did it conscript the men it could reach but it was none too considerate in requisitioning supplies for its own use. From the winter of 1917 to September 1918 the country was divided in two as the British occupied the south and the Ottomans the north. By the time the war ended entire settlements had been abandoned, whereas others were overcrowded with refugees; the total Jewish population had gone down by one-third.

Needless to say, the settlement of the Land of Israel could never have taken place without financial and other assistance from the World Zionist Organization abroad. Widely scattered, resting on an incredible maze of interlocking committees, staffed almost entirely by part-time volunteers, and wholly dependent on voluntary contributions, that organization itself was anything but streamlined and efficient. From the first day it was roiled with quarrels over power, prestige, and money. At any one time there were myriad ideas waiting to be realized but not enough funds to pay for them; land had to be bought, farms built, schools opened, and hospitals, libraries, and universities founded. Ottoman resistance and corruption, which was so widespread that hardly anything could be done without officials being bribed, did not help. For example, approving the expenditure of twelve thousand francs— twenty-four hundred U.S. dollars—to set up an agricultural station where Aaronsohn might experiment with the best methods for cultivating the Land of Israel took reams of correspondence spread over six years. By comparison, the establishment of Degania was a model of speed. Just five years separated the moment the lands were first earmarked for purchase and the arrival of the first pioneers.

In 1912–1913 the World Zionist Organization counted 172,000 due-paying members throughout the world, plus probably several times that number of people who sympathized with it to some degree. Inside it, the most important division was between "political" and "practical" Zionists. The former were led by Herzl in person; in part, perhaps, because he was enamored with his meetings with the great and the mighty, he did not want to invest "a single penny" in the Land before some kind of charter or declaration could be obtained that would stake it out as the place where Jews were allowed to settle.[18] His opponents considered this approach ill advised. Instead they hoped to proceed piecemeal, bringing in immigrants and adding "a dunam [about two-fifths of an acre] here, a goat there" (as the saying went) without worrying too much about international politics. In practice, from Herzl's death until 1914 it was the second approach, supported mainly by the Russian members of the organization (Russia, of course, also provided the greatest number of settlers by far), that prevailed.

Nevertheless, the organization's greatest single contribution to the cause bore a "political" character. Much of the credit was due to the greatest leader Zionism produced after Herzl, Haim Weizmann (1874–1952). Weizmann was born in Belarus, studied chemistry in Switzerland, and moved to Britain, where he took up a post at the University of Manchester. In 1910 he became a British subject; from then on he divided his attention between science and Zionist politics. Strongly pro-British, a brilliant conversationalist, witty (once, pressed by Ben Gurion to change his name into Hebrew as so many others did, he said, "Yes, you see, but I have a name to lose"), he was the ideal man to press the case. His chief contact was Arthur Balfour, a former prime minister who was as brilliant as Weizmann and with whom he shared an interest in history and philosophy.

Already during the very first days of the war Weizmann and others sensed that a great opportunity was coming their way. "We must," he wrote on September 8, 1914, "prepare for the coming peace conference so we can at least submit our demands."[19] According to British Prime Minister David Lloyd George, in whose cabinet Balfour served as foreign secretary, the subsequent Balfour Declaration was Weizmann's reward for inventing a process for the manufacture of acetone, a vital ingredient of the cordite used to propel artillery shells.[20] Of course, Lloyd George was writing tongue in cheek; in reality, things were a little more complicated. Originally the epicenter of Zionist activities had been in Eastern and especially Central Europe, so much so that English papers accused it of being simply one of the kaiser's arms. However, the war had the effect first of isolating the Central Powers and then, following the October Revolution in 1917, of throwing Russia into chaos. Consequently the center of gravity shifted to London, whose lines of communication with the rest of the world remained open; there Zionism had the support of some of the most respected Jewish families from the Rothschilds down.

From early on it was apparent that, should the Ottoman Empire collapse, the Land of Israel could not be allowed to fall into the hands of any other power. In 1917, with British armies preparing to take it, the question of what to do with it assumed a practical importance it had not previously possessed. Leading personalities such as Ian Smuts of South Africa, Winston Churchill, and of course Balfour, all continued

the nineteenth-century tradition of sympathizing with the return of the
Jews to their ancient homeland. Lloyd George himself once told Mrs.
Rothschild that the Biblical place names the Zionists were always
bringing up meant far more to him than those of the towns Britain's
armies were fighting for on the Western Front. Weizmann, he later
wrote, would go down in history as a second Nehemiah, the man who
delivered the Jews from Babylonian captivity.

Though Zionism at the time was hardly a major political movement, still its support was considered worth having. Coached by Herbert Samuel, the Jewish former home secretary, and assisted by Lord
James Rothschild, who came up with the formula of "a national home,"
Weizmann mobilized his troops and orchestrated a press campaign.
U.S. President Woodrow Wilson was consulted, and finally gave his
consent. When the Balfour Declaration of November 2, 1917, was issued it took the form of a letter to Lord Rothschild. It read as follows:

> Dear Lord Rothschild,
>
> I have much pleasure in conveying to you, on behalf of His
> Majesty's Government, the following declaration of sympathy
> with Jewish Zionist aspirations which has been submitted to,
> and approved by, the Cabinet.
>
> His Majesty's Government view with favor the establish-
> ment in Palestine of a national home for the Jewish people and
> will use their best endeavors to facilitate the achievement of
> this object, it being clearly understood that nothing shall be
> done which may prejudice the civil and religious rights of exist-
> ing non-Jewish communities in Palestine, or the rights and po-
> litical status enjoyed by Jews in any other country.
>
> I should be grateful if you would bring this declaration to
> the knowledge of the Zionist Federation.

"To Build and Be Rebuilt"

While the cabinet deliberated the matter, Weizmann was waiting outside. Told that "it's a boy,"[21] his first reaction was to express disappointment. And scant wonder: Rather than endorsing the principal Zionist

objective, the establishment of a Jewish state, the Declaration carefully avoided the term. Still, perhaps the best measure of what took place next is provided by the fact that when the British completed their conquest at the end of 1918, the number of Jews left in the country can hardly have exceeded sixty thousand. When they pulled down their flag thirty years later there were over six hundred thousand—ten times as many.

Yet there was more to Zionism than simply gathering as many Jews as possible in the Land of Israel. Right from the start, it also aimed at carrying out a far-reaching social transformation. Beginning in the mid-nineteenth century many European Jews engaged in self-criticism, often to the point where it was tantamount to self-hatred. Jews, wrote the German-Jewish industrialist, government official, and statesman Walter Rathenau (1867–1922) in 1897, had an "un-athletic build . . . narrow shoulders . . . clumsy feet . . . [and a] sloppy, rounded shape" that turned them into a "laughing stock."[22] To paraphrase Bialik, instead of working, they studied. Instead of earning their livings, they begged; instead of fighting back when attacked, they hid in "shitholes," suffered their wives to be raped in front of their eyes, and then proceeded to ask the rabbis whether they might still sleep with them.[23] Far too many of them were active in trade, especially petty trade. The outcome was an "inverted pyramid" made up of very few producers at the bottom and lots of *luftmenschen,* literally "air men," desperately struggling to make a living at the top.

As with most stereotypes, this one was part true, part false. After millennia during which they had been scattered, persecuted, pressed into the ghettoes, and banned from many professions, Jews differed considerably both socially and economically from the surrounding gentile society. They lived almost exclusively in towns; earned their daily bread by trade and services; put an extraordinary emphasis on education; and, once changes in the law permitted them to do so, entered the professions in very large numbers. Compared to their neighbors, their "military participation ratio," to use a phrase coined by the sociologist Stanislaw Andreski, was very low. This, in turn, led to such myths as the one that claimed Jews could not ride and that they "abjectly capitulated to every outsider," as one early Zionist put it.[24] Then as now, attempts to use biological criteria to decide who was Jewish came to nothing. Nevertheless, the strength of the myth was demonstrated by the attempts to correct the supposed physical deficiencies.

The term "muscle Zionism" was coined by Max Nordau (1849–1923). A physician, bestselling author, and close friend of Herzl, in 1897 he addressed the First Zionist Congress immediately after Herzl's speech. His words did not fall on deaf ears. Starting around 1900, Jews, who were often excluded from gentile sports clubs, began setting up their own so as to be able to "match themselves against the powerful northern barbarians," as Nordau put it.[25] The clubs were named after Jewish heroes such as the Maccabees and the leader of the last revolt against the Romans, Shimon Bar Kokhba. In 1903, Jewish athletes were invited to the opening ceremony of the Sixth Zionist Congress and gave a demonstration of their prowess. Briefly, in the words of a popular song of the 1920s, Jews did not come to the Land of Israel simply to escape anti-Semitism and build a new homeland. Rather, they themselves were to be rebuilt, transformed from what they half believed they were into what they hoped they would become.

In building their nation, the Zionists were greatly assisted by the change from Ottoman to British rule that took place in 1917–1918. True, the series of agreements in 1919–1923 which created the Palestine Mandate and was finally ratified by the League of Nations did not meet Zionists' aspirations in every respect. In particular, nothing was said concerning the Jews' historical right to the land. A Jewish "Agency," elected by Zionists all over the world, was "recognized as a public body for the purpose of advising and co-operating with the Administration of Palestine in such . . . matters as may affect the establishment of the Jewish National Home";[26] however, the language used left no doubt that the "Administration" had no intention of relinquishing control. With respect to the Zionists' final goal—establishing a state—His Majesty's Government went so far as to inform Weizmann that, if he persisted, they would refuse the Mandate.[27] Nor were the Zionists satisfied when Churchill, in his capacity as colonial secretary, redrew the country's borders in 1921–1922. He left out the entire area east of the Jordan, which later became the Kingdom of Transjordan. What remained were approximately 10,600 square miles—"from Metula to the Negev and from the sea to the desert," as the anthem of the first full-time Jewish fighting force, Palmach, was to put it in the 1940s.

The first high commissioner of the Mandate (1920–1925) was Herbert Samuel. For the Jews he was a good choice, but the Arabs saw his appointment as a deliberate insult. In 1923 he tried to hold country-wide elections for a consultative assembly that might one day develop into a legislative. However, the plan fell victim to differences between Jews and Arabs and could never be implemented. From that time to the present, any Arab leader in and out of the country who was suspected of cooperating with the Jews promptly put his life at risk. The list of those who were assassinated is a long one: Jordan's King Abdullah I (1951), Egypt's President Anwar Sadat (1981), Lebanon's President Bachir Gemayel (1982). . . . Perhaps more by default than by design, the outcome was a sort of benevolent totalitarianism. At the top was the high commissioner, who in turn reported to the colonial secretary in London. He was supported by an appointed council made up of senior civil servants, all of whom were British. Farther down, the administration was largely staffed by natives, some Arab, some Jewish.

Most British officials never really felt at home there. They called the Jews "towels," after the prayer shawls, and the Arabs "pots," after the fez, or Turkish headgear. Mostly they socialized among themselves. If an official attended a Jewish concert or watched an Arab football game, word would immediately spread that he favored either one side or the other; the Jews in particular had a reputation of mixing up politics with everything. Still, the achievements of the Mandatory authorities were impressive. After the first few years a balanced budget was established, based on a currency linked to the second-most important one on Earth, the pound sterling. A fairly well-paid, hence honest, administration and judiciary replaced the corrupt Ottoman ones. Efforts were made to exploit natural resources such as the potassium of the Dead Sea. The first power plant, located south of the Sea of Galilee, started operating in 1930 and was soon followed by others.

The fact that the Land of Israel is located midway between the old British colonies in Cyprus and Egypt and the newly acquired ones in Transjordan and Iraq helped. Slowly a modern infrastructure developed, including a telecommunications network, airfields, and a deep-water port in Haifa. By 1936 the tonnage the port handled exceeded that of all other east Mediterranean harbors combined, Alexandria aside; it also served as the terminal of a pipeline that brought oil all the way from Iraq. That the Arab population benefited greatly from these measures is proved by the fact that its size doubled between 1918 and 1948. Child mortality was cut from one in three to one in six, and growing prosperity attracted thousands of immigrants from the neighboring countries.

Still, there can be no question but that the principal beneficiaries of the Mandate were the Jews. Socially and economically they were modern. Proportionally six times as many adult Jewish males as Arab ones could read; indeed, the Jewish literacy rate in the Land of Israel was higher than that of several European countries. Excluding brochures, between 1923 and 1931 the number of new Hebrew-language books on the market exceeded that of Arabic ones by a hundred to one, no less. Being modern, the Jews ran their local government and their community as a whole on democratic principles. Backing them was the moral, political, and economic support of millions of Jews throughout the world. By 1936 the total raised and spent by the Zionist Organization was estimated at 90 million British pounds; in local terms this was a fabulous sum. Under such circumstances it was inevitable that they should pull ahead, and pull ahead they did. As we shall see, when the great clash with the local Arabs (the term "Palestinians" was still far in the future) came, the latter were no match for their neighbors.

Now as before, the key factor on which everything depended was immigration. The number of families allowed entry was fixed at 16,500 a year. Until the mid-1930s, when the reality or threat of Nazi persecution increased the pressure, this was far more than the number that actually arrived; as shown by the case of David Ben Gurion, who brought in his widowed sister and her children by claiming his sister was the wife of someone already in the country. The fact that families and not individuals formed the basic unit left room for interesting combinations. Immigrants who did not have sufficient means of their own had to be vouched for by the Jewish Agency, which thus acquired important powers in deciding whom to admit and whom to leave out. Especially during the 1930s, this often caused preference to be given to the young, the healthy, the well educated, and those who had some "practical" profession that might be useful in building the country—at the expense of everybody else.

The period from 1919 to 1926 saw the third and the fourth immigration waves, of which the former was again motivated by pogroms. The total number of immigrants may have been as high as thirty-five thousand, of whom about two-thirds stayed. Like their predecessors, most of the new arrivals originated in Eastern Europe, especially Russia (whose gates were not yet closed), Romania, Poland, and the Baltic countries. Among them, too, were some dedicated socialists who hoped "to redeem the people, nay the whole of humanity"[28] by hard work and a communal lifestyle; it was they who set up most of the moshavim, including the famous one at Nahalal, near Haifa, where Moshe Dayan grew up. However, the fourth wave differed from their predecessors in that they included, if not the wealthy—the truly wealthy seldom choose to live in underdeveloped countries—at least some of the relatively well to do. Most settled in Tel Aviv, Haifa, and Jerusalem, which was rapidly adding suburbs outside the ancient walls.

These newcomers made their livings as handymen, artisans, shopkeepers, small businessmen, teachers, "clerks" (anybody who could wield a pencil was called a clerk), and lawyers; whereas, around 1900, the Land did not yet have a single Jewish lawyer, the time was to come when, on a per capita basis, Israel would have more members of that noble profession than any other country. Thanks in part to the infusion of foreign capital, new institutions shot out of the ground, such as shops (in 1919 Tel Aviv had just one; six years later there were hundreds); coffeehouses; movie houses; theaters; restaurants; hotels; truck, bus, and taxi companies; newspapers and magazines; and schools. One such school was the Hebrew University of Jerusalem, which was established in 1925 on land purchased especially for that purpose during World War I.

The period 1927–1933 was marked by an economic depression, but thereafter prosperity resumed and, with it, immigration. Between 1933 and 1936 another 175,000 people entered the Land of Israel. By the time World War II broke out the Jewish population had risen to a little short of half a million, so that Jews formed about a third of the entire population. Furthermore, for the first time, most of the newcomers originated not in Eastern but in Central Europe, primarily Germany. Many of them were also relatively well to do. This in turn was due to the fact that the newly installed Nazi authorities and the Jewish Agency found they had something in common: Both wanted to move as many Jews as possible out of Germany, as soon as possible. Under the terms of an agreement signed by the Zionist Organization's "foreign minister," Haim Arlosoroff, Jews leaving for Eretz Israel could take some of their property with them in the form of German goods. The maximum sum permitted was one thousand British pounds, equal to about twenty-five thousand reichsmarks or five thousand U.S. dollars. Those who had that much were known as "capitalists."

Having enjoyed civic equality since the middle of the nineteenth century, German Jews tended to be both highly assimilated and extremely well educated. Like many of their "Aryan" neighbors, they thought of themselves as the highest *Kulturvolk* of all; had not "their" country produced Goethe, Schiller, Beethoven, and countless other luminaries? In almost every land to which they were driven they looked down on everybody else, stubbornly sticking to their dress, their food, their customs, their language, and even, it was said, their own way of laughing. In time stories about the *yekkes,* a derogatory term apparently meaning either "jacket wearing" or "slightly crazy," who spent their time saying "please, *Herr Doktor;* thank you, *Herr Doktor*" became part and parcel of popular culture. Conversely, the *yekkes'* response to the half-jocular hostility they met was to form their own institutions and communities, including at least one entire neighborhood, Rehavia in Jerusalem, and one entire town, Nahariya in the north, where pre-1933 German culture was preserved better than in Germany itself.

For decades on end, the cultural barriers proved very hard to break. This may explain why immigrants from Germany, for all their excellent education and high professional qualifications, never did very well in politics; they were no match for the Eastern European Jews who ran circles around them. Instead they entered such fields as banking, scholarship—the Hebrew University was largely built on German academic lines—medicine, and the law. Perhaps surprisingly, in view of their reputation as blockheads, another field in which they were to become prominent was the secret services. This in turn was due to the fact that the British during World War II needed German speakers for their own intelligence and counterintelligence services as well as the commando operations they mounted against German targets in the eastern

Mediterranean. From these beginnings grew the Israeli intelligence agency Mossad.

Life in the countryside was hard and poor. Agricultural labor and relative isolation left little room for pondering Spinoza. As one song put it, "The morning is for work, noon for a meal, and evening for rest"; this routine was repeated day in, day out. As is so often true, perhaps the worst affected were the women. With nothing but ordinary clothes, few if any beauty aids, and hardly even a feast to mark their wedding day, they worked in- and outside the home, causing them to wilt and look older than they were. By contrast, the towns bore a petit bourgeois character. In them, life was often as stifling as it was provincial. Since people were always comparing their community with the centers of contemporary civilization some of them had come from, town life was also marked by what can only be called an inferiority complex. If writer Meir Shalev's character nicknamed Chez nous a Paris (since she was always referring to life in that great and wonderful city) did not exist in reality, she should have.

For all these shortcomings, the Jewish community during the Mandate was marked by tremendous dynamism and creativity, as it still is. No doubt the need to build almost everything from scratch in a new country contributed to this. Having been despised and humiliated for so long, people were determined to show what they could do. They dared not falter, they dared not fail; there would not be a second chance. The city that personified much of the community's dynamism, creativity, and also—some would say—brash vulgarity was Tel Aviv. In the words of Oskar Neumann (1867–1946), a well-known German traveler who visited in 1933:

> As I step out along the broad, beautiful, and well-tended boulevards . . . with their central lines of palm trees and the flowering front gardens which flank them, with their motley, surging tide of jostling, vigorously gesticulating, suntanned people, with the chaotic mixture of the most varied languages (through which Hebrew emerges even more clearly as the basic melody), with the hum of motors, the car horns and all the richly nuanced sounds of pulsating life; as my eye wanders over the more or less beautiful and occasionally really ugly

tasteless forms of this stylistic Babel . . . [one is reminded of]
that question . . . one has heard over and over in Europe, in
lectures and at meetings, disparaging and sometimes no
doubt slightly contemptuous: Tel Aviv? Oh dear—a Nalewki
[a Jewish street in Warsaw] on the Mediterranean shore! An
unattractive city with unattractive people and houses and
other unattractive features.[29]

Right from the beginning Tel Aviv was tolerant and open to the
world. In 1924 it held its first international fair; twelve years later it
started building its own, albeit very small, port to take the place of
Jaffa. The contrast with Jerusalem—which lies relatively isolated in its
hills and swarms with people belonging to any number of very diverse,
often fanatical, Jewish and non-Jewish religious sects—could not be
more sharply drawn.

Tel Aviv also differed from Haifa, the third-largest city. First, Haifa's excellent deep-water port soon turned it into a magnet for industry,
including metals, chemicals, petrochemicals, cement, and, for many
years, textiles. This in turn made it into a "red" workers' town and, incidentally, the only one where public transport ran on the Sabbath;
wonder of wonders, it had some buildings four and even five stories
tall. Second, until 1948 Haifa had a large Arab population (which
tended to live close to the shore, whereas the Jews established themselves farther up the mountain). By contrast, Tel Aviv was a city of Jews
built by Jews for Jews, and one they had almost entirely to themselves.
It was a place where they could behave, or misbehave, as they pleased.

Between Tel Aviv, whose secular inhabitants preferred to work
in the services, and Jerusalem, whose secular inhabitants also preferred the services (whereas Orthodox residents preferred not to work
at all), the attempt to invert the "inverted pyramid" and turn Jews into
primary producers was not a great success. People were always complaining that the "miserable occupations characteristic of the Pale of
Settlement"[30] were being replicated. This complaint was not without
foundation. In 1939, the Jewish community in the Land of Israel had
the highest proportion of tertiary workers in the world.[31] The outcome,
a chronic balance-of-payments problem, could only be managed by *shnorr*
(begging).

Dismayed by the failure to build a proper "proletarian" society, Ben Gurion once called Tel Aviv "Nineveh," though this did not prevent him from building a house in the city and leading a comfortable life in it. The part of the population that corresponded most closely to the desired stereotype was that of the countryside in general, and that of the collective settlements in particular. The settlements did produce the muscular, calloused, and bronzed types earlier Zionists had dreamed of. However, at no time did their inhabitants represent more than a fifth of the total population. The towns, too, had some workers, mainly in construction and transportation. However, the exceedingly small size of most enterprises meant that a powerful feeling of class solidarity could not develop.

It was all the more remarkable, therefore, that for many years the dominant ideology was socialist; in fact, this remained the case until the mid-1980s. Probably the main reason for this was that the community was not, after all, self-governing. In the absence of a government, the most important institution was the Labor Federation, or Histadrut; but then, the term "labor federation" itself yields a false image. Normally unions are voluntary associations of workers, more or less protected by the law, that represent their members vis-à-vis employers. Not so Histadrut, which also acted as the largest employer. It founded and ran banks; factories; department stores; construction, transportation, and marketing companies; pension funds; insurance funds; hospitals, clinics; schools; newspapers and magazines; cultural associations; and sport clubs. It built entire neighborhoods and populated them with its members. No sooner was it established than it even started its own embryonic armed force known as Hagana (Defense).

The hydralike presence of Histadrut sometimes created curious situations. For example, the thousands of workers who filled the streets on May 1 each year never quite knew whom they were supposed to demonstrate against; this was another reason why a true "proletarian" spirit could not develop. In the early 1950s there were even occasions when the state borrowed from Histadrut to meet its obligations. The system put great power into the hands of the party hacks who ran the federation and who popular wisdom claimed could be recognized by their habit of drinking endless cups of tea during working hours. As

employers, it was they who decided who would get a job, in what part
of the country, at what task, on what conditions, and for what pay. As
marketers (the collective settlements were obliged to sell their produce
solely through them), they were able to dominate entire communities
and even to destroy recalcitrant individuals. Often Histadrut would
decide, by means fair or foul, what neighborhoods people would live
in, what health care and pensions they would receive, what schools
their children would attend, and so many other things as to make one's
head spin. As late as the 1960s, official identification documents issued
to immigrants included several pages left blank for Histadrut functionaries to put their stamps in.

The second important institution that the community developed
was the Vaad Leumi, or Jewish National Council. First elected in 1920,
its original purpose was to represent the community vis-à-vis the Mandatory authorities and also when it came to dealing with the Arabic
community. In 1927, after years of arduous negotiations with those authorities, it acquired the right to levy voluntary taxes; this brought about
a change in its activities, which were increasingly directed inward even
as the Jewish Agency took over responsibility for foreign relations.
During the 1930s it assumed responsibility for such fields as education,
health, social welfare, and religious services to the population. Later,
departments for physical training—also in view of the coming war—
culture, and press and information were added. After the establishment of the state some of its departments were turned into ministries.
In fact, it functioned as a state within a state.

At the top of the bustling, rapidly changing, ever growing community stood David Grün, aka David Ben Gurion. In 1896, at the age of
ten, he heard that "the Messiah had come. He is in Vienna, has a black
beard, and his name is Herzl."[32] Ten years later he moved to the Land
of Israel, spent some time working in agriculture, and studied law in
Constantinople, but did not take his degree. In 1915 he was one of
those whom Jamal Pasha sent into exile. He went to New York, where
he met and married his wife, Paula. She always called him by his surname; possibly because at one point he was unfaithful to her, for much
of his life she guarded him like a she-dragon. Having joined one of the
Jewish battalions that were then forming in the United States, he went

to London and from there to Egypt. After his discharge he returned to the Land of Israel, where he and his "Bolshevik" comrade Yitzhak Ben Zvi founded Histadrut. In 1921, following the first general elections held by that organization, he became its secretary general.

Physically Ben Gurion was of small stature with exceptionally short legs and a powerful torso. In his later years he added a considerable paunch, which was balanced by a truly leonine head and a famous white mane. Psychologically he was something of a tin-pot dictator, resolute—he won many a debate by sheer stamina—and possessed of an elephantine memory that never forgot or forgave. He could also be egocentric to the point of rudeness; hating small talk, he once greeted a visitor who had come for a chat with the words, "chat, chat." In addition to drafting his own speeches, throughout his life he wrote prolifically about Jewish history, Zionism, and socialism. Like many Eastern European Jews who grew up in ethnically mixed areas, he had mastered several languages, including Hebrew, Polish, English, and a smattering of Latin and Turkish. Late in life he started learning ancient Greek so as to study Plato in the original; no doubt he fancied himself the philosopher king. Yet to Amos Oz, the future writer who met Ben Gurion in 1955 when he was at the height of his power, it seemed that Ben Gurion had only two ideas, namely, (A) that there should be a Jewish state, and (B) that he should head it.

Thanks in part to the proportional system of representation, itself made inevitable by the fact that the community was a scattered minority, right from the start the Jewish community in the Land of Israel was blessed with any number of political parties. For a long time most of them had the word *poalim* (workers) as part of their title. Professing some form of socialism, they were secular in character. The members of those on the extreme left were not always above mounting a militant campaign against anything that smacked of Jewish traditionalism. Some of them provocatively worked on the Sabbath. Others demonstratively ate pork; still others launched occasional attacks on Orthodox youths and cut off their sidelocks. Yet in claiming that religion was the opium of the people Marx did not have the last word. Perhaps the idea that religion and socialism could go together—there are even some religious kibbutzim—was one of the more original contributions that Zionism made to world culture.

This is not to say that all religious Jews, let alone all the Jews now living in the Land of Israel, were socialists. There were the strictly Orthodox (some of whom intermarried almost exclusively and boycotted any kind of elections) who rejected the state in the name of religion, and the national-religious who supported it for the same reason. There were the "general" Zionists, the nonaligned Zionists, the communists, and the "Revisionists"—right-wing antilabor Zionists—to mention but a few. All jostled with one another, merged with one another, and fell out with one another in a game of musical chairs as complicated and vicious as that played at any other time and place. It may even have included at least one political murder, that of Haim Arlosoroff. In 1933 he was shot, execution style, on a Tel Aviv beach. The community's leadership was quick to blame the Revisionists, yet in reality the mystery of his death has never been solved.

Ben Gurion's own party, Mapai (Mifleget Poalei Eretz Israel, the Workers' Party of the Land of Israel) was formed in 1930 by merging two earlier parties, both of which also claimed to represent workers. From then until 1977 it and its descendants ruled first the Jewish National Council and Histadrut, then the World Zionist Organization, and finally the State of Israel without interruption; usually it did so in partnership with other left-wing parties, religious parties, and "general Zionist" (meaning nonsocialist bourgeois) parties. The main opposition, consisting of the Revisionists, was equally long lived. Their founder and first leader was Zeev (Vladimir) Jabotinsky (1880–1940). Russian born like most of the rest, by trade he was a journalist. He spent most of World War I in London, where he played a key role in setting up the Jewish battalions. He himself gave the example, donned khaki, and proudly carried the rank of a British lieutenant. As a linguist and writer he was at least Ben Gurion's equal. As a speaker, he was superior.

Above all else, Jabotinsky was a strong nationalist. As he once wrote: "I reserve my love for my own people alone, while treating the rest with cool courtesy."[33] Insisting that the entire Land of Israel belonged solely to the Jewish people, he refused to recognize the arrangements whereby the districts east of the Jordan River had been detached from it. He also rejected socialism and everything it stood for, including not least the collectivist settlements that formed one of the main pillars of Mapai's rule. Instead he emphasized liberal democracy and economic free enterprise, combining them with certain forms of ceremony, hierarchy, and discipline (his followers wore black shirts) that made his rivals accuse him, not entirely without reason, of militarism. Numerically he may have commanded the allegiance of perhaps 20 percent of the Jewish voters in the Land of Israel, whereas among Zionists abroad the figure was higher. In 1935 he took his supporters out of the Zionist Organization altogether. They set up a rival one, predictably called the New Zionist Organization, and only returned to the fold in 1946. Ben Gurion hated him during his life and continued the vendetta after his death. He even refused to have Jabotinsky's remains buried in the Land of Israel, with the result that they were brought there only after Ben Gurion was no longer prime minister.

Whereas World War II meant disaster for much of the globe, the Land of Israel experienced a vast boom. To be sure, Italian and German aircraft dropped a few bombs on Haifa and the summer of 1942 brought the possibility of an invasion by Rommel's Africa Korps perilously near. Yet in the end the threat from the air turned out to be negligible, and the invasion never materialized. As also happened in Canada, Australia, and South Africa, much of the boom in the Land of Israel was due to the disruption of foreign trade. Local industry, assisted by a five-fold increase in the number of British and Commonwealth troops stationed in the country, leaped at the opportunity; manufacturing of processed foods, textiles, cigarettes, and metals all benefited very greatly, as did construction. In each of the years between 1939 and 1945 the Jewish economy grew by 11.2 percent. This was four times as fast as the British economy did and a little faster even than the miraculous American economy. Real net domestic product went up 80 percent; manufacturing output increased by 133 percent. Since growth centered on industry it favored the Jews; the gap between them and the Arabs kept growing. On the eve of the 1948 War Jews owned 90 percent of all bank deposits. On a per capita basis, Jewish communities commanded ten times the resources of their Arab equivalents.

Zionism had its origins in the Diaspora. During the first four decades or so of its existence as an organized movement, it was the Diaspora that called the shots; even most of the parties into which the Land of Israel's community was divided were simply appendages of the ones abroad. Still, as early as the 1930s things started to change. One reason for this was because Russian Jewry, which had provided many of the Land's original leaders and almost all of its immigrants, was effectively isolated behind what was to become known as the Iron Curtain. From the early 1920s to the collapse of the Soviet Union, this community could hardly make its voice heard. At the same time a new and virulent form of anti-Semitism, emanating from Nazi Germany and spreading in all directions, was beginning to put the very existence of European Jewry at risk. Of course, the community in the Land of Israel could not compete with the Diaspora in terms of either numbers or the economic resources at its disposal. However, it was much better organized; thanks largely to the peculiar nature of Histadrut and its myriad branches, it was already beginning to bind its members with some of the coercive powers of a state in the making.

The shift in relative power became evident in 1935, the year when Ben Gurion was elected chairman of the Jewish Agency, the central organ of the World Zionist Organization. Up to that point he had been the semiofficial leader of perhaps 5 percent of the Jewish people who, heeding the call, left their homes to build a new existence in the Land of Israel. From that point on he was formally the one in charge of working toward the ultimate Zionist goal of a Jewish commonwealth. While that goal had never been a great secret, it was officially proclaimed for the first time at the Zionist Biltmore Conference in May 1942. And not a moment too soon; as the Holocaust was approaching its zenith, thousands of refugees were desperately trying to enter the Land of Israel only to be turned away by the British Mandatory authorities. To be sure, the community in the Land remained dependent on its Diaspora supporters for immigrants, funding, and political influence. On the other hand, Ben Gurion increasingly addressed Jewish-Zionist leaders abroad not as a supplicant but as an equal. They might conduct propaganda, raise money, and lobby. But he was already getting into a position where he could mobilize and command, causing Weizmann, as president of the World Zionist Movement, to complain that "we're being reduced to an embassy."[34]

Clearly half a century of enterprise—beset by all the usual problems that attend a young and struggling political movement as well as difficulties unprecedented in the annals of mankind, which has never seen anything similar—was beginning to yield fruit. Before it could do so, though, it still had to undergo the ultimate test—that of war, with all it entails.

"By Blood and Fire . . ."

The myth concerning the "cowardly" Diaspora Jew and the need to create a new, heroic type accompanied Zionism practically from its beginning. Also practically from the beginning, it was sometimes necessary to resort to violence in order to prevent "the tent-dwelling sons of Ismail" from "destroying the seed and uprooting the vineyards," as one nineteenth-century Zionist tract put it.[35] Thus, ideology and day-to-day life joined forces, creating an explosive mixture. As one of the earliest settlers, Jacob Cohen, wrote in a famous poem, "By blood and fire was Judea lost—by blood and fire it will rise again."

By the end of World War I the scattered clashes between Jews and Arabs that had accompanied the Zionist enterprise right from the start were well on their way to changing from socioeconomic to nationalist in character. Arab intellectuals in the towns, mainly Jaffa and Haifa, began using the press to warn against the Jews. They used every possible argument: from the claim that the Balfour Declaration was illegal in international law to the idea that Jews were "communists," "anarchists," "parasites," and "enemies of God"; and from the notion that the Land of Israel could not accommodate more people to protests against Jewish women who, as the mufti of Jerusalem once told a foreign visitor, were "shattering" Arab morals by running around in shorts. These, however, were no more than secondary issues. The real cause behind the hostility was the claim that "Palestine is a purely Arab land surrounded on all sides by purely Arab lands."[36] From then to the present day, the argument has not changed one iota.

Since the riots that broke out in 1919–1921 lacked any central direction, it is impossible to say what role each of these arguments played. Both in the towns and in the countryside, probably the vast majority of participants had never heard either of them or of those who enunciated them. All they knew was that the Jews, or *yahud,* were coming; also that the Koran has many bad things to say about them, and that they were to blame for everything and anything, including, one Arab official claimed, the fact that fathers were asking such high prices for their daughters that "Arabs in Nablus are no longer able to find wives in their own town."[37] Instigated by clerics and sheiks, they mounted attacks on Jewish settlements over much of the country. On both sides, people were shot, had their skulls crushed with blunt instruments, or were cut to pieces with knives. Houses and agricultural equipment were destroyed, and property of every sort was looted.

Some Jewish settlements had to be temporarily evacuated. In one of those, Tel Hai, Yosef Trumpeldor, a one-armed veteran of the Russo-Japanese War and a recent immigrant, allegedly died with the Hebrew equivalent of *dulce et decorum est . . .* "it is sweet and right to die for one's country" on his lips. He thus provided the community with a martyr whose memory was kept for decades thereafter; every Israeli has seen the monument that was erected in his honor, in the form of a roaring lion, or at least a picture thereof. Other settlements survived only thanks to determined British military intervention. Mixed towns such as Haifa and Jaffa also witnessed large-scale disturbances. The last outbreak took place in Jerusalem's Jewish quarter in November 1921. By the time British forces reached the scene and restored order, rampaging Arab mobs had killed five Jews and wounded forty.

Midway through these disturbances, Hagana was founded as an arm of Histadrut. At the helm was a five-member steering committee. The two most important members were Eliyahu Golomb (1893–1945), a highly cultured organizer who headed the Tel Aviv branch and acted as a kind of "minister of defense," and Levi Shkolnik (later, Eshkol, 1895–1969) who represented the collective settlements. Partly because many of these settlements were isolated, and partly because the British could not be everywhere, the latter played a major role in the community's protomilitary endeavors. The first de facto chief of staff, who was also the only full-time activist, was twenty-eight-year-old Yosef Hecht. Like the rest, he got what little military experience he had in 1917–1918 when he served with the Jewish battalions of the British army; so strict was the secrecy with which he surrounded himself that his name does not even appear in Hagana's *Who Is Who*.

At the time, the scale of "operations," if that is the right word, of which Hagana was capable was almost ridiculously small. In Jerusalem ten of its members, armed with pistols, took up positions and held off an Arab mob for as much as forty minutes. One of these members was Jabotinsky; for his efforts he was sentenced to fifteen years in prison, though he was released after serving less than one year. In Tel Aviv, in order to defend against attacks from Jaffa, all Hagana had available were eight rifles, twenty pistols, and five hand grenades. To escape the eyes of the authorities, these weapons had to be buried in the dunes. When the time for action came they could not be found. Ultimately, the town was saved only by the arrival of fifteen Jewish policemen in training. Alerted by telephone, they deserted their camp near Ramle, were issued ancient Turkish rifles by the British official in charge of the port of Jaffa, and marched to the rescue; for this, they were later dismissed.

Their fate, as well as that of the weapons earmarked for the defense of Tel Aviv, illustrates a wider problem that was to bedevil all Jewish attempts to set up an armed force, right down to the end of the Mandate. In the Ottoman Middle East, though weapon permits might have been few, weapons were plentiful. Absent a powerful police force capable of maintaining order, every Bedouin tent, every rural house, and many urban dwellings had them; upper-class households were veritable arsenals. Coming from long-established urban communities, the Jews in the Land of Israel had no such tradition and had to start from scratch. As long as the Ottomans were around they did well enough—though there was constant skirmishing, there were no countrywide disturbances and no major massacres. Later, though, they found themselves opposed at every step by the much more efficient British authorities. The latter permitted isolated settlements to store only so many weapons with only so many rounds of ammunition in case of an emergency. That aside, they systematically prosecuted anyone who had them— with the result that the Jewish community was in some ways less capable of taking care of itself than before.

By the time the next wave of riots broke out in 1929, Hagana may have had a few thousand members. In Haifa, for example, they numbered three hundred out of a Jewish population of sixteen thousand, virtually all part-timers. However, only about half could be provided with arms of any sort. Training, carried out by sergeants and corporals who had gained some experience by serving in foreign armies, had to take place in the members' free time and in secret. Weapons—mostly rifles and pistols, but already including the occasional machine gun—were acquired in Central Europe where, in the aftermath of World War I, they were plentiful and cheap. Next they were smuggled into the country by sea or by land; favorite hiding places were earthmoving equipment and the double walls of refrigerators. The weapons ended up in so-called *slikkim,* or hideaways, where tinkers did their best to maintain them and restore deficient ones to working order.

Such, roughly, was the state of Hagana when the Second Arab Uprising broke out in 1929. This time the focus was in Jerusalem, where Jews and Arabs had long been bickering over the former's right to pray at the Wailing Wall. After a few days in which the opposing sides demonstrated, threw rocks at each other, and pulled knives on each other, massive riots got under way on August 23 under the usual rallying cry *itbach al yahud* (butcher the Jews). From Jerusalem they spread over much of the country; so small was the number of British troops immediately available that they were powerless to react. On August 24 a mob armed with edged weapons put an end to the ancient Jewish community in Hebron, massacring dozens; people were set on fire with kerosene, tortured to death, castrated, and raped. At Beer Tuvia, far in the south, the women were already begging to be given poison pills when three British aircraft appeared and saved the situation by firing their machine guns. Even so, a number of rural settlements had to be abandoned. Only in Tel Aviv and Haifa was Hagana able to hold the line, more or less, though in the latter no fewer than three thousand houses inhabited by Jews had to be temporarily evacuated. Haifa also witnessed the first Jewish counterattack. A bus was commandeered and driven into an Arab market, where its occupants opened fire; a novelty at that time, and a harbinger for much worse to come.

By the end of August the British, having brought in reinforcements from Malta and Egypt, were able to quell the riots, though dealing with small-scale guerrilla warfare in the countryside took longer. In all, 133 Jews and 116 Arabs were killed; 339 and 232, respectively, were wounded. There was, however, an important difference. Almost all the Jewish casualties were the victims of Arab violence. Not so those on the Arab side, most of whom were killed by British fire. Hagana's perceived failure led to much squabbling among the principal Jewish leaders. In the end they compromised by bringing about the forced resignation of Hecht—by no means the last time when the so-called political echelon succeeded in evading responsibility by placing it on the shoulders of the military.

Though Golomb remained as the moving spirit, overall leadership passed from Histadrut to the Jewish Agency. In 1931, after a two-year interregnum, a new chief of staff was appointed in the person of Shaul Avigur. Under him, an attempt was made to transform the organization from a "primitive confederation" of local associations into a country-wide force; not an easy task, given that the work had to be kept secret from the British, who dominated all communications. Abroad, some eight hundred thousand British pounds were collected to rebuild destroyed settlements and provide them with patrol roads, fences, searchlights, and the like. On the whole the money seems to have been well spent. When the next round of hostilities got under way in 1936, not one Jewish settlement had to be evacuated.

Unlike the two previous outbreaks, which were directed almost exclusively against the Jews, the next one was also anti-British and was known to them as the Arab Revolt. The signal was given by the massacre of sixteen Jewish workers in the port of Jaffa in April 1936. As in 1929, the British government's preemptive measures—including censorship and controls over transportation and telecommunications—were unable to prevent the riots from spreading; instead, the Arabs organized a general strike that lasted until October of the same year. Previously, responsibility for security had been in the hands of the Royal Air Force. When its forces proved unable to put down the revolt, which at times was supported by Arab volunteers from Syria and Iraq, London was obliged to bring in an entire division complete with armored cars and some artillery. Its commander, a ruthless, rather eccentric major general by the name of Bernard Law Montgomery, was later to gain fame as Field Marshal Montgomery of Alamein.

Over the next three years the revolt took the form of widespread guerrilla warfare. It cost the lives of about two hundred Britons, four hundred Jews, and as many as five thousand Arabs. As in 1929 almost all of the Arabs were killed by the British, whereas the Jews fell victim to the Arabs. However, the consequences for the two communities could not be more different. To look at the Arabs first, the 1939 British White Paper, which was published by the imperial government in an attempt to end the crisis, went far to revoke the Balfour Declaration. It prohibited further Jewish land purchases in much of the country; limited immigration to fifteen thousand persons a year over five years, after which it was supposed to end; and even promised the Arabs "evolution towards independence" within ten years.

Yet in other ways the revolt decisively weakened the Arab community. Economically the community reached the end of its tether as agriculture and trade were disrupted and thousands of houses, including a whole quarter of Jaffa, were blown up either by way of punitive measures or in order to create fields of fire. Politically the community lost the one figure that might have acted as its supreme leader; namely, the mufti of Jerusalem, Haj Amin Husseini (1895–1974). He was arrested, escaped, and went into exile; World War II found him in Berlin, where he met Hitler in an attempt to get help for his people. His successors, to the extent that he had any, never even came close to setting up a central authority. So bad did things become that some of the more farsighted, better-off Arab-Palestinian families started leaving. Partly because they were being blackmailed for money by the rebels, and partly in well-founded fear of things to come.

For the Jewish community, the consequences were just the opposite. To be sure, the White Paper came as a cruel blow, and Ben Gurion promised to fight it tooth and nail. However, on a day-to-day level the situation was entirely different. During the revolt itself a number of new settlements of the type known as "stockade and tower" (after the prefabricated fortifications that formed their center) went up on land previously purchased by the Zionists, further strengthening their hold on certain areas in Galilee and the Negev. Another outcome was the decoupling of the Jewish economy from the Arab one. If anything could persuade Jewish employers to give up their ties with the latter, it was the revolt and the slaughter that accompanied it. Previously "Hebrew work" had often been little more than a patriotic slogan. Now it became an absolute necessity, and indeed, even the Histadrut's children's newspaper warned its readers to "tell mother she should always

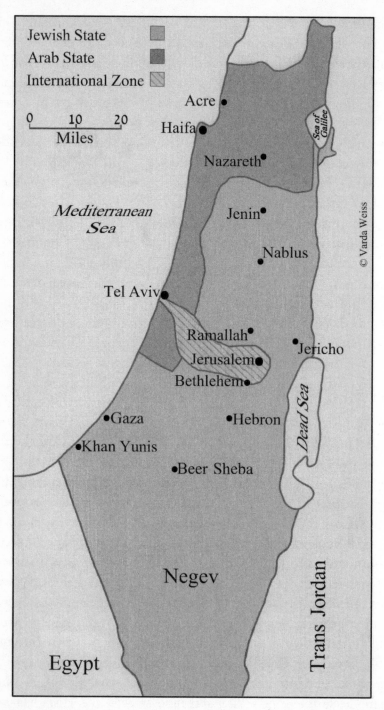

Peel Commission Partition Plan, 1937

buy products of the Hebrew economy."[38] The separation in turn made the gap between the two communities grow even faster than before, hastening the day when the Jews would be able to do entirely without the Arabs.

The revolt also initiated a period of limited military cooperation with the British, during which Hagana was able to set up new units and gain much-needed experience. By 1939 the organization could boast fifteen thousand members, of whom two hundred to three hundred worked for it full time. It was funded partly by the Jewish Agency, partly by Histadrut. Its magazines held six thousand rifles, sixty light machine guns, twenty-four thousand hand grenades, twelve thousand rifle grenades, and a million rounds of small-arms ammunition. In May 1941, in the face of a threatening German invasion, cooperation between Hagana and the British was resumed. A few dozen Jewish soldiers from the Land of Israel spearheaded the invasion of Vichy Syria; Hagana was even permitted to establish the nucleus of a mobile striking force, Palmach. When the German threat receded, the British lost no time in withdrawing their support and demanding that the force be dismantled. They could not be everywhere, however, and a way was found to keep the force in existence by basing it in the kibbutzim, where Palmachniks spent two weeks alternately working and training. Though British intelligence was aware of what was going on, there was not much they could do about it.

While Hagana was becoming stronger, the outbreak of World War II also created a situation where the British, desperate for manpower, agreed to take members of the Jewish community into their own armed forces. Eventually some thirty thousand, one in twenty of the entire Jewish population, served. Most did so as individuals; however, a few thousand were formed into the Jewish Brigade, whose base was in Egypt. Well aware that the expertise they were providing might one day be turned against them, the British dragged their feet. Consequently the Brigade, as an organized unit, saw action only during the last weeks of the war. Still, in and out of it, several thousand were introduced to military life, underwent training, and participated in combat. The most senior soldier of all was Haim Laskov (1919–1983), who made it to the rank of major and, in 1958, was to become the Israel Defense Forces chief of staff. Others served in the Royal Army, Navy, and Air

Force. Discharged into civilian life after the war's end, they joined Hagana, bringing with them invaluable experience such as very few Palestinian Arabs at the time possessed.

Another development during the period from 1936 to 1939 was the establishment by some of Jabotinsky's followers of a rival paramilitary organization called Etzel (Irgun Tzvai Leumi, National Military Organization). Its early operations were meant as retaliation against the Arabs. Individuals were waylaid and shot; markets were bombed in a terror campaign as cruel and indiscriminate as the one the Arabs themselves were waging, though the scale was much smaller. Later, as the revolt subsided, things changed. Etzel started directing its attacks against government targets such as telephone and electricity wires, railways, and, on one occasion, a Jerusalem radio station that Etzel itself occupied for a few hours. The outbreak of World War II caused the organization to divide. While Etzel suspended operations, a minority of its members, led by Avraham ("Yair") Stern, refused to do so. Instead they formed a breakaway faction known as Lehi (Lohamei Herut Israel), Israel's Freedom Fighters.

In 1942, Stern was killed in a shootout with the police. He left behind a poem, "Anonymous Soldiers," which said that "duty only ends with death"; his followers took up the message. As the war drew to its end during the second half of 1944, Lehi and Etzel began a classic terrorist campaign aimed at driving the British out. In August of that year Harold MacMichael, the departing high commissioner, narrowly escaped assassination. Two months later, two Lehi members killed Britain's resident minister in Cairo, Lord Moyne. Police officers and army camps were attacked (like so many other insurgents, Etzel in particular took some of its weapons from its enemies), communications cut, oil refineries set ablaze, railways demolished, trains derailed, air bases bombed, and cafés catering to British personnel blown up. Operations peaked in July 1946 when Etzel planted a bomb in Jerusalem's King David Hotel, one of whose wings housed the British Criminal Investigation Division. Almost a hundred people died, many of them Jews; if anything could show that the British no longer controlled the country, this was it. In two years, their losses amounted to 125 dead and 259 wounded.

From his position as de facto Jewish community leader, Ben Gurion watched the campaign unfold with mixed feelings. As he never tired of telling his British interlocutors, he fully agreed with the Revisionists' idea that the Mandate should be brought to an end and a Jewish state established as soon as possible. On the other hand, he wanted to rein in the insurgents. In part, this was because he was afraid that their activities would provoke the British into countermeasures as harsh as those they had used to break the Arab Revolt in 1936–1939. However, it was also because, as "dissidents," they refused to obey his orders; he called them "Jewish Nazis" and "a bubonic plague" and sought to eradicate them.[39] In the winter of 1944–1945 he directed Golomb to use Hagana units and personnel, specifically including Moshe Dayan (who emerged as a commander who would take orders from Ben Gurion even if they went against his principles), to arrest Etzel members. Some were tortured to make them betray their comrades, and over a hundred were turned over to the British. Yet the Season, as it was called, lasted only a few months before public opinion forced Ben Gurion to call a halt. In October 1945 Hagana, Etzel, and Lehi even signed an agreement that set up a united "Front of the Revolt."

From then on the three organizations divided the uprising among themselves. Hagana specialized in bloodless operations such as bringing in illegal immigrants from other countries in spite of the British blockade; here and there it also attacked the camps in which captive immigrants were being held. In just one night in June 1946, its strike force, Palmach, blew up ten of the eleven bridges linking the country to the neighboring ones, causing heavy damage. By contrast, Etzel engaged in a classic insurgency, which included killing and wounding British personnel, whereas Lehi, a very small organization with but a few dozen activists, specialized in what would later become known as "targeted" assassinations. In practice these distinctions were not always kept. Several Hagana operations went wrong, leading to the deaths of British troops who tried to intervene. Etzel carried out assassinations, whereas Hagana had a special unit that executed Jewish "traitors." Both Hagana and Etzel had agents in Cyprus, where seventeen thousand illegal immigrants were being held, as well as in Europe, where they recruited personnel, purchased arms, and, in the case of Etzel, tried to sabotage British targets.

Including civilian personnel who worked for the military, the British had one hundred thousand men in the country—in proportion to the population in which the insurgents had their roots, this was one of the highest ratios ever. Provided with everything from armored cars to aircraft and warships as large as cruisers, and drawing on their vast experience in colonial warfare, they engaged in every known form of what would later become known as counterinsurgency operations, from an air and naval blockade designed to keep out illegal immigrants, to cordoning off entire city quarters, to curfews, mass arrests, and executions. At peak on "Black Saturday," two hundred thousand people in and around Tel Aviv were confined to their homes while three thousand Jewish "leaders" and "instigators" were rounded up simultaneously. All to no avail—in part, no doubt, because the British, considering the Jews a "semi-European race,"[40] never really took off the gloves.

Perhaps more important in the long run, the British government's very strength worked against them. The more successful they were in keeping out illegal immigrants in particular, the easier it was for Zionist propaganda both in the world at large and in Britain itself to present them as a brutal *soldateska* fighting the homeless, the semistarved, and the sick. So effective was this propaganda that Britain's own papers began to speak of "manifest blunder[s]" and "the ultimate stage of lunacy."[41] In the House of Commons, Winston Churchill, an acknowledged expert on such matters, accused the troops of not knowing "how to behave like men."[42] By the end of 1946, the attempt by Field Marshal Montgomery, now serving as chief of the Imperial General Staff, "to smash [the Jews] forever"[43] had clearly failed. The British public was growing tired of the war; against the background of very great postwar economic difficulties, Montgomery was keeping one-tenth of His Majesty's entire armed forces busy at a cost of 40 million pounds a year.

At the end of 1946 the Labor government decided to dump the problem into the lap of the United Nations. Since Jews and Arabs refused to be reconciled, various plans for the partition of the Land had been floating about at least since 1937, only to be vehemently rejected by the latter. In the summer of 1947 the United Nations Special Committee on Palestine (UNSCOP) formulated another such plan and submitted it to the General Assembly. Following an intense lobbying effort by the Jewish Agency, the latter approved it on November 29. The resolution provided for the establishment of two states; Jerusalem, instead of serving as a capital for either or both, was to be internationalized. To the Jewish inhabitants of the country, who welcomed it by dancing in the streets, the decision represented everything they and their ancestors had dreamed about for almost two millennia. Amos Oz, who at that time was eight years old, described how his father, an extremely well-educated library worker, welcomed it by letting out a sound that was half shout, half groan. To the Arab residents, it represented an equally great defeat and the prelude to what, much later, they would call the Disaster, or *Naqba*.

On the very next day, open warfare between the two communities got under way as a Palmach squad patrolling a pipeline in the Negev came under attack and was wiped out. Though few people realized it at the time, in reality the two sides were unequally balanced. On one side there were about six hundred thousand Jews, of whom twenty-seven thousand were Hagana members. Most possessed only rudimentary training and were tied to their towns or settlements. However, four thousand to six thousand members (including perhaps six hundred to nine hundred women) formed part of Palmach, the striking force available for action anywhere in the country. There was a rudimentary military industry, secretly constructed under the noses of the British authorities, capable of repairing weapons as well as manufacturing some small arms, ammunition for them, explosives, and detonators. Medical, logistic, and intelligence services all existed in embryonic form. The chain of command ran from Ben Gurion as chief of the Jewish Agency to Ben Gurion as its minister of defense (he used to say that, with him, the prime minister went to see the minister of defense instead of the other way around) to the chief of staff of the Israeli Defense Forces (IDF), General Yaakov Dori. However, during most of the war Dori was neutralized by illness, so that real command was exercised by his deputy, the brilliant thirty-one-year-old Yigael Yadin.

To be sure, this was not yet a modern army. Even the Palmachniks were only half trained; in Ben Gurion's words, "Our men in the army are good Zionists, but they have yet to become soldiers."[44] Owing to the need to stay away from prying British eyes, few if any officers had commanded as much as a platoon. Since the British were in possession of the ports and would remain so until the end of the Mandate in May 1948, the heavy weapons Hagana agents were busily purchasing abroad

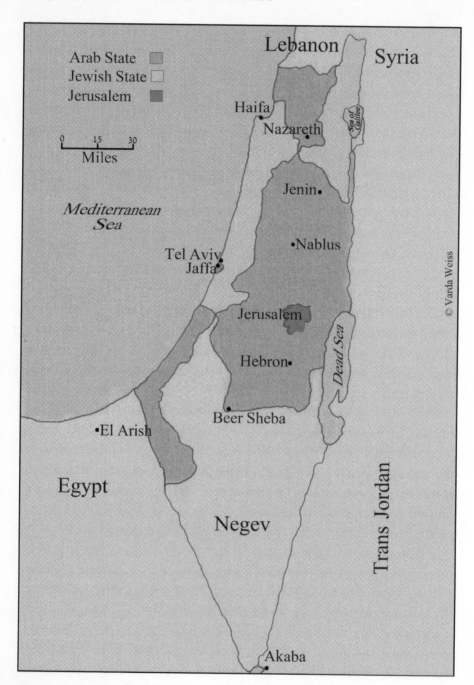

The UN Partition Plan, 1947

could not be imported. Even so, Hagana completely outclassed anything the Arab community could muster. The total Arab population was probably about twice as large as the Jewish one. However, only an estimated ten thousand of its members had received some military training by serving as policemen during the Mandate. In the towns of Jerusalem, Jaffa, and Haifa there were *jihadias,* voluntary associations of "holy" warriors, estimated at two thousand to three thousand men each. As in 1921–1922, 1929, and 1936–1939, the Arabs' greatest strength consisted of the fact that countless house owners had weapons of some kind. However, they had no central command structure, no logistic infrastructure, no intelligence service, no technical experts of any kind, and no mobile striking force.

Under such circumstances it was inevitable that the first phase of the war should consist of the so-called battle of the roads. All over the country, but especially on the slopes of Mount Carmel and on the road leading to Jerusalem, hordes of Arab villagers took up the traditions of 1936–1939 by setting up roadblocks. They shot up first individual vehicles, then convoys that tried to get through; the occupants of those that failed to escape were massacred. This phase lasted until April 1948, when Hagana felt strong enough to go on the offensive. Previously all it had tried to do was to clear the roads so as to enable convoys to get through. Now, for the first time, it started occupying the villages on both sides and demolishing the houses with dynamite. Doing so was necessary in order to open up fields of fire for defense. However, Hagana also made sure the inhabitants—among whom every adult male had to be considered an active fighter—would not come back.

In the same month, the first "major" battle—the total number of participants may have been around ten thousand—was fought against the so-called Arab Salvation Army. This army consisted of Syrian, Transjordanian, and Iraqi volunteers. Its commander was Fauzi Qawuqji, an Iraqi officer who had played a similar role in 1936 when he had come to assist in the revolt against the British. He crossed the Jordan well south of the Sea of Galilee and marched by way of Samaria, where there were no Jewish settlements to stop him. Reaching the southern end of the Valley of Esdraelon, the Arab Salvation Army encountered Palmach units and was forced to retreat to Nazareth. This in turn enabled Hagana and Palmach to occupy numerous towns in the northern part of the country, including Haifa, Acre, Beth Shean, Tiberias, and Safed. In an independent operation farther south, Etzel forces occupied Jaffa. Some of the inhabitants of these towns stayed in place, but most fled to Lebanon, Syria, and the Gaza Strip.

By the end of April, some two thousand Jews and probably far more Arabs had lost their lives. It was not a pretty war; atrocities such as Deir Yassin, where Etzel massacred about a hundred Arab civilians, and the Arab attack on a Jerusalem convoy carrying medical personnel on their way to the Hadassa Hospital on Mount Scopus have remained infamous. In the midst of this bloody butchery the State of Israel was proclaimed. The ceremony was held in Tel Aviv on May 14; this being wartime, only twenty-four out of thirty-seven intended signatories could attend. Ben Gurion read out the Declaration of Independence, whose key passages went as follows:

> The Land of Israel was the birthplace of the Jewish people. Here their spiritual, religious, and political identity was shaped. Here they first attained to statehood. . . .
>
> After being forcibly exiled from their land, the people kept faith with it throughout their Dispersion and never ceased to pray and hope for their return to it and for the restoration of their political freedom.
>
> On November 29, 1947, the United Nations General Assembly passed a resolution calling for the establishment of a Jewish State in Israel, requiring the inhabitants of Israel to take such steps as were necessary on their part for the implementation of that resolution. This recognition by the United Nations of the right of the Jewish people to establish their State is irrevocable. This right is the natural right of the Jewish people to be masters of their own fate, like all other nations, in their own sovereign State.
>
> Thus members and representatives of the Jews of Palestine and of the Zionist movement upon the end of the British Mandate, by virtue of "natural and historic right," and based on the United Nations resolution . . . Hereby declare the establishment of a Jewish state in the Land of Israel to be known as the State of Israel.[45]

On the very next day four armies, belonging to four neighboring states, invaded the country. There they joined the Arab Legion, a British-led Transjordanian force that was already there, and were soon followed by Iraqi units that came all the way from Baghdad.

The Arabs of the Land of Israel never had what it would have taken to wipe out the Jewish community, and by this time they were already well on the way to defeat. By contrast, the invaders represented a formidable threat. Between them they numbered about thirty thousand men; later the total reached sixty-eight thousand. They had artillery, armored cars, some tanks, and aircraft. Fortunately for the Israelis most of the troops, made up of illiterate peasants, were decidedly second-class. They had no common objective and no common command structure. Instead each was trying to beat the rest to parts of the Land of Israel; at the government level, if not the popular one, so little did they care for the Arabs of that Land that they did not even permit the mufti, who was living in Egypt, to recruit troops. Being dependent on their colonial masters, they also suffered from shortages of ammunition. On occasion this reached the point where they stole from each other.

From the Jewish point of view, the most difficult time of all were the first ten days of June. By that time Transjordanian forces had taken East Jerusalem, the Old City included, as well as some Jewish settlements (Gush Etzion) to the south of it. To the west they had penetrated as far as Latrun, a former British police fortress that they occupied and that enabled them to block the road to Jerusalem; but from then on they made no further attempt to extend their conquests. In the south the Egyptians had advanced with two separate armies, one passing through Beer Sheba and Hebron almost as far as Jerusalem and the other taking the coastal road before being brought to a halt at Ashdod, some thirty miles south of Tel Aviv. In the center of the country Iraqi forces passed through Nablus and reached Tul Karem, only some ten miles from the Mediterranean. By contrast, the Syrian and Lebanese forces that invaded Galilee never got very far.

On June 10, the "First Truce" went into effect. To the Israelis, as they were now called, it came like manna from heaven. By that time, the Israel Defense Forces (IDF) had officially taken the place of Hagana. An incident on June 22, when the Etzel ship *Altalena* tried to land a shipment of arms on a Tel Aviv beach, finally enabled Ben Gurion to deal with that organization, which, whatever its merits in driving out the British, he had long experienced as a thorn in his side. He summoned Yitzhak Rabin, then a handsome, freckle-faced twenty-six-year-old Palmach brigade commander who had gained his spurs in the fighting around Jerusalem. At his command, a few artillery rounds were fired at the *Altalena* and it was set ablaze and sunk. Thereupon the organization's leader, Menahem Begin (1913–1992), agreed to dissolve his fighters and have his men join the IDF, leaving Ben Gurion in undisputed control over Israel's armed forces. The process was continued in September–October when the assassination of a UN mediator, Count Folke Bernadotte, by Lehi provided Ben Gurion with the excuse to deal with that organization. It was completed in November when Palmach, which hitherto had operated very much as an army within an army, was dissolved.

By that time, the order for general mobilization that had been issued in December 1947 started bearing fruit. An infrastructure of bases and administrative facilities was stamped out of the ground, enabling tens of thousands to be called up. At peak, in January 1949, the IDF numbered some ninety thousand troops, including eleven thousand women. No sooner did the British leave than heavy weapons, funded by the Zionists abroad and secretly purchased in various countries, started arriving. The list included field artillery, armored cars, half tracks, some tanks, fighter aircraft, and even three World War II vintage heavy bombers. Thus came to an end the days when the Israelis had to face the invading regular forces with nothing but the light weapons that could be acquired or home-manufactured under the vigilant eyes of the Mandatory authorities.

The "ten days'" fighting (July 8–18) from the end of the First Truce to the beginning of the Second Truce were decisive. In the center of the country the two large, Arab-populated cities of Lydda and Ramle were occupied, creating another large wave of refugees who went to what was later to be known as the West Bank. Some thirty miles farther to the south, at Negbah, the last Egyptian attempt to advance in the direction of Tel Aviv was repulsed. From that point on, the initiative passed to the IDF. Only the attempt to capture Latrun failed, but the Israelis solved the problem by building a new road that bypassed it. By the time the Second Truce went into effect, the greatest danger had passed.

The last period of the war started in October and saw the eviction of the Syrian army—the Lebanese had already thrown in the towel and retreated—from almost all the very limited positions it was still holding in the northeast. In the center of the country Israelis and Transjordanians faced one another with hardly a shot exchanged. Apparently King Abdullah I had never intended to extend his conquests beyond the area that the United Nations had allocated for an Arab state. The scales having turned, all he wanted was to keep his gains; in this he was largely successful, though the Israelis did force him to give up some narrow strips of land along the borders. As Yigal Allon (1918–1980), the former Palmach commander who stood out as the most effective field commander of all, told Ben Gurion, at this point the IDF had it in its power to capture the West Bank "within 48 hours." Asked what would happen if the inhabitants chose to stay, he answered "leave that to me."[46] For reasons that remain largely unknown, the idea was rejected.

Instead the Israelis turned their fury against the Egyptians. An improvised division was formed—the first time the IDF operated such a large formation—consisting of four brigades and commanded by Allon with Rabin as his chief of staff. On October 21 they took Beer Sheba in a surprise attack, thus opening the road to the Negev; next, they invaded the Sinai. Had it not been for the threat of foreign intervention, which compelled Ben Gurion to call a halt, in January 1949 the IDF would have cut off the entire Egyptian expeditionary force. Instead, in March 1949, it rounded off its victory by advancing south and capturing Elat on the shore of the Red Sea.

Negotiations with the Arab states began in January 1949. They lasted until July of the same year, when an agreement with Syria was concluded; however, Iraq refused to sign, so that a state of belligerency between it and Israel continues to exist to the present day. Even so, the outcome was a series of armistices, not peace, since no Arab state recognized Israel or entered into diplomatic relations with it. Border incidents started almost immediately; an economic boycott imposed by the Arab League was to embitter relations for decades. In Jerusalem the places most sacred to the Jews were lost to Jordan, as King Abdullah chose to call his kingdom. So were half of the city and the 20 percent of the country later known as the West Bank. The Gaza Strip, consisting of some two hundred square miles, was left in Egyptian hands, though

Egypt never annexed it but set up a military administration instead. Still, Israel remained in possession of some eight thousand square miles, 30 percent more than the territory allocated to it by the United Nations. This included areas such as Galilee and the Negev that had been almost purely Arab.

To most people the establishment "by blood and fire" of the Israeli state represented the greatest achievement of the Jewish people in two thousand years (in those heady days, everything was done "for the first time in two thousand years"). However, the price was heavy. The total number of Arab dead was probably around twenty thousand. Six hundred thousand to seven hundred thousand Arab inhabitants of the Land of Israel fled their homes—often, apparently, in the hope of returning in a few weeks—or were expelled from them. This created an open sore that is as painful and as dangerous today as it was then. About 1 percent of the entire Jewish community were killed, a figure that, considering the size of the population and the time that hostilities lasted, is not far short of the French losses in World War I. Two factors account for the bloodletting. First, initially the IDF was desperately short of heavy weapons and sent its men "running over the hills," as the saying went, without them. Second, once the weapons had arrived, IDF forces lacked experience in using them. As Ariel Sharon, who in May 1948 found himself commanding the lead platoon in an abortive attack on Latrun without ever having attended officer school, once ruefully told this author: "There was so much we did not know."[47]

On the other hand, and as Nietzsche once wrote, "Victory is the best cure for the soul." The 1948 War was the most "total" one Israel ever fought. Not merely did it result in far heavier casualties than any other, but it was the only one in which the very existence of the Jewish community in the Land of Israel was put in jeopardy. At one point Jerusalem was cut off and Transjordanian forces advanced to within fifteen miles of Tel Aviv. Under such circumstances it was inevitable that the war should give rise to a myth, which continued to influence Israeli life for decades thereafter. As in most wars the main goal of the myth was to celebrate the achievement, and with very good reason. However, it also kept alive the danger, the heroism, the sacrifices, the losses, and the grief.

Nathan Alterman, one of the greatest modern Hebrew poets and a special favorite of Ben Gurion in particular, described in "The Silver Platter," a work dedicated to those who freely gave their lives, that the establishment of the state was a miracle beyond compare, brought about under flaming red skies and bought by the blood of the country's youth. To many inside and outside Israel, that remains true to the present day.

2

FULL STEAM AHEAD (1949–1967)

"The Rock of Israel"

Though the 1948 War of Independence did end in a victory for Israel, it left the country truncated—cut by a border that, on the map, looked like an ugly scar. Millennia-old trade routes were severed, disrupting transportation and trade and requiring major readjustments if economic life was to resume. Above all, divided Jerusalem remained stuck at the apex of a triangle. A bus line led to the wall between the two parts; as the driver reached it, all he could do was to turn back. The city was "lost in its dream," as a famous song was later to put it. People used to say that the best thing about Jerusalem was the road to Tel Aviv; though the distance between the two cities is only about forty-five miles, in the 1950s and 1960s being a Jerusalemite meant that one did not know how to swim. Furthermore, as far back as the record goes the Land had served as a bridge between Syria and Egypt and also between the Mediterranean and the rest of the Middle East. Now, cut off from its surroundings by continuing Arab hostility, it almost felt like a rotten tooth in a wide-open mouth, and indeed, caricaturists during the 1950s sometimes drew it in exactly that way.

In every postcolonial country, the hardest period is the first. Groups and people who for years have made their names, and often their livings as well, by breaking the law and perhaps waging irregular warfare must be brought back under the government's aegis. As the former rulers

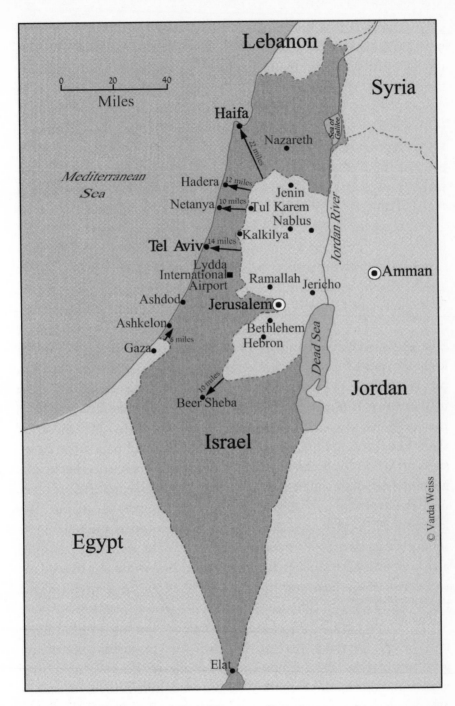

Borders and Distances, 1949–1967

depart, and often leave scorched earth in their wake, a new government must be created to take their place. In this respect the Israelis were doubly fortunate. First, by the end of 1948 "the sacred gun" (Ben Gurion) that had sent the *Altalena* to the bottom of the sea had broken the power of Etzel. Together with the dismantling of Lehi and Palmach, this created a situation where power was concentrated—some would say overconcentrated—in the hands of the government. Second, in the form of the National Council/Histadrut/Jewish Agency complex, Israel possessed an array of fully functional institutions that enjoyed wide recognition and for years had acted as a state within a state.

As the British retreated from one part of the country after another, they often left offices, communications, procedures, even entire military bases largely intact. To be sure, not all of them fell into Jewish hands. For those that did, though, often all that was necessary was to drop the English language (which, during the Mandate, had been official) and replace it with Hebrew (which had also been official). One outcome was that some forms bore expressions such as "I am your humble servant" that were quite foreign to the country's spirit. Many people continued to use pidgin English; this was especially true when it came to official matters. For example, a "traffic" stood for a traffic policeman. A "rapport" (with the "t" pronounced) stood for the ticket that he might give you. One crossroads in Haifa continued to be called the Check Post for decades on end, and a booth of the sort that houses a guard or a policeman became a *bootkeh*. Not merely was the currency unit, the Israeli lira, also known as the pound, but for years after 1948 it continued to be divided into twenty coins known as shillings. More seriously, because the Jews had a higher level of literacy, they had filled a disproportionate number of middle- and lower-ranking Mandatory civil servant positions. Now that the time had come, they were only too eager to take over.

No doubt because they are few in number but like to feel important, Israelis are fond of comparing their state to others ("the unique and the universal," as a famous history professor, Jacob Talmon, used to say), and this method will be followed here. Like Britain, the state is a parliamentary-type democracy. In contrast to Britain and also to the United States, there is only one chamber, known as the Knesset after an ancient Hebrew term meaning, roughly, "gathering." Elections must be held every four years and are proportional. Thus, the entire country forms a single electoral district; one casts one's vote for parties, not for individuals. Over the years, the Knesset has developed its own character. Ben Gurion himself saw the British political system as "the best democracy in the world"[1] (it was, of course, also the one with which he was most familiar). No doubt it was with this model in mind that he attended the first meeting in tails and a top hat; however, he only succeeded in making himself ridiculous. Since then, the debate as to whether jackets must or must not be worn, or whether jeans and sandals may or may not be worn, has been ongoing. The prestige of members of the Knesset (MKs) and of politicians in general is not high; in Israel as elsewhere, democracy seems to produce lots of petty rascals punctuated, here and there, by a real leader. Meetings tend to be fairly disorderly, with lots of catcalls and interruptions. Yet rarely, if ever, do they witness the kind of violence that often mars the parliamentary life of such countries as Taiwan and South Korea.

The Knesset elects the president, who, as in other parliamentary democracies, is largely a ceremonial figure. The first person to hold the office was Haim Weizmann; having been kicked into it by his former rival, Ben Gurion, he hated his enforced inactivity and died in harness in 1952. Albert Einstein, to whom Ben Gurion turned next, rejected the offer. In his letter he claimed that he lacked "both the natural aptitude and the experience to deal properly with people and to exercise official functions";[2] the real reason may well have been that he did not want to leave Princeton. Since then things have changed. The weaker the dominance of any single party—and no party after 1965 has ever succeeded in becoming as dominant as Mapai used to be—the more the post becomes the subject of fierce competition among senior—and sometimes not so senior—politicians. To get themselves elected they use, as they must, every trick in the book. Doing so is very difficult, yet finding a person who can do what it takes *and* maintain the somewhat Olympian detachment the job requires is more difficult still; some MKs come up with so many private law proposals that they should be given Ritalin.

Executive power is in the hands of the government. Though there is no legal requirement to that effect, its head, the prime minister, has always been the leader of the party with the greatest number of seats;

he and his government must command a majority. Originally there were twelve ministers, but the need to form coalitions has caused this number to expand. Usually there are between twenty and twenty-five, sometimes including a few without portfolio. The core posts have remained fairly stable over the years. They are those of the prime minister and the ministers of defense (this portfolio is sometimes held by the prime minister himself), the treasury, education (who commands the second largest budget after defense), foreign affairs, home affairs, and justice. Some other ministries, such as agriculture and health, have also led a fairly stable existence. Quite a number of less important ones appear and disappear, are separated and rejoined, and have their powers reduced or increased to suit the political demands of the moment. As a result there was and is a tendency to build governments within governments, the most famous case in point being Golda Meir's "kitchen cabinet," where five or six people made decisions about war and peace over cups of coffee and home-baked cakes.

Whereas many executive departments were already in existence, the judiciary had to be literally stamped out of the ground. One fine day the first minister of justice, Pinhas Rosen (born Felix Rosenblut, 1887–1961) called his law partner, Moshe Zmora, appointing him president of the Supreme Court; not the most regular procedure, but certainly an efficient one! The system that eventually emerged is modeled on that of the Mandate. However, it differed from the British (and the American) one in that there are no juries, so that all trials are held, and verdicts reached, by professional judges. Judges are appointed by a committee whose head is the minister of justice. Once they have taken their seats, they are independent and serve until they resign or retire; though disciplinary means to remove them from office do exist, they have been used very sparingly. As in most countries there are three tiers: magistrates' courts, district courts, and the Supreme Court. Over time, specialized traffic courts, family courts, and labor courts, all of whose decisions are subject to appeal at the Supreme Court, were added.

While the system draws on the traditions of many different countries, it still has one characteristic that is absolutely unique: The Supreme Court also serves as the High Court of Justice (Beth Din Gavoha

Letzedek, Bagatz in short). In this capacity it acts as a court of first *and* of last instance. This in turn means that anyone can address it (submit a Bagatz, as Israelis say) to obtain relief against any public agency that supposedly violates the law or simply behaves in an "extremely unreasonable manner," *without going through any other court first and even if he or she has no personal stake in the matter.* In the absence of a written constitution, the system empowers the court to exercise very broad supervision over both the executive and the legislature. Either it orders them to take action or it issues an injunction that will prevent action from being taken.

The first elections were held in February 1949 and were marked by a very high participation ratio of 86 percent. Remarkably for a country that was still technically at war, the 160,000 or so Arabs who had not fled were enfranchised; two were actually elected. Since then the Knesset has always had some non-Jewish members, though for all kinds of reasons their proportion is considerably smaller than the proportion of non-Jews in the population. Right from the beginning the system of proportional elections, combined with the low minimum number of votes required for entering the Knesset (at present 2.5 percent, formerly just 1 percent of the ballots cast), started producing numerous splinter parties that represented all kinds of special interests. Splinter parties, though they tended to be ephemeral, led to coalition building and hence to political instability. As in Italy, and in France under the Fourth Republic, few governments serve out their full terms. By 1961 there had been no fewer than nine; in over six decades, not once did any party succeed in gaining an absolute majority at the polls.

To read, let alone write, a detailed account of all of Israel's parties—their permutations, alliances, and mutual betrayals—is a punishment fit for the worst sinners in hell. The largest party continued to be Mapai, which reached the peak of its power in 1959 when it won 47 out of 120 seats in the Knesset. Originally Mapai had been strongly socialist; through its dominance of Histadrut, where it *did* have an absolute majority, it was able to operate a vast system of patronage (*protektzia*, or "preference," as it was called) in every field, from work to education and health care. Still, its long hold on power gradually caused it to take a more centrist line both as a matter of practical politics and because of the need to attract voters in Israel's rapidly developing towns. This cost it the support of some of its left-wing members, particularly in the kibbutzim and the moshavim. In 1948, and again in 1954, groups of them broke away and formed new parties. Both times, those parties promptly inserted the word "unity" in their names.

Except for a short period in 1954–1955, when he went into voluntary retirement, Ben Gurion continued to dominate Israeli politics. To his supporters he was "the one and the only," but in 1961–1963 disaster struck. Its instrument was the so-called Lavon Affair, a bungled attempt at sabotage in Egypt that had taken place in 1954 and led to the trial and execution of two Egyptian Jews. The blame was put at the door of the then-minister of defense, Pinhas Lavon. Seven years later in 1963, when an investigation was held and exonerated Lavon, Ben Gurion refused to accept the result. Since then all kinds of complicated reasons have been proposed to explain why he insisted on tearing his party to pieces, yet the real one was probably nothing more than an old man's obstinacy in getting his way at any cost. His successor was Levi Eshkol. Originally from Degania, for twelve years on end Eshkol had served as minister of the treasury. Blessed with a sense of humor that Ben Gurion never had, he was a moderate and a born compromiser; as one story had it, when asked whether he wanted tea or coffee he answered, "Half of each." Looking back, some people came to see him as the best prime minister Israel ever had.

The most important opposition party was Herut (Liberty). Its longtime leader was Menahem Begin. Polish-born Begin was an admirer of Jabotinsky, though the admiration was not always reciprocated. He began his career by joining the Revisionist youth movement in Poland, traveling from town to town to give speeches—he sometimes slept on park benches—and rising to become its leader. Aware that he was wanted by the Gestapo, at the outbreak of World War II he fled to the Soviet Union; that he left behind his entire family, who were exterminated, made him feel guilty and explains why he often spoke about the Holocaust as if another one were just around the corner. The Soviet secret police, aware of his identity, arrested him and sent him to an Arctic labor camp. After he was released he enlisted in General Wladyslaw Anders's Polish army. With it, he reached the Land of Israel in 1942.

Appointed leader of Etzel, Begin soon became the most wanted man in the country, forcing him to take on a new identity as a religious student complete with mustache, beard, and black hat. Yet he was no terrorist; he never participated in a single operation or killed anybody. Instead he moved from one safe house to the next, provided moral and political direction, and filled his idle hours by reading and playing chess. In 1948 he refused his supporters' plea to use force to resist Ben Gurion's handling of the *Altalena* affair, which, looking back, was one of the two best things he ever did (the other was surrendering the Sinai and making peace with Egypt). As leader of the opposition he cut a quaint figure. In a hot country where air-conditioning was rare if not unknown, he always dressed in dark suits; asked why, he explained that it was *snoblesse* oblige. In a supposedly socialist nation, he ceremoniously kissed ladies' hands. As a popular speaker able to incite the masses he had no equal. Which is why, time after time during the twenty-nine years he spent in the opposition while losing one election campaign after another, he was always able to fend off challenges from within his own party.

Certainly Herut was right wing in the sense of being nationalist. It claimed that not only the West Bank but Transjordan, too, formed part of the Land of Israel; for many years the party's newspaper, also called *Herut,* always put "Jordanians" in apostrophes. Begin himself would, if he only could, have started every day with a gun salute and a military parade. However, neither he nor his party was truly conservative either in a socioeconomic sense or in the backward-looking manner associated with Edmund Burke. Israel never developed any party like the American Republicans, let alone the British Tories. In Begin's own words, when he finally came to power in 1977 he did so with the votes not of the rich but of "those who are poor and those who believe."

A liberal—meaning mainly antisocialist, proprivate enterprise—stance was taken by some middle-of-the-road parties such as the General Zionists, the Progressives, and others. However, as the name of the latter in particular indicates, none of them was really conservative. Moreover, it is characteristic of Israel that, until the emergence of Sharon's Kadima (forward, also meaning "eastward," as it does in "Hatikva," Israel's national anthem party) in 2003–2004, centrist parties were never able to command much support. If the General Zionists were able to survive at all, then this was only because, in 1965, they merged with Herut to form a block known as Gahal. Kadima itself lacks any ideology whatsoever. It is neither right nor left wing, neither liberal nor socialist, but a haphazard meeting place for opportunists. Judging by its predecessors' fate, it will very probably prove short-lived.

The third important block was the religious one. Like everybody else, the believers were disunited. At any one time there might be two or three different religious parties represented in the Knesset; their shares of the vote were usually between 8 and 12 percent. Though some religious voters were socialist, their small number meant that they never played a very important role in politics. Others, particularly the National Religious Party (NRP), were bourgeois or petit bourgeois. The party's longtime leader was Yosef Burg (1909–1999). Round-faced and clean-shaven, he also dressed in suits like Begin, and he wore a skullcap and spoke with a strong Saxon accent. For thirty-eight years, this roly-poly epitome of middle-class contentment managed to secure a seat in every single Israeli cabinet. His own party shared the Zionist dream. Asked what was more important, "national" or "religious," he answered, "the hyphen." However, at any one time there was at least one religious party that regarded the dream, if not as outright apostasy, as essentially irrelevant to the real content of Jewish life, i.e., religion.

With that we come to some of the most important and most peculiar aspects of modern Israel—the ones that, for good or ill, truly make it unique among nations. Among the early Zionists some had been religious, others secular. Herzl in particular personified the latter type. As his critics never tired of pointing out, there was little about him that was specifically Jewish. Thus, right from the beginning there was a sharp debate as to whether the objective was simply a state of the Jews or a Jewish state. To the dominant socialists, a state controlled by religion was an abomination. To many Orthodox people, a state *not* controlled by religion was worse than no state at all. Thus, to them, Zionism was a product of "Satan and all his hosts" who had "come to mislead and intoxicate"; those who pretended to "ascend to the Land" had, in fact, "descended to the depth of hell."[3] The debate extended to symbols. Herzl, who appreciated their value, wanted the national flag to sport seven golden stars, one for each daily working hour, against a white background. His proposal was not accepted, and the one ultimately adopted carried a blue Shield of David and two blue stripes, both of them traditional Jewish symbols.

Throughout the years of Zionist struggle the secular minded and the religious, representing two radically different versions of the state to come, had clashed; now that the state in question had been established and its foundations were to be codified, the problem became more acute than ever. A foretaste of things to come was provided by the Declaration of Independence itself. The representatives of the religious parties, especially the ultra-Orthodox Agudat (Association of) Israel, made their consent conditional on concluding it with the words "putting our trust in the God of Israel." Ben Gurion, who hated religion as only a turn-of-the-twentieth-century socialist could, refused. To him the state was a human creation to be molded by him, not one that was subject to divine law and hence to the rabbis who interpreted it. Yet politically he simply could not afford to have these parties saying no to a step as fundamental as the state's proclamation. In the end a compromise was reached by using the rather mysterious term "the *tzur* of Israel." Ordinarily *tzur* can mean either "rock" or "strength." However, somewhat on the lines of "a mighty fortress is our Lord," it can also stand for God.

From then on, each time the question concerning the place of religion in Israeli life came up it gave rise to fierce political battles. It could, indeed, hardly be otherwise; given that Judaism is a religion that aims to control every aspect of life, both private and public. It does so by means of hundreds of Old Testament commandments, thousands of Talmudic regulations, and any number of answers to questions that have been issued by the rabbis over the ages. As one rabbi, Eliezer Yehuda Waldenberg, put it in 1952:

> No democracy, even the most perfect, can match the quality of divine rule, that which people call theocracy. More, even: any democracy that is not a theocracy—in other words, one that does not admit the absolute dominion of religion over political life—will necessarily end up by doing away with every kind of holy commandment.[4]

Democracy, another rabbi explained, is based on the opinion of the people and, which is as important, the right of that people to change its opinion should it want to. Not so Judaism, which has nothing to do with human will but is built on God's unalterable law.[5]

One can see these rabbis' point. Still, theirs are hardly the kinds of arguments that the majority of Israelis, even many religious Israelis, are prepared to accept. Many other rabbis have expressed themselves in less extreme terms. Precisely because they were not accepted, a lot of questions were left open. Were state and religion to be united or separate? What was to be the relationship between Jewish law and state law? What part of the state's authority, if any, was to be vested in the rabbis? Were the Sabbath and other Jewish festivals going to become legal holidays? If so, would people be obliged to observe them, and in what ways? To what extent was *kashrut,* i.e., Jewish dietary law, to be kept? How about food stores, restaurants, hotels, etc.? Who would be in charge of education, and what place would religion occupy in the curriculum? Would students in Talmudic high schools *(yeshivot)* be conscripted? Would the *yeshivot* themselves be accredited for professional purposes such as qualifying their graduates for public-sector jobs? Were women going to be conscripted as men were? Would abortion be legal? This is just a small sample of a vast number of problems that were in search of an answer.

An observer not familiar with Israeli life might well ask how a group that hardly ever managed to secure more than 15 percent of Knesset seats was able to influence a society to the extent that it did. The answer is twofold. First, the system of proportional representation has often created a situation where the religious parties, though they themselves could not form a coalition, held the balance in the Knesset; no wonder that, starting under Ben Gurion, they and other minority parties have done whatever they could to prevent any change in the system whereby the Knesset is elected. Second, though less than 20 percent of Israelis define themselves as observant Jews (and not all of those vote for religious or Orthodox parties), there exists a large group of so-called traditionalists, or *massortiyim.* Though their exact number is uncertain, it may have grown over the years. Privately they may not be very strict in observing religious law—for example, they may not always attend synagogue on the Sabbath and turn a blind eye to some of the more esoteric requirements of *kashrut.* Still, they do want a state that is unmistakably Jewish.

Even that, though, is only part of the answer. Seeking to integrate themselves into the surrounding society, nineteenth-century "emancipated" Jews always argued that Judaism was a religion much like all others—so that German Jews, for example, were simply Germans "of the Mosaic faith," as the saying went. By contrast, the entire Zionist discourse is based on the idea that Jews are a nation; it is as a nation that they are said to deserve to have a state of their own. The difficulty is that when it comes to deciding who does and does not belong to that nation, religion is the only possible criterion. From the late nineteenth century on, Jews and others have often tried to find some other criterion, whether based on the color of people's hair or on their genes; so far, all have failed.

It is quite possible to be a Catholic German or a Protestant one, a Muslim Iraqi or a Christian one. However, there is no such thing as a Christian or Muslim Jew—a Jew, in other words, who discards Judaism and acknowledges a God other than the one of Israel. To be sure, at any one time there have always been in Israel a few extreme secularists. During the 1950s, arguing that Israel would never achieve integration into the Middle East as long as it insisted on retraining its Jewish character, they called themselves Canaanites. In the 1990s people sometimes spoke of "Post-Zionism." Their objective was to cut the Gordian knot and define the nation in some other way than through religion. Some of these people, notably the poet Jonathan Ratosh (1908–1981) with his ideology of "Hebrewism," spoke and wrote very eloquently. However, in the end eloquence was all they had.

Given the well-nigh universal agreement among Jewish Israelis concerning the need to maintain *some* link between state and religion, it is not surprising that the above questions and many similar ones have led to a series of compromises. To go through them in reverse order: Abortions are legal provided they are carried out on medical grounds (in practice they have always been quietly tolerated). Women are conscripted, but religious ones can easily gain exemption. *Yeshivot* are not accredited except for the purpose of training rabbis. Their students are exempt from military service (in the midst of the battle for Jerusalem in May 1948, a group of rabbis calling themselves "the Central National

Guard Command" issued an order prohibiting them from signing up).[6] In one form or another religion—meaning the Old Testament, the Talmud, and some Jewish oral traditions—is taught at every level from kindergarten up. And how could it be otherwise, given that the Old Testament is also the Jewish people's history? While the ministry of education is in charge of secular schools and of national-religious schools, the *haredim* or ultra-Orthodox run their own, largely independent, school system.

Individual citizens and private businesses are not obliged to observe *kashrut* (though many of the latter do so voluntarily to attract customers), but the state, including the IDF, does observe it. The Sabbath and other religious holidays are official; between them, they define the calendar much as holidays such as Christmas and Easter do in Christian countries. As any visitor will notice, people are not obliged to follow strict Jewish law as to not driving, not working at home, etc., on these days. However, most public transportation and shops are closed. Public utilities such as water, electricity, telephone communications, and even broadcasting services are available. The one exception to this rule is the Day of Atonement (Yom Kippur). On that holiest of all holy days, broadcasting is also shut down and all traffic comes to a halt. Paradoxically this enables the children of secular families to have a ball by riding their bicycles over empty streets, which from a religious point of view is a most unholy activity. Finally, to provide the population with religious services such as *kashrut* and ritual baths, the state maintains a whole hierarchy of rabbis.

In all this, two issues have proved especially contentious. First, the fact that the rabbinate is in charge of marriages and divorces gives it enormous power over the lives of many individuals. To mention just two examples of the way things work, Jewish law does not allow marriages between Jews and non-Jews. As a result, the non-Jewish partner will have to convert; given that Judaism is not a proselytizing religion (during the centuries of the Diaspora, attempts by Jews to convert either Christians or Muslims were often subject to the death penalty), this can be a long and often difficult process. Couples who object to this on principle or simply do not want to jump through the hoops will have to go abroad and hold "a Cyprus wedding," as people call it. Next, if they wish to settle in Israel, they can only hope that the Ministry of the Interior will grant the non-Jewish partner some kind of permit to live in the country and participate in its life.

The system, whose origins go back all the way to the Old Testament, aims at preventing the children of Jewish parents from being lost to the Jewish people and also at preventing the Jewish partner from adopting the religion of the non-Jewish one. Whether it achieves this objective is debatable—in an increasingly open world, the effect may be just the opposite from what is intended. What it does do is to make Israel the only developed country where a Jew cannot marry whomever he or she likes. Furthermore, should the Jewish father die and leave his non-Jewish wife a widow, she and her children may very well face expulsion. Another peculiarity of the system is that, in principle at any rate, divorce is only possible if both sides agree to go through the procedure. One hardly has to be an Israeli to imagine the tragedies that sometimes ensue.

The other issue concerning state and religion I wish to discuss here is, if anything, even more fundamental. By virtue of the so-called Law of Return, which is based on the Declaration of Independence, the state is obliged to grant citizenship to any Jew who wishes to settle—after all, was the state not founded with the explicit purpose of providing a refuge for Jews, wherever they might be? By Jewish law, a Jew is either a person born to a Jewish mother—not, nota bene, father—or such as converted to Judaism. By Israeli law, carrying out the conversion process and issuing the necessary certificate is the task of the rabbinate. This puts the latter in a position to decide who is entitled to become a citizen and who is not. Not just individuals, but entire communities, such as the Ethiopian one, were affected. It is as if the Catholic Church were empowered to decide who can become a French citizen and granted that right only to those who could say at least some of the prayers in Latin and regularly attended mass.

In respect to these and other issues, the details are somewhat flexible and have changed over time. Now groups of would-be immigrants are recognized as fully Jewish, now they are not and have to undergo all kinds of procedures to become citizens. Now the Ministry of the Interior refuses to register mixed couples, now the Supreme Court forces it to. Now theaters and movie houses are ordered to shut down on Friday night, which is part of the Sabbath, now the Supreme Court authorizes municipalities to allow them to open if they so wish. Now religious women who do not wish to serve in the military have to provide some kind of proof that they are indeed observant, now they do not. At any given moment, the arrangements in question are the result of horse trading among various factions in the Knesset. Here and there a Bagatz is served and forces the Supreme Court to intervene. Surely this is a most unholy way of doing things, and one that many secularists and some religious people feel detracts from the dignity of religion.

That, in turn, may have been done on purpose. According to Professor Yeshayahu Leibowitz (1903–1994) the reason why Ben Gurion, with whom he claimed to have had many conversations, tolerated the various arrangements was because he wanted to "prostitute" religion by putting it on welfare.[7] In this he was successful up to a point. Waldenberg himself ended up by taking a post as president of the Jerusalem rabbinical court and pocketing the state salary that went with it. So have countless other rabbis who, while loudly denouncing the state, are serving it as judges, supervisors of *kashrut* and of funerary rituals, and the like. Only one small group in Jerusalem, known as Neturei Karta (Guardians of the City), has obstinately refused to accept the "Zionist" system and everything it implies. Yet even they had to make some compromises, such as gradually coming to speak Hebrew instead of Yiddish, using Israeli currency, receiving municipal services, and the like. All this makes the relationship between state and religion extremely problematic. Well may people wonder who is the prostitute and who the pimp.

To make things more complicated still, right from its beginnings Israel has had a sizable non-Jewish minority, which at present accounts for about 20 percent of the entire population. They have never been granted autonomy. Yet in matters of holidays, *kashrut,* and of course family law (marriage and divorce) the members of that minority are not subject to Jewish law. For example, Muslims are allowed to work on the Sabbath and Christians have always had the right to raise and eat pork. Just like the Jewish majority, Muslims, Christians, and Druze have their state-sponsored tribunals, staffed by judges who are state employees. To that extent equality before the law does exist, though only at the cost of applying different sets of laws to different groups of people. What Israel does not, and by its raison d'être cannot, do is to grant non-Jews equality under the Law of Return—in other words, the right to acquire citizenship and settle.

Taken together, these arrangements endow Israel with its unique character. But they also justify its existence; they are the real "Rock of Israel" on which everything else rests. However numerous the modifications in detail that have been, and still are being, introduced, they and the contradictions to which they give rise will not go away. As we saw, in practice decisions concerning the relationship between state and religion are made by the kind of haggling that is characteristic of democracy everywhere. As a result, in theory and perhaps in practice one may envisage a situation in which the decisions in question will be made by Arab Knesset members! Certainly the system, especially as seen from the point of view of the non-Jewish minority, is far from perfect. Jewish Israelis, too, are constantly grumbling about it. Some complain that the state does not do enough to impose values, especially Jewish ones. Others say that politicians, by "laying down all important aspects of thought and behavior," hold civil society captive.[8] Some consider that the system is not democratic enough—after all, Israel has neither a written constitution nor a bill of rights. Others point out that the system of proportional representation is too democratic and leads to chronic political instability.

In the end, the constant grumbling and power plays among various factions simply prove that the system works—*eppure si muove* (nevertheless, it moves), as Galileo might have said. On the whole Israel's democratic politics faithfully reflect society. They enable the latter to change without bloodshed; though the assassination of Prime Minister Rabin was a major tragedy, thankfully it has remained an isolated incident. Furthermore, not once in six decades has Israeli democracy been seriously challenged either from the right or from the left. This is not because everybody takes it for granted or is happy with it. The real reason is because the few people who seriously oppose it on religious and, even more so, ideological grounds have been almost entirely without influence, whereas the rest cannot agree among themselves as to what should replace it.

Perhaps the truth of all this is proved by the fact that there has never been even a shadow of an attempt to oust the government by a coup d'état, military or otherwise. To be sure the military, thanks to its size and its importance in defending the country, often makes its voice heard; in this respect Israel might be compared to a sailing boat with an exceptionally large and heavy keel. Retired officers also occupy a large, some would say too large, place in the upper echelons of government. At times, that government has looked almost like some South American junta. Still, as one story has it, when a future chief of staff, Haim Bar Lev (1924–1994), was asked about this scenario he answered that "no officer in his sound mind would want to take over such a mess."[9] Out of more than one hundred other colonial countries that have become independent since 1945, only India and Malta can say the same.

"Striking Roots"

"To be a free people in our own land": But what sort of country was it? At the time the state was created, only about 8 percent of its territory had been purchased by the Jews and was dotted by Jewish settlements. Both within that 8 percent and outside it, the vast majority of places and terrain features were still known by their Arabic names, as they had been for thirteen hundred years past; to that extent it was a foreign country, not a native one. Perhaps it is a tribute to Ben Gurion that, as early as the extremely difficult summer of 1948, he found the time and the energy to deal with this question. A committee made up of Biblical experts, Talmudic experts, historians, geographers, archaeologists, and linguists was assembled. Bringing their vast store of knowledge to bear, they systematically filled the map with new, Hebrew names. Of those names, quite a number were taken from the Bible or Talmud and referred to places that could be identified with some certainty. Others were translated from Arabic into Hebrew, whereas others still were simply invented to fit some kind of idea or the terrain.

To give the reader some idea of how things worked, well-known geographical features such as the valleys of Sharon and Esdraelon, the Sea of Galilee, and Mount Tabor, as well as ancient towns such as Jerusalem, Hebron, Beer Sheba, Haifa, Acre, Safed, Nazareth, Tiberias, and many others simply retained their age-old Hebrew (or foreign, as with Mount Kastel and Caesarea) names. By contrast, the town of Majdal (Tower) in the south became Migdal (also Tower, but this time in Hebrew); the coastal village of Isdud, not far from the Gaza Strip, became the town of Ashdod. Arab settlements whose inhabitants had stayed in place retained their names as, for example, the village of Abu Gosh near Jerusalem did. The often very apt Arabic names of countless terrain features were translated. Thus the river Al Auja (the Green) north of Tel Aviv became the Yarkon, its Biblical name. Jebel (Mount) Jermak near Safed became Har Meron. Kaukab al Hauwa (the Star of the Winds, a hill overlooking the Jordan Valley), became Kohav Hayarden (Star of the Jordan). Bab Al Wad (the Gate to the Valley) became Shaar Hagai, and so on.

Among newly invented names, the best known is Tel Aviv (the Hill of Spring, a Biblical expression). Others previously mentioned in this volume were Degania (from *dagan,* wheat), Tel Hai (the Mound of Life), Nahariya (from *nahar,* to come together), Negbah (Southward Ho) and Beer Tuvia (Tuvia's Well). The total number of new names is in the thousands, perhaps tens of thousands; certainly the foreigner traveling in Israel cannot be expected to understand all these names or keep them in mind. However, it is important that he or she be aware that most are of recent origin. Far from coming with the Land, as it were—in many countries place names tend to survive even as peoples and languages change—they were deliberately created as a cardinal part of the Zionist enterprise. As additional settlements are being established both in "Old" Israel and in the occupied territories, the process is still continuing every day. On the other side of the hill, Palestinian scholars have started using similar means to keep alive the memory of what they regard as *their* country. Hence, how the story will ultimately end is anybody's guess.

Not only places but people, too, received new names. Ben Gurion and Eshkol apart, Moshe Shertok (prime minister 1953–1955), became Moshe Sharett. Golda Meyerson (her divorced husband's name) became Golda Meir, Yitzhak Jazernicki became Yitzhak Shamir, Ariel Scheinerman became Ariel Sharon, and so on. Many people changed their names voluntarily by way of discarding the Diaspora and "striking roots." Others, especially those working for the military, the security services, and the Ministry of Foreign Affairs, were pressed by their superiors; serving soldiers using the military mail system to send their letters might find the envelope bearing this stamp: "Soldier, if you have a foreign name change it into Hebrew." Others still had new names assigned to them by immigration officials too busy to learn the original ones.

Some of the new names were translated from the old ones, so that Goldblatt might become Ale-Zahav (Golden Leaf) and Schwarz, Shahor (Black). Others bore a slight acoustic similarity to the original (e.g., Berezin became Razin, vaguely suggesting *raz,* a secret), whereas others still were freely invented. In particular, "Oriental" Jews with French or Arabic names (the former readily identified them as Moroccan) often felt that their names worked against them when it came to looking for work. In time Alphonse might become Aryeh (Lion). Morris was turned into Moshe, Suad (an Arabic woman's name) into Sara or Ada, and so on. Strangest was the fate of one Arabic woman's name, Freha (Hen). It came to stand for a coarse, cheaply dressed, and ill-educated woman; this in turn gave rise to *frehiada,* a gathering of *frehot* (plural of *freha*) and their male counterparts, the *frehim.* Mercifully, its use as a proper name was discontinued.

A comparison of present-day Israeli telephone books with the much thinner ones of half a century ago will show that several processes have been at work. First, the proportion of Hebrew names has greatly increased; even so, ongoing immigration from many different countries has probably caused the books to remain more heterogeneous than any others outside the United States. Second, though the names Cohen and Levi remain the most common by far, as the books became more Hebrew, paradoxically they also became less Jewish. The reason is that many non-Hebrew names that, especially in Europe, had been carried solely or mainly by Jews were abandoned; for example, Leisersohn might become Liraz. As this example also shows, most of the newly adopted names were shorter and, for Israelis at any rate, easier to pronounce than the old ones. Thus, when Rabin's father immigrated in 1917, one of the first things he did was to discard his original surname, Rovitzov. Of course, not everybody followed his example. As a result, some of those who failed to do so later found that their children, or at any rate their grandchildren, could not pronounce their own names.

Whereas changing geographical and personal names was relatively easy, absorbing new immigrants and turning them into Israelis was much harder. Throughout the critical years of World War II and the Holocaust the country's doors had been essentially closed. As a result, countless people either went elsewhere or lost their lives while desperately trying to escape the Nazis. Especially traumatic was the *Struma* affair of 1941–1942. The ship was an old, barely seaworthy Danube cattle barge. The Turks did not allow it to remain at Istanbul; when it went down in the Black Sea (probably after being torpedoed by a Soviet submarine), 769 Jewish Romanian refugees who had been denied entry to Palestine went down with it. If perhaps 50,000 people still managed to make it to Palestine by one route or another, then it was no thanks to the Mandatory authorities, which did everything they could to stop them.

Now, in keeping with the promise made in the Declaration of Independence, the gates were thrown wide open. The immigration figures were staggering. By the end of 1951, over 100,000 Jews from Poland, 120,000 from Romania, 40,000 from Bulgaria (the entire community there), and smaller numbers from Czechoslovakia and Hungary had arrived; counting Europe alone, the total number was around 320,000. A similar number were brought in from Iraq (over 120,000), Yemen (50,000), Egypt, Libya, Morocco, Turkey, and Iran. Within just three and a half years, Israel's population more than doubled.

It was taken almost for granted that anybody who voluntarily left the United States or Western Europe to try his or her luck in what still looked like a godforsaken country in the Middle East did so for some hidden reason; the standard phrase that greeted such immigrants was "Did you get into trouble?" Some immigrants brought their property along, but their number was small.

The vast majority of new arrivals were practically penniless, having lost their property either during the Holocaust or when the authorities in the Arab countries in which they originated confiscated it. Those who came from Europe were as well educated as Israelis were. Not so those of Oriental—the term stood for all those from Asia and Africa— origin. A few of them came from large cities such as Baghdad, Alexandria, and Rabat, where they had attended the best available British and French schools. At the other extreme were some Libyan Jews who, long isolated from the world, had literally lived in caves. Many were entirely lacking in modern skills, and indeed most of the women in particular could neither read nor write.

From 1952 until 1966 another 505,000 people, 60 percent of whom were Orientals, entered the country. The problems of absorbing such numbers were formidable. At times it was necessary to give preference to the educated—meaning, by and large, Europeans—and the young. The resulting bitterness has never quite disappeared. Most European immigrants went to the towns or else to the kibbutzim. Not so a great many Oriental immigrants, who initially lived in temporary cities made up of shacks or even tents, with one toilet for every fifty people and the nearest telephone six miles away. From there they gradually moved out into the towns' poorer quarters, often occupying more or less intact Arab houses that, having been deserted by their owners, were officially marked as "absentees' property." Others found themselves in "development towns," urban-type settlements erected especially for them, as well as in moshavim in outlying parts of the country that the government wanted to settle for strategic reasons. Large families were squeezed into one-bedroom prefabricated flats or into tiny houses that dotted the countryside. Schools, public transport, and medical services were rudimentary. Though nobody starved, living standards were very low indeed.

Without massive government aid, paid for by taxation as well as contributions from Zionists abroad, it could never have been done. Nor did the government operate on its own. Much of the burden was carried by the Jewish Agency, now transformed from a quasi-governmental body into one specifically responsible for bringing in and absorbing immigrants. Voluntary organizations did what they could. Their members taught immigrants Hebrew and distributed household articles, clothes, and the like. Each year before Hanuka (the Festival of Lights), *The Jerusalem Post* would launch a drive to collect toys. Kibbutz members in particular often shared their meager possessions, housing included, with the newcomers. Yet in many ways "native" Israelis treated immigrants as other people have always done—looking down on their culture, discriminating against them, exploiting them economically, and in general lording it over them.

Things were especially difficult for Oriental Jews. These, after all, were the dying years of colonialism; in many places, the idea that

Asians and Africans were the white man's equals was anything but self-evident. Too often it was supposed that, simply because they came from Asia and Africa, Oriental Jews had no culture and constituted "human dust" (an expression often attributed to Ben Gurion though in reality it was coined by Weizmann in a very different context). Moroccan Jews in particular were looked at with a mixture of fascination and horror. "The primitiveness of these people," one journalist wrote, "is unsurpassable. . . . What can be done with them?"[10] The horror was reciprocated. Unlike most European Jews, most Oriental ones were not "emancipated" but continued to define themselves by exercising their religion as their ancestors had always done. Arriving in the Promised Land, they could only rub their eyes at a "Jewish" country where a great many people walked around without head covers, did not particularly care about eating kosher food, and attended synagogue rarely if at all.

As young immigrants adapted faster than their elders, the authority of parents and of fathers in particular collapsed. Another urgent problem was the status of Oriental women. Israel at the time was a socialist country. In spite of the often very arduous conditions, and *pace* the complaints of subsequent feminists, it gave women a certain kind of equality rarely attained before or since. There was never any question concerning Israeli women's right to own property, receive the education of their choice, enter the professions, etc. Though some rabbis raised objections, women were fully enfranchised right from the start. For decades on end they were also the only female citizens in the world to be conscripted into the military and receive weapons training. Long before anyone had heard of "gender," full equality of the sexes was explicitly written into the Declaration of Independence. That is more than either the corresponding American document or the U.S. Constitution can say.

By contrast, Oriental Jews in many ways followed Arab custom. Unmarried girls were not supposed to go out on their own or choose their husbands but to take the ones their fathers had selected for them. Yemenite, Moroccan, and later Ethiopian Jews in particular were often married off while in their early teens. Even polygamy, which Ashkenazi rabbis as long ago as the Middle Ages had declared outlaw, was still practiced to some extent. Everywhere, the mere idea of women appearing in public while wearing pants, let alone short ones as many kibbutz women in particular did, went against their every notion as to how the world functioned or should function. Female soldiers working with Oriental immigrants had to be warned "to avoid hurting [the immigrants'] feelings by behaving in ways that are contrary to tradition."[11] No doubt inspired from above, popular poetasters wrote rhymes about how their hearts leaped at the sight of "the dark and beautiful" Moroccan girl, Simone. To what effect, is hard to say.

In 1962 only 2.3 percent of Oriental Jews were engaged in "free" and technical professions, as opposed to ten times as many among those with roots in Europe and the United States. Their participation, or rather lack of it, in the system of education reflected this fact. Thrust into the bottom of the social and professional heap, both in the towns and the countryside their lives were often very hard. It is scant wonder, then, that in 1959 some of them launched a wave of riots. The most serious disturbances took place in Haifa's Wadi Salib, a slum district that had been abandoned by its former Arab residents and that, to make things worse, was located downhill from the wealthier areas where Ashkenazis lived. In one of these riots the local Histadrut club and the Mapai House were wrecked. Demonstrations were held, many windows broken, some shops looted, and a few shots fired, though nobody was killed. How uncomprehending the establishment had been was perhaps expressed most clearly by one parole officer's surprised exclamation: "I came across Wadi Salib residents who felt they were discriminated against!"[12]

Yet in some ways the reception given to Holocaust survivors was even worse. As described earlier, right from the beginning one of the prime objectives of Zionism had been to create a new kind of "fighting Jew"—"a proud and cruel race," as the Revisionist anthem, written by Jabotinsky, put it. The way all too many "native" Israelis saw things, the very fact that immigrants from Europe had gone through the Holocaust proved that they did not correspond to that stereotype. Perhaps the "natives" were merely feeling guilty about the fact that, even as millions were being murdered by the Nazis, they themselves had done so little to help—although, in truth, it is not easy to see how a community numbering half a million, located on the eastern shore of the Mediterranean, and living under foreign rule, could have acted. So powerful were these feelings that Holocaust studies in Israel were dominated by the question, "Why didn't they fight?" Victims were described as "calves going to the slaughter"; schoolchildren during the late 1950s were even made to memorize and sing a poem to that effect. Surely a more sickening way of treating both the living and the dead can hardly be imagined.

To be sure, there were some signs of change even before 1960—in 1959, groups of survivors finally succeeded in pushing through the demand that the state recognize an official "Holocaust Memorial Day." Still, it was the Eichmann trial that really opened the floodgates of memory. Ben Gurion's announcement in the Knesset that Adolf Eichmann, "one of the main Nazi War criminals . . . responsible for . . . the 'Final Solution'" had been captured and would be tried in Jerusalem was greeted by stormy applause. Was it not a ringing confirmation of everything Israel had been established to achieve; namely, to provide a secure refuge for the Jewish people? Over the next year, no effort was spared to ensure that the full horrors of the Holocaust should be brought home to every single Israeli. As Hannah Arendt was later to write in her famous work *Eichmann in Jerusalem* (which Ben Gurion refused to have translated into Hebrew), things may have been carried too far. In particular Eichmann, an insignificant little man in ill-fitting clothes with hardly anything interesting to say, just did not fill the role allocated to him, that of an inhuman monster. To many, that fact came as a grave disappointment.

Some of the evidence heard in court was irrelevant or even manufactured. As the list of horrors was recited, people had to be reminded that Eichmann himself had never killed anybody. His area of responsibility included neither Poland nor the occupied parts of the USSR, where most Jews lived and where they were actually exterminated, but was limited to finding the Jews, concentrating them in ghettoes, and transporting them. One witness, a survivor who called himself Ka-Tzetnik (Concentration Camp Inmate), was well known as the author of semipornographic novels about his experiences in which truth and fiction could not always be told apart; the fact that he fainted on the witness stand did nothing to solve the mystery. Yet most people found the effect healing. To quote Nathan Alterman again, "All of us had known that there were among us some people *who had come from that world* [original emphasis]. We met them on our daily business. . . . As a clerk in some office was handing us a form . . . we noticed that he had a bluish number tattooed on his arm . . . However, it seems that only this awesome and sublime trial . . . made us realize that those people are not just a bunch of individuals but part of the terrible memories of our nation."[13] "Yes," wrote another popular poet, Haim Gouri, "we had always known . . . but only now do we really start to comprehend and to understand" what they had really gone through.[14]

Building a nation is always very difficult, and it would have been surprising if these and other problems had not often led to great hardship and perhaps even greater bitterness. Nevertheless, socially speaking, during the first half of the 1960s, in many ways the country was doing very well. Despite the divide between Ashkenazis and Sephardis, ethnically based parties never succeeded in attracting a large part of the vote. By the mid-1960s they were clearly at their last gasp. Conversely, "mixed" marriages slowly increased until, in 1965, they were accounting for one-sixth of the total.[15] Perhaps the greatest achievement was in the field of education. At first mass immigration after 1948 caused average standards to fall, but by the early 1960s they had started rising again. Instead rapid population growth was causing new schools to shoot out of the ground. With them came libraries, laboratories, and other facilities. Certainly the facilities were far from opulent and the quality of the schools, especially among Oriental Jews in new settlements, not always the highest. Still, the first nine years of education were free and compulsory. As a result, illiteracy, the curse of the countries where many Oriental immigrants originated, was gradually eliminated.

Particularly impressive was the increase in the number of high school students. It went up from a mere fifty thousand in 1958 to two and a half times that figure ten years later; in various international tests, Israeli students were doing very well. The language of instruction was always Hebrew. For Ashkenazis, at any rate, once they had mastered it the road to full integration was open. Though many foreign-language newspapers continued to be published, by the late 1960s their readerships were beginning to age. Another important factor in overcoming linguistic diversity was the IDF, and especially general conscription. Well into the 1960s mobilization orders targeting reservists (who were older than the regulars) were published in many languages, but other than that the army insisted on doing its business in Hebrew. Being technically progressive, it probably originated more new Hebrew terms than any other institution. It also held courses for soldiers with less than elementary school education to enable them to improve their language skills.

Compared to other developed countries, the crime rate, especially that of violent crime, was very low. In part this was due to the fact that Israelis hardly drank—so little that some doctors could confuse a drunk with a person who had suffered a heart attack. This, in turn, may have had something to do with the fact that customs duties made imported wine and spirits prohibitively expensive, whereas local ones, to put it mildly, were not always of outstanding quality; of one cognac, named 777, people said that it had been designed as a cure for malaria. Members of youth movements, recognizable by their colored shirts, ties, and round *tembel* (idiots') hats, thought nothing of spending a night on the beach or setting up camp in a wooded area in the countryside. In sharp contrast to most of their foreign models, these movements were sexually integrated; boys and girls used to sleep in adjacent tents or simply lie down side by side in the open. Though they did play pranks on each other, nobody had heard of sexual harassment or abuse.

Also in contrast to movements in other countries, the Israeli youth movements were led almost exclusively by sixteen- to eighteen-year-olds. For example, the "tribe" of Scouts in Ramat Gan, a town near Tel Aviv, numbered about a thousand youngsters aged ten to eighteen. Yet there was only one adult, assisted by a few twenty-year-olds, supervising them. Probably the extraordinary freedom young people enjoyed had something to do with the fact that they were soon going to be conscripted and, quite possibly, sacrificed to Moloch. They walked, cycled—though Israeli drivers have a bad reputation, there was little traffic—hiked and hitchhiked with little to fear from either criminals or the police; during the 1960s in particular, they could go anywhere on their own. To be sure, even then there was some cross-border terrorism. Still, there was no fence surrounding the prime minister's office, let alone other ministries, so that anybody could walk into the building without so much as being stopped or asked for an ID.

The man who occupied the prime minister's office at the time was

Levi Eshkol. His party, Mapai, continued to receive the support of large parts of the "labor settlements," i.e., members of the kibbutzim and the moshavim. However, the massive immigration of the 1950s in particular caused their share in the population, which had never been very large, to fall. This left "socialist" Mapai dependent on the petit bourgeois vote in the towns; meanwhile, the relatively few who had more to lose tended to vote for one out of several middle-of-the-road, liberal parties that never amounted to much. Mapai's own politics were becoming more middle of the road, a change that was accentuated still further in 1968 when, following a merger with some left-wing allies, it dropped the magic word "Workers" from its title and became known simply as "the Alignment." The party was also tainted by corruption, to the point that Golda Meir, before she herself became its secretary general in 1966, once compared it to "Tammany Hall."

Partly because the foundations of the state seemed to be firmly in place, and partly because he personally bore little resemblance to his fiery predecessor, Eshkol himself took a much more relaxed attitude on many questions. Perhaps his most important single move was made in 1966, when he abolished the military administration under which Israel's Arabs had been living for eighteen years. Originally put in place for security reasons, the IDF-run regime had survived the War of Independence, and kept about three hundred thousand people under night curfew while at the same time requiring them to obtain licenses to move out of their districts by day as well as for starting any kind of business.

By the early 1960s this regime had degenerated into a system of favoritism that enabled the ruling party to collect votes. This explains why an earlier attempt to do away with it was averted only by the vote of an Arab MK, Ziab Abid; and also why the right-wing Herut Party sided with the abolitionists. Eshkol himself was motivated partly by a growing shortage of labor both in the towns and in the kibbutzim and moshavim where many of his supporters lived. His trust proved well founded. Having been cut off from the rest of the Middle East by the 1948 War, and being discriminated against in many fields from employment to municipal services, certainly not every Israeli Arab liked the state. Some said so as loudly as they could, and a few tried to set up a

nationalist political movement, Al Ard (the Land), that was soon prohibited. However, before 1967 not a single one is known to have joined
a terrorist movement.

By holding regular meetings with Begin, Eshkol also improved relations with the parliamentary opposition. In particular, his granting
permission for Jabotinsky's remains to be brought and reburied marked
a "declaration of independence"[16] from Ben Gurion for which the latter never forgave him and who from this point on made Eshkol's life as
bitter as he possibly could. Last but not least, Eshkol reduced the powers of censorship. Previously they had tended to be rather extensive.
Ben Gurion himself once threatened to use the security service against
a recalcitrant weekly, *Haolam Haze* (This World), which he accused of
scandalmongering. Only Begin's intercession with the head spook, Is-
sar Harel, prevented the editors from being arrested. Greater freedom
made it possible to discuss the state's shortcomings, including cases of
corruption that used to be carefully hidden. Radio broadcasting services, which previously had been subordinated to the prime minister's
office, were transferred to a public authority that was at least nominally
independent. By the time Eshkol died in harness in 1969, the first TV
station, meant principally to wean people away from foreign ones, was
also in operation.

These on the whole very favorable developments were reflected by
cultural changes. Pre-1948 settlers were drawn to the Land of Israel as
the country of the Old Testament. In the words of the Declaration of
Independence, it was "the birthplace of the Jewish people [where] their
spiritual, religious and political identity was shaped." Yet it was also a
country for which many of them had no more liking than the kaiser
did. The climate was hot, arid, and, especially in the spring and autumn, dusty owing to the desert wind coming from the east. The hills
held lots of rocks but offered little vegetation and less shadow. As Ben
Gurion, quoting the Old Testament, put it to his dying wife, "I remember thee, the grace of thy youth . . . when thou wentest after me in the
wilderness, in a land that was not sown."[17] To make things worse, it was
populated by "the primitive people,"[18] exotic, mysterious, and always at
least slightly wild and dangerous. Hence, the Zionists' goal was not just
to settle it but to transform it—to "make the desert bloom," as the saying

went. Conversely, in a period when imperialists everywhere were making similar claims, the transformation itself would serve as an argument to justify the Zionist enterprise.

Younger Israelis growing up in the 1960s took a different view. To be sure, most also despised the Arabs and looked down on them. Had not those Arabs been beaten in 1948 and 1956, and would they not be beaten even more spectacularly in 1967? A common term of abuse was "Arabush," meaning, roughly, "dirty little Arab." The words "Arab work" stood for everything second-class and shoddy. Among Sephardis, to say that somebody's sister was sleeping with an Arab was a deadly insult; if that did not apply to Ashkenazis, then probably it was because the possibility was too remote to contemplate. Yet the same people were likely to eat Arab dishes such as *humus* and *tehinah,* not using cutlery but wiping them out of the dishes with the aid of Arab pita bread; herbs such as nana and *zatar* were also much appreciated. Above all, felafel acquired the status of a national dish and was celebrated in at least one popular song. *Keffiyehs* remained popular until the early 1970s, when they became the hallmark of terrorists. Young people often used Arab expressions such as *yallah* (hurry up), *tfadal* (thank you), *maalish* (never mind), and *mabruk* (congratulations), in day-to-day speech. This was particularly true of swearwords, of which Hebrew, a language long used almost exclusively for religious purposes, has very few. If Begin, who rarely swore, used Polish for the purpose, his followers, some of whom could do little else, definitely did not.

Disliking what they saw of the land, the founders had worked as hard as they could to transform it into a copy of their native one. They drilled for water and planted trees—at least one well-known writer expressed his longing for the "green color, semi darkness and profound silence" of Europe's forests[19]—as well as lawns and flowerbeds. Not so the sons and daughters who were much more sensitive to the land's often harsh beauty; "hills made of copper," as one song, referring to the Judean Desert, aptly put it. While water was and remains precious, those lucky enough to have gardens tried to incorporate that beauty into them. Rocks and ancient potsherds were gathered and put into position. First in the kibbutzim and then elsewhere some people started growing cacti, whereas discarded artillery casings, made of brass, often had a second career as flowerpots with thistles thrust into them. Artists sought to accentuate and enhance the native vistas by means of strategically placed "environmental" sculptures. In the words of Danny Caravan (1930–), one of the best-known sculptors of this school: "I tried to blend the structures [he was referring to a monument in honor of the capture of Beer Sheba in 1948] to the site. . . . They grow from the soil as variations on the neighboring hills."[20] Much of this was the usual rebellion of a younger generation against its elders. Yet it also showed that they had taken root in the country and were making it their own.

In other ways, the effect was just the opposite. As has often been said, Arab villages, whatever their shortcomings (lack of planning, and lack of modern facilities such as proper roads, running water, sewage, and the like), looked as if they had come with the hills on which they stood. That was not true of a great many Jewish-Israeli settlements, which looked as if a magic hand had taken them from Europe and planted them in the Middle East with no regard either to the climate or to the landscape. In particular, a combination of economic poverty and an extreme shortage of housing caused by immigration made its effects felt. In the near total absence of wood, almost all houses were built of cement blocks. Those in the countryside were simply cubes with doors and windows, ill finished, gray colored, and not nearly as neat as the children's picture books of the time suggested. Courtyards tended to be cluttered with plastic containers, old boots, and rusty bicycles, not to mention the occasional scorpion. While a water tower crowned every settlement, few were built with any kind of aesthetic effects in mind.

In the towns, blocks of flats were erected seriatim with the aid of "concrete cannons" during the 1950s and 1960s. These also tended to be ugly and ill finished, mere cubes with or without pillions and penetrated by narrow, dark stairwells. As happened in other countries as well, prefabricated dwellings in particular quickly deteriorated into slums and had to be rebuilt later on. To this day, the term "flaking apartment house" has remained synonymous with undesirable living quarters. Since elevators were rare, normally four stories were the maximum allowed, though buildings situated on the sides of mountains sometimes had three going down and three going up. Following a British Mandatory law, most Jerusalem buildings at any rate were covered with the local limestone, gray during the day but taking on a soft pink glow as the sunrays fell on them at sunset. Not so those of Tel Aviv and other coastal towns, many of which were badly corroded by salty particles originating in the Mediterranean and carried by the wind.

Almost everywhere conditions were Spartan and living space at a premium. During the 1960s, this caused many families to close off the balconies of their flats by all kinds of improvised, often very unsightly, contraptions made of asbestos or plastic. Acting with or without municipal permission, others erected makeshift structures on the flat roofs of the buildings in which they lived or else between the pillions that supported them. When one teacher told a group of middle-class high school students (since high school was not free and parents had to pay tuition, practically all students in such schools were middle class and upward) that ideally a house or flat had to have rooms equal to the number of occupants plus one, all they could do was stare at him in disbelief. In the entire class, there probably was not one whose family enjoyed such luxury.

To save money, many military headquarters and government offices occupied old British, German (Templer), or even Ottoman vintage buildings. Army bases, which by the force of circumstances take up relatively enormous spaces, tended (and tend) to be shapeless, haphazard gatherings of scattered, ill-maintained, and flaky structures. Half-legible signs, pipes running in all directions, strands of rusty barbed wire, and overflowing waste containers are everywhere; often the bases' only saving grace are the eucalyptus trees by which many of them were surrounded and which hid the worst eyesores. In Jerusalem both the Supreme Court and central police headquarters were located in buildings that had been taken over from the Russian Orthodox Church and modified until they looked like nothing in particular. By contrast, the Ministry of Education occupied a turn-of-the-twentieth-century Italian hospital that had been requisitioned by the British in World War II. It is a magnificent crenellated edifice that came straight out of the Florence of Lorenzo the Magnificent.

Some new buildings provided room for experiments in architecture. This was particularly true of the communal dining halls. In any kibbutz it was the most important structure of all and the first one that visitors would be taken to see; it was here, perhaps more than anywhere else, that diagonal lines first started breaking the monotony of the vertical and horizontal lines characteristic of Bauhaus and international-style buildings. On the other hand, the Histadrut headquarters complex on Tel Aviv's Arlosoroff Street could have been taken straight out of Walter Ulbricht's East Germany. The buildings erected to house various ministries on a hill outside Jerusalem in the late 1950s are simply rectangular blocks without any aesthetic pretensions; later, things became even worse as air conditioners dotted the exterior walls. The chief rabbinate's building on Jerusalem's Agron Street does have such pretensions, but with its symmetric lines and flat cupola it looks as if it was designed by Albert Speer for some particularly authoritarian government office. Also in Jerusalem, perhaps the most successful buildings erected in the 1960s were the Knesset, the Israel Museum, and the Hebrew University. Located close to one another with lots of greenery all around, separately and together they create a pleasant effect in spite of the vehement criticism to which they were originally subjected.

These cultural deeds and misdeeds reflected the haste with which everything was done as well as the scant available means. Yet other factors, too, were involved. This was a new country just being built, but claiming as its own foundations going back thousands of years. For all the talk about the need to "strike roots," nobody had an idea what "Israeliness" really meant. Part Jewish, to be sure, since very few people were prepared to give up on the state's Jewish character; but also part socialist (socialism being the ideology of the ruling party), part agricultural (in reality, the percentage of those active in agriculture was small and declining), part urban (petit bourgeois, often with little money and less grace), part Western, and part Oriental. Ostensibly the one thing everybody could agree on was the need for Hebrew, but even here there were some ultra-Orthodox groups that insisted on speaking Yiddish. In many ways it was a backward country, but already the foundations for a much more modern future were being laid.

Not counting Druze, Circassians, Christian Arabs, and Muslim Arabs, the country was filled with a bustling Babylon of people. Among the Jewish majority most were recent arrivals from all over the world. They adhered to very different forms of Judaism, spoke any number of different languages, and represented very different civilizations. In early 1966 a severe economic recession, the first since 1956, created a real crisis; yet among the Jewish population, at any rate, the sense of pride in the state and its achievements was well nigh universal. As events were soon to prove, it was also justified.

"A Car for Every Worker"

Under the British Mandate, the most outstanding feature of the economy of the Land of Israel had been its numerous contradictions. At the very bottom of the heap stood the seminomadic Bedouin, whose possessions consisted almost entirely of tents; a few camels, asses, and goats; and perhaps some gold coins that, instead of being deposited in banks, were worn by their wives. Only slightly better off were the great masses of rural fellaheen and, in the teeming towns, the crowds of Arab beggars and day laborers. The towns also held Arab craftsmen, moneylenders, merchants, and landowners, but their number was relatively small, and there was hardly such a thing as an Arab Palestinian industry.

Among the Jews, about 20 percent lived in the countryside. However, much higher standards of education and financial help from abroad translated into a very different rural environment. People might dwell in shanties, perform truly backbreaking work, and feed on a diet rich in cucumbers and tomatoes—red gold, as they are called—but somewhat poor in everything else. Yet as early as 1939 they were using more tractors per acre of land than their colleagues in any other country outside the United States;[21] Jewish yields per acre and per cow were much higher than among their Arab neighbors. Most Jewish town dwellers were employed in construction and the services, but by the 1930s early signs of industrialization appeared. Inside the Jewish community, the ever-growing power of Histadrut made for a socialist society with many collective institutions. Yet externally the Mandatory authorities instituted a laissez-faire regime. It was open to world trade and capital flows—some people never ceased wondering why British firms did not do more to deal with German, Austrian, French, and Italian competition in Palestine. Behind the regime stood what was then one of the two strongest currencies on earth, the pound sterling.

With the outbreak of World War II the situation changed. Imports from countries other than those of the British Empire ceased almost immediately. Britain's own economy was harnessed to the war effort, cutting imports still further. On the other hand, the arrival of large numbers of imperial troops raised demand by leaps and bounds. Though local industry did what it could to fill the gap, its capacity was limited. As in Britain's other colonies, the outcome was inflation, which the authorities tried to combat by imposing administrative measures such as price and wage controls. Also as in the case of Britain's other colonies, repressed inflation—a result of too much money chasing too few goods—caused large balances of sterling to accumulate in London. Sterling itself never really regained its convertibility into dollars as the only other currency worth having. Essentially, it became the forced currency of a bankrupt country.

When the State of Israel broke out in turn, its leaders inherited this system. Even more than their British predecessors during the War, their overriding, almost desperate concern was foreign currency. In part, this was because of the need to pay for the weapons now being imported, particularly from Eastern Europe; in part, because the British, in a fit of pique at their unruly former subjects, immediately took the 100 million Palestinian pounds deposited in London off sterling (a move that was only reversed in 1951). Nor was there any question of paying the local costs of the 1948 War by taxation. Instead it was necessary to resort to loans and, above all, print money; Moshe Dayan in his memoirs recalls how, in July 1948, his wife and he flew back from a mission in the United States while seated on crates filled with the first Israeli banknotes. To prevent inflation the existing system of controls was left in place and reinforced. Practical considerations apart, Israel's leaders were socialists with a strong belief in the virtues of a managed economy. Hence the system fitted them as a saddle does a horse.

Ben Gurion himself had a strong visionary streak in his character. This caused him to put great emphasis on long-term, sometimes almost utopian projects as well as distributive justice; what he wanted was not merely a Jewish state but one that would be good and just as well. Yet he was fundamentally uninterested in economics—"It is not a science," he once exclaimed—seldom carrying a penny in his pocket and leaving household finances to his wife. The one thing he spent money on was books; at the time he died he owned twelve thousand of them. By default, the task of financing the state fell largely to David Horowitz (1899–1979). Galician born, originally he had been a kibbutz member and left-wing socialist. Working as an economist in the Jewish Agency, he discarded most of his socialist views and in 1947 was appointed secretary general in the Ministry of Finance. Unable to make Ben Gurion understand that "economic facts, unlike the Egyptians, do not run away,"[22] in 1953 he left the treasury. However, a year later he returned to harness by founding the Bank of Israel and leading it until his retirement in 1972.

The task Horowitz faced was daunting—not just to pay for the recent war, but to somehow finance feeding, housing, and finding employment for hundreds of thousands of mostly penniless, often unskilled, not seldom sick immigrants. A rare entry in Ben Gurion's diary says it all. "Kaplan [Eliezer Kaplan, the first minister of finance]: in two months we shall run out of bread. Transportation takes 5–6 weeks. Nobody in Europe will give us a penny's worth of credit. Unless we do something, disaster will strike."[23] Yet Kaplan was a sick man. Each time a similar piece of news arrived he would send his deputy, Horowitz, into the big, wide world to beg for a million here, a million there. In fact, it is almost impossible to exaggerate Israel's economic difficulties during these years; they were sometimes compared with those facing the Soviet Union in 1941–1945. If in coping with them, errors, even grave ones, were committed, then *tant pis*, as the saying goes.

In May 1949, an austerity program (*tzena*) was put in place. Under its terms, all foreign purchases were to be made exclusively by government-licensed firms. First the owners had to hand in a request to receive foreign currency from the government; predictably, the outcome was endless bureaucratic difficulties and, of course, increased costs. To "equalize the burden" between rich and poor, a rationing system was instituted. At first it applied only to a few staple foods such as oil, sugar, and margarine. Later, most other foodstuffs were added to the list. The resulting diet, calculated at twenty-six hundred calories per person per day, was more or less adequate. However, since it consisted mainly of bread, codfish, powdered milk, and powdered eggs, it was also monotonous.

Foodstuffs such as butter and cream were banned so that possessing them became, in theory, a prosecutable offense; pregnant women, needing calcium, were particularly hard-hit. The following popular song captured the atmosphere of the times:

> *A young guy, big and strong*
> *enters a restaurant that's been there for long.*
> *No sooner done, than he breaks into song:*
> *"Meatballs! I am dying for meatballs!"*[24]

Manufactured goods, too, were rationed. The list included textiles, shoes, furniture, and assorted household utensils. Local producers of such items were instructed to focus on single lines known as *lakol* (for everybody). Whatever was on sale was cheap but shoddy; in fact, even the rationing books themselves kept falling apart. To obtain any kind of goods one had to stand in line, hand in one's coupons, and obtain a receipt. Next one had to make one's purchases, stand in line again, and pay. Since food coupons were only valid for the days that were stamped on them, the burden all this put on housewives was immense, to say nothing of administrative snafus that often prevented goods from being where they were supposed to be at the time they were supposed to be there.

In charge of the system was Dov Yosef (1899–1980), originally a lawyer from Canada. He had a passion for detail and no sense of humor; as has been said, with his mustache, black suits, and stiff manner he looked and acted like a Mandatory civil servant whom the British had forgotten to take along.[25] In the Knesset, he and the opposition debated the system's ability to provide sufficient eggs, meat, fish (big or small), pants, shoes, diapers, and, of all things, gowns for newly created physicians and lawyers.[26]

The outcome of this system was a thriving black market, fed partly by the kibbutzim and moshavim and partly by some better-to-do new immigrants who brought their goods along specifically to sell them later on. A small army of inspectors was appointed and citizens' courts established to deal with the phenomenon. However, their members tended to sympathize with the accused—a reminder, perhaps, of a centuries-old Jewish antigovernment tradition that may still be seen in many cases. Rich people, not so rich people lucky enough to receive goods from friends and relatives abroad, and officials able to claim expenses for hosting foreigners fared best. One day a journalist knocked on Yosef's door and asked his wife how she got along. "Nobody will believe I can live on rationed goods alone . . . ," she said, "yet I cook and bake and do what I can. My conscience only feels responsible to those who died for the country, the one we must maintain to honor their memory!"[27] Her own daughter had been killed in the battles for Jerusalem.

Though some rationing remained in force until 1959, much of the system was abolished as early as 1953. One reason for this was growing unrest in the form of strikes and demonstrations that Mapai feared might favor its rivals, the liberal General Zionists; another, the beginning, in the same year, of reparations payments from West Germany, which considerably eased the foreign currency situation. The decision to enter into negotiations with Bonn was made in December 1951, and a month later the Knesset voted to ratify it. To the Germans, it marked one step on the way back from pariah status to the family of nations. In Israel, a state formed partly in response to the Holocaust, its reception was predictably stormy. Tens of thousands took to the streets of Jerusalem to demand that the Germans be sent to the devil and "tainted" money be refused; as so often Begin, a man always liable to be carried along by his own fiery rhetoric, set the tone. During one demonstration he threatened Ben Gurion—"that dwarfish dictator and big egomaniac"—that "today I shall order bloodshed—as I did not do at the time of *Altalena* affair—yes! You will not grant us quarter and we'll do the same . . . it will be a life to death war."[28] Yet this was the same man who, a little earlier, had accused Dov Yosef of trying to fill people's bellies with statistics instead of food.

Begin's antics earned him a three-month suspension from the Knesset, but in the end even his own party members backed away from his more extremist statements. On September 10, 1952, an agreement was signed. By the best available calculation, individual survivors who were living in Israel received about 7 billion German marks (1.75 billion U.S. dollars), a huge sum that helps explain the growing gap between Europeans and Orientals. The state received about half as much. In the words of a Bank of Israel study:

[In 1953–1964] German reparations financed 9 percent of all imports and 17 percent of the balance of payments deficit. Directly or indirectly, the reparations also paid for 15 percent of all investments. During the period in question GNP grew threefold, and the reparations were probably responsible for 15 percent of that increase; in 1964 they accounted for 10 percent of GNP. These investments provided work for 45,000 people. . . . The reparations played a major role in developing shipping, power systems, railways, fishing, and several major industrial plants. . . . They prolonged Israel's dependence on imported capital, but made possible increased production, consumption, and a higher rate of economic growth.[29]

And here lies the rub. Since 1945 numerous so-called developing countries have received foreign assistance, some of it fairly massive. However, too often it has been frittered away—either to buy consumer goods or ending up in rulers' secret Swiss bank accounts.

Certainly Israel did not always invest its money wisely. For example, the attempt to gain more agricultural land by draining the Hula Lake turned out to be an ecological disaster and had to be reversed. The copper mines at Timna north of Elat proved unviable and had to be closed. Cotton raised for export demanded too much water, and the few civilian aircraft built by Israel Aircraft Industries found no customers. Still, reparations financed 26 percent of all imported Israeli capital goods, 11 percent of imported production factors (mainly fuel), but only 3 percent of consumer goods.[30] Like their foreign opposite numbers, government officials and Histadrut functionaries tended to live off their expense accounts, but apart from that probably little money was diverted from the public purse to private ones. Several Israeli prime ministers died with hardly a penny to their names—the best known being Begin who, leaving office in 1983, did not have a flat to live in. Others were very well off, thank you, but none became a billionaire (as far as we know), or ended his or her career by having to flee abroad.

Even taking reparations into account, for decades the main economic problem remained the country's chronic balance-of-payments deficit. Given the need to absorb immigrants and put them to work, inevitably the government's primary goal was rapid growth. As the recession of 1966–1967 proved, in the absence of growth not merely would immigration, as the state's real source of strength, come to an end but people with the appropriate education and skills would leave. Yet capital for investment was always short; one reason for this, of course, were the heavy expenditures caused by defense, which, during the period in question, was eating up about 9 percent of the GNP each year. Except in agriculture, which thanks to the social makeup of farmers and kibbutzniks was very progressive, too often the outcome was primitive manufacturing methods and low productivity.

When it came to the more sophisticated consumer products, another problem was small production lines. The local market was quite limited, whereas war and continuing hostility among the Arab states had isolated the country and cut it off from its traditional customers in the Middle East. All this explains why, in the 1960s, watching the "native" Israeli cars (Carmel, Sussita, and Sabra, all three of them using cheap fiberglass bodies mounted on a foreign chassis with a foreign engine) being glued together by hand, one did not know whether to laugh or to cry. That these and similar cars had no prospect whatsoever of being exported hardly requires saying. Not merely were they mechanically unreliable, but legend had it that camels liked to eat them. When it comes to corporations, Israel never succeeded in building either a Honda or a Hyundai. Finally most Israelis, instead of taking to "productive" work in the fields and the factories, stubbornly stuck to the centuries-old Jewish tradition of preferring the services. Neither Zionist ideology nor government homilies were able to change this fact.

Part of the gap could be bridged by means of even more foreign aid, primarily from the United States and from individual Jews abroad. Another source of income were the bonds sold by the Jewish Agency; though they did bear interest, many saw them more as a charity than as an investment. The rest had to be dealt with by instituting extremely high tariffs on many goods; whole series of prohibitions on the purchase and possession of foreign currency; and differential exchange rates for exports, imports, tourism, and foreign travel. At moments when nothing else seemed to work and bankruptcy was looking the state in the face, it was always possible to resort to devaluation. From the end of the Mandate until 1964 the lira lost about 85 percent of its value against its parent, the pound sterling; yet the latter itself was repeatedly devalued vis-à-vis the almighty U.S. dollar. With devaluations came inflation, which Horowitz, now acting as chief of the Bank of Israel, always regarded as the great enemy but which he did not have the authority to restrain. Nor did the process end in 1967. Then and later, as people used to say, to make a small fortune in Israel it was necessary to bring in a large one first.

Other aspects of the economy were also managed from the top. Among the most important was and is land ownership. By 1948, less than 10 percent of the total amount of land had been purchased by Jewish individuals or organizations. The rest consisted either of state land inherited from the British, who had inherited it from the Ottomans, or of abandoned Arab land; in the Negev there was some land that was owned on a collective basis by Bedouin tribes, or so they claimed. To manage all this land a special authority, known as the Custodian of Absentee Property, was established under the Ministry of Finance; later all land was put under the Israel Land Administration, which was part of the Ministry of Agriculture. As early as the summer of 1948 rural communities asked for, and received, permission to harvest crops left behind by Arab farmers. Later the lands in question were leased to the communities in question on condition that they should be used solely for agriculture. More requisitioning followed, especially during the period of military administration. In the end, the 20 percent or so of Israelis who were Arabs were left in possession of somewhat less than 4 percent of the land.

The land thus made available made it possible to set up as many as seven hundred new settlements all over the country. To this day, whenever some new settlement or city neighborhood is to be built, land must first be obtained from the administration. In a small country where land is scarce, this puts the administration in a position where it wields truly enormous economic power. Starting in the 1990s, there has been a tendency to permit agricultural land to be used for other purposes, too. Does a large garden or park, rented out for couples to get married in, count as "agriculture," and may one use it to raise horses and start a riding school? At the same time, the status of built-over land started to change as leases were canceled and property was privatized. As might be imagined, both processes give rise to many disputes—partly economic, given the vast opportunities for profiteering; and partly ideological, as people questioned whether state-owned land should really be transferred into private hands. As a result, progress was very slow. At present, the Administration still controls 92 percent of all land.

In distributing land as in much else, preference was given to agricultural settlements. In part, this was due to the perceived need to invert the inverted pyramid and create a new Jewish people whose members would be attached to the soil. Also important was the wish to settle outlying parts of the country so as to consolidate the gains made during the War of Independence. Only a strong rural sector, consisting of many settlements and based on agriculture, could secure Israel's continued existence, or so Ben Gurion, Eshkol (who as minister of the treasury was personally responsible for establishing many new settlements), and their fellow senior Mapai leaders believed. Over time, a whole theology was stamped out of the ground to explain how the Crusaders had failed precisely by not paying attention to this point. Yet at the same time as the system favored cultivators of the soil, it also subjected them to production quotas. As a result, the strong producers had, and have, their wings clipped so as to support weaker ones.

Another favored sector were the numerous companies linked with Histadrut. Largely run by Mapai functionaries, in many ways they acted as de facto arms of the state, carrying out projects nobody else would touch. In the words of Meir during her tenure as minister of labor (1949–1956), "I have not yet seen a private entrepreneur who would go to Beer Sheba . . . and construct modest housing which could be rented to new immigrants at a low price";[31] no fewer than 83 percent of all dwellings earmarked for immigrants were built by Solel Boneh, Histadrut's earthmoving and construction company. Other Histadrut companies also received preferential treatment when it came to leasing land, submitting tenders, and finance; Histadrut, after all, owned a bank, a large insurance company, and many pension funds. Finally, there was a political dimension to all this. Like the rural settlements, Histadrut formed a critical pillar in Mapai's rule. Also like the rural settlements, it had to be shown some favor if the party were to remain in power.

From 1953 to 1968 the government's, Histadrut's, and private enterprise's relative shares in the economy hardly changed. The first and the second accounted for about 20 percent of the GNP each, whereas the third was responsible for the remaining 60 percent. Their relative shares in providing employment were not much different, which in turn meant that productivity in all three sectors was broadly similar.[32] Desperately in need of capital, the state could not go too far in (mis) treating either large local companies or what foreign investors could be lured into the country. The former also had their own accountants and attorneys with whom to fight back. This did not apply to small independent businessmen. Regarded as just the type that labor Zionism had set out to eradicate, they were the milk cows on whose teats the establishment fed. In response they developed an entire culture of tax avoidance and evasion. This could not have continued without the assistance of the general public, who felt some sympathy with them and was quite happy to cooperate with them by not demanding receipts, etc.

To meet the population's minimum demands, basic foodstuffs such as flour, bread, milk, sugar, and oil were heavily subsidized and so cheap that consumers often wasted them. The same was true of public transport; during the 1960s a bus ticket in Jerusalem cost only about four U.S. cents. Intercity bus services, though uncomfortable and not always reliable, were likewise very cheap. Many other products, especially imported ones, were extremely expensive both in world terms and, even more so, in terms of local purchasing power. Disregarding the extraordinarily high tariffs on coffee, which were designed to protect local manufacturers and became the subject of many jokes, throughout the period vehicles were so heavily taxed that the idea of "a car for every worker" (a slogan used by Ben Gurion's Rafi party during the 1965 election campaign) sounded hopelessly utopian and may very well have backfired. Also, the country did not have one real motorway. Even in the early 1980s men using the newspapers to meet women would advertise that they possessed *rehev* (a vehicle), indicating both that ownership was an important requisite for finding a mate and that it was anything but self-evident.

Not just cars, but anything with an electric motor in it was defined as a "luxury." The same applied to electronic equipment such as television sets—which until the late 1960s were extremely rare—radios, record players, tape recorders, and even telephones. Not merely were the last-named very expensive, but outside the great cities they could only be had by paying a deposit and putting one's name on a years-long waiting list; only when electronics began to take the place of mechanical exchanges in the 1980s did the countryside finally see the construction of a proper telephone network. To protect the local industries, textiles were taxed at no less than 231 percent, causing Israelis to dream of London's Marks & Spencer as a sort of promised land. Yet the single product that carried the highest tariff of all was rugs. The largest local manufacturer was Avraham Shapiro. He was an enormously wealthy—to his hangers-on he was known as the Master—and enormously obese Orthodox MK; his party, Agudat Israel, often held the balance in the Knesset. For decades he kept the inhabitants of an entire township, Or Akiva, working for his firm, Carmel Industries; only in the late 1980s was his stranglehold over this part of the economy finally broken.

In many ways, those who suffered most under the system were housewives. Unless they were middle class or higher, they had to do their laundry by hand. Unless they could afford an electric refrigerator, which until the late 1950s remained a fairly rare and precious item, they had to either use an icebox or do their shopping on a daily basis. They also had to clean their homes without a vacuum cleaner (to say nothing of the fact that many homes were too small for one to be efficiently used in them). In summer they did not enjoy the benefit of air-conditioning. In winter, given that central heating was very rare, they had to buy kerosene from street vendors and schlep it home. Some did not even have cooking gas but continued to prepare the family meals on kerosene stoves. As in other socialist countries toilet articles, deodorants, cosmetics, beauty aids, hair driers, and similar items, though not officially banned, were disapproved of and made prohibitively expensive. Certainly the lives of most 1960s Israeli women were no longer as hard as those of some of their predecessors who, settling the country, had worked in the fields along with the men. Still, they were hard enough; in the words of yet another popular song, "Her eyes are tired, but her legs quite nice."

Inevitably, the outcome was a lively black market. Concentrated in

Haifa and Tel Aviv, it dealt with products imported either by sailors or by new immigrants as well as in hard currency needed for speculation or for foreign travel. Tel Aviv's Lilienblum Street in particular was a precinct where shady characters gathered, accosting passersby, leading them into dark stairwells and hidden courtyards, and sometimes stealing from them. From time to time the police raided that street and similar ones, but it was typical of the regime that the penalties the courts imposed were very low and that no real effort was ever made to close the market down for good. As Eshkol, quoting the Old Testament, once put it, "Thou shall not stop the mouth of an oxen during threshing."[33] During the *tzena* he himself had once been caught eating his fill in a "black" restaurant in the same district; almost certainly he believed that a little smuggling acted as a safety valve.

Another field where socialism led to strange results was wage negotiations. In a country where inflation ran at about 5 percent a year, strikes aimed at obtaining a cost-of-living supplement were frequent. In a country where Histadrut was as strong as it was and where citizens were drafted—every individual was vital for national defense—it was also inevitable that most strikers should be handled with kid gloves. Negotiations were conducted by the Association of Industrialists on behalf of all private employers. At the other side of the table sat the head of Histadrut, or his representative. This arrangement ignored the fact that Histadrut itself was the second-largest employer after the government; anyone who reads the organization's publications of those years will get a good idea of what schizophrenia is all about. Furthermore, any agreement would also apply to the civil service. This meant that the government, while officially not taking part in the talks, had a strong interest in making sure that they did not run out of hand. The system favored public-sector employees and "strong" unions in large companies capable of throwing their weight around; in particular, unions of workers in the ports, in the airports, in the Israel electricity corporation, and in the banking industry were and are powerful. The system was least effective in protecting those employed by small businesses, whereas to the self-employed it did not offer any kind of protection at all.

As one group of popular comic entertainers, the Gashashim (Trackers), put it, people lived "from hand to mouth, from mouth to mouth, and under the counter"; at this point, everybody would join in the song. Everybody and his neighbor also seemed to operate on a permanent overdraft. Since most people received wages or salaries, employment was often guaranteed, and labor mobility was low in proportion, the banks were quite ready to grant overdrafts and grow fat on the proceeds. On the other hand, the interest banks could charge was limited by fiat—in the late 1960s it stood at 9 percent, which, considering inflation, was not too much. In response they developed a unique arrangement whereby they acted as brokers for private lenders and vouched for the loans.

Compared to Western Europe, let alone North America, living standards were very low. This is perhaps best illustrated by the fact that grocery stores carried only two kinds of cheese, yellow and white. In the whole of Jerusalem there was just one small supermarket; even so, nobody thought it should be provided with a dedicated parking lot. Low living standards, plus a travel tax, ensured that foreign travel was reserved for a privileged minority (for many years the stairway leading to the boarding area at Tel Aviv Airport was nicknamed "the gate through which the righteous will pass," after a phrase in the Old Testament). All this, plus the peculiar nature of Israel's relations with neighboring countries, helped create a somewhat stifling atmosphere.

Yet the coin had another side. Between 1954 and 1965 growth proceeded at a very high 10 percent annually. Part of this could be attributed to the rapid increase in population, yet per capita growth still amounted to over 5 percent each year, every year. Thanks in part to German reparations, which provided the wherewithal for importing capital goods, in 1960–1965 even manufacturing, a latecomer to the Zionist scene, was starting to find its feet. It expanded at almost 14 percent annually, focusing on metal, electric, and electronic products as well as textiles. By far the most important product was that traditional Jewish specialty, polished diamonds. In 1968 the first skyscraper devoted to that trade went up in Ramat Gan near Tel Aviv. Since then it has developed into a huge complex, the largest of its kind in the entire world; here billions of dollars in precious stones are bought and sold by means of a simple handshake. With the growth of industry came employment opportunities. Not merely was essentially full employment established from 1957 on, but the share of those employed in agriculture started to decline.

On one hand, workers moved from the countryside to the towns, where they entered the factories. On the other, some kibbutzim, realizing that agriculture was fast approaching its limits, started expanding into industry (and tourism as well). By the late 1960s, 70 percent operated at least one industrial plant. Whereas in 1950 agriculture had accounted for a third of all exports, fifteen years later its share had fallen to about one-eighth. Jaffa oranges, though still important, were starting to lose their luster. The time would soon come when most groves were systematically uprooted to make room for housing. Polished diamonds apart, the most important industrial exports consisted of processed food, chemicals, and textiles; after all, Israel at the time was a low-wage country, and competition from the Far East was yet to get under way. Exports as a whole now covered 60 percent of imports, which was more than twice the 1950 figure. Though they were often accused of living in an ivory tower and not being commercially minded, the Hebrew University of Jersualem, the Technion in Haifa, and the Weizmann Institute of Science in Rehovot provided first-class higher education and research facilities unmatched by anything from Tokyo to Rome and from Moscow to the south pole.

Could Israel have grown even faster if, instead of adopting a managed economy, it had given greater rein to free enterprise? Right from the beginning, some people thought so. For a long time the most important of these was Zalman David Levontin (1856–1940) who waged a lifelong battle against Zionist socialism. Russian by origin, he first visited the Land of Israel in 1882 and helped found the aforementioned settlement of Rishon Lezion. In 1903 he became a permanent resident. From then until 1924 he headed the APC (Anglo-Palestine Company), and after his retirement he served on its board of directors. He strongly believed that only by capitalist methods could a sound economy be created. "First we'll build factories," he wrote, "then other people will . . . set up plantations at their own expense and on their own responsibility. Then poorer people will come (if they are allowed to lease land), and finally people without means who will start as laborers and gradually acquire land. . . ."[34] From then on, hardly a year has passed that his criticism of socialist ideology and methods, the preferential treatment given to the rural sector, and the power of Histadrut to lay down the rules of the game and run the economy on collectivist lines without regard to profit has not been echoed by his General Zionist and liberal successors, down to and including Benjamin Netanyahu.

On the whole, the argument does not carry conviction. For reasons that are only too understandable, right from the start the Zionist enterprise attracted the poor rather than the rich. To the extent that the latter were interested at all, they tended to contribute money rather than emigrate and invest. No Baron Edmond Rothschild or Baron Maurice de Hirsch, no Jacob Schiff, Bernard Baruch, or Henry Morgenthau (all three of them famous Jewish-American figures in American finance) packed their belongings, moved, and set up shop in the Land of Israel. Had they done so, then, operating on strict capitalist principles, no doubt they would have turned to cheaper Arab labor, as did indeed happen to some extent. Except for a relatively short period in the 1920s and 1930s, most immigrants were young and penniless. Partly for this reason, and partly because they were surrounded by hostile neighbors, the new arrivals *had* to adopt socialist and collectivist ways of life. The land at their disposal was bought, and many of their economic enterprises erected, on behalf of the Jewish people as part of a national enterprise. Transferring it to individuals did not make sense; had this been done and become widely known, it might have hurt fund-raising. During the difficult years after 1948, almost certainly no capitalist-minded state could have coped with the problems of mass immigration and the urgent need to settle the remote, less inviting, regions of the country. Had it not been for Histadrut, there is a very good chance that even Hagana, as the parent of the IDF, would not have been able to come into being.

Socialism, meaning a system whereby much depended on the ability of entrepreneurs to get senior government officials on their side (and that, on occasion, required them to "contribute" to the parties, mainly Mapai, to which those officials belonged), certainly distorted the economy and may well have held it back in some respects. Yet during the 1960s it also made Israel into a complete welfare state, in many ways even more so than such countries as Labour Britain and Social Democratic Sweden. Throughout the 1950s and 1960s the government regarded it as a duty to provide work, mainly in such categories as road construction and forestry, albeit often at very low wages. A system of social security, originally established by Meir among others, was in full operation, though it only barely managed to keep its beneficiaries afloat. In both the public and private sectors workers with over six months' seniority were automatically given tenure. From then on they could be dismissed, if at all, only after compensation had been paid. Services for delivering mothers and for new mothers and their infants, educational services (a year of kindergarten and eight years of school), and burial services were free. Medical services were cheap and, in the towns, often excellent.

All this, plus heavy taxation, meant that gaps between rich and poor were smaller than in any other Western country, contributing to social solidarity. It is true that the government owned the electronic media. It also exercised strict censorship over questions of national defense, banned publications originating in enemy countries, and, until the 1960s, did not allow German films to enter the country. Yet Israel never came close to imposing thought control. A vibrant press hotly debated almost every aspect of public life. Foreign papers and magazines were freely available—perhaps more so than in some other countries, owing to the heterogeneous background of the population. From Begin down, many people tuned in to foreign broadcasting stations as a matter of course; others listened to Arab stations, especially the Jordanian one in Ramallah.

Socialism apart, much of this good feeling—and the relative prosperity on which it rested—was based on imported capital. While exports grew at an impressive rate, they could not prevent the balance-of-payment gap from widening in absolute terms. In 1965 German reparations came to an end. Israel's minister of finance at the time was Pinhas Sapir (1906–1975). He was a bulldozer of a man who slurped so loudly during meals that (allegedly) restaurant owners put on the radio so other guests would not be disturbed. His carefully shaved bald pate made him the ideal butt of caricaturists; the fact that he tried to run the economy out of a black notebook as if it were his father's grocery store helped. To attract foreign investors to development towns such as Kiryat Gat in the south, he would take them in his own car, at five in the morning, to show them how small the distance was to Tel Aviv. His response to the end of reparations was to do what the Bank of Israel had been demanding for so long, i.e., stop the printing presses and cut government spending. The result was a severe recession (*mitun*). Immigration all but ceased, growth went down to just over 2 percent, and unemployment soared to over 10 percent.

As the frequent use of superlatives in day-to-day language shows, Israelis are a volatile people—a legacy, perhaps, of centuries of persecution. The psychological consequences of the interruption in what had previously been a story of almost continuous success were severe. People started making inquiries and taking out foreign passports. Some voted with their feet; bitter jokes such as "The last person leaving should not forget to turn off the light" abounded. When one group of high school students declared that they did not know why they should live in Israel, of all places, their elders were shocked. Yet, understood in another way, what they were saying was that they themselves had never experienced anti-Semitism, thus proving how well Zionism was carrying out its self-imposed mission. For all the difficulties it caused, the Ministry of Finance did achieve its objective of reducing the balance-of-payments gap, which went down by 20 percent in a single year. Had things been allowed to run their course, in time no doubt the economy would have recovered and the country continued to gather steam.

"On the Fifth of June . . ."

"On the fifth of June—the armored battle broke out." Casting off the camouflage nets, hidden in a cloud of dust, three Israeli divisions stormed across the Egyptian border. Within hours they were hotly engaged with Egyptian tanks and infantrymen, turning the former into blazing pyres and making many of the latter run as if the devil were on their heels.

Israel's War of Independence did not bring the conflict between Jews and Arabs in and around the Land of Israel to an end; in fact, by initiating a twenty-five-year period of major wars against the neighboring Arab states, it did no more than open a new chapter in that struggle. The declared objective of the Arab states, endlessly repeated, was always

to terminate Israel's existence, albeit that the hope of doing so was remote and that until May 1967 there was never a serious attempt to set
up a united front for that purpose. To understand the true extent of the
threat, all one had to do was open a map. There they were, the enemies.
On the one hand, the Arab states, with a population measured in the
tens of millions and territories comprising many hundreds of thousands
of square miles; on the other, Israel, with a population of a little over a
million, eight thousand square miles of land, and a border that, at one
point, came within nine miles of the sea.

Fear of Arab intentions translated into a feeling of *en brera,* "no
choice." For decades on end, it was to become the strongest single mo-
tivating factor in Israeli life and the true engine that drove the country.
It was in the name of "no choice" that hardships were willingly under-
taken and the most stupendous sacrifices demanded and made. Lose
a single battle, and not only would the Zionist enterprise be doomed
but Israel's Jewish population would be massacred, or so many people
believed—not without reason, given the bloody way Arabs have often
treated and still treat one another when the opportunity arises. These
anxieties were reflected in the parlance of the time. It tended to refer to
the Arab leaders as the successors of Hitler—some of them had, in fact,
harbored Nazi sympathies during their youth, whereas others invited
German scientists to devise rockets for them or gave shelter to Nazi
war criminals. Israel itself was seen as an "ember salvaged from the
fire" or "a state under siege."

In the absence of peace, early on the most important immediate
problem was the constant attempts made by refugees—their number is
estimated at six hundred thousand to seven hundred thousand—to return to their former homes from the refugee camps in Lebanon, Syria,
Jordan, and Egypt. They did so either on a temporary basis, in the hope
of gathering crops, livestock, belongings, etc., or else with the idea of
permanently resuming their lives. Some came armed, but most did not.
Some engaged in theft, robbery, killing, and sabotage, but most did
not. Later some worked for the intelligence services of Egypt, Jordan,
and Syria. From 1949 to 1956, they were responsible for some two hundred Israelis killed, many more wounded, and property damage running into millions of Israeli pounds.

Beginning in 1949, Israel's reaction to the activities of the so-called *mistanenim* (infiltrators) was harsh. Unarmed ones were turned back if they were lucky—sometimes with shots fired over their heads—and injured or killed if they were not. Armed infiltrators were hunted down, as they deserved to be, and were either killed or captured. The IDF, which was in charge of these operations, used similar methods to drive entire groups of Arabs, who had been designated as "illegal residents," back across the border from where they had allegedly come. Responding to more serious incidents, the IDF, commanded by Ben Gurion, who was serving as both prime minister and minister of defense, would launch retaliatory raids into the neighboring countries—mainly Jordan, but later Egypt as well—in an attempt to avenge itself on the perpetrators and their supporters.

The instrument Ben Gurion used for the purpose, the IDF, had come out of the 1948 War with flying colors. The population worshipped it, so much so that when the first Independence Day parade was held, enthusiastic spectators mobbed the troops. However, the glory soon began to tarnish. The dismantling of Palmach in November 1948 left deep wounds, causing some of the country's best and most experienced commanders to leave the forces. In 1951–1952 the need to look after immigrants led to deep budget cuts, which in turn made Yigael Yadin resign his post as chief of staff. Though the number of youths of military age increased, a great many were new to the country. They had little education, and did not possess an adequate command of Hebrew. The same, of course, applied to reservists, who, not having done their conscript service in Israel, could only be given perfunctory training. On top of all this Israel came under an international arms embargo. This restricted the weapons the country could purchase, and for some years prevented the IDF from being modernized.

Emerging from Hagana as Athene did out of Zeus's head, the IDF was less original a creation than has sometimes been supposed. In essence it resembled the most important European armed forces as they had been from 1871 to 1945, combining general conscription, a standing corps made up of professional and noncommissioned officers, and a large number of reservists who had done their service and could be called up either for refresher training or for active duty. Perhaps its most distinctive feature was the fact that women, too, were conscripted—the only time in history this has been done—and the fact that officers, instead of being preselected and going through a military academy, were commissioned from the ranks after attending officer school. Another remarkable characteristic was the numerous nonmilitary functions it was made to fill; setting up new kibbutzim, helping absorb immigrants, training paramilitary youth, providing emergency relief, and even assisting archaeological expeditions. In all these ways it became the school of the nation, a role that itself was similar to, though perhaps more important than, the one played by other armed forces during the above-mentioned period.

Whether Israel at the time was an "expansionist" state has been hotly debated. Certainly many on the right never acquiesced in the fact that the West Bank and the Gaza Strip, comprising a little over 20 percent of the Land, had fallen into foreign hands. In the IDF General Staff, the planning department, led by Lieutenant Colonel Yuval Neeman—who later became a world-famous nuclear scientist—drew up plans to conquer not only the entire West Bank but large parts of Lebanon and Transjordan as well. Yet in assuming that foreign powers would help Israel realize this project, Neeman and his superiors were deluding themselves. When Moshe Sharett, who during the period in question was serving as prime minister, heard of the plans, he wrote—not being familiar with everyday slang—that they "farted."[35] Ben Gurion himself once told Sharett that Churchill, who had returned as Britain's prime minister in 1951, had to be convinced of the need to allow Israel to occupy the entire West Bank.[36] Instead Churchill's successor, Anthony Eden, hatched a scheme that would have taken part of the Negev away from Israel and turned it into a corridor between Egypt and Jordan that British forces might use.

From time to time attempts were made at peace talks with the neighboring countries, but all came to naught. In 1949 Syrian strongman Hosni Zaim wanted peace, but only in return for half of the Sea of Galilee and, with it, a third of Israel's water. Before he was assassinated in 1951 King Abdullah I of Jordan wanted peace, but only in return for a broad corridor from the West Bank to the sea that would have cut Israel in half. Even Gamal Abdel Nasser, the de facto ruler of Egypt from 1952 on, generously told an American mediator that he was prepared for peace if only he could have the southern port of Elat on a platter. All three rulers also demanded that a great many refugees be allowed to return, a condition that Israelis understood, and in their negotiations with the Palestinians still understand, as tantamount to the destruction of their state. Meanwhile, all three countries served as bases for *mistanenim* and *fedayeen* (Arabic for freedom fighters) acting against Israel. In the case of Syria and Egypt this was because they wanted to do Israel the greatest harm they could. In the case of Jordan it was because Abdullah's successor, King Hussein, was powerless to stop the raids.

The great powers of the time were the United States, Britain, France, and the USSR. During the War of Independence the USSR had greatly assisted Israel, recognizing it and providing it with desperately needed weapons by way of Czechoslovakia. As the Korean War got under way, however, Ben Gurion—worried lest a world war might break out and cut off Israel's maritime communications—took the country into the Western camp. Whatever else may have motivated their policy, it was a move the Soviets never forgot nor forgave. From then until the end of the Cold War they were always found on the side of the Arab states—those Arab states, at any rate, that were prepared to have them and that themselves did not join the pro-Western, pro-American side.

Considering itself a "Western" country, Israel would very much like to become a recognized part of "the West." However, the West, for its part, was never quite certain it wanted Israel. Without Western economic support—which, during the period in question, consisted above all of German reparations and of tax-free bonds sold to American Jews—Israel might not have survived. On the other hand, the West, with the United States at its head, had its own interests in the Middle East, including, above all, the Suez Canal, oil, and the need to keep them from falling into Soviet hands. Hence, most of the time, Israeli attempts to get closer were rebuffed. For example, Jerusalem was not asked to participate in the anti-Soviet Baghdad Pact. Nor did President Dwight D. Eisenhower agree to provide it with weapons. Whenever Israel, incensed by the ongoing minor hostilities along its borders, launched an "excessive" military strike into its neighbors' territory, it could expect to be roundly denounced by those who proclaimed themselves its friends. Ben Gurion's response to the condemnations was to declare that what mattered "was not what the gentiles said but what the

Jews did"; it was left to Moshe Sharett, who served as foreign minister during most of the period in question, to try and repair the damage.

In the end, three events broke the not-so-merry-go-round of half-hearted peace talks, minor skirmishes, and the great powers' jockeying for position in an attempt to turn things to their own benefit as much as they could. First was the outbreak in 1954 of the revolt in Algeria, which made the French more ready to cooperate with Israel. Second was the Czech-Egyptian arms deal of the summer of 1955, which marked the entry of the Soviet Union into the Middle East and seemed to present Israel with an unprecedented threat. Last was Nasser's nationalization of the Suez Canal in July 1956. In this way a firm basis for a triple French-Israeli-British alliance was created, which in turn led to the Suez Campaign of November–December of the same year.

At the end of 1953 Ben Gurion resigned, leaving his posts as prime minister and minister of defense to Moshe Sharett and Pinhas Lavon, respectively. His self-imposed exile did not last long; in early 1955, following Lavon's resignation in the wake of the Lavon Affair, he returned as minister of defense, and soon resumed office as prime minister as well. Throughout this period the chief of staff was Moshe Dayan (1915–1981). Dayan was the greatest soldier Israel has ever produced, aggressive, courageous to a fault, devious, a highly original strategist, and positively dripping with charisma; the fact that he wore an eye patch (one eye had been shot away in 1941) contributed to the effect. He was also an extremely political operator, deeply conscious of the interaction between war and politics and an expert at intrigues, backbiting, and avoiding responsibility. On the other hand, Sharett, proud of his diplomatic skills and of his perfect knowledge of Arabic, always tended toward moderation. Together, Dayan and Lavon turned his life into a misery while he was prime minister by repeatedly launching retaliatory raids far larger and more deadly than had been agreed on.

Though Dayan was certainly capable of trifling with Sharett and Lavon, playing similar games with Ben Gurion, who was probably the only man he feared, was a different matter. During much of 1955 the bellicose chief of staff (he once wrote that, to deter the Arabs, Israel had to behave like "a rabid dog nobody dares to touch"[37]) seems to have tried to convince his superior that a war against Egypt—meant to forestall an attack by the latter, end the terrorist threat from Gaza, and open the Straits of Tiran (which the Egyptians had closed to Israeli shipping)—was necessary. However, it was only in early 1956 that he succeeded and that preparations started in earnest. Thanks largely to the efforts of the young then–director general of the Ministry of Defense, Shimon Peres (1923–), France agreed to provide modern weapons, including jet fighter aircraft, tanks, and trucks needed to take Israeli troops across the Sinai Peninsula. Plans were put together, and in the summer Britain, too, was brought into the plot. In October Ben Gurion, French foreign minister Christian Pineau, and British foreign minister Selwyn Lloyd met at Sevres and sealed the secret agreement. Essentially Israel agreed to an attack on Egypt so as to give France and Britain an excuse for entering the fray soon after. In return, on top of aid already supplied, the allies also provided assistance with some air and naval cover.

Aware that he was about to be attacked by Britain and France, Nasser had withdrawn about half of his forces from the Sinai, giving the Israelis rough numerical parity with their opponents. This is not to say that Dayan's plan, first put down in just a few moments on the back of a cigarette pack, was not brilliant. First, to deceive the Egyptians, a crack unit was deployed opposite Jordan so as to give the impression that the Israeli mobilization, which could not be concealed, was directed against that country. Next, a battalion of paratroopers was dropped at the Mitla Pass deep in the Sinai. This confused Nasser, who, according to his close aid Mohammed Heikal, exclaimed that "the Israelis are attacking sand."[38] Third, a brigade of paratroopers, commanded by then–Lieutenant Colonel Ariel Sharon, was sent by land to link up with their comrades. Meeting little opposition, the brigade accomplished its mission within thirty hours.

The Israeli plan had been to postpone the main attack until the French and the British came in, but the IDF commander of the southern front did not know this and sent in his troops ahead of time. Heavy fighting developed around the stronghold of Um Katef, in the center of the Sinai, where the Israelis suffered several reverses before they finally got through; in the end, though, the Egyptians broke and retreated. Heavy fighting also marked the northern part of the front near Rafa, but here, too, the Israelis prevailed, sending their forces to pursue the Egyptians to the west while at the same time occupying the Gaza Strip.

An advance on the Straits of Tiran, coming from two separate directions, sealed the victory. All this was achieved in just six days and in spite of the fact that France and Britain, violating the Sevres agreement, allowed forty-eight anxious hours to pass before they intervened.

In terms of Arab divisions broken per Israeli casualty taken, the Sinai Campaign was very much the most successful of Israel's wars, more so even than the famed 1967 Six-Day War. To be sure, as Dayan himself repeatedly said, the IDF was fighting Arabs, not Germans (in Israel and abroad, everybody took it for granted that Germans were the best soldiers of all). As he also said, the war revealed a "limitless capacity for misadventure."[39] This was partly his own fault; some of the problems experienced at Um Katef resulted from his contradictory orders. Several of his commanders acted without orders or else lost control over their subordinates. Israeli units opened fire at one another, and the Israeli Air Force mistakenly attacked both its own ground forces and a British destroyer that was patrolling the Red Sea. On the plus side were the Israelis' resourcefulness, flexibility, speed—one future chief of staff later wrote that fighting the Egyptians was like playing chess against an opponent who was only allowed to make one move for every two of one's own[40]—and, above all, the utter determination that only "no choice" can produce.

In the end, the political results of the campaign were meager. When he heard of what was happening, America's president, Dwight D. Eisenhower, was livid. His angry words, as well as Soviet threats concerning long-range rockets and nuclear weapons, forced the British, the French, and the Israelis to give way and surrender their conquests. Yet the Straits of Tiran remained open to Israeli traffic, which in view of the growing importance of the Far East was not an insignificant achievement. The three Western powers even promised to keep it so—a promise that, when the time came, they did not keep. The Sinai was demilitarized, and a UN peacekeeping force put in place to supervise the arrangements. Perhaps the most important outcome was the boost to Israeli morale. The test had come, blood had been shed, and the country had showed what it could do. Pictures of thousands of Egyptian prisoners, most without shoes so they could run better, helped. The fact that Israeli forces had captured Mount Sinai even gave the victory a religious-mythical aura. Much later, Shimon Peres called the campaign "one of the most brilliant of all time." Others claimed that it was "unequaled since the days when Hannibal crossed the snow-covered Alps and Genghis Khan, the mountains of Asia."[41]

Judging by the fact that the next decade was, from a security point of view, perhaps the best Israel ever had, Arab leaders of countries around Israel must have shared this assessment to some extent. To be sure, "infiltrators" kept coming. From 1965 on, they included some working for the newly founded Palestine Liberation Organization (PLO). There were also some major border incidents, especially with Syria and, late in the period, Jordan. Yet the total number of Israelis killed during the ten years in question was extremely small—far fewer than during the preceding period and, of course, during the one that followed. The time thus gained was well used. By 1967 the IDF had become the strongest armed force in the Middle East, capable of fielding a quarter million men and women out of a Jewish population of just over two million. It also possessed an array of fairly modern weapons, including supersonic fighters, fighter-bombers, tanks, and self-propelled artillery. Not only did it acquire the weapons but it also assimilated them and learned to use them. Vis-à-vis the Arab states, most of whose rank and file consisted of semiliterate peasants, this was perhaps its greatest advantage of all.

The basic fact of life, i.e., the Arab's hostility to Israel and their refusal to make peace with it, was unchanged. In 1958 a formal union between Israel's main enemies, Egypt and Syria, caused a scare, but just three years later the two countries again went their separate ways. As the Soviet Union rearmed Nasser and also provided weapons to Syria and Iraq—the latter, after the coup that brought down the monarchy and led to the establishment of a military regime there in 1958—relations with it remained as strained as they had been. The arms embargo had been broken, and Israel was able to obtain what it needed from a number of countries including France, Britain, West Germany (again, Peres had a hand in this), and later the United States. Given that Eisenhower had always refused to sell weapons, making his successor do so was a particularly great achievement. And not a moment too soon; though the French did sell Israel fighter aircraft during the 1960s, Charles de Gaulle, trying to rebuild France's status among so-called neutral countries, was already starting to distance himself from Jerusalem.

Meir, whom Ben Gurion appointed foreign minister in 1956 and who stayed in office until 1966, put great emphasis on making friends with "our neighbors' neighbors," as she put it. Israel, it was thought, had something to offer newly independent countries in such fields as nation building, education, farming methods, and military training. This being the time of "the ugly American," many of the relevant programs were financed by Washington, D.C., as part of the Cold War. People thought that an Israeli presence would receive a warmer welcome than a U.S. one. In Meir's own words, "We helped to build the self-confidence of the Africans."[42] Thus, Israeli agricultural and military experts went to Burma and Iran. Slipping into Iraq, they also helped the Kurds in their revolt against Baghdad. Others went to Ethiopia, Uganda, Ghana, and several other African countries, where they helped organize the military and set up experimental farms; yet on the whole, what ties they succeeded in creating proved flimsy.

In spite of all this, the single factor that occupied most Israelis as well as the government and the media during 1966 and the first half of 1967 was not foreign affairs but the ongoing economic recession. By this time, even Begin and his Herut followers had more or less given up the idea of expanding Israeli rule to the Jordan River, let alone to the eastern bank. Terrorism, most of it originating in Syria even if the terrorists often came by way of Jordan so as to direct Israel's anger against that country, remained an irritant. The principal "current" defense problem was the escalating situation on the Israeli-Syrian border. In 1964 Israel's national water carrier went into operation, pumping water out of the Sea of Galilee and taking it to the Negev. In response, the first Arab summit meeting, in December 1964, resolved to divert the Jordan River.

Throughout 1965 and 1966 numerous border incidents took place. As Dayan was later to describe it, first the Israelis would drive an armored tractor so close to the border as to provoke fire. Next they would use the excellent 105-millimeter cannon on their British-made Centurion tanks to destroy the Syrians' heavy earthmoving equipment. In return the Syrians, whose tanks were nowhere near as good, regularly rained down artillery shells from the slopes of the Golan Heights on the Israeli kibbutzim below. When the Syrians tried to resume the works at a point farther away from the border the Israelis called in their air force. By the summer of 1966, they had forced their enemy to suspend operations.

Serving under Eshkol, who never pretended to be an expert in the field, the man in charge of national defense was Yitzhak Rabin. Appointed chief of staff in 1964 when he was forty-two years old, he was humorless, clear-headed, and systematic, an excellent trainer, organizer, and staff officer. A man better suited to prepare the IDF for war could hardly be imagined. However, his experience in operational command was limited. If Peres, admittedly not always the most reliable witness, may be believed, Dayan in 1956 had made him the officer commanding the northern front specifically so he would not "get in our way" during the forthcoming Sinai Campaign.[43] Even after the Syrians had stopped trying to divert the Jordan, Rabin pressed on—the rationales being the need to put an end to terrorism, as well as Israel's right to cultivate some very small plots of land along the border that had been demilitarized in 1949. Looking back, the most surprising thing about this policy is the near unanimous public support it enjoyed.

Things came to a head on Friday, April 7, 1967, when an Israeli attempt to work one of the disputed plots "right up to the border," as the saying went, led to another major incident. Syrian shells demolished Kibbutz Gadot in the upper Jordan Valley. In response, the Israeli Air Force, having shot down no fewer than six Syrian MiG aircraft, flew over Damascus. Apparently the IDF chief of intelligence, General Aharon Yariv, had convinced Rabin that, since Nasser's troops were busy fighting in Yemen, this was the time to take serious action against Syria, even to the point of bringing down the regime in Damascus if that was what it took to put an end to terrorism. In the days just before Israel's Independence Day, which fell on May 15, Rabin gave no fewer than four different interviews threatening to do just that. Yet things did not go the way he and Yariv had planned. As the chief of staff was watching the Independence Day parade in Jerusalem, news arrived that massive Egyptian forces had crossed the Suez Canal and were streaming into the Sinai. A week after that Nasser also expelled the UN peacekeeping force and closed the Straits of Tiran, presenting Israel with a fait accompli.

At the time, Nasser explained his actions by claiming that Israel had concentrated ten army brigades opposite Syria. This particular piece of information originated in Moscow, which, as it later turned out, knew it to be untrue. Nasser's own generals knew better; based on their own sources, they told him that "there is nothing there, no massing of forces, nothing."[44] Such being the case, Nasser's real motives remain a mystery. Possibly all he wanted was to remilitarize the Sinai, but he was pushed to go further by Egyptian public opinion as well as his own success. It's quite possible, too, that his move should be understood as a last-ditch attempt to halt Israel's nuclear program, which was just then preparing to produce the country's first bomb. Be this as it may, there is no doubt that Israel, and Rabin more than anyone else, was taken by surprise. While the country was always prepared to take border incidents in stride, war, a serious war in which its very existence might be called into question, was the last thing it had expected.

As Arab mobs danced in the streets, Syria, Jordan, and Iraq joined Egypt. Ahmed Shukeiri, chairman of the PLO, said that in case of war "no [Jews] will survive."[45] In response, Israel mobilized. First tens, then hundreds of thousands streamed to the colors. Since many motor vehicles were also called up—the IDF at the time relied heavily on them for its second-echelon transport—the streets took on an eerie, deserted look. Military morale, it soon turned out, was excellent. Many units had supernumerary personnel as all kinds of men whom the IDF manpower division had discharged or overlooked crawled out of the woodwork and begged to be given a job, any kind of job. "We'll screw them," the troops roared, "and if once is not enough we'll pull out and do it again!" It was not all fun and games. People in the cities started hoarding food, soap, candles, and toilet paper. High school students dug trenches in the parks; nearby, rabbis consecrated the same parks so they could serve as cemeteries. Especially among the older generation, there was frequent talk of a second Holocaust. Visiting one air base, the IDF chief rabbi, Shlomo Goren, broke down and wailed that "even if Israel is destroyed the Jewish people and Jewish faith will survive." Thereupon the base commander told him to leave and issued orders that he should not be admitted again.[46]

IDF doctrine at the time demanded that any war be fought on enemy territory, causing the General Staff to press for an immediate offensive. At one point the deputy chief of staff, General Ezer Weizman, who was a nephew of the Zionist leader, ripped off his epaulets and threw them on Eshkol's table. Every additional day of waiting, he shouted, would cost the country so-and-so many casualties; a dramatic gesture, to be sure, but far from the attempted coup d'état some people later claimed the IDF had been trying to mount. Chain-smoking one cigarette after another, Rabin himself seemed to stagger under the weight of the responsibility suddenly thrust on him. On May 24, following a conversation with Ben Gurion in which the elderly statesman rebuked him for his "adventurism," he had to be sedated for twenty-four hours before resuming work. Speaking on the radio, Eshkol himself made an unfortunate slip of the tongue and seemed unable to make up his mind, an error that cost him dearly in terms of public confidence.

Amid much coming and going, the cabinet decided to see what the international community could do to help. Israel's foreign minister at the time was Abba Eban (1915–2002). He was an accomplished diplomat with a pompous manner, an amazing mastery of English (along with half a dozen other languages, Arabic included), and an ever-growing number of chins. In Henry Kissinger's not entirely complimentary words, his "sentences poured forth in mellifluous constructions complicated enough to test the listener's intelligence and simultaneously leave him transfixed by the speaker's virtuosity."[47] In Israel he was known as Papa Balatah, which, punning on his name, may be roughly translated as "Daddy Stonehead." This was the man Eshkol sent to tour Western capitals in order to enlist sympathy and see whether the powers would stick to their 1957 undertaking to keep the Straits of Tiran open. To no avail; in Paris, in London, in Washington, D.C., Eban was told that Israel should avoid going to war and wait.

To wait, however, was the one thing Israel could not do. The three weeks' period during which its units were mobilized enabled the IDF to engage in refresher training and complete its preparations. However, those weeks were absolutely nerve-wracking. As a large part of the labor force donned uniform, the economy all but came to a standstill. Advice came from every direction. Test a new and awesome weapon that had recently entered the Israeli arsenal, said the man mainly responsible for building Israeli's nuclear reactor in Dimona, Shimon Peres. Bring back Ben Gurion, said the members of the former prime minister's party. Set up a national unity government and appoint Dayan minister of defense, said the National Religious Party (Dayan was also supported by a group of society ladies known as the Merry Widows of Windsor). Avoid Dayan at all cost in favor of Yigal Allon, the 1948 Palmach commander, said Eshkol's coalition partner, Ahdut Haavoda Party. In the end, the National Religious view won. Begin and one of his cronies joined the cabinet as ministers without portfolio. On June 2 Eshkol's place as minister of defense was taken by Dayan. The intention was to avoid war—the NRP leaders considered him a dove. Israel's best-known caricaturist of the time, Dosh, knew better. He drew Nasser challenging Israel and posing a question mark to it. In response it produced Dayan, in the form of an exclamation mark.

On the next day the U.S. defense secretary, Robert McNamara, finally gave the green light—not to Eban but to the head of Mossad, Meir Amit, who was acting as a special emissary. Early in the morning of June 5, wave after wave of combat aircraft took off. They flew low over the Mediterranean, avoiding Egyptian radar (Jordanian radar picked up the movement, but for some reason did not inform the Egyptians), and hit the enemy's airfields at 0745, Cairo time, just as the Egyptian pilots were having breakfast. First, specially developed bombs rendered the runways unserviceable. Next, some three hundred Egyptian aircraft were destroyed. By 1100 Weizman, bellowing over the telephone, was heard telling his wife, Reuma, that "we've won the war."[48] At 1000 Dayan himself spoke on the radio. In his well-known, Russian-accented, slightly nasal voice he said that Israelis were "a small people but brave," promised that the IDF would fight as only it knew how, but provided no details.

At that time, three Israeli divisions were already driving into the Sinai. Many of the men had tuned their transistor radios to the "Voice of the Thunder" (Kol HaRaam; originally an acronym for United Arab Republic, as Egypt, following its failed union with Syria, still insisted on calling itself). A not-too-bright spokesman was explaining something about Israel's unemployed *boalim* ("fuckers," since Arabs cannot pronounce *poalim,* "workers") and how the Arab armies were winning in all the "brassieres" (*haziot,* instead of *hazitot,* "fronts") and would soon meet in Tel Aviv. Fierce fighting followed on the road from Rafa to El Arish in the north, at Jebel Livni in the center, and at Um Katef in the south. It was not easy, but by early next morning the Israelis had broken through at all three points and the campaign had been effectively decided. Caught between the advancing Israeli divisions and the Israeli Air Force, which was systematically shooting up anything that moved in the desert, the hapless Egyptians broke and ran. Thousands were killed, thousands more probably died of thirst, thousands were captured, and an unknown number injured. Out of a force comprising five divisions, only one brigade was able to make it back across the Suez Canal as an intact unit.

Like every other army worth its salt, the IDF had detailed contingency plans for fighting its enemies, Jordan and Syria, but no very clear idea as to whether they were to be carried out and what might trigger them. At first Eshkol hoped to keep Jordan out of the war. On the morning it started he even sent King Hussein a message to that effect, telling him that Israel would not attack any country that did not attack it first. However, the king felt that public opinion gave him no choice. In any case, his own armed forces were now being commanded by an Egyptian general to whom, foolishly enough, he had entrusted them just a few days earlier. When Jordanian troops started attacking objectives in Jerusalem and shelling Israeli targets along the coast and in the Valley of Esdraelon, Israel responded. This author was in Jerusalem at the time. Coming after a day during which Jordanian shells landed all around, the sound of some Israeli heavy mortars opening fire around 2000 hours that evening was the sweetest he ever heard.

When Dayan first authorized his forces to respond to the Jordanian moves, he had in mind only limited land grabs. However, his front commanders were extraordinarily aggressive—after all, these were men in their early forties who, as one general once explained, had reached their posts "by natural selection."[49] Once they had taken the bit between their teeth there simply was no stopping them. They were cheered on by the Israeli nation, which as the campaign succeeded beyond anyone's wildest dreams was rapidly exchanging fear with the greatest imaginable excitement. Though the Jordanians fought bravely, such was Israeli superiority in the air—Jordan's small air force was destroyed even more easily than the Egyptian one—and on the ground that they stood no chance. In just three days the entire West Bank, East Jerusalem included, was in Israeli hands. Iraqi forces that were making their way west in order to participate in the battle were intercepted and bombed, and the Israeli Air Force even paid a visit to Iraq itself. As the opposition melted away an IDF unit crossed to the East Bank. Only an urgent call from Washington, which did not want to see Hussein toppled, caused the unit to be called back.

It remained to deal with Syria, whose activities during the previous years had done much to bring on the war and for which many Israelis, following some incidents when IDF soldiers were captured and tortured to death, had developed an intense hatred. Whatever Dayan himself may have felt, he did not allow such emotions to cloud his judgment. For several years past he had been telling anybody who was prepared to listen that in provoking Syria, Rabin and Eshkol were "out of their minds."[50] As the war broke out the Syrians joined in. They resorted to their usual method of shelling kibbutzim, demolishing "205 houses, 9 chicken coops, 2 tractor sheds, 3 clubs, 1 dining hall, 6 haystacks, 50 tractors, 15 cars," as one report pedantically put it.[51] Yet they only succeeded in killing two people and wounding sixteen. Nor did they even try to invade Israel, which, in any case, would have been impossible since their air force was also destroyed.

With the war in the Sinai going well and the occupation of the West Bank completed, Dayan came under intense pressure to have the IDF settle accounts with the Syrians, too. At a cabinet meeting held on the evening of Thursday, June 8, he found himself in a minority of one. The war with Egypt had not yet ended, he said; the Soviet Union might intervene (it is possible that he knew more about this than he could tell his colleagues at the time), and Israel stood in danger of swallowing more than it could digest. Later that night news that Nasser was asking for a cease-fire arrived and caused him to change his mind. Without so much as consulting Eshkol, who had gone to bed, or Rabin, who allegedly could not be reached, he called up the commander of the northern front, General David Elazar, and ordered him to attack as soon as possible.

Elazar, who had been roaring to go for days, lost no time in carrying out his mission. First he hit the Syrian positions with an intense air bombardment. Next several Israeli brigades, spearheaded by bulldozers where necessary, started climbing up the Golan Heights and took them in the face of what was often strong resistance. Other troops were lifted there with the aid of helicopters but arrived too late to see action.

Admittedly a greater part of the Syrian army was able to escape destruction than in the case of Egypt and Jordan. With the Syrian troops went most of the civilian population, so that the district was captured empty. By the next evening the Israelis, having achieved all of their objectives, were standing within line of sight from Damascus, and the Middle East had been forever transformed.

3

THE NIGHTMARE
YEARS (1967–1980)

"The Third Temple Is in Danger!"

If the war took Israel by surprise, the swift and total victory in which it ended presented an even greater one. Israeli losses stood at just under eight hundred dead, one-seventh as many as in 1948–1949 and only one-twentieth if one takes population growth into account. For this price, a threat the like of which had not been seen since the 1948 War or even the Holocaust was lifted. Three enemy armies were shattered. More than four hundred enemy aircraft were destroyed on the ground or shot down, hundreds of tanks turned into smoking wrecks, immense amounts of equipment captured, and the territory under Israeli control quadrupled. To put the icing on the cake, East Jerusalem, with its numerous holy places, now came under Israeli rule. All this had been achieved by Israel on its own without the kind of external aid it had gotten in 1956. In the West at any rate, admiration for Israel and its army was almost universal—for a few weeks in London, Paris, and Tokyo, some young women even paid them the ultimate accolade by wearing an eye patch.

No wonder the country responded with a feeling of euphoria. Even many secular-minded people were swept along by a wave of messianic feeling: "When the Lord turned again the captivity of Zion," they recited, "we were like those that dream. Then was our mouth filled with

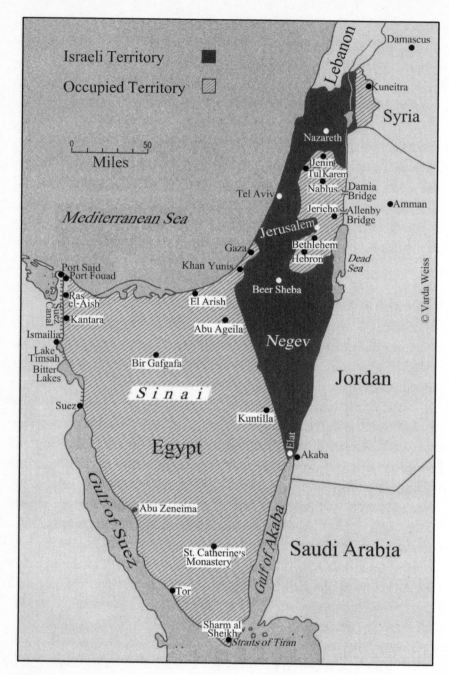

Israel's Post–1967 War Borders

laughter, and our tongue with singing."[1] Just ten days after he had shed tears over the anticipated fate of his people, Rabbi Goren was found rushing to the Wailing Wall in order to blow the shofar in triumph. A few weeks after the war Dayan, in a typically bold move, decided to open the borders, enabling hundreds of thousands of Israelis to tour the occupied territories; Arabs from the territories also came to see Israel, but the numbers were much smaller. Often this involved visiting familiar sites or even those where they themselves had lived before the Jordanian conquest of 1948. Public pressure to resettle some of those sites, notably the Jewish quarter in the Old City of Jerusalem and Gush Etzion further south, started almost immediately. The airwaves were filled with hastily written, often quite kitschy victory songs. Dozens of coffee-table books celebrated the IDF and the war. Some came with empty pages so people would be able to write down their memoirs of the great days.

Perhaps it was Rabin who best captured the prevailing mood. He was shy and introverted, looking like some wide-eyed boy from the provinces. Eloquence was hardly one of his virtues; his knowledge of poetry was limited to the Palmach songs of his youth, his vocabulary was limited, and his delivery was flat. Yet this time he chose the right person to write his speech for him. Accepting an honorary doctorate from the Hebrew University on Mount Scopus, posed against the impressive background of occupied territory (the Judean Wilderness), with the Dead Sea visible in the distance, he said:

> I take the honor you are bestowing on my comrades, the soldiers, by way of my person as recognition of the unique nature of the IDF and the entire Israeli people. . . .
>
> [Our victory] is entirely a result of the spirit. Our fighters surpassed themselves not because they have better weapons, but because they are supremely conscious of their sacred mission. They recognize the justice of our cause; they deeply love the fatherland; and they are deeply aware of their task. To wit, to secure the existence of the nation in its land; and to maintain, even at the cost of their lives, its right to live in its own country, free, independent, in peace and quiet.[2]

Future hopes were best summed up by Moshe Dayan: "We are waiting for the Arabs to call."

It was not to be. Ignoring the events that led to the war, "The Kings, Presidents and representatives of the other Arab Heads of State," regarded it as pure aggression on Israel's part. On September 1, having met at Khartoum, they came up with the famous resolution: "No peace with Israel, no recognition of Israel, no negotiations with it";[3] rather than opening a window toward peace, the war only caused the conflict between Israel and its neighbors to escalate. Nor did the victory do much to change the country's overall foreign policy position. The realization that the Arabs were broken reeds and that Israel was now the strongest power in the Middle East did not cause the superpowers to compete for the benefit of entering into an alliance with it, as some had hoped.

Instead the war caused the Soviet Union and all the remaining Eastern Bloc countries except Romania to sever diplomatic relations with Jerusalem. From then until the end of the Cold War Moscow and the rest always treated "Zionism" as if it were their greatest enemy after the United States; by no means the first or last time when the power of the movement, that of a small people (not all of whom were involved with the cause) desperately trying to maintain a small country in the Middle East was vastly exaggerated. As most Israelis saw it, Soviet support for the Arabs was strong and consistent. Not so Western support for their own country, which was always tempered by the need to placate the Arabs. To be sure, the place of France as Israel's principal diplomatic and military backer was taken by the United States, with its vastly greater power and resources, a most welcome change. Yet when de Gaulle called Jews "a self-assured, dominating people," imposed an arms embargo, and prevented fifty Mirage V fighter-bombers that had already been paid for from being delivered, his move rankled. Until native production of aircraft could start, and the switch to American arms could be completed, the embargo also caused the IDF, and the air force in particular, considerable difficulties.

In November Security Council Resolution 242 was adopted. It required "the establishment of a just and lasting peace in the Middle East"; demanded the "withdrawal of Israel's armed forces from territories occupied in the recent conflict"; mandated "termination of all claims or states of belligerency and respect for and acknowledgement of the sovereignty, territorial integrity and political independence of every state in the area and their right to live in peace within secure and recognized borders"; and emphasized the need for "guaranteeing freedom of navigation through international waterways in the area" and "achieving a just settlement of the refugee problem."[4] It was a finely chiseled document, but one that each side could read as it wished.

During the first weeks after the war Israel's government was probably prepared to return most (though not all) of the occupied territories in exchange for peace. However, as time went on and "the Kings, Presidents and representatives of the other Arab Heads of State" refused to negotiate, attitudes hardened. Particularly important was Jerusalem, the holy city, which was declared "one and indivisible." Not merely was the eastern part of the city formally annexed, but the construction of new neighborhoods in occupied territory—intended among other things to make any return to the prewar status quo impossible—started almost immediately. Just three years after the war, residents who bought the heavily subsidized flats because originally nobody wanted to live "among Arabs" moved into Ramot Eshkol, the first such neighborhood. Many others followed.

As problematic as Jerusalem was the question of "defensible" borders, a concept invented by Yigal Allon, who served as deputy prime minister from 1969 on. Previously the IDF had considered the country's borders so hard to defend that any war had to start with an offensive into enemy territory. By contrast, the post–1967 borders were seen as ideal. In the east and south, the Jordan Valley and the Suez Canal ("the best anti-tank ditch in the world") presented formidable obstacles to any attack from Jordan and Egypt. In the north, the capture of the Golan Heights exposed Damascus, deprived the Syrians of an even more formidable defensive line, and prevented them from shelling the Israeli kibbutzim below. All these borders were also much farther away from Israel's population centers, thus adding strategic depth and providing warning time.

"Defensible" though they may have been, the new borders were much more volatile than the old ones. The Soviet Union rapidly reequipped the armies of Syria and Egypt, so that on paper, at any rate, they soon recovered their prewar strength and even surpassed it. To hasten the process, thousands of Red Army advisers arrived in both countries. In return, the Soviets were granted naval bases in Alexandria and Latakia; from there their forces could easily intervene in the conflict if Moscow so decided. On the Golan Heights, as well as along the Suez Canal, irregular artillery duels took place with the Syrians and the Egyptians. Yet the most serious incident of all occurred at sea. In October 1967, Soviet-built Egyptian missile boats based on Port Said sank the Israeli destroyer *Elat,* killing forty-seven sailors and injuring another one hundred. In response, Israeli artillery shelled the Egyptian oil refineries along the Suez Canal and set them on fire.

In the Jordan Valley, too, things were anything but quiet. At first Israeli and Jordanian forces exchanged artillery fire. Later, a more serious threat emerged in the form of the Palestinian Liberation Organization (PLO) and its military arm, Fatah. The way the Arab masses saw it, Fatah and a whole series of smaller, ever-changing Palestinian terrorist organizations, were the only Arab armed forces that had not been defeated. Their prestige, and their willingness to engage Israel, soared; training films, broadcast on TV, showed fighters tearing up live chickens with their teeth. Hundreds of rockets were launched at the Israeli settlements in the Jordan Valley. Farther south, groups of terrorists started crossing the river in an effort to commit sabotage. In response the IDF erected obstacles, launched patrols, mounted ambushes, and much more. In March 1968, they tried to cut off the snake's head by launching a large-scale raid into Jordan itself. The Jordanian Army fought back fiercely, gaining time and allowing Yasser Arafat, known to Israeli military intelligence as "a Syrian-Palestinian who is operations officer of the Fatah gang,"[5] to seize a motorcycle and escape. Having suffered thirty dead, the Israelis did not consider the raid a success and it was not repeated.

In the midst of all this, in February 1969, Eshkol died. He had never really recovered from the humiliation of having to surrender the defense portfolio to Dayan, the very man whom, considering him mercurial and hard to work with, he had once called Abu Jilda after a well-known Palestinian-Arab terrorist leader of the 1930s. Eshkol's successor was Golda Meir. Aged seventy, for many years she had served Ben Gurion, "taking orders as a soldier does," to quote her own words. Personally rather austere, her last post had been that of Mapai secretary general. This made her highly unpopular among many Israelis who identified her with everything unsavory and corrupt in the ruling party; each time a case of this kind came to light she would profess to be "shocked." So self-righteous was she that, with her, "objectivity meant nothing less than one hundred percent support."[6] Caricaturists loved her heavy shoes—which she did not wear for fun but because her feet were being painfully deformed by old age—black handbag, and prominent nose. Yet as she proved her iron nerve in rejecting international pressure on Israel to retreat from the post-1967 lines, her approval ratings soared.

This was the person who, barely a month after taking office, had to face a formidable challenge in the form of Nasser's "War of Attrition." From then until August 1970 it went on without a break, with hardly a day without casualties. Spending a last carefree summer on the beach before being drafted, high school students used to tell each other, "See you in the IDF cemetery." Though the IDF had prepared by constructing what was later to become known as the Bar Lev Line (after Haim Bar Lev, Rabin's successor as chief of staff) on the Suez Canal, it was hopelessly unable to withstand the Egyptians, with perhaps a thousand artillery barrels, on the ground. The IDF tried to bring the fighting to an end by conducting commando operations and bringing in the air force, but to no avail. Thousands of Egyptian troops, including one visiting chief of staff, were killed. Their aircraft were shot out of the sky; their strongholds raided; their radar sets attacked, dismantled, and taken to Israel for examination. Yet they kept coming—"like ants," as Anwar Sadat, who took over from Nasser in October 1970, later put it.

In the fall of 1969 Meir, Dayan, and Rabin, who was proffering advice from his new post as ambassador in Washington, D.C., decided to "change the military reality of the war of attrition" by "deep-bombing" Egypt and "severely hitting Nasser and his regime."[7] The plan, which was also meant to foil a scheme by the U.S. secretary of state, William Rogers, to make Israel give up part of the Sinai, backfired. First it turned out that the Israeli Air Force did not have nearly enough planes for the purpose. Next the Soviets, on Nasser's urgent request, rebuilt Egypt's antiaircraft system and sent thousands of Red Army personnel to run it. Worst of all, Soviet pilots started flying combat sorties over the Canal, where four of them ran into an air ambush and were downed. For several weeks in April and May, it looked as if the Soviet Union might join the war against Israel—which, if it had happened, might have resulted in the country's destruction. In response, it was rumored, Israel was preparing some of its new nuclear-capable Phantom fighter-bombers to fly one-way suicide missions to Odessa.[8] Throughout all this the Soviet-Egyptian antiaircraft defenses on the Canal were evolving until they grew into the most powerful system the world had ever seen. In the early summer of 1970, even the Phantoms were starting to be shot out of the sky.

In any event, his "awesome apocalypse," as one contemporary put it,[9] was averted, but only by a hair's breadth. In August 1970 a cease-fire brought the War of Attrition to an end, though the Egyptians immediately violated the agreement by pushing forward their antiaircraft defenses right up to the Canal. A month later King Hussein of Jordan, worried that the various Palestinian terrorist organizations were getting out of control—they had hijacked four Western airliners, flown them to the Kingdom, and blown them up—launched a major offensive against them and, massacring thousands, broke their power. From then to the present, almost the only terrorists active along the Israeli-Jordanian border have been those who somehow succeeded in avoiding the armies and security services of both countries, a very hard task.

While these two threats were terminated for the time being, others remained or soon emerged. The border with Syria was mostly quiet, but from time to time the calm was interrupted by "battle days," when both sides shelled each other and sent fighter jets to buzz each other's cities. Having been expelled from Jordan, Palestinian terrorists went to Lebanon, hitherto the most peaceful of all Israel's neighbors. From there they fired rockets, launched raids, and planted mines, provoking the first Israeli reprisals. In the occupied territories and in Israel itself, terrorism, though it did not yet take on the dimensions it was to assume from 1987 on, was an ever-present irritant. Abroad, too, Israeli passenger aircraft, embassies, and other organizations, as well as all sorts of Jewish targets, were beginning to come under terrorist attack. The worst incident of all took place during the 1972 Olympic Games, when terrorists belonging to an organization known as Black September took hostage, and later killed, eleven Israeli athletes.

All this put Israeli society under a tremendous strain. To banish its own fears and those of the population, the leadership kept saying, "Our security situation has never been better," a sort of magic incantation that was endlessly repeated, by Rabin among others, up to the last days before the October 1973 War. Yet that leadership's real feelings were perhaps best expressed by defense spending. In the years that followed 1967 it rose to 21.6 percent of the GNP, more than twice the 1957–1966 figures.[10] The standing army was enlarged, taking up an even greater share of the country's precious manpower. For males, the period of conscript service was extended from two and a half to three years (for females it remained as it was, two years); reservists were called up so often that some men found themselves wearing uniform for as many as three months each year. The IDF purchased unprecedented quantities of new military hardware, primarily fighter-bombers; tanks; heavy, self-propelled artillery barrels; armored personnel carriers; missile boats; missiles; and all kinds of electronic equipment.

In the summer of 1972 Sadat, in a surprise move, expelled the Soviet advisers from his country. Time after time he promised his people "a year of decision" when the struggle with Israel would be renewed. Time after time he failed to carry out his threats, causing both the Israelis and their American supporters to mistake him for a clown. In May 1973, following an episode when Israeli intelligence correctly predicted there would be no war and thus made fools of those—Meir and Dayan included—who had ordered a partial mobilization, their self-confidence was strengthened still further. Though Israeli intelligence had singly failed to predict the 1967 war and, in misinterpreting Nasser, may even have helped bring it on, victory caused this fact to be forgotten. Allegedly the intelligence agency knew everything that was happening on the other side, down to the names of individual pilots and their girlfriends; the one thing it did not know was that, right under its nose, half a million Egyptian and Syrian troops were making ready for the attack. Around noon on October 5 the head of military intelligence, General Eliyahu Zeira, was still telling Meir's secretary, Lou Kedar, "There won't be a war."[11]

Belatedly realizing how vast the Egyptian and Syrian buildup was—between them, they had about one thousand combat aircraft and four thousand tanks—the IDF during the first days of October had at least taken some precautions, such as putting the air force as well as regular forces on the borders on high alert (though not all units received the orders). Little of this was known to the public, however, with the result that most ordinary Israelis only learned that their country was at war when the air-alarm sirens started howling at 0200 on Yom Kippur, the sixth of the month. Everywhere, people's immediate reaction was to switch on their radios—normally there are no broadcasts on the holy day. Next, telephones started ringing, and the deserted streets were filled with traffic. More than two hundred thousand reservists took leave of their families, many for the last time. Soon they were on their way to the emergency depots to be formally inducted, issued with their gear, and sent to the front. If the state of the emergency depots left something to be desired, the men's willingness and determination to defend their country at all cost did not.

Much worse was to come. Having known little but victory for many years, the Israelis had grown self-confident, not to say arrogant. Their attitude was perhaps best summed up by the repeated references to the need "to wave the Egyptians back across the Canal," as if the enemy were some kind of towel and the IDF, the person holding it.[12] For the first few hours in the north, and for the first two days in the south, the General Staff just did not understand what had hit it; hence, its response was totally inadequate and only caused the troops, who threw themselves into the fight, to be frittered away in dribs and drabs. When a major counterattack was launched against the Egyptians on October 8, it was badly mismanaged and repulsed with heavy losses. Only then did the Israelis, to quote Dayan again, realize that "the Third Temple [was] in danger," meaning that, unless the struggle was brought to a victorious end, Israel might end up by being destroyed as the two earlier temples had been in 586 B.C. and A.D. 70, respectively.

Nevertheless, on October 9, the wheel began to turn. Counting both fronts, on Yom Kippur fewer than two divisions had stood between Israel and its enemies. At the time the war broke out, mobilization having been completed, the number rose to six (another was hastily formed during the war itself). The Israeli Air Force, which during the first three days had suffered heavy losses at the hands of the Egyptian and Syrian antiaircraft defenses, started learning how to cope with them, though it never regained the freedom or the impact it had had in 1967. Proving their mettle, the reservists stopped the Arabs in their tracks and took the offensive. By October 11, not only had the Golan Heights been cleared but the IDF was also threatening Damascus, having beaten off an Iraqi counterattack on its way. In the south the turning point came on Sunday, October 14, when the Egyptians tried to advance beyond their initial bridgehead but were decisively defeated with the loss of over 250 tanks. Thereupon Bar Lev, the former chief of staff who was now serving as commander in chief of the southern front, allegedly told Meir that "we have returned to our old selves, and so have they." Sharon, whose division bore the brunt of the fighting, put it less politely. "They came," he said, "they saw, and they got f—ed."[13]

Four days later, having fought their way to the Canal, it was the Israelis' turn to cross it. Still, another ten days, and much ferocious fighting, had to pass before a cease-fire went into effect on October 24. By that time Israeli units were standing just sixty-five miles from Cairo and a large part of the Egyptian Army had been surrounded. Only massive American pressure, applied in the hope of getting Sadat to move his country out of the Soviet camp and into the U.S. one, prevented the IDF from exploiting its success and defeating the Egyptians as badly as it had done in 1967. Several more months had to pass before separation-of-forces agreements were signed with the Egyptians and the Syrians, allowing the IDF to disengage and withdraw across the Canal (in the south) or to a line just inside the one they had held before the war (in the north).

It is a tribute to Israeli democracy that, in the midst of these extremely difficult circumstances, elections were held in December 1973. They proceeded in good order and brought the Labor Party, as the Alignment was now calling itself, back to power with fifty-one Knesset seats. Since then, no party has been able to win that many. Still, the most impressive change was the growing power of Likud, the heir to Herut. In 1970, not long after the War of Attrition had ended, Begin in the Knesset heard Meir say that Israel was prepared to "withdraw" from some of the territories. Slowly rising from his ministerial seat, he returned to the opposition and took his party with him. Now he got thirty-nine seats, up from twenty-six in 1969. For Israel's traditional leadership, the writing was clearly on the wall.

In April 1974 Meir, in her own words, "was beginning to feel the physical and psychological effects of the past few months";[14] those who met her at the time could see she was at the end of her tether. When she resigned she took with her Dayan, the former idol whom public opinion blamed for the war even though the Agranat Commission set up to investigate events absolved him. The man who now carried the burden was Yitzhak Rabin. Fortunately for him, and almost certainly for Israel, too, in October 1973 he was serving in a junior post as minister of labor, leaving his image as the victor of 1967 intact. Fifty-two years old, he was probably at the height of his intellectual powers. He was also deliberate, prosaic, and not artistic whatsoever—typical, to use a term coined by Amos Oz, of the "circumcised Cossacks" Palmach produced. Thanks in part to his experience in Washington, D.C., he got along well with U.S. president Ford and the secretary of state, Henry Kissinger. At a time when the country's survival appeared to be at stake, he performed as well as circumstances permitted.

By the time the last reservists went home in the spring, Israel had suffered almost three thousand casualties in dead alone. Perhaps even worse were the psychological consequences. Probably few countries in history have experienced a more abrupt transition from peace to all-out war. Pearl Harbor comes to mind, of course, but then the United States is a huge country and Hawaii, which at that time was not even a state, is thousands of miles from the mainland. The closest analogy may be the series of small countries that were attacked by Hitler and Stalin in 1939–1940; but whereas they succumbed, Israel fought back and emerged intact. Still, fears of the future persisted. Flush with victory—or with what they claimed as victory, ignoring the fact that the IDF inflicted perhaps seven times as many casualties as it took and ended the war well forward of its starting positions—Egypt's Sadat and Syria's Hafez Assad periodically threatened to reopen hostilities. As they had done in 1967–1973, they also rearmed with remarkable speed.

Every few months there was a crisis. First it appeared that the Syrians might not renew the agreement—it had been signed for six months only—that allowed a UN peacekeeping force to be stationed on the Golan Heights and separate the two sides, with God knows what consequences. Next there were fears that Syria, Iraq, and Jordan might form an "Eastern Front" capable of fielding armed forces even larger than the ones that had attacked in 1973; and then high-flying, Soviet-built, MiG-25 fighters violated Israeli airspace while the Israel Air Force did not have what it took to intercept them. So fearful did people become that when listening to the news, they would pay close attention to the announcer's voice so as to guess, ahead of time, whether anything bad had happened. Not even the second separation-of-forces agreement with Egypt, which was signed in September 1976 and led to half of the Sinai being evacuated and demilitarized, brought much relief. As Kissinger, who brokered the agreement, told Rabin at the time, "The Egyptians are only prepared to discuss the practical aspects of non-belligerence, but not non-belligerence as such."[15] As late as the second half of 1977, when the first covert contacts toward peace with Egypt were already well under way, Israeli military intelligence still feared that Egypt was about to attack; as Sadat prepared to visit, the IDF chief of staff, General Mordehai Gur, thought it might all be a bluff.

Though the quiet that had descended on the borders with Syria, Jordan, and Egypt ultimately held, a new front was being opened between Israel and Lebanon. Border incidents, including the attack on the town of Maalot in 1974 when twenty-two schoolchildren died, became a daily occurrence. Other terrorists, also coming from Lebanon, were able to reach as far as Tel Aviv. On several occasions they took hostages and massacred people before they themselves were finally overpowered. Still others tried to blow El Al aircraft out of the sky, though a combination of defensive measures and luck prevented them from succeeding. All this took place in the shadow of the civil war that started to engulf Lebanon from 1975 on, an unrest that provided the Syrian army with an excuse to enter that country in force, thus threatening to open a second front against Israel.

To deal with the terrorism the IDF mounted countless cross-border raids, commando raids, and air strikes at Palestinian targets all over Lebanon. It also established a kind of protectorate over the Shiite population in the southern part of that country, setting up a militia and allowing limited numbers of people to cross the border to find work, undergo medical treatment, and the like. Some operations, such as the one called Spring of Youth, in which future chief of staff and prime minister Ehud Barak dressed up as a woman, were extremely daring and tactically successful. Others, such as Operation Litani (after a river in southern Lebanon) in early 1978, were cumbersome and heavy-handed and achieved nothing. It was like trying to hit a swarm of mosquitoes by using either a needle or a sledgehammer; no wonder it did not work. Stern Israeli warnings to Damascus not to extend its involvement in Lebanon and, in particular, to leave the Christian community in that country alone did not have much of an impact, either.

Even before October 1973, some "developing" countries had begun severing diplomatic ties with Jerusalem, though whether this was because their leaders were still not confident enough or because they had grown *too* confident is not clear. During and immediately after the war, their example was followed by many others. These were the years of the energy crisis, and oil was speaking loud and clear. Accordingly bodies such as the Organization of African Unity and the Non-Aligned Movement started passing resolutions that condemned Israel, though in the end few if any of their members succeeded in making the Arabs give them anything in return. Nor was "the diplomatic landslide," as it was called, restricted to the developing world. During the war itself, when the United States tried to organize an airlift in order to help its beleaguered ally, it discovered that no NATO country except Portugal would grant it landing rights. Throughout the 1970s, Israel could expect little from its self-professed European "friends."

The full extent of Israel's isolation came to light in November 1975. The UN General Assembly, in its wisdom, adopted Resolution 3379, declaring that "Zionism is a form of racism and racial discrimination."[16] Equally humiliating was the decision of the Asian section of the World Soccer Federation to expel Israel. For two decades, the Israeli team could play only in Australasia and Latin America. Not until the Europeans did it a favor by including it in their part of the world did this state of affairs come to an end. By the late 1970s the number of countries that still had embassies in Israel was down to thirtysomething. Along with Taiwan and South Africa, both of which it maintained close ties with, it had turned into a true pariah state. Israel was being criticized even in the United States, where some people objected to the continued occupation of the territories whereas others preferred oil to Jews. Using more refined language, General George S. Brown, chairman of the Joint Chiefs of Staff under President Gerald Ford, twice said that Israel was "becoming a burden" to the United States; speaking in private, Sam Lewis, the American ambassador to Tel Aviv, said Washington was growing "tired" of Israel.[17]

Flanked by Shimon Peres and Yigal Allon, who were serving as ministers of defense and foreign affairs, respectively, Rabin navigated the stormy waters as best he could. Everything considered, he did not do badly. By late 1975 a degree of "normalcy" had been restored. Most Israelis agreed that he was a good, though far from exciting, helmsman. However, in December 1976 his main coalition partner, the National Religious Party, using the pretext that some new F-15 fighters had been flown in on the Sabbath, deserted him. When elections were held in May, Likud, with Begin at its head, won.

Their victory did nothing to ease Israel's military and foreign policy situation. Abroad, some people had not forgotten Begin's past as a terrorist leader. Nor did his republishing his book on that period, *The Revolt,* help them do so. In what can only be called an anti-Semitic remark, *Time* magazine claimed—falsely, as anybody familiar with modern Hebrew knows—that his name rhymed with Fagin, the villain from Dickens's *Oliver Twist.* In the words of one contemporary, "We have lost the active support of our old friends, and become more isolated than at any time since World War II."[18]

Begin was well aware that he and his party had an image problem. He quickly sent one of his old Etzel cronies, Shmuel Katz, to explain his position in the few foreign capitals that were prepared to receive him, but to no noticeable effect. For weeks after being elected prime minister, he used to start each day by asking his secretary "what the foreign papers have written about [him] today."[19] Upon reading the answer, he would explode in anger; not without reason, for some of the same people who called him a terrorist were extolling Arafat as a great Palestinian statesman. Initially his repeated claims that he would work toward peace in the Middle East and that his government recognized Security Council Resolution 242 were overlooked or dismissed. Again, this was partly his own fault. Begin was an ideologue who was in love with his own voice. He also had an unfortunate tendency to hold speeches and patronize—he once antagonized the Egyptian foreign minister by calling him "young man." Meeting President Jimmy Carter, he even managed to get on the nerves of Israel's only real supporter.

To employ a slang expression that came into use many years later, the sirens tearing through the peace of Yom Kippur left an entire generation of Israelis "scratched" like a defective record. Their worst nightmare was that they might hear that sound again; did not practically every one of the countless intelligence publications in Israel during those years end with the conclusion that the possibility of a surprise attack, though it might be guarded against, could never be eliminated? However brave the face people put on the situation, being an international outcast led to considerable difficulties and was no fun to boot. Looking around them many, all too many, Israelis could see nothing but darkness ahead.

"An Economy in Tailspin"

Whereas Israel entered the 1967 war in a state of economic recession, no sooner did the war end than the country started experiencing an unprecedented boom. There was nothing mysterious about this: Had not the great economist John Maynard Keynes, whose influence peaked during those very years, written that the best cure for a recession was a massive injection of government money such as the war had provided? Whatever problems it may have caused, doubling the defense budget created demand as well as jobs. This was all the more true because, made wise by de Gaulle's arms embargo, Israel soon started straining every muscle—in industry, science, technology, finance, and intelligence—in an effort to become as self-sufficient in defense as its resources allowed.

All of a sudden the country was awash with money. Much of it came from abroad as the war led to a dramatic rise in voluntary contributions by Jews around the world as well as an increase in the purchase of bonds; by the end of 1967 Bank of Israel's foreign currency reserves stood at almost $1 billion, a record level. Then there was a wave of immigrants, mainly from the Soviet Union, whose gates had opened a little. The total number of new arrivals may have been around two hundred thousand to three hundred thousand. Though not all of them were highly educated, the skills they did bring with them were often equal or even superior to those of the native population. On the whole the "Russians"—a misnomer, since many of them were actually Georgians—were welcomed with open arms. Some were later to emerge as self-made millionaires. The unexpected influx of workers notwithstanding, unemployment disappeared almost overnight, so that by 1973 it was down to just 2.6 percent. Before long it was replaced by its opposite, a shortage of labor.

Thanks to Dayan's policy of "open borders," first thousands, then tens of thousands of Palestinian Arabs poured across the border in search of work until, in 1972, they formed one-seventh of the entire labor force. It is true that there was always some terrorism, a bomb here and a shooting there. However, for twenty years after 1967 its impact was minor. As a result, personal relations between Jews and Palestinian Arabs remained fairly amiable; on both sides, people felt free to go almost anywhere without taking any special precautions. The fact that many Israelis knew Arabic (Arabic, after all, is an official language) and that even more Arabs quickly learned some Hebrew helped.

While the Israelis claimed that they were "enlightened conquerors," the Arabs, once the first shock of defeat had passed, were able to participate in the economic boom to a considerable extent. Most of the Arab laborers were recruited by their own leaders (rais, in Arabic), who were also responsible for disciplining and paying them. Most were employed in agriculture, for example in digging ditches (men), or else picking oranges (both men and women) and strawberries (women and children). However, one could also meet them at street markets, gas stations, automobile workshops, and similar places.

Another field where Palestinian Arabs made themselves indispensable was construction. Partly because the recession had ended, and partly because the IDF was steadily moving into the occupied territories, there was a tremendous building boom; within a relatively short time, Jewish workers had all but disappeared. One curious outcome of this was that the term "Arab work" began to change its meaning. Instead of standing for everything shoddy, after a time it came to be used as a compliment. After all, one only had to visit the better-to-do neighborhoods of East Jerusalem, Ramallah, and other West Bank towns to see that Arab architects were paying far more attention to aesthetics than many of their Jewish counterparts did; often the outcome was beautifully proportioned buildings that made full use of the local white, rosa, and gray stone. Tourism, too, flourished as never before, benefiting both Jews and Arabs. Not merely did Israelis flood the occupied territories in search of bargains, but hundreds of thousands of foreigners from all over the world flocked to the country about which they had heard so much and which had just displayed its prowess in such a spectacular manner.

Perhaps the biggest winner of all was Jerusalem. To start with, the Jewish, i.e., western, part, previously had been stuck at the apex of a triangle. Now it assumed its rightful place in the center of the country and as a transportation hub through which most of those traveling from north to south or from west to east simply had to pass. Partly for this reason, and partly because of the wave of enthusiasm that swept the country, people flocked to the city. Traffic increased many times over; whereas previously almost the only people who could be seen walking the streets on the Sabbath were Orthodox Jews on their way to or from synagogue, now many of those streets woke up to a new life. So expensive did housing become that "Jerusalem prices" became notorious. North of the city, and later to the south and to the east as well, entire new neighborhoods shot out of the ground.

Yet even these changes paled in comparison with the ones that swept newly occupied East Jerusalem. Previously foreigners could get there only by way of the Mandelbaum Gate, a ramshackle border-control point that Israelis and Jordanians maintained for the purpose. The alternative, namely, traveling first to Jordan and from there by road into the West Bank, was complicated, time consuming, and expensive. Now all of a sudden East Jerusalem could also be reached from the west by way of Israel's Lydda Airport, hardly the world's most highly developed transportation hub but still a lot better than Amman Airport. Following the city's annexation, its residents were issued "blue" Israeli IDs, which enabled them to vote in the municipal elections and gave them access to Israel's highly developed system of social services. In the Old City the infrastructure, much of which was totally

inadequate, was repaired. The results were spectacular and almost immediate. Within a few years, the gangs of rheumy-eyed, ragged, bare-
footed children pestering visitors for alms had melted away; in spite of
everything that has happened since then, they have not returned. No
wonder that when plans for some kind of peace with Jordan were
discussed during the 1970s, the representatives of Bethlehem always
insisted they did not want to be separated from Jerusalem.

Macroeconomic data and social indices reflected the change. Calculating in fixed 1970 prices, per capita GNP (in U.S. dollars) surged
from $1,590 in 1965—a peak year—to $2,410 in 1973. Israelis, including Israeli Arabs, ate more and better food. They also lived in larger
apartments; owned more cars, electronic appliances, and telephones;
enjoyed better health—in particular, there was a sharp drop in infant
mortality—and traveled abroad much more often than they used to.
Scant wonder that when French filmmaker Claude Lanzmann, who
visited in 1973, tried to interest workers in the Port of Ashdod in class
warfare, he found that nobody would listen to him.[20] Even that peren-
nial problem, the negative balance of payments, looked as if it was capable of being solved. By 1972, exports, stimulated by a 20 percent
devaluation of the pound in 1971, were financing about two-thirds of
imports, compared with one-half in 1960 and just one-seventh in 1950.[21]
The rest was easily covered by means of unilateral transfers—during
these years, U.S. government aid rose from practically nothing to about
$ 250 million a year—as well as long-time loans. As inflation picked up
toward the end of the period, the economy began showing clear signs
of overheating. However, at the time that was something Israel had in
common with much of the rest of the world.

Then the October 1973 war came and upset the national accounts.
The best estimates have it that the war cost the economy a billion
pounds ($238 million) per day. If so, then the total price tag must have
come to approximately $4.2 billion, which in turn compared with a
GNP of $6 to $6.5 billion. Above all else, it was necessary to rebuild
the armed forces. During the war itself losses had been very heavy. In a
mere eighteen days of fighting, one-quarter of the air force's aircraft,
and a similar proportion of the ground forces' tanks, were destroyed or
damaged; so prodigious was the expenditure of artillery rounds,
bombs, and missiles that the General Staff came to see the "fire-soaked

battlefield" as perhaps the most important feature that distinguished "modern" warfare from its predecessors. Another cardinal "lesson learnt" was that the IDF was too small for the task it faced. As people said at the time, never again should a situation be allowed in which just three divisions stood between the Egyptians and Tel Aviv.

In response, over the next few years the number of divisions was more than doubled; to control this enormous force, it was even necessary to form corps for the first time. Prewar plans to shorten the period of obligatory service were put aside. The IDF Manpower division reassessed the available manpower, enabling tens of thousands of new personnel to join the armed forces either as professionals or as conscripts. Thousands of new tanks and armored personnel carriers, as well as hundreds of self-propelled artillery systems and combat aircraft, were bought in the United States or manufactured at home; the navy, which during the war had done better than any other service, received generation after generation of new missile boats. The outcome was inevitable. As the shift from F-4 Phantoms (which came at approximately $5 million each) to the F-15 Eagle (which carried a price tag five times as high) illustrates, costs rose into the stratosphere, prompting some people, including Dayan, to question how long this could go on.

To make things worse still, the IDF was seized by a mania for fortification—on the Golan Heights, in the Sinai after the two successive separation-of-forces agreements, and also in the Jordan Valley. Everywhere bunkers were built, antitank ditches dug, minefields laid, and listening posts established. Later it also became necessary to build a number of new airfields to replace those lost when the Sinai was returned to Egypt. Still, most of the IDF order of battle continued to consist of reservists. The result was that the new arms, instead of being distributed among combat units, had to be stored in the emergency depots—which, of course, had to be constructed first. Even taking into account U.S. financial aid, which at this time amounted to approximately $2.2 billion annually, the strain on the country's finances was enormous. In 1976–1980 defense spending was consuming 28 percent of the GNP. Even factoring in American aid, this was three to four times the corresponding figure for most other developed countries.[22] Meanwhile, the growing defense industry soaked up the best available technical and managerial talent. At peak, it accounted for one-quarter of all industrial workers.

These were the years of the so-called energy shock, which got under way in 1973–1974 and lasted throughout the rest of the decade. While Israel itself has no oil or any other form of energy, the 1967 war had put it in control of the Abu Rhodeis oil fields, on the southwestern shores of the Sinai, from which it was able to draw about half of its requirements. However, after Rabin signed the second separation-of-forces agreement in 1976 the fields were returned to Egypt. As a result, the second crisis of 1979 had an even greater impact on Israel than it did on many other countries. The terms of trade worsened and the Achilles heel of the economy, i.e., the balance of payments, took a hit. By the best available calculations, between 1973 and 1982 the cost of imported oil rose from 1.5 percent of the GNP to 10 percent, no less. Overall, the additional price tag during those years may have been around $12 billion; even taking into account the declining value of the dollar, this was well in excess of a year's GNP. Scant wonder that, by 1978, the trade deficit was running at three times the 1972 figure.[23]

As external and internal debts mounted, it is not surprising that investment in everything except defense declined. The result was that productivity growth, which among other things is a function of investment, slowed to a crawl even more than was the case in other countries following the global crisis of those years. Another direct outcome was a slight rise in unemployment. Still, the expansion of the public sector from 24 percent of the workforce in 1973 to almost 30 percent seven years later prevented it from ever going beyond 5 percent. To pay for the steadily expanding public sector a value-added tax was introduced for the first time, helping increase the share of taxation in the GNP from 38 percent in 1972 to 47 percent just seven years later. Above all growth, which for so many years had been the showpiece of the Zionist/Israeli economy even though many other things were wrong with it, came to a halt. Still calculating in fixed 1970 prices, by 1981 per capita income had only risen to $2,550.

Prices, though, were anything but fixed. Even before the October 1973 war, inflation, reflecting both internal conditions and those of the world at large, had raised its ugly head and was running at over 10 percent annually. Now, stimulated by massive government spending that led to equally massive deficits, it exploded. Not once during Rabin's three-year term as prime minister did it go below 25 percent; in 1976 it reached 38 percent. As prices went up the pound went down in proportion. In April 1974, in a stunning move, the official exchange rate against the U.S. dollar was lowered from 4.2:1 to 6:1. In June of the same year the minister of finance, a soft-spoken former mayor of Tel Aviv by the name of Yehoshua Rabinovich, felt constrained to introduce a "sliding" system of paltry devaluations in the hope that people would not notice and would go on doing business as if the world had stood still. Needless to say, people *did* notice and the system did not work. Very soon devaluation was fueling inflation and inflation, devaluation.

The rise to power in May 1977 of Begin and Likud made things much worse still. A demagogue first and foremost, Begin knew nothing about economics, not even home economics, which, like his political rivals Ben Gurion and Rabin, he gladly left to his wife. Nor, apart from a good understanding of how to use people's plight to attract voters, did he care for them. Like his master Jabotinsky he had turned his back on socialism. Still, he was possessed by a vague feeling concerning the need to fill citizens' pockets so as to put a chicken on everybody's table and a roof over everybody's head—"to do well by the nation," to use his own words. To carry out this task, he brought with him as deputy prime minister and minister of finance Simha Ehrlich. Sixty-two years old at the time, Ehrlich was a veteran of the General Zionists, a party that had practically ceased to exist twelve years earlier and whose heads were known as "generals without troops." He was, however, a long-time friend of Begin's; his qualification for the job consisted of the fact that, as a businessman, he had run a firm that manufactured optical products.

Though he was the least charismatic of men, Ehrlich resembled his boss in that he, too, was an ideologue, albeit one with a different idea to propagate. Rejecting the warnings of professionals at the Bank of Israel and within his own ministry, he threw caution to the wind and carried out what became known as the Upheaval. He started by devaluing the pound by 43 percent, no less. Next, administrative restrictions on foreign currency, which throughout Israeli history had been rather tight, were relaxed. Citizens traveling abroad were suddenly allowed to purchase $3,000 or its equivalent, instead of a mere $450 as previously; at the time, this was a considerable sum. Even better for them, they were permitted to open foreign currency accounts in Israel as well as overseas. By way of a special bonus Ehrlich also abolished the hated travel tax, a move that, in a country where foreign travel has always been a status symbol, did much to make the Upheaval popular. Later it was reinstituted, but that is part of a different story.

Had Ehrlich had any sense at all, he would have started by balancing the budget and postponing the liberalization of the economy to the end of his program. Since he did the opposite, the result, to quote the title of a book written by a former director general of the treasury, was to send the economy into a tailspin.[24] Over the next two years inflation, which had been running at 35 percent, rose first to 50 percent and then to 80 percent. It is true that Ehrlich himself was forced to leave the treasury in November 1979. However, his successors were no more able to ride the tiger than he had been. The first to try was a sharp-tongued industrialist by the name of Yigal Hurwitz. Exclaiming that "I ain't got it" and dramatically displaying his empty trouser pockets, he cut subsidies and tightened the money supply until the pips squeaked and labor unrest grew even worse than usual; on one occasion he told those who objected to his policies, "Madmen, get off the roof!" Hurwitz's boss, Begin, may not have grasped all the details. What he did realize was that the new course might very well lose him the 1981 elections.

To forestall such a possibility, in January of that year Begin fired Hurwitz and replaced him by a Likud functionary named Yoram Aridor. Adopting a policy he had the gall to call "correct economics," Aridor printed even more money than before. At the same time he used up the country's dollar reserves to try and slow the devaluation process. To make his policies more popular he cut tariffs on such things as motor vehicles and electronic appliances, incidentally enabling hundreds of thousands of Israelis to buy color TV sets for the first time. At one point, so overvalued was Israel's deteriorating currency that even orange juice, once a major export item, started to be imported; overall, the effect of his measures was like feeding sugar to a diabetic. In the midst of all this a currency reform was carried out. The pound was abolished and replaced by the shekel at the rate of one to ten; however, changing names did no more to halt inflation than did the government-inspired

TV and radio broadcasts that called on people to stop buying things. By the end of 1984 inflation was running at almost 1,000 percent.

So far, the causes of the problem and the acres of red ink that it produced. But what did life under inflation *feel* like? The answer is, like some surrealist dream. One of the first effects, which was becoming visible as early as 1974, was the growing use of the U.S. dollar as a ghost currency. At first the system whereby calculations were carried out in dollars and payments were made in pounds applied only to major items such as houses, flats, and, increasingly, cars as well. Later it was extended to less important goods and services such as monthly rents. Then it was the turn of other things such as child support, lawyers' fees, and the tuition paid at private kindergartens; more than one mistress proudly put a note on her door saying that "the price is fifty dollars, and so it will stay!" At one point Aridor suggested that, since all calculations were being made in dollars anyhow, Israel should give up its economic sovereignty, either linking its currency to the U.S. dollar or simply adopting that currency as its own. Insofar as it would have ended inflation at a stroke, the plan was perfectly sensible; however, it was too bitter a pill for the membership of the ruling, nationalistically minded Likud Party to swallow. Not only was the idea rejected, but it also played a role in Aridor's eventual resignation.

As inflation accelerated, life became more and more weird. Each time there were rumors that this or that subsidy would be cut, products disappeared from the shops, only to reappear a few days later with new price tags attached to them. Here and there attempts were made to end the practice by sending in inspectors, but never with success; most people simply sighed and paid the new sums demanded of them. Supermarket employees, armed with price-tag guns, spent much of their time desperately moving from shelf to shelf trying to keep up, with the result that many products carried several price tags glued on top of one another. Gas-station owners and operators faced a similar problem. At this time most pump mechanisms were still mechanical rather than electronic. They simply could not keep up with the ever-rising increases; instead, calculations had to be made by hand or the figures rounded off to the nearest decimal.

So fast did the mail service raise its prices that the post office no longer saw fit to issue new stamps. Instead it chose to print a standard one that did not show the cost and whose value was adjusted from time to time. Some people accumulated mountains of practically worthless coins. They put them into sacks, hauled them to the banks, and insisted that they be deposited or exchanged for bills. At one point the value of the copper in some of the coins exceeded their nominal value, with the result that they were taken out of circulation and melted down. Other people bought masses of tokens of the kind used for public telephones, making them also hard to get. The bills themselves replaced one another at bewildering speed. New ones carrying different portraits and colors were constantly being issued and old ones, having lost most of their value, withdrawn.

All these were minor nuisances. They generated a certain nervousness and made day-to-day life more complicated than it should have been; however, once one got used to them they were not really disruptive. Much more serious was the fact that when drawing up major contracts, it became necessary to decide in advance not only the date on which the transaction would be carried out but also the hour at which this would be done. Normally this was 11:00 A.M., the time when the Bank of Israel published the exchange rate of the day. Since buyers had to obtain liquid funds first and vendors had to reinvest any sum they received as quickly as they could, the banks also became the favorite meeting places where many transactions were carried out. An unforeseen accident, a traffic jam, or simply a sick child at home that prevented people from keeping their appointments could easily cause buyers to gain large amounts of money, and vendors to lose similar sums. This again made people turn to lawyers, who invented complicated procedures to protect their clients, and so the merry-go-round went on and on.

On one hand, those caught with pounds or shekels in their pockets lost their pants; one result of this was the growing use of credit cards, which reached Israel and gained in popularity precisely during those years. On the other hand, people fortunate enough to have taken out mortgages in 1970–1974—the only time in the whole of Israeli history when they were not indexed—saw their monthly payments melt away until the banks finally gave up and no longer bothered to cash them at all. The impact on wage and salary earners on one hand, and on corporations and the self-employed and corporations on the other, was also unequal. The former continued to have income tax deducted at source as usual (wages, salaries, and tax grades were all indexed fairly effectively, so that the relative burden remained more or less as it had been). The latter were able to avoid almost all income tax by simply demanding payment at the beginning of each fiscal year and postponing the time when they themselves paid the treasury as much as possible.

As is so often true, best of all was the situation of those able to claim government or company apartments, cars, telephones, and so on. Rabinovich at one time made an effort to change the situation by subjecting such "fringe" benefits (in reality, they were often anything but "fringe") to income tax. So numerous were the beneficiaries, though, that he was only moderately successful; the harder he and his successors tried, the more people found expedients to circumvent the regulations. Perhaps this explains why, for many years, each time the cabinet met the cameras would catch the table groaning with food and (nonalcoholic) drinks until it looked as if it was about to break. Yet curiously enough, people did not resent this privilege. On one occasion, when food intended for Begin's household was being carried through the streets of Jerusalem, they stood and applauded.

By the late 1970s, inflation had created a situation where simply to calculate the GNP and similar figures became an exercise in futility. So did the government's many successive "budget cuts," which were nullified even before they could be implemented. By the summer of 1983, at the very latest, it was becoming clear that Aridor's policies were leading to a massive drain on Israel's foreign currency reserves and might lead the country into a real catastrophe. In October of that year his place was taken by yet another former businessman, Yigal Cohen-Orgad. Cohen-Orgad well understood what the problem was—not that doing so required any particular genius. As part of his efforts to deal with it, he had the Knesset pass a law known as Taxation under Inflationary Conditions. However, with its hundreds of paragraphs the law was so complicated that not even the accountants who wrote it, let alone the MKs who voted for it, could understand what it was all about. As a result, it was never implemented. Nor was Cohen-Orgad able to keep his promise to send out "divisions" of inspectors to root out tax evaders. In any case, to a large extent these divisions only existed in the public imagination as well as his own. Given how fast money was losing its value, evading taxes simply no longer made sense.

As receipts from taxation fell, the government deficit grew. As the government deficit grew, receipts from taxation fell, further increasing inflationary pressures. Now inflation proceeded faster than devaluation; now things worked the other way around. Israeli economists, a highly qualified lot with professional connections all over the world, wrote learned treatises to determine which was the chicken and which the egg, but everybody knew all too well that the spiral was heading nowhere but down. The effect on ordinary people was what might be expected. People bought foreign currency on the black market—Israel at the time was the only country where black-market rates were published in the daily press—and stashed it away in the banks' safety deposit boxes. There, withdrawn from circulation, it neither earned interest nor did nobody any good.

In response, Hurwitz used a cabinet meeting to propose that the boxes be put under guard—it was a Friday afternoon, the right time to engage in such a move—opened, and the owners summoned and asked to explain their contents. The results would no doubt have been very interesting. However, this plan was blocked by Begin, who, to his everlasting credit, told his underlings that "this is something one just cannot do in a democratic country." When news of the abortive plan leaked out people's confidence in the deposit boxes was understandably shattered. Many of them preferred to take whatever they had and stow it away under their mattresses; in one or two cases that came to light and were reported by the press, people had stuffed it into frozen chicken inside their refrigerators. Thus, Hurwitz's hope to walk away "like a bridegroom from his wedding canopy," as he himself (quoting a Hebrew proverb) put it, was not to be realized.

Many ordinary people started each working day by gathering at the banks' gates. Come rain or sunshine there they stood, reading the latest financial wisdom as it appeared in the dailies—Israel at the time had few if any popular papers specializing solely in economics—and exchanging views as to what was best to do with their money. Meanwhile, they waited for those gates to open as if they gave access to some sort of Ali Baba caves or secular temples. Once admitted, they engaged in an orgy of speculation. They bought and sold not only foreign currency but also every conceivable kind of share, bond, and other financial "products" that investment councilors dreamed up and put under their noses. One very visible outcome of the process was the increase in the number of bank branches—when the IDF invaded Lebanon in 1982, it took along special mobile banks to enable the troops to continue speculating in the field. Banks came to be positively hated. When they advertised themselves as "the Oxygen of the State," popular wisdom quickly turned this into "the Nitrogen (*hankan,* which in Hebrew is associated with "to choke") of the State." Conversely, to people who went abroad the relaxed atmosphere that prevailed inside foreign banks, as well as the fact that it was possible to calculate one's own budget ahead of time, came as a pleasant surprise.

As the saying went, the best money was *"yarok verahok"*—green and far away. Black humor abounded. One story claimed that using money to buy a meal in a restaurant was preferable to putting it in the bank, since the ultimate result would be the same in both cases. Another had it that the shekel was going to be linked to the Greek drachma in order to create a new currency known as the *dreckel* (little piece of dirt). There was, however, also considerable bitterness. As the placards carried by one group of demonstrators read, AFTER THEM—THE DELUGE! Yet even skyrocketing inflation and daily devaluations of the currency formed only part of the problem. In late March 1983 the stock market started declining as people, feeling insecure, took out their money and put it into foreign currency or index-linked government bonds. In the autumn, it collapsed.

With the exchange went the shares of the four most important banks. For several years before this those banks, competing with each other, had been "regulating" (read "buying") their own shares. Their objective was to turn those shares into alternatives to state bonds so as to show the world, and themselves, how stable they were. Now the banks' reserves were exhausted. Amid scenes of pandemonium reminiscent of America's Black Tuesday—people did in fact talk of October 6, 1983, as "Black Thursday"—their shares dropped 17 percent in a single day. As had also happened in 1929, many people had accepted the banks' advice and taken out loans to buy their shares. Since they might now be unable to meet their obligations, the crisis threatened to develop into a general financial meltdown. Following two weeks during which trade in the shares was suspended, the government saw no choice but to pour $8 billion in public funds into the banks, essentially nationalizing them. At the same time it promised those who were willing to wait that they would receive their money back after so-and-so many years. A commission of investigation was set up, and in 1990 some of those responsible were put on trial (but not convicted). Only then was the mess finally sorted out.

In 1982 Israel engaged in yet another war, this time in Lebanon, thus further increasing the economic burden. The gap between its foreign currency holdings and its obligations widened to over $15 billion. This was five times the 1973 figure and twenty (!) times the 1965 one that had so worried Eshkol and Sapir that they engineered the recession of 1966.[25] Had it not been for U.S. aid, which in 1984–1985 was raised to $3 billion annually (a further $1.5 billion arrived in the form of emergency assistance), the country would have faced financial ruin. In fact, aid was more extensive than these sums indicate. To them should be added two brand-new air bases built in the Negev; American orders for Israeli-made military hardware; joint military-technological R & D; and the construction on Israeli soil of depots in which U.S. military equipment was stored. Some of this may have reflected real sympathy, but most of it was based on realpolitik as America's leaders understood it. Still, the process of obtaining aid was often humiliating. For many years each time an Israeli dignitary visited Washington, his hosts would carefully assess his worth and decide how much money, usually in the form of an extra loan, they should throw his way. Thus, Ezer Weizman, at the time he was minister of defense, once got $200 million. Others were less successful than he was.

Had the situation been allowed to continue, Israel might have been forced to suspend payments to its foreign and domestic creditors. The outcome would have been a crisis of confidence, mass unemployment, social unrest, and, quite probably, political instability and a threat to democratic government. Alternatively government spending would have had to be cut, as world-famous economist Milton Friedman, whom Ehrlich had actually recruited as an economic adviser but who quit in disgust, recommended. Since defense was the largest item in that budget by far, inevitably the first step in such a program would have been to pare down Israel's conventional forces by cutting back the number of armored divisions and air force squadrons, reducing training periods, postponing work on all sorts of innovative projects, and the like. Either way, the Arab rulers might have sensed an opportunity to settle accounts with their enemy, as to some extent happened during the run-up to the June 1967 war. This in turn might have forced the country to bare its nuclear teeth to a greater extent than it actually did; a most unwelcome possibility both to Israel and to much of the rest of the world, and one that was almost certainly not unrelated to the willingness of the United States to extended additional aid.

As we shall see, thanks very largely to Uncle Sam, collapse was averted at five minutes to zero. In the meantime, though, the growing economic difficulties, as well as Israel's international isolation and the equally difficult military problems it faced, led to a profound cultural crisis deeper than anything the country had experienced until that time. And it is to that crisis that we must now turn our attention.

"I Am Going to Look at the Sea"

"I Am Going to Look at the Sea" was the title of a poem as well as an essay, both written (in Hebrew) by Jonathan Geffen, then twenty-six years old and already seen as one of Israel's up-and-coming writers, immediately after the October 1973 war. Geffen, a nephew of Moshe Dayan, had spent part of his youth living in his uncle's home. Now, having experienced the full fury of war while fighting the Egyptians in the Sinai, he and his generation felt their illusions coming apart around their ears—hence the urge to go and look at the sea in the hope that it, at least, was still beautiful.

One of the greatest strengths of the Zionist enterprise had always been its ability to mobilize culture. Countless artistic works celebrated the enterprise and sought to assist it; partly because nonconformists could expect to be ostracized, and partly because the artists believed in the cause as fervently as anybody else. The importance of Bialik in this context has already been mentioned. As he wrote in one of his early poems, "Bless the arms of our brothers who [are] building our land."[26]

Merely to list all the poets who celebrated "the Jewish nation in its re-emerging ancient homeland" (as the saying went) would require an entire volume. Among the most important was Aaron David Gordon (1856–1922). A Tolstoy-like character, with a flowing white beard, his verse—written in pretentious Hebrew that has since become almost unintelligible—celebrated the virtues of the simple farmer's life and working the soil. Then there was the great lyrical poet Rahel Bluwstein (1890–1931, known simply as Rahel) who sang the beauty of "my country" and of her own insignificance in trying to work it. Another was Saul Tschernichowsky (1875–1943). In "I Believe," he wrote that his people would flourish again. When they had settled in the Land of Israel, their chains would be broken and they would look into the light.[27] In other poems he glorified the heroism of the Biblical King Saul and the "wall and stockade" movement of the 1930s. Along with Bialik, all three were studied by generations of schoolchildren. All still have streets named after them in older Israeli cities and towns.

Once the War of Independence had been won, the torch passed to a new group of writers known as "the generation of 1948." Unlike their predecessors, they had spent most or all of their lives in the Land. Also unlike their predecessors, their principal virtue was that they had fought for their country. The general contents of their works may be recognized from the titles: e.g., *Gray as Ashes* (Yigal Mosenzon, 1917–1994), *He Walked through the Fields* (Moshe Shamir, 1921–2004), and *They'll Arrive Tomorrow* (Nathan Shaham, 1925–). All were resolutely secular, paying little attention to religion and thus breaking with Bialik, who, though he was not observant, always remained firmly rooted in religious tradition. Though the best of them did acknowledge their heroes' frailties, all were also resolutely nationalist. And how could it be otherwise? After all, in 1956 the Ministry of Education had the following to say about the objective of studying literature at school:

> [It] is to bestow upon the student and to commend to him the ideals, reflections and experiences of the nation in its development during various periods and the recognition of the unbroken historical link between the nation and its land and culture. In particular the efforts and achievements of our

generation and the generations close to it in the national establishment and the cultural and social regeneration must be revealed.[28]

Similarly, by merely listing some of the works of the most important Israeli composers, one can get a fair idea of the depth of their involvement with the Jewish-Zionist-Israeli tradition. Take the opus of Paul Ben Haim (originally Frankenburger, 1897–1984). Born in Munich to a well-to-do Jewish family, he served in the German Army during World War I. In March 1933, soon after the Nazis came to power, he left for the Land of Israel. Seeking to break his ties with his native country and start over again, he put everything he had written up to that point in storage with the intention that it should never again be performed. Among his patriotic compositions are "To My Country" (1947), a "Fanfare to Israel" (1949), "Views of Israel" (1951), and the famous version of "Hatikva" for orchestra (1950). Likewise, Mordechai Seter (1916–1994) wrote "Valiant Woman" (1957), "The Daughter of Jephtah" (1966), and *Jerusalem* (1971). Perhaps unsurprisingly, there is hardly an Israeli composer who did not at some point try his or her hand in putting parts of the Old Testament, especially Psalms and the Song of Songs, to music.

Whereas "serious" music reaches only a relatively small public, the impact of popular music is much greater. This is nowhere more the case than among the Zionists in the Land of Israel, who, both before and after 1948, deliberately harnessed it to their cause. Neither the music, much of which was hijacked from foreign sources, nor the words, nor the performances were always of the highest quality. Yet their impact cannot be overestimated; indeed, there existed, and continues to exist, a whole class of music known as "songs of the Land of Israel." The list of titles is endless: "The Land of the Deer Is Calling us" (one of the many names the Old Testament has for the Land of Israel), "On the Mountains, the Sun Is Rising" (words by Nathan Alterman), "In Galilee, at Tel Hai, Yoseph Trumpeldor Fell" (words by the subsequent mayor of Haifa, Abba Hushi), "Sleep, Beautiful Valley, We Are on Guard" (in honor of the Valley of Esdraelon), "The Song of Cameraderie" (a great favorite with Yitzhak Rabin), "Let's Build the Country, the Fatherland, for It Is Ours, Ours," and so many others as to make one's ears ring. This kind of patriotism swelled during the period after 1967, culminating in the world-famous "Jerusalem of Gold," written just before the war and quickly adapted to reflect the victory.

Some of the most popular songs and sketches were written for, and performed by, the military ensembles. First emerging during the early 1950s, the ensembles presented a unique Israeli phenomenon with no equivalent in any other country. They were made up of ten to fifteen young, more or less talented conscripts of both sexes under more or less professional direction. Originally their purpose was to help maintain morale among IDF units by means of songs such as "Oh My Army Post," where the only heating was "the warmth of the heart in the fire of combat," and "Dina Barzilai," a beautiful female soldier whom some soldiers, having seen her file, would love to meet. Still, it speaks volumes about the mood of the period, and especially about civil-military relations, that these ensembles were also very welcome among the general public; many of the ensembles' members later developed successful careers in music and on the stage. If they sometimes poked fun at the military and at the country, then it was gentle fun indeed.

Also enlisted to assist the process of "striking roots" were the visual arts. Take the painter Abel Pann (born Abba Pfefferman, 1883–1963). The son of a Lithuanian rabbi, before and during World War I he spent time in Paris and New York but in 1920 took up permanent residence in the Land of Israel, where for many years he taught at the Bezalel School of Art. He spent much of his career trying to forge a link between the Old Testament, which after all was the basis on which the Zionist claim to the Land rested, and the present. The outcome was works with titles such as *And Rebecca Loved Jacob* (1932); *And It Came to Pass That His Master's Wife Lifted Her Eyes to See Joseph* (1945); and *Rahel Came with Her Father's Flock, for She Was a Shepherdess* (1950).

The difficulty was that nobody had the faintest idea what Rebecca, Jacob, the handsome Joseph, and the beautiful Rahel might have looked like. Hence, Pann and his fellow Orientalists—there was a whole school of them—presented them as Oriental types, by which they meant either Arabs or Sephardi Jews who, to them, looked more or less as Arabs do. Their hair was black, their eyes dark—as one of Pann's critics wrote, artists "should not populate ancient Canaan with Scandinavian types"[29]—and their skin tanned by the Oriental sun. Male figures wore *keffiyes* and many of them carried *shebariyas* (short, curved knives).

Female ones invariably wore gold jewelry around their heads as Bedouin women do, including, in some cases, nose rings. Thus, far from Zionist artists despising and denying "the Orient," as Edward Said claims in his book on the subject, they took it as a model, embellished it, and idealized it. To them, it represented everything that their own people had been and, if that people wanted to reestablish an authentic identity in its own country, had to become again.

Israel has never been a totalitarian dictatorship. In the 1950s and 1960s the universities enjoyed extremely high status; though it was the government that paid most of the bills, the arrangements under which they operated gave them almost complete independence in respect to curricula, teaching, and conducting research. All the more impressive, therefore, was the fact that most of the scholarly establishment voluntarily enlisted to serve the cause. In particular, Jewish history, the "history of the Land of Israel"—a field centered on Jerusalem's Yad (Institute) Ben-Zvi, after the president who had died in 1963—Talmudic studies, and Biblical studies were used to demonstrate the "unbroken historical link between the nation and its land." This was even more true of archaeology, a field that assumed extraordinary importance and on which fortunes were spent. It provided, as its greatest find, the Dead Sea Scrolls, including the entire book of the prophet Isaiah; if ever there was proof of continuity, this was it. Scant wonder, then, that no sooner had the various territories been occupied in 1967 than Israeli archaeologists followed the flag and started excavating wherever they could. Each time they discovered some Jewish remains the news was trumpeted in the media. It is so still.

The fact that during the 1960s Israelis, especially young Israelis, were too busy fighting and building their country goes far to explain why the sixties' counterculture, beat culture, hippie culture, yuppie culture (both of which presupposed a certain material affluence that Israelis had not yet attained), psychedelic culture, and drug culture never really struck roots among them. To a considerable extent, the country was their drug. Foreigners and new immigrants often wondered why Israelis would not talk of anything else. This is not to say that *all* Israeli culture and scholarship was patriotic, let alone deliberately designed to serve patriotic ends. Returning to the subject of universities, side by side with the above-mentioned fields Israel also developed excellent engineering schools, natural science schools, medical schools, and any other number of schools. In the same vein, Ben Haim did not focus solely on patriotic works, he also wrote "Symphonic Metamorphosis on a Bach Chorale," "Five Pieces for Piano," and "Pastorale Diverte," not to mention preludes, études, and other kinds of music for everything from choruses to full orchestras, to quintets, quartets, and solo instruments.

To repeat: Israel, tucked away in the Middle East and preoccupied by the need to defend itself against external enemies, was in no position to compete with the great centers of world culture in terms of wealth and the abundance of talent. Some of its culture, specifically including the military ensembles, bore a somewhat provincial, even naive, character. Still, Israelis always stayed in touch with those centers and often tried to emulate them as best they could; perhaps the best demonstration of this is the world-famous Israel Philharmonic Orchestra. Compared with the citizens of other "third-world" countries, Israelis have always been highly educated. Furthermore, theirs is a country with an astonishing mix of people, originating in an astonishing number of countries, and representing an astonishing number of different cultures. The early Zionists' encounter with local people and conditions made the culture even more fertile. This was as true of literature as it was of music (both "serious" and popular), of painting as of scholarship; as shown, among other things, by the rise of a large, high-quality community of experts on Arabism and Islam superior to anything found in almost any other country. Under such circumstances, Israeli culture could not help but be varied, creative, and dynamic. It also could, and did, give expression to almost every conceivable human emotion and need.

Again, this is not to say there were no cracks in utopia. As early as the 1950s songs designed to imbue people with love of their country as well as some of the more martial tunes began to be spoofed with the aid of humor, some of it black indeed. Youngsters about to be drafted, instead of promising that after being killed, they would be buried in a winery, "where girls serve glasses of red wine," expressed the fear that their bodies would be left in Shaar Hagai, "where armor-piercing bullets whistle." Instead of swearing that they would "overcome" and "march towards the luminous future," they welcomed one another to the hospitals' emergency wards. In 1958 the writer S. Yizhar (aka Yizhar Smilansky, 1916–2006) published a truly great novel, *Yemei Tziklag* (Philistia Days). Yizhar, who incidentally looked just like the typical *sabra* (Hebrew native) with an open shirt and forelock, had fought the Egyptians in 1948 and knew only too well what he was talking about. Following the deeds and thoughts of a group of soldiers day to day, he described the horrors of war as well as the atrocities some Israeli troops had committed. It is true that he only questioned some of the means, not the end; still, his reward was to be denied the Bialik Prize for literature, the most prestigious of all. When Ben Gurion at one point denounced Israeli writers for their alleged lack of social responsibility, he may very well have had Yizhar in mind.

As with the economy, what caused much of this patriotic, flag-waving worldview to be shattered was the "October Earthquake," as it was called.[30] Without question, the war was the sternest test Zionism and Israel had undergone since 1948. It was also a test that, in the eyes of many, should never have taken place, had military planning, military doctrine, military organization, and, above all, military intelligence done their job; and that the country and its leaders passed only with mediocre grades, if at all. Instead of victory, all the war yielded was heartbreak. The dead, the crippled, the injured, the psychiatric casualties (who entered the public consciousness for the first time), the widows (but not widowers: Though almost one in ten IDF soldiers were female, only two or three women were killed), the orphans, and the bereaved parents and siblings were everywhere.

During the cold, rainy winter of 1973–1974 hundreds of "memorial parties" were held. Relatives, friends, and fellow soldiers gathered to discuss the merits of each of the fallen; they would describe his looks, his behavior, the clothes he wore, and anything else they could remember. Diaries and letters of the heroic dead would be produced and read aloud—some people, having gone through the experience, claimed they would destroy their own—and pictures of him distributed as souvenirs. Next, what the mourners had said would be written down, and the results published in private editions. More often than not, these brochures were amateurish in form; as far as their contents went, they tended to mix the sublime with the banal. Still, they and the memorial parties on which they were based reflected the public mood as nothing else did.

They also constituted a cultural phenomenon in themselves, and one that some Ph.D. student might find interesting.

This was just the tip of the iceberg. Until 1973 most Israelis had regarded the IDF as the peak of the Zionist enterprise. The best anybody could be was "a Hebrew soldier," as one song put it; too often, war itself was presented almost as if it were a lighthearted adventure. Now it resumed its rightful place as a bloody, serious business, and *mehdal*—a term that manages to combine the meanings of negligence, oversight, blunder, and failure—was on everybody's lips. Previously people believed any statement coming from the IDF spokesman almost as if it were holy writ. Now doubts entered; wits claimed that, whereas hitherto the Israelis knew how to fight, and their enemies, how to cover their defeats with lies, things were turning the other way around. The coming decades were to see many ups and downs in civil-military relations. For good or ill, the positive feelings that had prevailed before 1973 were never completely restored.

Among the casualties of the war were many of the IDF's nonmilitary activities as well as the military ensembles. Partly because that was how their members felt, and partly because their message was dictated from above, for two decades they had spread a fresh, youthful kind of optimism. Now, although the IDF continued to invest in them, that optimism no longer fitted the darkening public mood. When Israel invaded Lebanon in 1982 a young writer by the name of Ephraim Siddon kicked them in the stomach by changing the lines of one of their most popular songs; in the new version a little girl, her bones broken, stood up and asked why the war had to be fought. The reference was to the 1973 war when Elazar, as chief of staff, had promised to "break the Arabs' bones." After that, it is no wonder the ensembles lost their audience until they were finally dissolved.

Still, in regards to the military, a very good illustration of the change is *The Joker,* a play by Joshua Sobol (1939–). The play opens during the last days of the October War in a bunker on the Golan Heights—"the asshole of the country," as its occupants, a handful of haggard, rather bedraggled reservists, say. The background is formed by the constant quacking of wireless apparatus and an occasional artillery shell exploding in the distance. In walks Eyal—the name means something like "strength"—a fresh-faced, twenty-two-year-old soldier with a large pack and a red suitcase, who immediately starts boasting. First he tells some tall story about a hair-raising episode he had allegedly witnessed on a base where he had undergone his basic training. Next he explains how the war "caught [him] with [his] pants down, in the midst of coitus, after a good meal complete with meat and wine," with another man's wife.[31] Both stories are quickly exposed, the first by a soldier who recalls hearing an even more improbable version of it and the second by another soldier who asks whether all that took place on the Day of Atonement. In the end all that is left of Israel's once-proud heroes are a group of tired, frightened men with mortgages to pay and relatives who need looking after.

Moving from the military to civilian society, an early sign of change was the rise to fame of Moshe Kroy (1948–1989). Kroy taught philosophy at Tel Aviv University and was a follower of the best-selling self-styled "objectivist" Ayn Rand. He developed a theory of "rational egoism" that rejected altruism, let alone socialism, as mere stupidity, and advocated utilitarian self-sufficiency instead. Never having had a friend himself, he claimed that nobody else should have them, either. When people visited him at home he charged them for the tea they drank; he and his wife would leave their infant daughter on the stairs leading to their flat so as to toughen her character. Yet in 1973–1974 this confused young man grew into a media star. Moving beyond the confines of academia, many of his lectures were held in the homes of the elite, where they succeeded in attracting businessmen, politicians, generals, and their wives. Later, convinced that some mysterious powers were plotting to kill him, Kroy left for Australia, where his wife was mistakenly shot by his son-in-law. Later still he returned to Israel but was unable to reestablish himself and ended by committing suicide.

Though Kroy was an extreme case, he was far from alone. The entire country seemed to prepare for incoming, as military men say, and withdraw into its shell. Inside the shell was a greater emphasis on private as opposed to public life. Previously people spent the hot summer evenings on their balconies playing cards; now they started buying air conditioners and remained in their living rooms in front of their TVs. Previously they had celebrated Independence Day by going into the streets to watch shows and dance; now they increasingly did so by means of private picnics and parties. To observe the changing mood, it is enough to compare Jerusalem's French Hill, built just before the war and consisting of widely spaced, free-standing, eight-story-tall buildings flaunting themselves against the sky, with Gilo, a huddled, fortress-like beehive of a neighborhood in the same city that dates to 1974–1975. A similar difference emerges from a comparison of the Hebrew University campus at Givat Ram with the newly rebuilt one on Mount Scopus. The former was constructed in the mid- to late 1950s. Until it was surrounded by a security fence in the 1980s, it used to be completely open to visitors. The latter was erected mostly between 1973 and 1980. With only a few gates, all of them guarded, it looks like an (ivory) fortress; perhaps it is no accident that the manager in charge of the entire project was a retired IDF colonel.

In the whole of Israeli literature, perhaps the man who did most both to reflect the change and to bring it about was another playwright, Hanoh Levin (1943–1999). A native of Tel Aviv, he came from a religious background, a fact that gave him an edge when it came to attacking Orthodoxy. Personally he was just the opposite of the native-born "new" Israeli that Zionism had tried so hard to create: small, delicate, and anxious looking, more an ascetic scholar than a burly pioneer or a swashbuckling hero. He first became notorious in 1970 when, in *Bathroom Queen,* he poured ridicule on everything people at the time held most sacred. As one contemporary critic fumed: "A scene in which a journalist coming to interview a young widow whose husband had been killed on the [Suez] Canal makes love to her could only have been invented by a Satanic brain or a madman. . . . This play deliberately sets out to torment thousands of bereaved parents."[32] When it was produced, shocked spectators started breaking up the hall and attacking the actors. This, as well as government threats to withhold money from the theater that dared produce it, caused it to be withdrawn after only nineteen performances.

Levin was not defeated. Switching from Israeli politics to the private lives of its citizens, throughout the 1970s he wrote and produced plays that focused on the latter's seamier side. The stage saw a grotesque parade of petty bourgeois characters, most of them town dwelling and male. They are held prisoner by their petty ambitions, their fears, and their unfathomable narrow-mindedness. Even more powerful is their helpless desire for greedy, often sluttish women with large breasts and moldy vulvas who torment their would-be lovers, enslave them, and drive them to suicide; "A Hunchback Finds a Whore," the title of one of Levin's less well known poems, goes a long way to sum up his opus. Still, he could not leave politics alone. In 1982 *The Patriot* featured an Israeli whose fondest wish is to leave the country for the United States. Following the instructions of the American consul, he is prepared to spit on his mother and kick an Arab boy in the face. Only extensive cuts to the script prevented the attorney general, quoting the imperative need to maintain good relations with the United States, from taking the theater that produced the play to court. Sharp tongued, courageous, and exceedingly productive, Levin kept up the barrage into the late 1980s. By then he had begun to repeat himself.

While social critics such as Sobol and Levin thrived, anybody trying to defend the regime suffered. Among the most important victims was the party press. Israelis, and before them Zionists, have always been exceedingly politically minded, and throughout the country's history many of the daily papers had been associated with political parties. Thus *Davar* (best translated as "Word") was the mouthpiece first of Mapai and then of the Alignment. *Al Hamishmar* (On Guard) represented the left-wing Mapam party and its kibbutz movement; *Lamerhav* (Into the Open), the equally left-wing Ahdut Haavoda; *Kol Haam* (The Voice of the People), the communists; and *Herut,* the party by the same name. All these carried long-winded, heavy-handed articles full of ideological fare. Many were written by, or on behalf of, elderly party hacks trying to show off their learning. Partly for this reason, and partly because of the belated rise of television, all lost readers and ended by having to close. Apart from some papers representing the religious parties—so different are the needs of the religious community that they cannot be served by the secular press—only three or four commercial dailies were left. Competing for readers, even the best of them concentrated more and more on sex and crime. A new generation of young, brash journalists saw their task as not educating readers but titillating them. Doing so, they also moved farther and farther away from the "high" language literature used.

As the press became less cooperative—the party papers aside, it had never been subservient—cases of corruption that previously would have gone unnoticed began coming to light. An early case was that of

Asher Yadlin. The son of an important Mapai, Hagana, and Histadrut functionary, he was convicted and imprisoned for bribery and embezzling funds. Later he wrote a book in which he claimed that "this is not the story of Yadlin alone, but of the growing defilement of Israeli society in general and the Labor Movement in particular";[33] for years on end, a half-finished building he left behind him, carrying a huge red graffito that read YADLIN'S HANDIWORK, could be seen at an important crossroads north of Tel Aviv. Another spectacular case of corruption was that of Rabin's minister of housing, Avraham Ofer. Rather than face the accusations directed at him, he preferred to commit suicide. Standing over the grave, the prime minister addressed the dead man, saying, "Avraham, I believe you were innocent." Soon thereafter Rabin himself was tried, convicted, and fined because of a small but illegal foreign currency account his wife and he were keeping in Washington, D.C. These cases, as well as others like them, did as much as anything else to end the reign of the Labor Party.

Taking a wider look, and as was also happening in other countries, political life was changing. Probably the main reason for this was television; it enabled leaders to address followers without having to bring them together first. As people retreated into private life, the percentage of those taking an active part in politics by attending rallies and the like went down. Cultural clubs such as Tzavta (Togetherness), which was closely associated with the Labor Party, lost members and some had to close their doors. Previously many politicians, including Ben Gurion, Ben Zvi, and Moshe Sharett, had been almost as good at wielding the pen as they were at politics. Now, more and more, politics and culture came to be seen as opposites; when one Labor MK claimed that a book he had written would get him to the cabinet table, he sounded pathetic. Among other things, this explains why Shimon Peres, a very well-read man, never really caught the people's imagination. Even Begin, who knew how to play on his followers' heartstrings, sometimes came close to spoiling the effect by his excessive use of Latin quotes. Parties, instead of representing well-defined groups and classes, were coming to be seen as little but organized mafias where hacks—sometimes, hacks who could not make it anywhere else—competed among themselves for power, money, and glory.

The change was perhaps best illustrated by the rise of a new terminology. Meir, who was a good socialist and, by the time she wrote her memoirs, well beyond her prime, followed the established tradition of Mapai leaders in saying that she took on this and that post, went here and there, "on mission from the movement." Had it occurred to Ehud Olmert, an ambitious young lawyer who was first elected to the Knesset in 1973, to use such words, he would have covered himself with ridicule; in 1974, indeed, a satiric TV program by the name *Cleaning Heads* did ridicule Rabin and Co. by presenting them as they pretended to be: hewers of wood and drawers of water. Instead the purpose of politics became "to get things moving" and, of course, to do oneself good in the process. Years later a Likud minister of education tried to set the clock back by turning to a hall packed with her party members and rhetorically asking them whether what they were after was jobs. "Yes," a thousand throats roared back at her.

Among the clearest sign that values were shifting and that social change was well under way could be found in the decline of those showpieces of the "First Israel," the kibbutzim. From early on their role in the Zionist enterprise had been out of all proportion to the number of their members. They were "pioneers" who settled the country and worked the land, literally "making the desert bloom" and thereby helping justify the Zionist enterprise—or so people thought. In the entire Zionist ideology, no myth was more powerful than this one; accordingly, throughout Mapai's long rule the communal life was held up as a model to emulate. In particular, Ben Gurion always did his best to convince the country's youth that the best thing anybody could do with his or her life was to join a kibbutz. Following his retirement, he actually went to live in one.

Another factor that explains the kibbutzim's unique status was their role in defending the country. Early during the War of Independence some of them had served as strongholds. Their members, taking up weapons, had joined with Palmach and later IDF fighters to repulse the invading Arab armies; while Negbah was the most famous case, it was hardly the only one. For decades after 1948 kibbutzniks were greatly overrepresented among combat troops and pilots, enabling them to claim elite status and put everybody else to shame. However, the world is round. In 1973, when Israel faced the most powerful onslaught in its entire history, the military role of the kibbutzim was reduced to zero. Those established on the Golan Heights from 1967 on had to be hastily evacuated just before the Syrian attack, and their inhabitants were allowed to return to their homes only after the war had ended.

Previously kibbutzniks had been perceived, often with good reason, as idealistic pioneers who worked hard and led exemplary, if austere, lives. Now many of them developed a rather comfortable lifestyle in parklike settings complete with trees, lawns, and that ultimate provider of comfort in a hot country, swimming pools. Dressed in shorts and sandals, people moved around on ancient bicycles. Children tumbled among the bushes, spent time at the ubiquitous petting zoos, or did light gardening work. Thanks to their collective purchasing power kibbutzniks often enjoyed cultural facilities—access to movies, plays, concerts, and the like—far superior to anything most townspeople could afford. Discarding their ideology, they also started hiring outside labor to do their heavy work for them. As one novelist later put it, they looked "like well fed Dutch cows."[34] Though everything was becoming more expensive all the time, they did not have to worry. Increasingly, this caused them to be regarded with envy rather than admiration. The fact that, whereas the kibbutzniks themselves were almost exclusively Ashkenazi, many of those they employed were Sephardi also caused resentment to grow. It was a factor Begin knew how to exploit. As prime minister, he once started a speech with the words: "Lo, a kibbutznik is sitting beside the swimming pool. . . ."

With the parties and the kibbutzim went the youth movements. Right from the beginning, most of them had been associated with one political movement or another. Proceeding from left to right, Hashomer Hatzair (Young Guards) was an arm of Mapam. Maccabee Hatzair was affiliated with the General Zionists (who had merged with Herut in 1965); Betar, with Herut; and Bnei (Sons of) Akiva, with the National Religious Party. Except for the last-named, which found a new mission in life in the form of settling the occupied territories, all suffered steep declines in membership so that fewer and fewer members could be seen on the streets. The same fate overtook the one "nonaligned" movement, the Scouts. For many years their great aim in life, too, had been to form "nuclei," groups of lads and lasses who would do their military service together and then either join an existing kibbutz or, best of all, set up a new one. As the kibbutzim changed their mission from "pioneering" to providing their members with the good life, though, they became less attractive to idealistic youth. In the end, all that was left of the Scouts were clubs where a few middle-class children played.

Traditionally Israel's leadership had been almost entirely Ashkenazi; "a Russian tale," to use the original title of a novel by Meir Shalev known, in English, as *The Blue Mountain.* Perhaps because they were new to the country, most of the Oriental immigrants who arrived during the 1950s were prepared to defer to that leadership. Not so their sons and daughters who grew up in the country itself. Wadi Salib apart, the first rumblings of discontent could be heard even before the 1973 war. A movement calling itself the Black Panthers was formed, and its members took to the streets in protest against the dire socioeconomic conditions under which they and their families lived. They held speeches, published some literature, and broke a few windows. Some of their young and rather aggressive leaders even met with Meir. She offered them cigarettes—she was a heavy smoker—took an interest in their personal stories, and tried to persuade them that "Black Panthers" was a bad choice for a name. However, she refused to recognize that they represented a serious social movement growing out of a serious socioeconomic problem. Later—how typical—she said that they were "not cute."

The war postponed these problems for a time, if only because many of its heroes—including most of the troops of the Golani Brigade who shed their blood copiously in an attempt to recapture Mount Hermon—were themselves Orientals. However, after the Rabin government took over they quickly resurfaced. Instead of striving "to integrate the different Diasporas," it was claimed, Israel was being divided into two. The "First" Israel consisted of often well-educated, relatively well-to-do, mostly secular, Ashkenazis, sometimes known as *vuzvuzim* (plural form of the Yiddish *vus,* meaning, "what") with light skin and, sometimes, blond hair. They originated in Europe or North America (though the number of immigrants from Latin America was growing, there was no separate statistic for them) and spoke with a "soft" accent. They ate *kneidlach* and gefilte fish, looked down on everybody else, occupied most important positions, and occasionally stole public funds as Yadlin and perhaps Ofer had done.

The "Second" Israel consisted of Orientals. They had dark skin, eyes, and hair; spoke a guttural Hebrew (one name Moroccans in particular were called was *tshah-tshahim*), and were often "traditional" in outlook. Most were stuck in city slums or in godforsaken development towns where they enjoyed few leisure and educational facilities. In 1974, they formed 55 percent of the population, but accounted for just 3 percent of all academic degrees.[35] They ate *khraime*—fish cooked in tomatoes and spicy peppers—as well as *mufleta,* a sort of unleavened bread made with lots of oil and served with any amount of sweets. Too many of them made their livings as hewers of wood and drawers of water; indeed, the mere sight of a cleaning lady who did *not* have dark hair was enough to make passersby stop and stare. Poverty explains why Orientals were disproportionally responsible for property crime, violent crime, and prostitution. Poverty, plus the feeling that they were being discriminated against, also explains why, in 1977, most Orientals voted against Labor and for Herut—even though, in truth, the leadership of the second was no less Ashkenazi than that of the first.

Coming as it did after almost half a century during which Mapai and its successors ruled Israeli society, Begin's victory in the 1997 elections certainly revealed the depth of discontent in that society. Yet even that discontent paled beside the most serious problem of all: namely, the growing doubts that now surrounded the Zionist enterprise itself. In the words of Walter Laqueur, himself an Israeli (though he spent most of his time abroad) and the author of a standard work on the subject: "The basic aim of Zionism was . . . to regain Jewish self-respect and dignity in the eyes of non-Jews, and to rebuild a Jewish national home, for Jews to 'live as free men on their own soil, to die peacefully in their own homes' [Herzl]."[36] Until 1967 the enterprise, whatever its shortcomings and limitations, seemed to be overcoming all difficulties and going from one success to another. The victory caused many Jews throughout the world to take a new pride in "plucky" Israel, even to the point that they became Zionists for the first time. However, the 1973 war and the events that followed it spoiled the effect. It offered proof, all too clear proof, that the struggle to build a safe haven for Jews was far from over.

As the threats mounted, or seemed to mount, during the 1970s, both Israelis and others saw little but trouble ahead—after all, Israel was now the only place on earth where Jews, just for being Jews, were in real danger of losing their lives. Inevitably, the news that this was indeed the case spread. More and more, Soviet Jews who had been permitted to leave preferred to choose the United States, Canada, Australia, or similar countries over Israel as their new homeland. As one country after another cut its diplomatic ties with Jerusalem and Zionism was condemned in every international forum from the UN General Assembly down, gigantic question marks started popping up. Had the medicine been worse than the disease it sought to cure? Might Zionism, instead of leading to the gradual disappearance of anti-Semitism as Herzl and his followers had hoped, be producing the opposite effect? Had the establishment of the state, with all the tremendous sacrifices that it involved, in fact been the worst error ever committed by the Jewish people?

At least the sea, that sea at which Geffen went to look and into which Israelis had always feared the Arabs might push them in case they ever lost a war, was still beautiful.

Hallelujah!

While the 1970s and early 1980s represented an exceptionally difficult period for Israel, not everything was darkness. Perhaps most impressive of all was the military recovery and buildup that followed the 1973 war. By the end of the decade Israel, a small nation of no more than about 3.5 million Jews, was capable of fielding a force that, according to international sources, numbered six hundred thousand men and women. The number of fighter-bombers increased by more than 50 percent. That of artillery pieces went up by 75 percent, whereas that of tanks doubled. At peak, Israel was able to deploy more tanks than France and Britain combined. Had the Chinese owned proportionally as many tanks as the Israelis did during those years, then the figure would have exceeded a million.

Side by side with quantitative expansion went qualitative improvements. Certainly before 1967, and to some extent even in 1973, technologically speaking the IDF—the army of a relatively small country—was backward in many respects. By contrast, many of the weapons received from the United States from 1974 on, including fighter-bombers and missiles, were the most modern of their kind anywhere. The outcome was that Israel became a vast military laboratory to which foreign experts could, and did, look in preparing for future conflicts. Nor is this the entire story. Already during Mandatory times, Hagana had set up underground workshops where technicians repaired weapons and maintained them. During the 1950s and 1960s the military industries, now operating in the open, expanded until they were capable of producing small arms, explosives, most kinds of ammunition, and many sorts of electronic gear.

The events surrounding the 1967 war, which showed how vulnerable Israel could be to an arms embargo imposed from outside, provided an additional impetus. By the late 1960s the Ministry of Defense was determined to press ahead in building at least one major indigenous weapons system for each of the three services, i.e., the ground forces, the air force, and the navy. In any event, the dream of self-sufficiency proved beyond Israel's grasp. However, the vast sums spent, and the outstanding talent mobilized both from within the country and, when necessary, abroad, did yield a powerful and highly innovative military-industrial complex. By the late 1970s it was capable of designing many excellent weapons and weapons systems from scratch, producing them at reasonable cost, and exporting them to many countries around the world.

Forming the background to this entire issue was the growing shadow cast by nuclear weapons. Israel's first reactor, constructed with French aid, was completed in 1964.[37] One or two primitive nuclear devices may have been available even as early as 1967, and more started entering the arsenal from 1968 on. By the time of the 1973 war a dozen or so are said to have been available, complete with delivery vehicles in the form of Phantom fighter-bombers and Jericho I surface-to-surface missiles with a three-hundred-mile range. If Egypt and Syria nevertheless dared to attack, then this was only because they never intended to cross the pre-1967 border. True, the war did not cause Israel to change its formula, first introduced by Eshkol, according to which "it would not be the first to introduce nuclear weapons into the Middle East." However, in late 1974 statements by former Minister of Defense Moshe Dayan and then President Ephraim Katzir made the threat hard to miss. In March 1976 the IDF censor even permitted Israel's leading daily to reprint a story published in *Time* magazine about how, on October 8, 1973, Israel had come very close to using its nuclear arsenal.

Though it took time, these developments caused Israelis to regain some of their self-confidence. In July 1976, that confidence received an unexpected boost. In a brilliant operation that has few equals in history, Israeli commandos carried out a surprise landing in the Ugandan city of Entebbe, twenty-five hundred miles away. They had come to rescue 105 Israelis and French Jews who had been hijacked inside an Air France plane and were being held hostage at the airport there. Their safe return to Israel, complete with hostages, was marked by an explosion of joy; here was tangible proof that the effects of the war were being overcome and that IDF was returning to its old self. Better still, previously Israeli military ventures had often been condemned in every possible international forum. This time, by contrast, much of the Western world, at any rate, stood by and applauded. For weeks after the operation foreign producers flocked to Israel in the hope of persuading the IDF spokesman to cooperate with them in making films about it. Eventually, four different movies (one with Elizabeth Taylor) reached the screen, each kitschier than the other; the raid also became the subject of a computer game.

As the decade ended, Israeli defense spending amounted to 80 percent of that of Egypt, Syria, and Jordan combined. This compared with 50 percent in 1960 and just 33 percent in 1954.[38] Abroad, war-gamers struggling to reproduce the military balance in the Middle East on the hex maps of the time found themselves facing an unexpected problem. So small was Israel in relation to its neighbors, but so huge its army, that the maps simply could not contain the necessary counters. To be sure, the cocky self-assurance that had characterized Israel in the years 1967–1973 in particular never returned. In its place was a grim determination to survive at any cost. So tremendous was the IDF's quantitative and, in many ways, qualitative expansion that there could be little doubt as to the direction in which the balance of power was tilting. In 1981, when another brilliantly planned and executed Israeli air attack destroyed an Iraqi nuclear reactor under construction near Baghdad, that direction became clearer still.

In the midst of this, the 1977 elections were held. For the first time in Israeli history private advertising agencies were asked to lend a hand. Parties introduced modern techniques, had jingles written and broadcast, and the like. A televised debate even took place between the two main candidates, Peres and Begin; considering that Ben Gurion had always refused to call the latter by his name (he referred to him as "the man sitting next to MK Bader"), this represented progress. Yet the most important innovation was the appearance out of nowhere of a new, center-of-the-line, vaguely liberal, largely Ashkenazi party known as Dash. Formed with the specific intention of punishing Labor for its sins, it won thirteen seats, largely at the expense of the latter. The outcome was the victory of Likud. As the continuing deterioration of the economy was soon to show, some of those who now "had suits sewed" (as Israelis say) for themselves were anything but responsible or competent. Still, the elections had the virtue of clearing the air. They rid the country of an elite that, in the eyes of many, had turned into little but a slogan-spouting, money-grabbing mafia with no ideology and no sense of what it wanted except to hold on to as much power as it could for as long as it could.

Perhaps even more important, the elections provided decisive proof that Israel was what it had always claimed to be: namely, a functioning, if sometimes chaotic, democracy. This was a time when Leonid Brezhnev's Soviet Union was at the peak of its power, crushing dissidents from the Elbe to the Pacific Ocean and soon about to invade Afghanistan, too. From Buenos Aires to Phnom Phen and from Kinshasa to Beijing, much of the "developing" world was in the hands of tin-pot dictators; some were so vicious that they practiced genocide on their own people. By contrast, the number of democracies was down to just a few dozen. Under such circumstances, the orderly way in which Israelis went to the polls and the transfer of power was carried out commanded respect. Begin, whom Rabin during the campaign had called an archaeological exhibit, made his own important contribution by prohibiting his followers from carrying out far-reaching purges in the civil service. Conversely, after the elections' results were announced Peres called the winner and congratulated him. Amid the rough-and-tumble of Israeli politics this was an innovation, and a welcome one at that.

Economically difficult as the 1970s were, they were not entirely without their bright side. To return to defense, certainly not all of the investments made in this sector bore fruit. Some projects turned out to be white elephants. Thus the Lavi, a fighter-bomber then being developed by Israel Aircraft Industries (IAI), proved to be beyond the country's capabilities. Equally abortive was a revolutionary artillery system. After a few years during which they built the hulls of new missile boats, the Israel Shipyards in Haifa went bankrupt. Still, not everything went down the drain—as time went on, these and similar projects made an important contribution in building up plants, organizations, and skills. They did so, moreover, in a field in which Israel—thanks to its relatively large armed forces, low wages, system of universal service (which permitted exceptionally close ties between engineers on one hand and soldiers on the other), and, above all, plentiful combat experience—possessed a comparative advantage over many other countries. By 1980, arms exports amounted to perhaps $1.3 billion a year—and growing fast.

Thanks to generous—perhaps too generous—government spending and the expansion of the public sector, unemployment never really turned into a problem. Throughout the decade it hovered between 3 and 4 percent, which was less than in most developed countries at the time.[39] Taking 1967 as a starting point, the distribution of income, already the most egalitarian in any country outside the Soviet Bloc, became a little more egalitarian still. Israel's welfare state, which had been constructed during the previous two decades, remained intact. Basic foodstuffs, bus transportation, and some housing were all heavily subsidized. So was healthcare, with the result that Israel had more doctors per thousand people, and that people visited those doctors much more often, than was the case in any other developed country.[40] Certainly the lives of those at the bottom of the socioeconomic scale was often hard. Yet nobody starved and there were few if any homeless. The share of subsidies and transfer payments in the GNP actually increased, rising from 14 percent in 1968–1972 to 24 percent in 1975–1978.

In 1974 Rabin—a man whose heart was usually in the right place even if, with his brusque manner, he did not always know how to show it—introduced child allowances (previously only mothers with more than ten children had received them). Given their exceptionally high fertility rates, the principal beneficiaries of the reform were Orthodox

Jews on one hand and Arab-Israelis on the other. The difference between the two groups was that, especially among the Bedouin (a fiercely
independent population that in many ways consists of only half citizens), polygamy was, and is, occasionally practiced. Before long, stories
started circulating concerning *paterfamilias* who, bravely girding their
loins, had produced as many as thirty children, all of them supported
by the public purse. Since then, right-wing parties in the Knesset have
often tried to cut back payments to Arab families by suggesting that
those payments be made conditional on the recipients serving in the
military first. However, thanks to the fact that the percentage of Jews
who do conscript service has been declining—see more on this in
chapter 5—there is little chance that they will succeed.

In 1979 a slight increase in social security payments made it possible to raise the age of obligatory education from fourteen to sixteen
years and the age at which it was free from sixteen to eighteen. Another indication that living standards kept rising, albeit much more
slowly than before, was the fact that among the Jewish population, the
number of persons living three or more to a room went down from 7.5
percent in 1970 to a mere 2.2 percent in 1978. It is true that a combination of higher fertility rates and poverty, itself due to a combination of
fewer skills and discrimination, made the situation of Israeli Arabs
much more difficult in this respect. Still, even among them, the re-
spective numbers fell from 45 to 37 percent. Considering how difficult
and worrisome the postwar period was, these achievements, modest
though they were, sometimes appeared little short of miraculous. Certainly they enabled the above-mentioned Gashashim, whose popularity was at its peak, to make their point even more loudly and more
clearly than before.

Israel's international isolation during these years, which culminated when the UN General Assembly declared Zionism to be a form
of racism, has already been mentioned. For a nation as well as for an
individual, to be humiliated in this way is no fun. Still, the resolution
had some unexpected consequences. Although the vast majority of Israelis have always been fiercely patriotic, by the 1960s the younger
generation in particular had become sick and tired of the term "Zionism." To them it stood for the preaching of their elders who, like all elders at all times and places, never tired of contrasting their own

(alleged) heroism, stoicism, and self-sacrifice with the (allegedly) easy life led by their offspring. This revulsion was taken to the point where "Zionism" was put into quotation marks. In popular culture, and elsewhere, it came to stand for everything that was moralizing, fake, and, ultimately, stupid.

But cornered, with their backs to the wall, confronted by a multitude of snarling enemies, most Israelis reacted as people in such a situation will—by putting on a show of defiance. At the UN, Israeli ambassador (and future president) Haim Herzog declared that the resolution was "devoid of any legal or moral value"[41] and dramatically tore a copy to pieces. Back in Israel, all of a sudden Zionism started emerging from the quotation marks. T-shirts reading I AM A PROUD ZIONIST appeared on the streets, and there was a renewed interest in the history of the Zionist movement. Furthermore, the international offensive against Zionism and all its alleged evils probably had the unintended effect of strengthening the ties between Israel and at least part of the world's Jewry. Jews were worried about the fate of the only state certain to provide them with a safe haven in case of trouble; hence, they, too, embraced Zionism in a new way. Quoting Samson, the Old Testament has a phrase reading, "Out of the strong, sweetness came forth."[42] It certainly applied in this case.

All these were welcome developments, yet they were overshadowed by the prospect—which was to be realized in 1977–1981—of finally reaching a peace agreement with Egypt. Ever since the decision to establish Israel had been made, the latter country had been Israel's most powerful enemy. This caused five major wars to be fought—in 1948, 1956, 1976, 1969–1970, and 1973—as well as countless border incidents from 1953 to 1956 in particular. Starting at least as early as 1950, there had also been numerous attempts to conclude a peace; however, all had been frustrated for one reason or another. Before 1967, the problem was that neither Egypt nor any other Arab country with which Israel tried to talk—in most cases, negotiations were too strong a term for what went on—was prepared to grant peace except in return for far-reaching concessions Israel felt it could not make. For a long time after 1967, those countries simply demanded the restoration of their territories while refusing to promise anything in return.

Then the 1973 war came and reshuffled the cards. To the extent

that the war restored the Egyptians' lost honor and set in motion a diplomatic process that ended in the return of the whole of the Sinai Peninsula to them, they were justified in proclaiming it—as they did, at the
top of their voices—as a victory. To the extent that it seems to have put
an end to the Arab, or at any rate the Egyptian, desire to fight Israel
once and for all, it constituted a clear victory for the Jewish state—does
not Carl von Clausewitz say that the objective of war is to break the
enemy's will? At the same time, the war shattered Israel's confidence in
its own ability to deter another round of hostilities by sheer force of
arms, thus making it more prepared to consider other possibilities, too.
It is true that, in the immediate aftermath of the war, these mental
shifts were only beginning to emerge, let alone to be understood. One
of the first who did understand them was Henry Kissinger. From then
on, as he once quipped, he did no more than any genius would.

Undoubtedly, one very important reason why Israel suddenly showed
itself prepared to make greater concessions than previously was the
Second Separation of Forces Agreement of 1976. First, by demilitariz-
ing the western half of the Sinai, the agreement gave both sides a
breathing space. Second, it presented a model of how they might secure
themselves against future aggression. Third, by leading to another massive influx of up-to-date American arms, it did a lot to put Israel's fears
at rest. When Likud gained power in 1977 and Ezer Weizman, the
former air force commander and deputy chief of staff, was appointed
minister of defense, his subordinates told him that he would hardly
recognize the army he had left ten years earlier. They turned out to be
right. From then on Weizman, who for a long time had been considered so hawkish that in 1967–1968, Eshkol refused to appoint him chief
of staff, started changing his mind; as he talked to the Egyptians and to
Sadat in particular, they identified him as their most dovish partner.

On the Israeli side, the second man to spearhead the efforts toward
peace was Moshe Dayan. Though the post–October 1973 commission
of investigation had acquitted him, public opinion forced him to resign,
and from then on he kept only his Knesset seat. Begin, following his
victory, asked Dayan to join his cabinet as foreign minister—the two,
after all, had known each other for thirty years past, and while they did
not belong to the same party, they had established feelings of mutual
respect. Much to the chagrin of his own party comrades, who competed

with one another in calling him a traitor, and of some Likud members, who coveted the post that Begin had earmarked for him, Dayan accepted. Long the most political of generals, he could be the consummate diplomat when he wanted to, outwardly frank but capable of stripping a man of his underwear without taking off his pants first. He was also well known for his sympathy for the Arab language and culture; he turned out to be the ideal man for the job.

Begin's own motives during this period remain something of a mystery. By instinct he was a militarist. His dearest wish had long been to review an Independence Day parade as his great rival, Ben Gurion, used to do; however, his advisers talked him out of the idea. In respect to the Arab-Israeli conflict he was an extreme hard-liner. In both 1974 and 1976 he had done his best to sabotage the separation-of-forces agreements with Syria and Egypt. Had he lost the 1977 elections, and assuming his party would not have gotten rid of him as a result, no doubt he would have continued on the same course. Yet shortly after entering office he changed his position—probably the greatest feat any statesman can perform, and one that lost him the support of some of his right-wing friends.

In the absence of any real evidence of his thought processes, one can only guess at them. Perhaps Weizman and Dayan, both of them military men with global reputations, persuaded him that, provided the Sinai was demilitarized and proper arrangements to monitor Egyptian military movements put in place, Israel would be safer without the peninsula than with it (as actually turned out to be the case). Perhaps he hoped that by giving way in the Sinai and driving a wedge between Egypt, Israel's most powerful enemy, and the other Arab states, he would be in a better position to keep the remaining territories. Perhaps it was simply the fact that, for the first time since 1948, he had nobody else to pass the buck to. As Rabin, in one of his few recorded sayings that were truly witty, once put it, "Begin's greatest advantage as prime minister was that he did not have to cope with Begin."[43]

On the Egyptian side, the man in charge was Anwar Sadat. Having stepped into Nasser's rather large shoes as a compromise candidate, during the first three years of his rule few foreigners took him seriously. In the Arabic (but not the English) version of his autobiography he says that his brain functioned like a "Swiss watch"; Egyptians called him "the black ass," after the dark skin he inherited from his mother, a Sudanese slave. Then came 1973, and the war forced many people to change their view of him. From then on, using his pipe as a diplomatic weapon, he worked assiduously to change his image into that of a moderate, peace-loving, almost avuncular figure. In some ways Sadat's motives are easier to grasp than those of his Israeli counterparts. What he wanted was to complete his "victory" by taking back the Sinai. Knowing that he could not do so by means of war, he chose to make the necessary concessions and pay the necessary price. Besides, Egypt at the time was being racked by bread riots. American money was what Sadat needed, and some American money was what, in the end, he got.

As was disclosed later on, attempts to establish contact between the two countries started very soon after Begin set up his government, when he personally asked the Romanian dictator, Nicolae Ceauşescu, to mediate. Next Dayan, wearing sunglasses and a false mustache, flew to Morocco. There he met first King Hassan II and then Sadat's special envoy, Hassan Tuhami. By September 9, 1977, the two men had uncovered sufficient common ground for Sadat to inform the Egyptian National Assembly that he was prepared "to go to the end of the world and even to the Knesset in Jerusalem" if doing so could help in establishing peace. So unexpected was the announcement that Yasser Arafat, whose PLO had more to lose from the move than anybody else but who happened to be in the audience, rose and applauded along with all the rest.

Needless to say, from the first moment, Dayan had acted in concert with Begin, whose emissary he was. Nevertheless, the prime minister was as stunned by the news as Arafat had been; his first recorded reaction was, "He will really come!" When Sadat did arrive on the evening of Saturday, November 19, excitement peaked. As Israeli dignitaries jostled one another to obtain a spot along the red carpet, the IDF chief of staff, General Mordehai Gur (served 1974–1978) worried about possible treachery. To be on the safe side, he had snipers stationed around the Egyptian leaders' aircraft. In any case, there was no treachery, only a perspiring, serious-faced Sadat walking down the stairs. When the time came to shake hands with Gur he said, "You see, this was no bluff."[44] Dayan, who had probably done more than anybody else to bring the meeting about, greeted the event by jotting down a poem. It was preserved by his office manager, Elyakim Rubinstein, and only published after Dayan's death. Using Biblical language, he expressed his surprise and delight at the fact that, after all those years, Sadat had landed in Israel and seemed ready to talk peace. To an overwhelming extent, the nation reacted as its leaders did. If, in the midst of what can only be called an orgy of joy, there were some extremists who, fearing for the future, opposed the visit and tried to disrupt it, they hardly succeeded in making their voice heard. The media reported the Egyptians' every move, including their request to visit a restroom, as if it were a miracle; in a sense, watching Israel's long-standing enemies behave like ordinary men *was* a miracle. Thousands lined the road from the airport to Jerusalem, cheered, waved Egyptian flags, wept, and prayed. As Sadat addressed the Knesset on the afternoon of the following day, the Israeli people were riveted to their TV sets. To many his words, "I wish to tell you today and I proclaim to the whole world: We accept to live with you in a lasting and just peace," were the sweetest they had ever heard.

This is not to say that the way to peace was now wide open or that reaching an agreement was easy. The two sides had fought one another for too long for trust to be established immediately—as Sadat spoke, the Israeli security service even put his voice through the appropriate electronic gadgetry to try and see whether he was sincere. One of the most important hurdles was reaching agreement on the extent of the withdrawal (early on, Begin seems to have hoped to retain at least the Israeli settlements in the northeastern corner of the Sinai). Others were the fate of the two military airfields the Israelis had built in the peninsula, its demilitarization, the question of the Straits of Tiran and the Suez Canal (which Israel insisted should be opened to its shipping), what to do with the Gaza Strip, and the precise meaning of the "peace that was to follow." Israel insisted on establishing diplomatic and commercial relations, communications, air and bus transport lines, border controls, and so on, and in the end it got its way. Perhaps most difficult of all was the question that, in Israel, was known as "linkage." On one hand, Egypt could not be seen as forsaking the populations of Gaza and the West Bank in their attempts to rid themselves of their Israeli occupants. On the other, the agreement had to be formulated in such a way that it would retain its validity even if the occupation did not come to an end.

At first the talks were bilateral. Like some traveling circus, they were held now in Jerusalem, now in Ismailia, now in various neutral sites around the world. Both parties proved obstinate, and things did not move as quickly as Sadat had perhaps imagined they would. Almost from the beginning, he and Begin did not work well together. While both were flamboyant, if Sadat thought that by merely visiting Israel he could solve "seventy percent" of the problem, he was deluding himself; rather than gracefully smiling and saying yes, that's wonderful in response to Sadat, the Israeli prime minister instead delivered homilies on Israel's past or else raised point after legal point. Having failed to obtain a breakthrough at Ismailia, Sadat apparently considered breaking off the negotiations and resigning.

Later, too, there were moments when it looked as if progress was impossible. Each time this happened, the Israeli media, which were only too well aware of what was at stake, grew shaky. Might not the dream of peace prove illusory after all? At one point Dayan, to stave off disaster, in a typical flip-flop—this one that surprised his fellow Israelis, however—proposed that the Americans be asked to mediate. Probably his real objective in doing so was to soften up Begin, who from this point on would answer his own party members' anxious questions by asking, "Do you really want to quarrel with the U.S.?"[45] Thus President Carter; his gentlemanly secretary of state, Cyrus Vance; and his hard-nosed national security adviser, Zbigniew Brzezinski got involved. Over the next months messages were exchanged, meetings held, compromises reached, and formulae hammered out.

In the end, the Camp David Accords agreement that was formed at Camp David and signed in a public ceremony at the White House on March 26, 1979, left both sides fairly content with their achievements. The Egyptians got what they wanted most, i.e., the whole of the Sinai exclusive of any Israelis who might have been stationed in it or settled in it. The Israelis, on their part, got most of what they wanted, i.e., peace, recognition, demilitarization, early warning posts in the Sinai (which, however, were manned by American troops, not Israeli ones), and freedom of navigation. While Gaza and the West Bank were not mentioned in the text, a letter approved by the parties that Carter sent to Egypt did promise that Israel would start negotiating with the Palestinians to withdraw the military government—another Dayan idea—and achieve autonomy within five years. In this roundabout way, the question of "linkage" was solved or, at any rate, supposed to be solved.

It remained for Begin to steer the agreement through the Knesset. A few people went on hunger strike in front of his home, and a few MKs engaged in histrionics. True democrat that he was, the prime minister did not enforce party discipline (had he tried to, most probably he would have failed). As a result some Likud members, including Ariel Sharon, who at that time was serving as minister of agriculture; Moshe Arens, a future minister of defense; and Ehud Olmert, voted against. Nevertheless, thanks to the support of Labor and the left, the resolution passed with an overwhelming majority. It was a triumph—a triumph for everything that was most enlightened, most decent, most peace loving, and, yes, most patriotic in Israeli life. As to Begin himself, had he died later that night—he had already suffered several heart attacks—his epitaph would have read, "Here lies a great man." Instead he saw the move not as a first step toward withdrawal from the remaining territories but as one that would render such a withdrawal unnecessary. Overcome by hubris, his future actions were to take him from a peak where much of the world applauded him into a pit from which he did not emerge.

Certainly the process by which the treaty was carried out had its ugly side. First Sadat, in a move that was probably meant to appease his critics, refused to accept the 1978 Nobel Peace Price, leaving Begin to receive it on his own. Next, in October 1979 Dayan, feeling that Begin had no intention of seriously negotiating with the Palestinians about autonomy or anything else, resigned. His brother-in-law, Weizman, soon followed suit. While Weizman's post remained vacant for over a year, the one Dayan had held was taken by a real hard-liner, Yitzhak Shamir. Meanwhile, Sadat in Cairo had his own problems. The agreement with Israel left Egypt isolated in the Arab world. A few of his collaborators resigned, and he personally came under fierce attack both by his foreign enemies and by domestic ones. On October 6, 1981, while watching a parade held to commemorate the 1973 "victory," he was gunned down. Pompous to the last, apparently he thought that his assassin, an Egyptian officer, was about to salute him.

The IDF's evacuation of the Sinai went without a hitch, but doing the same to Yamit, a town the Israelis had built in the Peninsula's northeastern corner, was more difficult. Hard-liners argued that the move might create a precedent and that Jews should not evacuate other Jews. Some used the word "transfer," to draw a parallel between the inhabitants of Yamit and that of Holocaust victims. Only in April 1982 did Sharon, who had been appointed minister of defense in August of the previous year, resort to some of his usual brutality to solve the problem. In marched the frontier guard and the police with batons, water cannon, and cages to hold people so they would not return. The settlers pleaded, swore, and used planks to beat off their assailants. In the end, amid fierce scuffles, not merely was the town evacuated but it was razed to the ground and its ruins were buried in the dunes; "an ass's burial," as Israeli newspapers, using an Old Testament phrase, put it. Perhaps with a view to restoring his standing among right-wingers, by then Sharon had picked a quarrel with the Egyptians over Taba, a small strip of territory just south of Elat, where some Israeli entrepreneurs had built a beach club and a hotel. Not until 1988, and not before it was subjected to international arbitration, was that issue resolved.

Though Israeli feeling toward Egypt remained positive on the whole, the opposite was not true. Some Egyptians, notably the radical Muslim Brotherhood, which had long been fighting first the monarchy, then Nasser, and then Sadat, rejected the agreement in principle, claiming that it presented a betrayal of Allah's will, the Koran, or whatever. As time went on and Israel not only strengthened its hold on the remaining occupied territories but went on to invade Lebanon and fight Syria there as well, many others reacted with considerable bitterness. In particular many Egyptian intellectuals, not just clergymen but doctors, engineers, lawyers, journalists, and writers, continued to see Israel as evil incarnate. Some would not even talk to Israelis. Normalcy in terms of trade, tourism (numerous Israelis went to visit Egypt, but only very few Egyptians have visited Israel), cultural relations, and so on was only half achieved.

For example, whereas Israel has set up a BESA (Begin-Sadat) Center for Strategic Studies, nothing similar has emerged in Egypt. Whereas Israel has returned to Egypt antiquities its archaeologists had dug up in the Sinai—this was the first time in history a peace treaty included such a clause—Israeli official representatives in Egypt continue to lead an isolated, sometimes somewhat scary, existence. Some Israeli visitors to Egypt, and especially the Sinai, have come under terrorist attack. One Egyptian diplomat was forced to leave because of allegations that he had sexually attacked an Israeli belly dancer. His Israeli counterpart in Cairo, surrounded by Egyptian security personnel who do what they can to prevent their fellow citizens from approaching the embassy, would not have gotten the opportunity if he had tried. Much more problematic is the fact that Sadat's successor Hosni Mubarak has visited Israel only once, to attend Rabin's funeral. Though Israeli prime ministers do visit Egypt on occasion, most of the time they are only allowed to go as far as the resort city of Sharm el-Sheikh, at the southern edge of the Sinai; out of sight, out of mind, as people say.

Still, there is no denying that compared to the extremely difficult period from October 1973 to September 1977, the last years of the decade were a considerable improvement. In large part, this was due to the blessing of peace itself. Having gone to war five times in a quarter century, not counting countless skirmishes and acts of terrorism, what people knew its horrors better than Israelis did? First in his Nobel Prize acceptance speech, and again during the White House ceremony signing, Begin himself went out of his way to praise it. Rolling out what, in private, he called his "Shakespearean" language, he intoned: "Peace is the beauty of life. It is sunshine. It is the smile of a child, the love of a mother, the joy of a father, the togetherness of a family. It is the advancement of man, the victory of a just cause, the triumph of truth!"[46] In part, it was the improving strategic situation. While not everybody may have understood the military details, it was easy to see that once Egypt had left "the circle of hostility," as Israelis say, Israel was more secure than ever in its history; the more so because, in September 1980, the outbreak of the Iran-Iraq War ended any fear of an "eastern front." As Gur's successor as chief of staff, General Rafael Eytan, put it with characteristic bluntness, "Both belligerents are so obstinate—may they go on fighting forever."

With the clouds lifting, an immense feeling of relief swept the country. As so often, it soon found expression in a popular song. Luck was with Israel; not only was the song televised to tens, perhaps hundreds of millions of spectators, but it ended up winning the 1979 Eurovision. As if to crown the triumph, the contest was held in Israel's own capital, Jerusalem, making Israeli hearts swell with pride in front of much of the world.[47]

And what was the song's title? "Hallelujah!"

4

~~~

NEW CHALLENGES (1981–1995)

"Two Legged Beasts"

While the Israeli-Egyptian peace did take the largest and most powerful Arab state out of "the circle of hostility," it fell very short of solving all the outstanding problems between Israel and the remaining Arab states as well as between Israel and the Palestinians. As already indicated, in a sense it was not even meant to do so. On the contrary: In the eyes of Begin, if not in those of Dayan and Weizman, the intent was to free Israel's hands in retaining the territories it had been occupying in 1967. In December 1981 he had the Knesset pass a law annexing the Golan Heights—thus making clear that intent for the entire world to see and, since the annexation was a clear violation of international law, achieving absolutely nothing except, perhaps, pleasing his own followers.

The Knesset that passed the law, and indeed the coalition that gave Begin the majority he needed, was very different from most of its predecessors. For decades on end, first the Jewish community in the Land of Israel and then the State of Israel had been governed by Mapai, aka the Alignment, aka the Labor Party. It did so with the support of various left-wing, center-of-the-line, and religious groupings—"anybody except for Herut and the Communists," as that angry old man, Ben Gurion, used to say. On the whole, the result was a regime that was Ashkenazi-led (though always aware of the need to have a few token Sephardis as well). It was also secular minded (though mindful of the need to maintain Israel's "Jewish" character, whatever that may have meant), and socialist (though tending to be increasingly pragmatic as time went on). In terms of the electorate, its supporters consisted mainly of members of the urban petite bourgeoisie and the so-called labor settlements, i.e., the kibbutzim and the moshavim, in the countryside.

From Begin, Weizman, Dayan, Ehrlich, Sharon, Aridor, Hurwitz, Shamir, and the young Olmert down, the leadership that came to power in 1977 and was confirmed there by the elections of 1981 also consisted almost entirely of Ashkenazis. Begin, who well knew his followers, understood he had a problem on his hands. In 1978, the year when the Knesset was supposed to elect a new president, it could no longer be avoided. The Labor candidate was a highly cultured Sephardi activist by the name of Yitzhak Navon (1921–) who had once served as Ben Gurion's secretary. To appease his own electorate, Begin had to find a token *frenk* (a derogatory term for a Sephardi) who would run for the job. Eventually he settled on Yitzhak Shaveh (1924–). Shaveh at the time was on sabbatical in Paris. As the journalists descended on him, they found a worthy, if totally unknown, professor of physics whose sole claim to fame consisted of the fact that he used to repair his little Citroën Deux Chevaux with his own hands. In the end Shaveh withdrew his candidacy, allowing Navon to be elected. Thanks partly to his friendly character and partly to his beautiful young wife, Ophira, Navon proved an excellent choice.

Ethnic makeup apart, in other ways, the leadership in question also differed considerably from its predecessors. First, as already mentioned, its members were not socialists but self-proclaimed liberals. No sooner had they come to power than they tried to practice what they preached, with consequences that can only be called catastrophic. Second, they were nationalists, which apart from the relevant rhetoric and symbolism meant that they were committed to retain the occupied territories— Gaza, the West Bank, and, though it had never been part of Israel, even the Golan—not merely for strategic reasons but also for ideological ones. Third, they brought with them a different attitude toward Judaism and the role it should play in the state. True, neither Begin nor, even less so, his principal colleagues were practicing Jews. Still, Begin's very first act after winning the elections was to go to the Wailing Wall. In front of the cameras, he thanked the Lord for his good luck. He also peppered his speeches with expressions such as "the Lord willing," insisted on eating kosher food even in private, and wore a skullcap more often than his predecessors. In this he was not alone; shortly after the elections, somebody in the Jerusalem municipality apparently ordered that, from then on, male heads painted on the doors of public toilets should wear a skullcap, too.

Likud was not the only force pulling Israeli society in a right-wing nationalist direction. The peace agreement with Egypt and the withdrawal from the Sinai cost Begin in terms of support within his own party. In 1979–1981, some diehards broke away and set out on their own. The most important ones were Yuval Neeman, already mentioned on these pages; and Geula Cohen, the veteran Yemenite-born radio broadcaster who, at the time Lehi struggled against the British, used her lugubrious voice to read the organization's blood-curdling pronouncements over the radio. Their party, Tehia (Revival), was soon divided in two, giving birth to Tzomet (Crossroads). Later a third right-wing party, called Moledet (Motherland) joined the fray, only to be followed by yet a fourth, Israel Baaliya (Israel in Immigration) during the early 1990s.

Of the four, Tehia was elitist and, once Tzomet had seceded from it, quickly lost its appeal. Tzomet, which lasted longer, was populist; Moledet, which replaced both, was nationalist in a way reminiscent of the old "activist" tradition (its founder, Rehabam Zeevi, a retired general said to have ties to Israel's mafia, always claimed he was merely following in the footsteps of Ben Gurion); and Israel Baaliya was anticommunist (as the name indicates, those who voted for it were recent immigrants who arrived from the USSR after the latter broke up) as well as nationalist. What all four had in common was their secularism and their demand that not a square inch of the Land be given up. At least one, Moledet, also suggested that the "solution" to the Palestinian problem was to "voluntarily" transfer the inhabitants of the occupied territories into the neighboring countries.

In terms of both parliamentary and extraparliamentary power, probably even more important than the above changes were the ones that took place among the religious and "traditionalist" segments of the population. From 1948 to 1977, Labor's principal partner had always been the National Religious Party. During most of this period it held the portfolio of interior affairs, a vital post since this was the ministry in charge of deciding who was and was not a Jew. From time to time the party also tried to throw its weight around over such questions as kosher food, daylight saving time (which its leaders opposed, sometimes with success, sometimes without), and observance of the Sabbath. In all this it behaved almost as if it were Labor's skullcap-and-tassel-wearing pet, occasionally pulling at the leash but rarely doing any real harm. Contrary to what one might expect, the NRP's real enemies were not Israel's secular parties, with whom it got along well enough, but Orthodox ones such as Agudat Israel. The latter was always berating NRP members for not taking religion seriously enough in their private lives and not pressing their demands hard enough in their public ones, as they still do.

In the mid-1970s leadership of the NRP passed to a younger and much more dynamic generation headed by Zebulon Hammer (1936–1998). By discarding suits in favor of jackets over open collars, the new leader immediately set himself apart from his predecessors. Whenever possible he and his followers also wore "Biblical," meaning extremely light, sandals. Riding the messianic wave that had started forming after the "miracle" of 1967, Hammer made "Eretz Israel Hashlema" (the Complete Land of Israel) into the party's most important mission by far. In the *yeshivot* associated with the movement, above all the one known as Merkaz Harav (Rabbi's Center) in Jerusalem, the old, moderate, political attitude was put aside. In its place there appeared a nationalist, some would say bellicose and terrifying, spirit. The NRP rabbis strongly believed in the superiority of the people of Israel to all the rest—if this was not racism, then it came pretty close. Above all, in the words of one graduate, they taught that "the [complete] Land of Israel must be in the hands of the Jewish people—not just by having settlements but by being under Jewish sovereignty."[1] Even if by filling the "commandment" they would go in the teeth of the entire world; even if it meant circumventing or disobeying the orders of the Israeli government of the day; and even if, while engaged in "self-defense," it involved using armed force against the local inhabitants.

While not every NRP voter took up an Uzi submachine gun and went to live in the territories, the rabbis taught their disciples to consider themselves Israel's new elite—"the salt of the earth," as they liked to say. The way they saw it, Labor and the kibbutzim, lacking a belief in

God, had necessarily lost their ideological fervor. They had turned into mere *nehentanim,* "seekers of the pleasures of life." Therefore, it was up to them to assume the mantle of "pioneering," so that the future of the Zionist enterprise rested in their hands. The heady mixture of nationalism and religion often manifested itself by crowds of bearded men taking up Torah books, chanting and dancing at suitable occasions such as dedicating a new synagogue in a new settlement. Others walked the streets toting the submachine guns the IDF had issued them for self-defense. Thus, NRP leaders and followers moved from the margins of Israeli society into a position where, in their own eyes at any rate, they constituted its spearhead. By settling in occupied land they could also get cheap housing—all while executing God's manifest will.

Another marked change in Israel's sociopolitical landscape during these years was the emergence of new, ethnically based religious parties. The 1950s and 1960s had seen a few parties claiming to represent various kinds of Orientals. However, partly because of the "Uncle Tom" syndrome, partly because they were secular minded, these parties had no mass appeal; by 1969, the last of them had disappeared. Left high and dry, some practicing Orientals tried to join long-established Ashkenazi Orthodox parties such as Agudat Israel. Not, however, with success, since the rabbis who led those parties probably formed the most racist group in the whole of Israeli society, as they still do. In the early 1980s, an attempt to set up Tami, a religious party of Sephardis, by Sephardis, and for Sephardis, also ended in failure. Several of its leaders, some of whom were former Black Panthers, were caught embezzling funds and jailed. However, as the 1984 elections approached things changed. The place of Tami was taken by a much more powerful group known as Shas (Observant Sephardis).

For a long time, the principal driving spirit behind Shas was a Baghdad-born rabbi by the name of Ovadia Yosef (1920–). His religious adherents consider him a genius and often quote his rulings. The nonreligious majority is more inclined to note his racism—in 2005 he blamed the flooding of New Orleans on "the Niggers over there" who, as everybody knows, do not study the Torah. In one of his vicious attacks on the Supreme Court, he called the judges "wicked . . . apostates . . . religionless, lawless . . . [men who] sleep with menstruating women and violate the Sabbath" (presumably another thing they did was to pick their noses, which, he once ruled, was not permitted on the holy day).[2] Judging by his white beard, the gold-embroidered robe he almost always wears, and the sometimes outlandish Hebrew he speaks, one might mistake him for a benevolent wizard out of *One Thousand and One Nights*. In reality, there is nothing comic about him; coarse, ambitious, and occasionally brutal, he made himself into the most powerful extraparliamentary political figure in the whole of Israeli history.

Yosef's stated objective is to "restore lost laurels," i.e., bring about a religious revival among Sephardis so as to rival the Ashkenazi rabbinical establishment. This in turn may cause Israelis to turn their backs on secularism and pay greater heed to religion, and the rabbis who represent it, in both private and public life. For example, they oppose gay rights, want to prohibit women from wearing short sleeves and trousers, and want to confine women to the rear seats of buses so that men may avoid any accidental contact with those of them who may be menstruating. To achieve its objective, Shas, pulling its weight in the Knesset (at peak it had seventeen seats), set up numerous interlocking educational foundations, charitable foundations, and the like. The foundations, which attract both public funds and private money, provide their heads with endless opportunities for corruption. It is mainly because of them that several leading Shas luminaries have followed their Tami predecessors in being put on trial, convicted, and jailed.

Perhaps in order to maintain the bargaining power of Shas vis-à-vis Likud—the groups that vote for the two parties overlap to a large extent—Yosef's acolytes have often claimed that his personal views are on the dovish side. Even if this is true, he must take heed of his Sephardi backers, most of whom entertain far more powerful anti-Arab feelings than Ashkenazis do. In part, the problem has to do with the fact that many of the people in question, or their parents, were deprived of their property and expelled from their Arab homelands. In part, it is socioeconomic. As one Sephardi told the writer Amos Oz in the early 1980s, if Israel withdrew from the occupied territories, and Palestinian laborers were prevented from crossing the border, then "[his] sister" would have to go back to "washing floors."[3] Be this as it may, since the middle of the 1980s Shas has almost always joined forces with the NRP, Likud, and one or more of the secular right-wing parties in opposing anything that might lead to a withdrawal. With the exception of

Gaza, which will be discussed later, by and large they succeeded in having their will.

Thanks in part to the system of proportional representation, which makes it relatively easy to set up new parties, all these groupings were able to join the endless game of musical chairs known as politics. Together they played a decisive role in pulling Israeli society to the right. Whether for ideological reasons or, later, to help their followers obtain housing on the cheap, they also did what they could to promote settlement in the occupied territories. As a result, those settlers not merely multiplied but gradually turned into a force that no party, no coalition, and no government could ignore.

The very first settlements on the far side of the "Green Line" border went up almost immediately after the 1967 war on the Golan Heights and in the Jordan Valley. Their principal sponsor was Meir's deputy prime minister Yigal Allon, the former Palmach and IDF commander and "activist" Ahdut Haavoda leader. The way he saw it, the objective was to make certain that Israel would keep the areas in question, which in his view were critically important for its defense. But whereas those who followed Allon's call were secular-minded kibbutzniks and moshavniks—"educated in a youth movement, with hot blood,"[4] as one of them put it—those who soon started trickling into such West Bank sites as Hebron came with a religious, even messianic, purpose in mind. Thanks largely to the antics of their leader, an unwashed, haggard, pistol-waving graduate of Merkaz Harav by the name of Moshe Levinger, and his equally obnoxious wife, Miriam, they were also constantly in the headlines.

Excluding those in annexed East Jerusalem, until 1977 the number of settlers remained very small—no more than twenty thousand or so. For all the noise the religious ones among them in particular made, their political influence was limited. It was Begin who, to ensure that no future Israeli government would ever be able to let go of the territories even if it wanted to, started changing this situation. His chosen instrument was Ariel Sharon. Born in 1928, Sharon was a bona fide war hero. At twenty he commanded a platoon without ever having gone through officer school, and later he fought in every one of Israel's wars. Famous for his appetite—he ate huge steaks along with several portions of felafel—and his bulk, his chief quality was his extraordinary, some would say brutal, dynamism. He was known, affectionately, as "Arik," and, not so affectionately, as "the man who does not stop at the red light."[5] Meeting with Caspar Weinberger once, he lost his cool and started pounding the table, upon which the secretary of defense asked him whether he would like it replaced. As minister of agriculture he built new settlements right and left. It is estimated that, by the time Begin resigned in 1983, the number of settlers had gone up to a hundred thousand.

These, moreover, were settlers of a different type. Neither socialist— in Israel by the 1980s, to be a left-winger meant opposing settlement, not advocating it—nor particularly religious minded, they were run-of-the-mill Israelis. Typically their background was petit bourgeois: a young couple out for a place where they could have a subsidized mortgage and pay less income tax; the ambitious bus driver and his wife, a teacher or a nurse, who hoped to add another room for themselves and their two children with one to come; or else the colonel who, along with his comrades, was offered a "once in a lifetime" chance to buy a townhouse—a cottage, as Israelis say—with a small garden attached to it. The last thing most of these people had in mind was ideology. Some apparently went to their new homes with a bad conscience, telling themselves that they would willingly return to their previous ones if peace ever came (and if they were paid compensation). Most continued to commute to work inside "old" Israel, as the phrase went. Realizing this, the authorities, when advertising homes for sale, always claimed that the settlements in question were located "just five minutes away" from the Green Line; many of the newcomers did not see themselves as "settlers" at all.

While Israel was strengthening its hold on the territories, Palestinian resistance to the occupation, though always simmering just under the surface, remained fairly muted. Since September 1970, when King Hussein of Jordan crushed the PLO in his country and sent its leaders fleeing for their lives (some were so terrified of the king's legionnaires that they ran straight into the Israelis' arms), the Jordan Valley had been almost completely peaceful. Close cooperation between the security services of Israel and Jordan also made it very hard for the PLO in the West Bank to obtain arms. Both there and in Israel proper there were occasional incidents in the form of stabbings, shootings, bombings, and the like. Yet their impact on day-to-day life was relatively minor. Proof of this is the fact that foreign tourism continued rising throughout the period; in 1980, visitors to the region topped one million. Finally, Gaza in 1970 did witness a limited PLO uprising against Israeli rule. However, Sharon, who was then serving as commander in chief of the Southern Command, succeeded in suppressing it.

From about 1968 to 1977, Labor leaders such as Eban, Dayan, and Allon often met with King Hussein in an attempt to settle the differences between Israel and Jordan. Most of the meetings took place in London in the house of Hussein's doctor. On at least one occasion Hussein, wearing disguise, visited Tel Aviv. Time and again the sides got on well together (all three Israelis spoke fluent Arabic, whereas the king prided himself on his Western manners and on being a bon vivant, a quality his interlocutors thought they knew how to exploit). In October Hussein even informed Meir personally that war was coming. Time and again the Israelis came up with plans to divide the West Bank between the two countries along either territorial or functional lines. In the fall of 1974 it looked as if an agreement was just around the corner. The Israelis even built a new road, later called Allon Road, around Jericho, which was designated as the first city to be returned to Jordanian rule. Yet in the end the talks led nowhere. To Dayan, Hussein said, "You must get it into your head that no Arab king can propose that a single village be taken away and become Israeli . . . without being accused of treason."[6] And that was that.

Unlike his predecessors, Begin had no use for "Hussi," as Israelis, half contemptuous, half affectionate, used to call the king. Instead he sought to break the power of the PLO and its supporters both inside the occupied territories and abroad. To deal with the former, Sharon, during his term as minister of defense, appointed Menahem Milson, a professor of Arabic literature at the Hebrew University in Jerusalem, to head the civil administration in the territories. Together they encouraged the establishment of "rural fraternities" in the southern half of the West Bank in particular. The fraternities would provide Israel with an alternative to the urban-based, ideologically more sophisticated PLO, or so the theory went. An ignorant Palestinian villager who spent his days playing with his prayer beads was preferable to one who spouted patriotic slogans, let alone one who knifed people or planted bombs to tear them apart. In reality, factionalism and corruption dominated. Some of the fraternities' leaders were assassinated, with the result that they never amounted to anything and soon collapsed. Yet in their preoccupation with Islam they did leave behind an explosive legacy—one that, in time, was to develop into the Hamas movement.

Throughout all this, Palestinian terrorism from Lebanon continued. Raids were mounted, mines planted, and rockets fired, causing military and civilian casualties. As the Israelis, using air strikes and commando operations, hit back, the country became destabilized. Partly for this reason, and partly because of demographic changes that upset the balance among the various Christian, Druze, Sunnis, and Shiite communities, in 1976 it slid into a vicious civil war. As the Lebanese militias—at peak there were some fifty different ones—battled each other, Syria's ruler, Hafez Assad, was engaged in a tricky game of his own. On one hand he kept the Palestinian population in his own country under such tight control that the Golan Heights became one of the safest areas in the whole of Israel, as they still are. On the other, he used the opportunity to send thirty thousand of his own troops into Lebanon, more or less putting an end to its existence as an independent state. He also supported the PLO, providing it with weapons, training, and shelter. Thus he was able to have his cake and eat it, too—attacking Israel while making sure that Israeli retaliation, when it came, would hit other people and not his own.

Across the border Ariel Sharon was watching. As a commander, he was impetuosity itself; as a politician, he knew how to wait. Just when he conceived his "grand plan" for dealing with the Palestinians, the PLO, Lebanon, and Syria, we do not know. By mid-1981, when there was heavy fighting along the Israeli-Lebanese border and when Begin put him in charge of the most powerful army the Middle East had ever seen, his ideas must have already been well advanced. Never one to be content with half measures, he and then-chief of staff Eytan started preparing a full-scale invasion of Lebanon. Their intent was to destroy the PLO; push Assad's forces back across the border; link up with the Christian militias north of Beirut; help them overcome their enemies; make their leader, Basher Gemayel, president of Lebanon; and, by way of a crowning achievement, have that country sign a peace treaty with Israel—six flies with one stone.

At that time Begin was already a very sick man on two different kinds of medicine—one against heart disease, the other (which worked at cross-purposes with the first) against depression. Whether he understood the full extent of his subordinate's ambitions remains moot. Publicly Sharon presented his plan as if it were intended solely to push the rocket launchers and their PLO operators to a distance of twenty-five miles north of the Israeli border. Later Begin's son Benjamin claimed that his father had been misled. In a way, it was scant wonder. Sharon had long been notorious for his tendency to take the bit between his teeth and for not always sticking to the truth as he did so, with the result that Ben Gurion refused to make him a general. Begin, on his part, admired Sharon as a "hero," but knew almost nothing about modern war. A decent, somewhat prudish man—he once expressed his astonishment at the idea that some women might actually like to have sex with each other—he could be surprisingly innocent about other people's motives. Still, following his son's account, when told that he had been lied to, he replied, "No, no, it is impossible that [Sharon] had planned to reach Beirut from the start."[7]

On the other hand, it will not do to dismiss Begin as a simpleton, as some have done. Sharon apart, compared with him all the other cabinet members were pigmies. Not for nothing had Begin led his party for decades despite all the electoral defeats he suffered; whoever dared oppose him, he quashed. We know how obsessed he was with the need to defend Israeli citizens against terrorists; whether he had the military understanding to judge the probable outcome of a campaign against them is another matter. In 1974 he had called the PLO, leaders and activists, "two-legged beasts."[8] He also pretended to be, and in all likelihood was, deeply affected by the fate of the 40 percent or so of Lebanese who are Christians and who, he claimed, were facing a "holocaust" at the hands of the Syrians and their local allies. In one letter to President Reagan he compared Beirut to Berlin and Arafat to Hitler. Furthermore, according to Sharon himself, in a cabinet meeting held in the middle of May 1982 he said that "there are rumors that Arik is pushing me into war. I have stated that I am not easily pushed."[9]

After a year of searching for an excuse for war—the border, as it happened, was absolutely quiet—the General Staff finally found one in the form of the shooting of the Israeli ambassador in London, Shlomo

Argov. Knowing that the PLO would respond, the Israelis opened fire in southern Lebanon. When the PLO did respond, the Israelis started their invasion on June 6, 1982. The sight the IDF presented was an impressive one. Six hundred combat aircraft, including some of the most modern ever deployed until that time, guided to their targets by the first ever operational use of AWACS (airborne warning and control system) aircraft; six divisions, with two more standing ready to handle any problems the Syrians might cause on the Golan; some nine hundred tanks with active armor, another first ever; and armored personnel carriers and artillery to match. As one senior Israeli commander said, "Never in its history had Israel gone to war so well prepared."[10] The enemy consisted of two fledgling PLO brigades, one and a half Syrian ground divisions, the Syrian Air Force, and the Soviet-built anti-aircraft defenses that Syria had deployed in Lebanon.

Against the juggernaut that was coming at them, these forces simply did not stand a chance. First the Palestinian brigades were sent running in all directions and thousands of their troops were killed or captured. Next the IDF, using innovative technology in a series of truly brilliant operations, destroyed the Syrian missile defenses that had decimated the air force in 1973. Then, the Israeli Air Force demolished the Syrian Air Force, shooting down one hundred enemy aircraft against the loss of a single friendly one. While carefully avoiding any infringement of the border between Lebanon and Syria, it also pushed back the Syrian ground forces, though it did not succeed in destroying them. In just six days Israeli troops reached the suburbs of Beirut, some sixty miles from their starting point. On Sharon's orders, they stopped short of entering the city proper.

In August, following a siege and a bombing campaign that helped turn Beirut into an even bigger shambles than it already was after six years of civil war, Begin and Sharon celebrated a last triumph. Just before the start of the invasion Arafat, using an intermediary, had sent the prime minister a personal message, saying, "I have learnt more from you as a resistance leader than from anyone else. . . . Do not try to break me in Lebanon, you will not succeed."[11] Now, as the TV cameras whirled, he and five thousand of his fighters were forced to leave Beirut and go into exile in places as far apart as Syria, Egypt, and Tunisia. The IDF had positioned snipers around the embarkation area, and at one point they had Arafat in their sights. For good or ill, the order to kill him was not given.

By that time the IDF, which during the early days of the campaign had sometimes been welcomed by rice-throwing Lebanese, was already beginning to feel the effects of a vicious guerrilla war. Soon not a village, not a building, not an orange grove, and not a road were safe; ambushes were mounted, shots fired, bombs planted, and one entire headquarters blown to pieces with the loss of thirty dead. In trying to cope, the Israelis were no more successful than most other late-twentieth-century armed forces have been. Meanwhile, public opinion, which at first had been all but unanimous in its support for the campaign, was becoming increasingly worried by the endless nature of the task as well as the growing losses. Here and there soldiers, including one major general and one well-known brigade commander, raised their voices in protest or refused to carry out orders. A few were fired from their posts or jailed; however, fearing lest harsh measures would only lead to more opposition, on the whole the authorities treated them with kid gloves.

Both at the front and in Israel itself, people, lampooning a famous kindergarten song, chanted:

> *Aircraft, come down from the cloud.*
> *Take us far to Lebanon*
> *we shall fight for Mr. Sharon*
> *and return, inside a shroud.*

On September 14 Sharon's main ally Gemayel was assassinated by Syrian intelligence, the latest, but almost certainly not the last, in a long list of Arab leaders who lost their lives by making or pretending to make peace with Israel. In response, his enraged followers entered the Palestinian refugee camps of Sabra and Shatilla—in reality, crowded slum suburbs of Beirut—and systematically started massacring their populations. While the IDF commanders around Beirut did not take an active part in the massacre, they did not do anything to prevent it, either. Some of them, either unable to understand what was going on or simply looking the other way, may have provided the Christian militias with logistic support. By the time a journalist's report caused the alarm bells to start ringing in Tel Aviv and the General Staff ordered its frontline troops to rein in their allies, between eight hundred and three thousand men, women, and children may have died.

At first Begin tried to make light of the matter by claiming that "Arabs have killed Arabs, and the world is blaming the Jews." To the immense credit of most ordinary Israelis, they did not buy this argument. A few weeks after the massacre the dovish "Peace Now" movement organized a huge demonstration in the center of Tel Aviv. People claim there were four hundred thousand participants, which if true would have meant one-eighth of the entire population attended; the real number was probably about half that. They carried signs that read BLOOD ON YOUR HANDS, HAST THOU KILLED AND ALSO TAKEN POSSESSION (a pointed reference to the Biblical story of King Ahab and the prophet Elijah)[12] and CRY, BELOVED COUNTRY. Above all, they demanded an investigation. Begin's half-hearted efforts at stalling were brushed aside, a clear sign that he was losing his hold both on the cabinet and on the Knesset. When the Kahan Commission published its findings early in 1983 Sharon, Eytan (whose term of office was about to end anyhow), and two other generals were forced to go. The dead remained dead, of course, but it was the least a country that has always considered itself civilized could do.

Sharon's replacement was Moshe Arens (1925–). American educated, a true technocrat (he had run Israel Aircraft Industries), he was soft-spoken and lacking in charisma. Politically speaking he was not a bit less hawkish than his predecessor. He did not, however, have the latter's brutal drive; having done little if anything by the way of party politics, he did not have his clout, either. A more important change took place in August 1983, when Begin resigned. Barely a year earlier, having completely failed to understand how badly things were going in Lebanon, he had visited Washington. Meeting the media, he spoke and acted as if he were some kind of conquering hero. Now, each time he entered or left his residence, he had to face vigilantes who lit candles in honor of the growing list of Israeli dead. He was a semi-invalid—having slipped in the bathroom, he had broken his hip and had to use a stick in order to walk—and freshly a widower as well. Seldom in history can any man have fallen so deep, so quickly. As he himself said, he "could not carry on." Throughout his life he had been something of a manic-depressive. Now, seized by the blackest of black moods, he retired into a Jerusalem flat from which he only rarely emerged until his death nine years later.

Into Begin's shoes stepped foreign minister Yitzhak Shamir (1915–). "The man from Lehi," as he has been called,[13] was a born conspirator. During his time as the organization's operations officer—in plain words, terrorist in chief—he took the code name Michael, after Michael Collins, the Irish revolutionary leader. As such he had played a major role in the assassination of the Swedish mediator Count Folke Bernadotte back in 1948. Wits said he was like an electron, "small and negative." He was small, barely reaching the floor with his feet, as Israelis say. He was also as prosaic as his predecessor had been dramatic. Having risen by way of the secret service, Mossad, he was as hard as nails; had he tried to break the wall with his head, no doubt he would have succeeded. Sporting a small, white mustache that almost made him look as if he had an extra pair of lower canine teeth, he seemed to breathe defiance even when he laughed; genuinely uninterested in public opinion, in his dealings with the media he could be quite rude. Yet in private he could be surprisingly open and gentle, as shown in his letters to his wife, Shulamit, written in Eritrea while the British held him prisoner.

Barely a month after entering office Shamir bowed to the inevitable. Supported by Arens, he took the IDF back from Beirut to the Awali River, giving up central Lebanon and implicitly admitting that the campaign had failed to achieve its objectives. The number of Israeli dead up to that point was around six hundred. Given the financial crisis of the same month, the miracle is that when elections were held in the winter of 1984, Likud still managed to gain almost as many Knesset seats as Labor did—an indication of how deep the cleavage between left- and right-wingers, secularists and traditionalists, Ashkenazis and Orientals, had really become. An attempt by a well-known left-wing publicist, Dan Ben Amotz, to make people vote against Likud by means of a giant newspaper ad showing the graves of IDF soldiers and saying, "Let's see you vote for this!" backfired; apparently people were not prepared to see their dead used for such a purpose.

In the wake of the elections a coalition government was set up. Peres, who had taken over from Rabin as Labor leader in 1977, became prime minister for two years. After that period he was supposed to change places with Shamir, who served as foreign minister under him. Still, the man who walked away from the table with the greatest gains was Yitzhak Rabin. Having lost office in 1977, in 1981 Rabin was defeated by Peres when the latter was elected leader of the Labor Party; from that time on, he started drinking more than was good for him. In 1982 he had acted as an informal adviser to Sharon, but came up with no better idea than to "tighten, tighten, tighten" the siege of Beirut. Now, thanks to Shamir who admired him as "Mr. Security" and worked well with him, he was to serve as minister of defense for the entire four-year period until the next elections.

Rabin and Peres had long been bitter rivals. In his memoirs, published in 1978, Rabin had written that "knowing [Peres], [he] did not believe one word he said."[14] Now he went out of his way to emphasize that he owed the prime minister nothing. Each time they met, Rabin blew cigarette smoke right into Peres's face. Yet in this emergency they were able to overcome their differences to a large extent. Early in 1985 they pulled the IDF out of the whole of Lebanon except for a narrow "security zone" in the south, which they fortified and where they set up a sort of protectorate. A militia known as the South Lebanese Army (SLA), trained, equipped, and paid for by Israel, was established. Under an arrangement known as "the good fence," some Lebanese citizens were allowed to work in Israel and receive medical treatment there.

The PLO in Lebanon had indeed been smashed. Its leaders rented villas for themselves in a well-to-do suburb of Tunis, capital of Tunisia; they never regained their military might. However, their political power, which rested on the fact that the PLO was internationally recognized as the sole representative of the Palestinian people (it had an emissary, with observer status, at the UN), remained intact. That power kept on growing throughout the next decade until, in 1993, Yasser Arafat finally met Rabin, Peres, and President Bill Clinton on the White House lawn. Meanwhile, along Israel's northern border, the PLO's fighters were already starting to be replaced by those of Hezbollah. In time the Iran-assisted, Shiite-based, determined, and fanatical guerrilla organization was to prove a much tougher nut to crack than its predecessors had ever been.

As the overwhelming consensus by which it was initially greeted shows, the Lebanese adventure was not just the product of a conspiracy by Sharon, Begin, Mossad (which, its agents having been dined and wined by the Christians, went against the advice of military intelligence and supported it), or whoever. Instead, it grew out of grandiose nationalist-religious dreams. Widely shared by many Israelis, those dreams concerned the need for, and the feasibility of, keeping Israel's hold on "the complete" Land along with the three million or so Arabs under occupation; before the war went sour, indeed, some people talked of settling southern Lebanon. To this was added what at the time looked like towering military power, as well as the determination to prove that the inconclusive 1973 war had been an aberration and would not be repeated; had not Sharon said that the IDF was capable of overrunning the entire region "from the Atlantic to the Persian Gulf"?[15] The combination might have caused a less volatile people than the Israelis to lose their heads. As one popular song put it, the IDF entered Lebanon as if it were going on safari, "Hey ho, hey ho, a hunting Arabs." Others joked that the Ministry of Tourism had come up with a new slogan: "Visit Israel before Israel visits you."

Yet looking back, the adventure also had a positive side. The year 1985 marked the end of any desire on Israel's part to wage large-scale offensive war against its neighbors—though this may still happen if, one day, its leaders feel that they have absolutely no choice. It also ended any illusion that the country would ever be able to impose peace on its neighbors through force of arms. Considered in terms of lives lost and resources squandered, the lesson had been dearly bought. In particular, the relatives of some of those who died never forgave Sharon. Carrying the Cain's mark of a dangerous man, for almost two decades after his forced resignation he remained in a kind of political limbo, occupying this post and that but never regaining his former stature. When he finally returned to power, he soon showed that he was no longer the same. Yet nations, like individuals, only learn through failure. Provided the lesson sticks, perhaps the price was worth paying after all.

"Eliminating the Zeroes"

Around the time when Peres, Rabin, and Shamir took Israel out of most of Lebanon, the economic crisis peaked. In any but the simplest societies money is what makes the world go round; as the saying goes, in God we trust but the others pay cash. Should money lose its value, then many of the ties that bind people together and enable them to communicate and cooperate will be disrupted. Perhaps it says something about Israeli society that, even faced with these tremendous external and internal pressures, it did not collapse.

To be sure, the atmosphere was tense. Just how tense was proved most dramatically in February 1983 when one Yonah Avrushimi, a religious man, threw a hand grenade into a Peace Now assembly. A young activist by the name of Emil Greenzweig was killed. Also, some of the political groups that emerged around this time, such as the right-wing/religious Kach movement, with a clenched fist as its symbol, were truly terrifying. The leader of Kach—the word means "thus"—was an American-born and -raised rabbi, Meir Kahane. Repeatedly he declared that "democracy and Judaism are two opposite things"[16] and promised to make the country Jewish again. Had it depended on him, he would have sanctified the Sabbath, banned the sale of pork, disenfranchised Israel's Arab population, and prohibited sexual intercourse between Jews and non-Jews. He would also have used armed force to empty the occupied territories of their Palestinian inhabitants. Nevertheless, the 1984 elections, in which Kahane was elected (only to be removed from the Knesset two years later because of his "racism") came and went without a hitch. In 1990, while on a visit to New York, he was assassinated; he who lives by the sword will perish by it, too. As to Avrushimi, he still remains where, in the near unanimous opinion of Israelis, he deserves to be, i.e., behind bars.

Though the establishment of a security zone in southern Lebanon did not put an end to terrorism from that quarter, for a number of years it remained muted. On one hand Hezbollah, which at that time was in its infancy, took time to get organized. On the other, it did not yet get as much support from Iran as it later did. This enabled Peres and his minister of finance, Yitzhak Modai, to look after the economy. Modai himself was a real piece of work. Born in 1926, married to a former beauty queen, he held degrees in chemical engineering as well as economics and law. He served in the IDF, retiring as a lieutenant colonel. Later he became a successful businessman and, like many of his kind, joined the liberal General Zionists. In 1974 he was elected to the Knesset as a

Likud member. Though his intelligence was unquestioned, after he lost a daughter to a traffic accident some people saw him as unstable; he was normal on some days and abnormal on others, they said, but one could never know which was which. Ezer Weizman, who was equally intelligent and equally ready with a biting phrase, called him MK Lipstick, a reminder of Modai's time as CEO of the Israeli branch of Revlon.[17]

By this time economic disaster was staring Israel in the face. The worst part of it was the dramatic drain on the state's foreign currency reserves. At one point they went down to just $1.6 billion, barely enough to pay for a single month's worth of imports. Without imports, a country that had no indigenous energy, very few raw materials, and was only barely able to feed its people was bound to fall apart. As is so often true in these situations, there was no shortage of advisers. Everybody knew what had to be done. Slash the budget; cut subsidies; increase government revenues, if possible without imposing new taxes that might stifle economic activity; abolish the system of indexation that fueled inflation; and get rid of as many public employees as possible. The difficulty was in making socialist politicians (although, by this time, little was left of their socialism), liberal politicians (whose record, starting with Ehrlich, had been disastrous), industrialists, Histadrut leaders, bankers, and academic economists who had been called on for help agree on a single plan and implement it. Later both Peres and Modai took the credit, and the former ended by firing the latter. Let it be said that, had it not been for both of them, Israel would have gone bankrupt and might have collapsed.

In a way, Israel was lucky. Energy prices, which peaked in 1981, were declining quite sharply. In 1980 imported oil accounted for 10 percent of the GNP, no less. Four years later the figure had fallen to 6.3 percent, a falling trend.[18] A huge, coal-fired power station near Caesarea, on the Mediterranean coast, that went on line around this time helped. Probably even more important was the fact that Jimmy Carter, who never had much use for Israel, was gone, and Ronald Reagan had taken his place. In 1985, having been reelected, he was at the peak of his popularity. He personally was strongly pro-Israel. After all, Israel, whatever its other problems, had always been able and willing to fight its own wars. As the Balkan struggles of 1991–1999 were later to show, in this it differed from many of America's other allies, including some of its most important ones.

Furthermore, this was the time when terrorists, mostly Arabs originating in Lebanon and Libya, started attacking U.S. targets in Europe. But whereas Carter had been halfhearted in his approach to terrorists, Reagan, claiming to take a page out of Israel's book, was determined to confront them head-on. In the United States, T-shirts were sold showing an F-16 fighter and the words, DON'T WORRY AMERICA, ISRAEL IS BEHIND YOU. Considering Israel a useful ally in the struggle for hegemony in the Middle East and, perhaps, against the Evil Empire, too, he and Secretary of State George Shultz agreed to help Israel in its plight, but only if it did its share and put in place drastic economic reforms. Their support helped Modai and Peres hammer out a domestic consensus. Peres's own favorite device for getting his way was marathon sessions in which everybody was permitted to make speeches until they dropped. As he later wrote, "When it came to hanging on I was as strong as any of them—indeed, as all of them together."[19]

The critical moves were made in July–September 1985. The state budget was cut by $1.25 billion. This reduced the fiscal deficit from 17 percent of the GNP—a huge gap—in the first half of that year to only half as much in the second one; 1986 actually saw a budget surplus. To increase government revenue, various benefits that went to various sectors were abolished and some new taxes imposed. In particular, the travel tax was restored, a most unpopular measure that was supposed to both bring in revenue and save foreign currency. While prices and wages were frozen, the shekel was devalued by 24 percent and the value of the new Israeli shekel (NIS) was fixed at 1.5 to the U.S. dollar. A currency reform caused three zeroes to be taken off each denomination, so that 1,000 shekel were turned into 1 NIS (New Israeli Shekel), 10,000 into 10, and so on. Keeping its given word, Washington played its part by providing grants. It also canceled some debts and lowered interest rates on others. Thus the aid was spread over a number of years. Moreover, in calculating the sum involved, one cannot ignore the fact that had Israel gone bankrupt, it would have been forced to suspend payments to the United States as its largest creditor. These considerations make the cost to the American taxpayers hard to estimate. Coming on top of the annual $3 billion, probably it was in the order of $1.5 billion.[20]

Not everybody agreed with the above measures. Take Milton Friedman, the Jewish-American, Nobel Prize–winning economist who, at that time, was widely regarded as the world's economic guru in chief. According to him, they were "insufficient, and headed in the wrong direction."[21] Inside Israel, the cuts in subsidies and transfer payments—from 22 percent of the GNP in 1979–1983 to 17 percent in 1980–1984 and 15.4 percent in 1985–1989—made many people extremely unhappy. Still, Modai and Peres proved right and their critics wrong; one caricature showed the latter as St. George, spearing the dragon called inflation that was eating Israel's wage earners alive. During the first critical month inflation went down to zero. This came as a complete surprise and, to people who had long grown accustomed to seeing their money go down the drain almost as fast as they could earn it, as a most welcome one. Later, inflation stabilized at about 1 percent a month. Still too high, to be sure, but what an improvement on the previous situation! Devaluation slowed to a crawl, and foreign currency reserves started rising again. As confidence returned, real interest rates dropped.

From this point on, inflation slowly went down until it reached single-digit figures in the early 1990s. Thus, one can only agree with two well-known foreign economists who wrote that, in their opinion, "Israel's stabilization program was among the most successful in the entire world." It is true that, for some time after 1985, growth—especially per capita growth—remained very modest. Still, anybody who left Israel in June of that year and came back two years later, Rip van Winkle–wise, could not but be impressed with the change that had taken place. The morning queues in front of the banks melted away. Here and there, some banks even found it necessary to close a branch or two. So much did the gap between the official exchange rate and the black market rate diminish that Lilienblum Street was hardly worth visiting any longer, and many speculators were forced to starve or find other jobs. More seriously, ever since 1973 the country's economic heart had been suffering from semiparalysis. Much of it was caused by the war but some of it was self-inflicted, first by Histadrut functionaries who ran their companies as if profit did not matter, and then by Ehrlich and Co. Now it started beating again.

From 1985 to 1992, real wages rose by 15 (private sector) and 25 (public sector) percent. During the same years foreign investment in

Israel (excluding bonds) went up approximately fourfold, with much more to come.[22] In part, this favorable outcome was due to noneconomic factors. To be sure, Labor and Likud kept quarreling. Wits maintained that, instead of a "government of national unity," what Israel got was a "government of national paralysis"; on TV, the two parties were often represented by a slide that showed lightning in a thunderstorm. Nevertheless, an uneasy political stability prevailed. In late 1986 Peres, keeping his promise, changed places with Shamir. He did so even though his approval rating at the time (74 percent) was the highest ever received by any Israeli prime minister until then; and even though some of his own supporters accused him of wanting nothing better than to become an ex–prime minister.

Next, when the results of the 1988 elections came in, they left the balance between the two principal parties almost unchanged. As a result, the broad coalition, with Shamir as prime minister, Peres as minister of finance, and the indispensable Rabin as minister of defense at its head, was able to last until 1990. In fact, the period of stability lasted longer; though Peres, relying on the promises of Shas, took Labor out of the government (this was known as "the stinking trick"), Shas betrayed him and, by joining Shamir instead, enabled him to last until the end of his term in 1992. Partly because of the "national paralysis," and partly because Shamir himself was at his best when he tried to do nothing in particular, Israeli society, which had been smothered by the state for so long as to become almost identical with it, finally started casting off its socialist shackles.

It was, indeed, high time. Certainly until 1965, and to some extent even thereafter, Histadrut in many ways had acted as if it were a state within a state. In others it had come close to running—from Levontin on, some would say, ruining—the state. After all, of the two institutions it was the older one, and by a considerable margin; originally, as discussed previously, even Hagana had been an arm of Histadrut. From the state Histadrut demanded, and very often obtained, exemptions, privileges, and subsidies of every kind. To its members (anybody who worked for one of its numerous companies had to be a member, whereas kibbutzniks and moshavniks were members from birth) Histadrut offered a medical insurance program. Though it was widely regarded as the worst in the country, they were unable to leave without giving up some of their accumulated benefits; which goes far to explain the hold of the organization over the people as a whole.

Nor was this all. Acting as a de facto arm of the state, Histadrut's medical insurance fund was the only one that would take in new immigrants straight upon arrival regardless of their physical condition or ability to pay. From the point of view of the state, this system had the advantage that it permitted those immigrants to be looked after, no questions asked, thus relieving the state of a heavy economic and administrative burden. At the same time Histadrut was provided with a steady stream of new members. Once they had joined—often they were made to sign the relevant papers at the airport itself, before they had the time to understand their new surroundings—those members, like their predecessors, were held in a vise. Held in that same vise, Histadrut's own employees were forced to accept relatively low pay. Too often the sole exceptions to this rule were senior managers who, as managers will, lived on their expense accounts.

Does all this sound strange? To anybody brought up on the knees of free market capitalism, there can be no doubt about the answer. The system whereby the state ran the economy owed everything to left-wing ideology as carried by Ben Gurion, Eshkol, Sapir, and Meir (neither Rabin, a gruff soldier, nor Peres, who as a founding member of Rafi belonged to Labor's right wing, were true socialists). Yet the same system also had the state act as a mediator, and sometimes enforcer, in disputes between employers and labor. In this respect it bore a surprising, though probably accidental and certainly unintended, resemblance to Italian fascist corporatism. In some ways Israel was a command economy where the government did, or tried to do, almost everything. In many others it was simply a mess where state, Histadrut, and private interest crisscrossed one another. The net effect was to blur the distinction between the private and the public. To this should be added the country's small size. Very often it made for an intimate working environment where everybody knew everybody else, did favors for everybody else, and intrigued against everybody else. Marinate, stir well, and let them stew in their own juices; doing so, one may perhaps begin to understand something concerning the kind of socialism that Israel created or, to be more precise, that created Israel.

To proceed with the analysis, it is true that the labor laws Histadrut upheld provided both its own workers and most others with a kind of security that their successors could only dream about. Those laws also provided many employees with a variety of tax-free benefits, some of which they still maintain. On the other hand, by limiting labor mobility they created a situation whereby employers and employees almost held one another prisoner. Often the laws acted as a mask for corruption, nepotism, and, above all, gross inefficiency. They also led to the creation and maintenance of what Israelis call "eight zero five jobs," i.e., jobs whose holders arrive at eight, do zero work, and go home at five. Perhaps even worse, the system of nationwide collective bargaining that Histadrut enforced failed to distinguish between different companies. By so doing it ignored problems such as productivity and profitability, driving some companies into bankruptcy and enabling others to operate as if those things did not exist.

By 1993–1994, notwithstanding their privileged position, many Histadrut-owned and -operated companies and funds were on the verge of failure. In some cases this was because, having enjoyed the state's support for so long, they mistook the never-never land in which they lived for the real one. In others it was because their managers were party hacks with no professional qualifications except for their proven loyalty to Mapai and its successors. In others still it was because they had invested their money in the stock exchange, only to see it go down the drain when the exchange crashed in the fall of 1983.

Among those who lost their treasure in this way were many kibbutzim. Like everybody else in their situation, their response was to turn to the government for help; in the end, after much infighting among the coalition partners, help was what they got. In most cases, help involved "defreezing" agricultural land so that it could be built on, a procedure that increased its value many times over by a simple stroke of the pen. Some "rescues," especially in the center of the country, were successful and eventually made the kibbutzim that benefited from them almost filthy rich. Others, especially in the periphery, were not, and left the members living in poverty. Some of the better-to-do kibbutzim tried to help the poorer ones, but there were limits to what they could do.

The catch was that the land in question did not really belong to the kibbutzim in the first place. Some of it had been put at their disposal by the Zionist movement (before 1948) or else by the state (after that date). The rest had been conquered from the Arabs during the War of Independence itself; thereafter, the kibbutzim were allowed to work it, often without any formal contract to establish ownership. Insofar as "defreezing" land meant bailing out a specific group at the expense of the nation at large, the arrangement gave rise to much bitterness. Certainly it did nothing to improve the status of kibbutzniks in the eyes of the rest of Israeli society. In the long run it proved to be one more milestone in the process that turned them from a self-conscious elite into ordinary people just as much, or as little, concerned with money grubbing as everybody else.

The role that government played in all this was somewhat ambiguous. Certainly the Likud or Likud-appointed ministers who ran the Ministry of Finance from 1977 to the time when Peres took up that post in 1988 were a mixed lot (Peres himself, incidentally, once said that his knowledge of economics equaled that of a second-year college student). Some of the ministers were utterly useless; others, including Modai's successor, Moshe Nissim, mediocre plodders with no particular agenda. Modai himself was almost a genius, though a highly unpredictable one. If only because most of them had started their careers as businessmen, none of the finance ministers had any sympathy with socialism, the kibbutzim, or Histadrut. All did whatever they could to pull the latter in particular down from its pedestal.

Still, not even the most "liberal" of Israel's ministers tried to treat labor the way Ronald Reagan did the members of PATCO (Professional Air Traffic Controllers Organization), or the way Margaret Thatcher treated Britain's miners. Reagan's solution of firing the controllers and replacing them with military personnel would not have worked in Israel because the IDF consists largely of conscripts and reservists and also because such a step would have alienated wide segments of the population. As to the miners, it should be kept in mind that Likud was and is not the same as the British Conservatives. While there were exceptions, most Israelis who voted for it belonged to the lower socioeconomic strata. They lived in "the neighborhoods," as Israelis say, worked in blue-collar jobs, and rode buses. They did much of their shopping in the cheap, sweaty, open-air markets of Jerusalem, Tel Aviv, and other cities. As a result, many a right-wing politician has tried to gauge his or her popularity by visiting the first-named in particular. Those who cannot get a round of applause from "the pickle-peddlers," as the saying goes, had better stay at home.

Shamir's main concern was always to maintain and strengthen Israel's hold on the occupied territories so as to ensure they would *never* be relinquished. In private conversations, he used to say that the greatest measure of autonomy he was prepared to grant the Palestinians was to paint their own lines on their parking lots. Much like Begin, he cared little either for state economics or for his personal ones—with the result that, in his memoirs, the word "inflation" merits only two very brief mentions. Still, he well understood the side his party's bread was buttered on. In his typical uninspiring manner, at the time he formed his first cabinet in 1983 he "pledged to continue the social welfare programs directed at disadvantaged neighborhoods and at a reduction of the social gap."[23] Later, had he tried to go too far in the opposite direction, no doubt he would have been stopped by his coalition partners, who would have been only too happy to use the move as an excuse to pull out of the coalition and call new elections. Thus, Israel's shift toward a less socialist, more liberal economy was not merely the result of a deliberate policy, but also grew out of the perceived, and often very real, failures of the previous regime and Histadrut in particular.

As Histadrut sold its profitable companies to cover the losses of the rest, during the second half of the 1980s its grip on the economy began to be relaxed. One critical step was taken in 1987–88, when the system whereby the head of Histadrut negotiated countrywide wage agreements with the chamber of employers was abolished. Good-bye, hallowed ritual; good-bye, nerve-wracking negotiating sessions; good-bye, countless cups of tea! The process was completed in 1995 after the organization held new elections. A young and dynamic secretary general, Haim Ramon (1950–), was installed. As he never ceased pointing out, he himself was a product of "the neighborhoods." Previously, in his post as minister of health, he had laid the groundwork by passing a national medical insurance law. By obliging every fund to take in every citizen—previously, the one run by Histadrut had been the only one to do so—and allowing people to move feely from one fund to another, he effectively broke the stranglehold in which Histadrut had held its members.

What was left of the organization was renamed the New Histadrut. No longer did the head of Histadrut, as the workers' representative, negotiate with himself as a large employer; stripped of its manifold enterprises, with many of its members voting with their feet, the organization lost much of its impact on Israeli life. In essence all it could still do was to represent workers vis-à-vis employers, be they the state or private companies. Even this it did without much of an ideology and without waving the red flags of old. The strikes' objective had always been money, not helping the poor or class solidarity or such. The weakening of Histadrut also helped relax the vast complex of Israel's labor law. Having been built up over decades, it helped create, in the words of Yigal Hurwitz during his tenure as minister of finance, "a mafia of parasites." As is so often the case in Israel, it was less a question of abolishing the laws than of circumventing them. First private-sector employers, then, increasingly, public-sector ones changed their hiring practices. As long-time employees left or retired, employers took on new ones on the basis of so-called personal contracts. By 1992 over one-third of all workers were hired in this way. Among them, two-thirds worked in jobs where they did not have unions to represent them.[24]

Though no politician has dared touch the right to strike, sympathy strikes—work stoppages meant to express solidarity with another group of workers—were prohibited. All this could not but affect the labor courts. As their authority was undermined, more and more often they found themselves mediating disputes rather than adjudicating them. Unsurprisingly, the main losers were ill-educated, low-skilled workers in industry and the services (in Israel, as in other developed countries during the 1980s, the massive influx of newly liberated women into the labor force led to a rapid expansion of this tertiary sector). Only too often they found themselves working for manpower companies that paid them minimal wages while providing no job security, no pensions, and few, if any, benefits. Equally unsurprising, the main winners were well educated, highly skilled workers able and willing to dictate their own terms.

Of these two groups, the former were left in a position where the "New" Histadrut, for all its occasional rhetoric concerning "mutual assistance" and "social responsibility," could do very little for them. By contrast, the latter did not really need it to represent them. Indeed, they not infrequently looked at it with some contempt. That said, some of the "strong" or "big" unions kept their power intact. The most important among them were the unions of port workers, airport workers, telecommunications workers, Israeli Electrical Corporation workers, Tahal (the government company in charge of managing the water supply) workers, bank workers, and teachers.

Of these, the first six earn high wages because they have it in their power to strike and bring the economy to a halt. The seventh earns low wages but, by preventing parents from going to work, can achieve the same result. In theory Histadrut, as an organization that unites all the various groups, continues to represent them all—though in reality the power of the "big" unions is often so great that it is difficult to say who, the head or the arms, is ruling whom. Some critics argue that since Histadrut has reformed itself, it has focused on "protecting" the strong while only paying lip service to the weak. As became evident once again in mid-2008, when Histadrut threatened to launch a general strike so as to prevent the Ministry of Finance from taking away some tax privileges that only the former enjoy, the charge contains more than a grain of truth.

From the time of Eshkol on, many Israeli leaders had often spoken of opening the economy to foreign competition so as to encourage productivity and lower prices. Yet most of this remained empty talk and never left the government offices in which the ideas were discussed. Tariff walls remained high and, with them, the price of a great many consumer goods. As one story had it, when a man caught trying to pass coffee through customs was asked why he had declared it was bird food, he answered that "either the birds will eat it, or they won't." One outcome was that, as late as the mid-1990s, anyone going abroad was besieged by friends and relatives thrusting money into their hands and asking for this and that. Often unable to afford items that the citizens of developed countries took for granted, Israelis became famous for their shopping sprees. They brought back clothes, sneakers—a highly desirable item that, at home, could cost three times as much as in the United States—cosmetics, cigarettes, alcoholic drinks, cameras, electronic gadgets, even rugs, and anything else that could be picked up at what were, by Israeli standards, bargain prices, and hopefully smuggled in.

Though the process was slow and hesitant at first, this situation, too, started changing in the late 1980s. Duties on American and European goods in particular were lowered, and many administrative restrictions designed to make the lives of importers as difficult as possible were eased. Particularly important in this respect was a 1995 deal with the European Union that granted Israel associate status. The stabilization of the shekel and the lifting of some restrictions on foreign currency deals also helped. Today, in many cases the price gap has been closed, if not in comparison with the United States—with its low indirect taxation and exceptionally efficient retail industry—then at any rate with Western Europe. To be sure, the small home market, which often translates into insufficient competition, means that some items remain much more expensive than they should be both absolutely and in relation to the average income. Still, the difference is no longer nearly as great as it used to be. If ordinary Israelis still try to smuggle products through customs, normally they do so only for themselves and their immediate families.

Shall we go on listing all the changes in insurance law, banking law, stock exchange regulations, and so on? Surely in any modern society that aims at economic development, such things are supremely important and must be as well managed as circumstances permit. As surely, they are extremely technical and only understood by a handful of people such as economists (of which Israel has plenty), accountants (ditto), and bankers. One can sum up the process by saying that during the entire period when Likud ruled either on its own or along with Labor, i.e., from 1977 to 1992, it did much to push Israel away from state- and Histadrut-directed socialism toward a market economy, complete with a very active and often volatile stock exchange. This was particularly true of the years from 1985 on. Had Ben Gurion been able to witness what was happening, no doubt he would have spun in his grave—but he would also have admired the extraordinary progress made in what he used to call "building the country."

When Rabin and Labor came back to power in 1992 they did nothing to stop the process. One indication of this was the new prime minister's own behavior. Rabin himself may not have cared about money—he was famous for his rumpled suits—but his wife, Lea, who looked after the household finances, certainly did. They lived in a flat in one of Tel Aviv's most expensive neighborhoods. It had been purchased with his fees from speaking tours during his time as ambassador in Washington, D.C. Wits claimed that over the entrance there was inscribed the Herzl-like motto, "If you lecture, this is no dream." Previous prime ministers had run cream-colored Volvos indistinguishable from those their colleagues used. Not so Rabin, who preferred to be driven around in a conspicuous black Cadillac with heavy police escort, blue lights flashing. Claiming the need to attract investors to the economy, he liked to hobnob with millionaires; his daughter Daliah married one (later they were divorced). Though he never grew rich, the contrast with some of his predecessors, especially Begin, could not have been more sharply drawn.

Under Rabin's minister of finance, Avraham ("Beiga") Shobat, who like his Likud predecessors was a businessman, the shift toward liberalization and privatization continued. Certainly it did nothing to make Israel into a kinder, gentler place. While Israel grew much richer than it had been, the waning of socialism also made it less friendly and more competitive. To speak with Shimon Peres, too often the free enterprise capitalism that it created was of the most "swinish" kind.[25] For example, whereas a 1970s-vintage popular song "The Good Life," claimed that "nobody has been thrown into the streets because of an [unpaid] mortgage," since then such cases have become all too commonplace. A contributing factor to the change in labor conditions in particular was the outbreak in late 1987 of the First Palestinian Uprising, or Intifada, which led to many Arab workers being either fired from their jobs or prevented from reaching them. To replace them Israel, no longer a poor country, started attracting foreign labor from abroad. Romanians took the place of Arabs in construction, Thais in agriculture. Chinese workers were rumored to have emptied the country of dogs, which they killed and ate; Africans cleaned city sewers, and "a Philippine" became synonymous with a female person who looked after an elderly invalid.

Unsurprisingly, the results of this new immigration differed little from those long familiar to other developed states. Especially in Tel Aviv, the newcomers took over entire neighborhoods, turning them into "Little Manila," "Little Bangkok," "Little Lagos," and so on. Nor was this all. Starting in 1989, as many as a million immigrants from the former Soviet Union flooded the country. This had the effect of increasing the Jewish population by about 20 percent. To help them settle down, the government of Israel, generously assisted by the Jewish Agency, provided each household with an "absorption basket." The terms offered were far from unattractive—as is proved, among other things, by the fact that in cities such as Moscow, Saint Petersburg, and Kiev there grew up an entire industry that counterfeited the documents, chiefly Jewish wedding certificates, would-be immigrants needed. Still, there were limits to what the state could do to assist the new arrivals.

Many of the newcomers were highly educated (the median number of years of schooling they had received stood at 14.5). However, the skills they brought with them were not always the ones Israel needed. As also happened in other countries that absorb immigrants, sometimes this was a question of "not made here"—the idea that foreign courses and qualifications were inferior to native ones. For example, immigrant physicians were often unable to pass the necessary exams, which in Israel are modeled after those used in the United States. Some of the immigrants later closed the gap by reentering school, whereas others did not. Among the latter, many were forced to accept paramedical jobs. Israel's clinics and hospitals are full of them—much to the benefit of patients.

Being new to the country and unfamiliar with its language, many "Russians" shared the fate of immigrants at all times and places and were thrust toward the bottom of the socioeconomic heap. Among them, as among guest workers, there were plenty of hardship cases; after all, how many musicians can a small country absorb? Some left the country; others were forced to find another occupation. Others still tried to make a meager living by playing on street corners. For the first time in Israeli history, one could see blond maids cleaning floors; not such a bad thing, perhaps, since it may have helped break a stereotype that only Orientals did such work. People who had run the kinds of computers that regulate rail transport found themselves working in travel agencies; the guy who renovates your house is able to quote Pushkin by the yard.

As had also happened in the case of previous waves of immigrants, some women found life so hard that the terms "Russian" and "prosti-tute" came to be closely linked. Some prostitutes are simply guest work-ers of a peculiar kind who came in the hope of making some money and leaving again; others are single mothers who, having come to set-tle, were unable to make a living in any other way. Since guest workers and immigrants form a sizable part of the workforce, the terms under which other Israelis were employed could not but be affected, too. Job security declined; labor mobility increased. By definition, a more heterogeneous workforce meant greater differences between differ-ent groups of workers. Briefly, it is true that the tenor of Israeli life un-derwent a not-so-subtle change and that there were numerous cases of exploitation. However, in many ways that change was a consequence not of failure but of the country's outstanding success in attracting new people, just as bees swarm over a honey pot.

Even so, the extent of the shift should not be exaggerated. Be-tween 1985 and 1995 the Gini Coefficient, which measures inequality, only went from 0.468 to 0.497, hardly a dramatic change.[26] Though the power of Histadrut declined, there remained some situations where it could and did call general public sector strikes and threatened to bring the country to a halt. The role that government plays in the economy, as measured by the share of GDP that it collects, also re-mains very considerable. In proportion, Israeli government spending is much larger than that of the U.S. government and resembles that of most Western European ones; though unfortunately the high cost of defense means that less is spent on social welfare than perhaps should be the case.

Many state companies were privatized during this time (this pro-cess actually got under way before 1973, but was interrupted by the war and the period of economic hardship that followed). Yet the state is very far from having sold all its assets. As always, the greatest asset is land, both that which is directly owned by the government and that whose use it controls. The state also continues to hold on to water re-sources, natural resources (stone quarries, for example, are leased to entrepreneurs, not sold to them), and much of the transportation net-work including most roads and all railroads, rolling stock, and sta-tions. It also owns a great many enterprises, including ports, airports, the Israel Electricity Corporation, IAI, the Rafael Advanced Defense

Systems, a housing company, an oil-exploration company, an export-insurance company, hospitals, and others.

If some Israelis grumble about the system, most seem either to be fairly happy with it or to have resigned themselves to it. In any case, for anybody who thinks he or she knows what its nature is and where it is going, it also contains some surprises. To return to mortgages, the fact that hardship cases are often publicized in the media—and that almost every time this happens the response is overwhelming—speaks for itself. What other prime minister besides Ehud Olmert keeps pictures of three kidnapped soldiers always on his desk? Where else do the media report any citizen who happens to be killed, or injured, or lost while on a visit abroad? How to account for the fact that nonprofit organizations take up a higher share of Israel's GNP—15 percent—than in any other country?[27] Are we to conclude that the government is trying to divest itself of its responsibilities as fast as it can? Or that some people have discovered a new and legal way to embezzle money and gain power over their fellows? Or instead that many Israelis, both individually and as a nation, still care for each other and are prepared to help in case of need?

The answer, dear reader, is probably somewhere in the middle, forever moving among the three axis points and never coming to a final halt. Without question the government of Israel, motivated by budget considerations, *is* trying to divest itself of its social responsibilities by putting as many of them as possible on the shoulders of not-for-profit organizations. Without question some people, sensing an opportunity, *do* find in these organizations legal ways to embezzle money and gain power. Last, many Israelis *do* care about their countrymen and countrywomen and *are* prepared to help them more often, and in more different ways, than is the case in many other developed countries. In the new system, as in the old one, the good and the bad are hopelessly mixed. Without doubt, they will continue to be mixed for a long time to come.

"The Jewish Head Invents Patents!"

While the reforms that Peres and Modai instituted had the effect of putting the economy as a whole on the right track, some of the greatest beneficiaries turned out to be the defense industries. Even before Israel invaded Lebanon in 1982 defense was consuming about 30 percent of national resources; some economists, factoring in such things as the opportunity cost of the youths who, instead of studying or working, spent three years doing their conscript service put the figure higher still. The runaway inflation of those years made it impossible to calculate the cost of the war itself, but it must have involved the expenditure of additional billions. As Rabin took over from Arens in 1984–1985 he realized that the state would not be able to carry this burden forever. Perhaps only somebody with his kind of authority—it had, indeed, become almost mythological—would have been able to do what he did next: to wit, slash the defense budget, reduce the standing army, and cancel some of the R & D projects then under way.

The largest, as well as the most prestigious, project of all was the aforementioned Lavi aircraft. A brainchild of Weizman, Arens, and some other air-power and technology enthusiasts, had it been completed it would have resulted in a smaller, lighter version of the American-built F-16 fighter-bomber that was then considered the best in the world. Its cancellation, which was due at least partly to U.S. pressure (understandably, America's defense corporations did not want the Israelis to compete with them at their own taxpayers' expense), threatened to bring down the manufacturer IAI as well as many of its subcontractors. Yet IAI was wholly government owned, so its downfall might have caused the politicians to look bad. It was also the firm with the largest number of employees in the entire country; in an economy that was only just beginning to recover, the decision to terminate the program constituted a courageous step.

Some of the firms whose projects were cancelled at this time did, in fact, go bankrupt. Others, including IAI, not merely survived the cuts but soon started flourishing as never before. One reason for this was the impressive growth of exports. For political reasons, many countries around the world would not buy major weapons systems made in Israel that they would later have to put on parade; for example, no foreign army has ever purchased the excellent Merkava tank. Yet many of the countries in question were more than happy to buy the components of those systems as well as smaller, less conspicuous weapons. As a result, IAI became a major exporter of such items as battlefield computers, electro-optic gear, communications gear, radar sets, avionics, remotely piloted vehicles (RPVs), and, later, unmanned aerial vehicles (UAVs). It also sold many kinds of missiles, some of them so advanced that they were purchased by the U.S. armed services or else taken over and manufactured by American firms. Looking at the list of buyers, one finds that they start with Argentina and end with Zimbabwe.

The high reputation these products enjoyed is made clear by a yarn that used to circulate in 1982–1983. In this story, meteorologists, physicists, and other scientists have discovered that a new deluge is in the making and will soon put an end to life on earth. Thereupon Brezhnev, going on TV, raises production quotas and demands that people work harder. Reagan, also going on TV, suggests that his fellow Americans eat and drink all they can before they die. Not so Begin. Turning to the experts at Rafael, he tells them that they have forty-eight hours to invent a device that will enable people to breathe underwater.

To illustrate these developments at the hand of a single company, take Magal (Sickle) Security Systems Ldt. Founded in 1969 as a subsidiary of IAI, in 1984 it was privatized, though IAI still held 26 percent of the stock. The company's home base is in Yehud, originally the Biblical Yehud.[28] Later the site was occupied by an Arab village called Yehudiya (in Arabic, "Yahud" means Jews). Having been deserted by its inhabitants during the 1948 War, it was subsequently resettled by new immigrants, many of them of Oriental, especially of Iranian origin. It was here that Magal, whose specialty is security systems such as electronic fences, surveillance equipment, and the like, set up shop; the location, not far from Tel Aviv's Ben Gurion airport, proved well chosen.

By the early 1990s Magal had grown into the largest manufacturer of its kind in the entire world. Originally its products were meant to help close Israel's borders to terrorists. Now they were used to defend not just military installations but every kind of high-value target such as airports, nuclear reactors, power stations, sensitive research facilities, and so on; in all, over six thousand miles of its security fences have been installed or erected. Partly to be close to its customers, and partly to help circumvent the usual hurdles that governments like to put in the way of foreign competitors, the company busily bought subsidiaries in places as far apart as Germany and Canada. Yehud itself was transformed from a neglected dump where Tel Aviv housewives recruited their illiterate or semiliterate maids into a satellite town where thousands of highly qualified academics, engineers, and technicians, many of them IAI employees, live.

Ultimately, what made this development possible were the microchip, the personal computer, and the Internet. Though all three were invented in the United States, in many ways they seemed tailor-made for Israel. Israeli scientists had long been interested in computers, and the first computer was built at the Weizmann Institute as far back as 1950. Later in the same decade Israeli computer experts are said to have helped France develop its first atomic bomb. Still, as long as mainframe computers dominated the industry, few Israeli organizations could afford them. In 1961 Ezer Weizman, who at that time commanded the Israeli Air Force, questioned whether a computer was really needed and whether the money—several million Israeli pounds—should not be used to build a new runway for one of his bases. As late as 1968, when the IDF manpower division put the computer it was using on show, it caused a sensation. Yet the IDF was the largest organization in the country by far. That the other organizations were unable to compete with their long-established, much bigger and richer counterparts abroad is not surprising.

The spread of microchips as well as personal computers, and the rapid reduction in the cost of data processing that followed, changed this situation. It permitted anybody to own and operate a computer and, somewhat later, to link it to the Net—thus, to a certain extent, leveling the playing field and enabling David to take on Goliath.

Throughout Jewish history, people had tended to make their livings by engaging in the services. Though the Zionist movement had done its best to change this preference by emphasizing the need to settle the land, its success in doing so had always been limited. The failure meant that the share that services occupied in the Israeli economy was always abnormally high. During the 1970s, when those services were deliberately expanded to prevent a rise in unemployment, it rose higher still. To be sure, the digital revolution could not wean Israelis away from the services—for most of them, doing hard labor in agriculture or industry was all but inconceivable. At the time, in any case, advanced countries, with the United States at their head, were already starting to deindustrialize. Hence, even if Israel had chosen another road, doing so would have been counterproductive.

Ever since 1948 Israel, cut off from its natural markets by the hostility of the neighboring countries and subject to the "Arab boycott," had found it hard to export its products. Being limited to the local market, and often protected by high customs walls as well, most industrial firms remained small and inefficient. In Israel's small and intimate society, instead of looking for ways to improve productivity these firms spent their time lobbying for subsidies and tax breaks; one 1960s-vintage cartoon portrayed such benefits as whales, followed by a perspiring entrepreneur intent on harpooning them. Many firms were not really industrial at all, being more correctly classified under "arts and crafts." They had neither resources nor much incentive to invest in R & D. As late as 1984, whereas defense-related R & D accounted for no less than 4.5 percent of the GNP, the civilian sector, exclusive of the universities, spent only 0.7 percent on it.[29]

The effect of the digital revolution, with its emphasis on "small is beautiful," was to do away with many of the constraints on exports. Neither distance nor customs barriers mattered much. Israel was able to reap the benefits of globalization; as of 2007, high-tech industries, employing 7 percent of the workforce, accounted for 23 percent of foreign sales.[30] What is more, these changes took place without any need for people to dirty their hands with mud or grease. Instead they sat in front of computers and either wrote programs or invented little devices by which those programs could be transmitted and stored. Thanks partly to the heterogeneity of the population, partly to a literacy level much higher than that of any other country between Japan and Italy, and partly perhaps to the traditional tendency of Jews to live by their wits—too often they were prohibited from doing anything else—relative to its size, Israel had always been bubbling with creativity. Now, after many failed attempts, its residents had finally found a way to channel that creativity in a direction where it could be used to make the cash registers ring.

At the time IAI was forced to cancel the Lavi and turn its attention to smaller projects, it was already a large corporation. This was not true of most of the rest, which were often started by a handful of people. Many of these people first met during their military service—in particular with Mamram, the computer unit that is run by the Ministry of Defense and the IDF in common. Taking in promising conscripts, Mamram makes them sign up for an additional number of years as a condition for putting them through the appropriate computer-training courses. Once they graduate, it almost immediately entrusts them with heavy responsibilities that their counterparts abroad can only dream about. Thus, one twenty-two-year-old lieutenant I knew had ten people, including several computer engineers, working for him. He was running a network with no fewer than seventeen thousand computers!

Where Mamram is unique is that it is not a commercial organization. Having invested so much in training, it does not fire its employees when they make an honest mistake but allows them to experiment—even if, as sometimes happens, the experiments consist of little more than play. In the view of some insiders, this is probably the real reason why, over time, it has acquired a well-deserved reputation for turning out bright young men (as of 2009, incidentally, it was commanded by a woman). After their discharge, making use of the informal character of Israeli life and the country's small size, they stay in touch. They latch on to some interesting idea and start a new company in one of their homes or else in a garage. They then spend the next years working sixteen hours a day—the typical pattern of young entrepreneurs everywhere. A willingness to take risks helps; in 2007, Israel was said to have the highest number of start-up companies per capita in the world.[31]

As also happened abroad, some firms failed, but many succeeded. By the mid-1990s their success could be measured by the sixty-mile stretch of road from Tel Aviv to Haifa. Lined with row after row of shining new glass buildings, it was developing into a second Silicon Valley. Inside these buildings are sparkling clean reception desks, luxurious offices where management works, and cubicles cluttered with every kind of data-processing, -storing, and -transmission device known to man. The buildings are air conditioned as a matter of course—which, compared to even as recent a period as the 1970s, represents a big change. The entire complex is dotted by restaurants, coffee shops, barber and beauty shops, and similar facilities that workers need; in other words, by urban sprawl, though the fact that land is expensive means that distances are usually very small and movement from one building to the next is much easier on foot than by car.

As any visitor will soon note, Israelis are utterly lacking in social discipline. They gesticulate, they raise their voices, and they treat any queue as an invitation to jostle one another. They drive like madmen (and -women) and will smoke a cigarette right under a "no smoking" sign. As in many other "Mediterranean" countries, public life tends to be somewhat disorderly; as the saying goes, what is permitted is permitted and what is not permitted is also permitted. Certainly the system, supposing the term is not an oxymoron, is not without disadvantages. Plans are considered no more than bases for change, as another saying goes, and anyone who does not have a loud voice and sharp elbows tends to be pushed aside. This may explain why Israeli firms seem to be better at inventing than at building and managing large-scale enterprises. This, in turn, may explain why they have so seldom succeeded in translating their ingenuity into the kind of consumer products that crowd the shelves of developed countries, as Canon, Seiko, Sony, Toshiba, Samsung, and, increasingly, Chinese and Indian companies do.

On the other hand, this lackadaisical, disrespectful, and often noisy approach to life is not without certain advantages, too. It probably helps dispense with some problems that are not really problems at all—of which public smoking may very well be one. More pertinent to our purpose, a certain kind of mental rebelliousness is almost definitely an indispensable prerequisite for creativity and inventiveness. What do these qualities mean if not the breaking-down of barriers and the construction of new combinations? Surely he or she who always sticks to the rules will never invent anything. In both English and Hebrew, such people are "squares" and "pinheads." Israelis have added the expression "plywood [brains]." Though Israel certainly has its share of them, perhaps their proportion in the population is a little lower than elsewhere; after all, Jews have always been famous for their tendency to argue about everything under the sun. It is not for nothing that companies such as IBM, Hewlett-Packard, Intel, Microsoft, Motorola, and Sun Microsystems have set up research labs in Israel.

All this may explain why Israelis, though they may not have developed and sold many famous consumer products, do provide many of the programs and devices that go *into* those products. For example, take the LZ algorithm for compressing data. Dating to 1977, it was the brainchild of two Israeli researchers, Abraham Lempel and Yaacov Ziv, who called it after their own surnames. Later versions were incorporated into various other programs, of which the one perhaps most familiar to laypersons is PDF. Other Israeli inventions include VocalTec—the first program that, long before Skype, made it possible to talk on the Internet by phone and thus drastically reduce long-distance costs—FireWall-1 (one of the first antivirus programs, produced by Check Point Ltd.), the Babylon translation program, and the little gadget known to tens of millions as a jump drive. A few of the companies involved, including Check Point and an outfit named Amdocs that specializes in the storage and management of documentation, developed into international giants. Some did not know how to market their products, so others reaped the profits. Most worked for the export market, especially in the United States; in 2000, high-tech firms exported over 45 percent of their product.[32] Hence, it is not surprising that a great many ended by being bought by foreign corporations for a great many dollars.

Israeli engineers and technicians are everywhere—witness the fact that they won a Pentagon competition for an autonomous vehicle capable of crossing so-and-so many miles of desert terrain without a driver. Building on their success, they are selling automated vacuum cleaners and lawn mowers. Nor is the list of inventions limited to computers. To mention but a few, it includes an innovative laser-based system for locating explosives (useful for catching terrorists); a system for preventing birds from colliding with aircraft, a vital necessity in a small country that, owing to its geographical position, has half a billion birds crossing it during their annual migration; and a system for monitoring fatigue in drivers and waking them if necessary. Israeli-developed desalination plants, as well as automated watering systems for agriculture that are able to save both water and labor, are exported all over the world.

On a per capita basis Israel manufactures and operates more square yards of clean, cheap solar energy receptors than any other country. Israeli-bred and -raised cows and sheep yield more milk per head per annum than those of any other nation. Some Israeli scientists have developed a miniature camera that can pass through the small intestines, taking pictures all the way. Others devised a nanotechnology-based gadget for monitoring the level of sugar in the blood of people who are suffering from diabetes. Some scientists produced a revolutionary medicine for the treatment of multiple sclerosis, whereas others still have come up with an ointment for treating people stung by jellyfish, whose pervasive presence along the eastern Mediterranean coast has turned into a real problem during the last few decades. Israeli scientists have developed an innovative treatment that makes many hysterectomies unnecessary. One Israeli professor who works for the Technion in Haifa even invented an air-conditioning system for motorcycle riders. An excellent idea, no doubt, though not one that seems to have found many buyers.

For some obscure reason, Google Scholar hits that combine the words "education" and "Israel" are dominated by articles about the allegedly deficient education of minorities, the education of women, and the education of disadvantaged groups (including what is currently the most disadvantaged group of all, immigrants from Ethiopia). One may even find something called "Children's reports of emotional, physical and sexual maltreatment by educational staff in Israel."[33] These are certainly important problems, and there is no denying that they need to be attended to. Equally certainly, though, the resulting impression is misleading and does Israel an injustice. Whereas the 1950s brought tens of thousands of illiterate immigrants into the country, two decades later illiteracy was limited almost entirely to elderly Oriental women who did not work outside the home. Among the young, it had all but disappeared. Even during the 1970s, and in the face of all the security-related, economic, and social difficulties, secondary education continued to expand. By the end of the decade education accounted for 8.4 percent of the GNP; as of 2008 the figure was 8.5 percent, which is higher than any of the OECD (Organisation for Economic Co-operation and Development) countries. The median number of years of schooling that Israelis received is also rising, though whether this means that people are really better educated than they used to be is an open question.[34]

The record of higher education is even more impressive. During the early years Israel had just one school of engineering, the Technion;

one university, the Hebrew University in Jerusalem; and one scientific research center, the Weizmann Institute in Rehovot. Thanks in large part to Hitler, whose policies drove numerous scientists and scholars into emigration, right from the beginning they were able to command excellent faculty members—an advantage that few if any other developing countries have enjoyed. In 1955 Bar-Ilan University, a quasi-religious institution located at Ramat Gan not far from Tel Aviv, was added. In the 1960s and 1970s three more universities were established in Tel Aviv, Haifa, and Beer Sheba, thus raising the total to seven.

All these institutes of higher learning were largely government funded (the rest of the money came from voluntary contributions, mainly by non-Israeli Jews, and tuition). In spite of being government funded, they were not run like state institutions. Rather, they were independent public corporations. Each of them elected its own leaders and was responsible for running its own affairs. Central authority was in the hands of a body known as the Malag (Council for Higher Education), two-thirds of whose members had to be academics and the rest public figures; it was presided over by the minister of education. Thus, Israel's universities occupied a position midway between those of countries such as Italy and France, where faculty are simply state employees, and the private universities of the United States. For many years the arrangement worked very well. It kept tuition relatively low—even today, it stands at less than three thousand dollars or so. It also permitted a great deal of academic freedom, yet it did not subject the universities to the whims of the commercial world or, what can be even worse, those of their students.

Of late there have been growing complaints about the supposedly declining quality of Israeli scientific research, specifically including the humanities and the social sciences. As so often, there is no agreement about the roots of the problem. Some point a finger at the "present generation of students." Having abandoned the libraries in favor of that terrible monster, the Internet, they "have no intellectual curiosity whatsoever," "do not possess the slightest courage," and no longer devote "all their energy, their time, and their abilities to acquiring knowledge."[35] Others blame the faculty. Running the universities as if they were their private fiefdoms, they have created a democracy of mediocrity and block any reform, such as individual contracts and reduced job security, aimed at producing excellence. Still others blame the government, which has refused to increase funding so as to keep up with the growing number of students. Indeed, it did the opposite, depriving the universities of some money and using those funds instead to assist colleges in remote parts of the country (to the extent that anything can be remote in tiny Israel). While the universities are being starved, the system enables the colleges—whose faculty members are not expected to engage in research—to take in students who did not qualify for the larger universities. Under such circumstances, mediocrity is almost preordained.

Even if we accept these claims, few people doubt that Israel continues to maintain the best system of higher education from Tokyo to Rome and from Moscow to the South Pole. But should we even accept them? Some of them are clearly ridiculous—for example, the idea that students no longer want to study goes back at least as far as the thirteenth-century collection of songs known as the *Carmina Burana.* In one of them, titled "Let's Play Hooky," the anonymous authors suggest that "the fruits of love" are better suited to youth than the "mountains of books" old men prefer.[36] Certainly Israeli students—the country now has no fewer than 250,000 of them—are no worse than the rest. If anything, the opposite applies. Israeli students differ from their foreign counterparts in that, before they enroll, they serve two, three, or even four (if they get a commission) years in the military. There, some of them may carry heavy responsibilities indeed. After their discharge they are wont to spend a year or so traveling abroad, seeing the world and sowing their wild oats. As a result they are older, and much less childish, than their counterparts. Indeed, the boring nature of Israeli student life, and the near complete absence of juvenile pranks, have often been commented on.

When it comes to money, one cannot help but wonder whether things are really as bad "as the lass yells," to use a Hebrew expression taken from the Old Testament that refers to false accusations of rape.[37] After all, it is by complaining that universities both inside and outside Israel make their livings; as far back as 1965, a committee appointed to look into the matter wrote that "since the government refuses to pay the bills, the universities are always in a state of financial crisis."[38] Last, it is not at all clear that the decline is real. The following cumulative data, which cover the quarter century from 1981 to 2005 and are thus not subject to quirky changes any single year may bring, will shed some light on the matter. During this period Israel led the world in the number of papers in computer science published per one thousand of population; whereas the Israeli figure was 58.12, the runner-up, Canada, managed only half as many. Israel also took first place in economics, business administration, and mathematics; second place in biology and biochemistry; third place in chemistry, material science, and molecular science; fourth place in space science; and fifth place in clinical medicine and the social sciences.

Perhaps even more interesting are qualitative measures. In terms of citations per published paper in computer science, Israel led the world; this means that each paper written by an Israeli was cited 9 times on the average, vis-à-vis 7.95 for the runner-up, the United States. By the same criterion the country came second in economics, business administration, and engineering. It also came second (along with Switzerland and the Netherlands) in material science; fourth in physics; fifth (along with three other countries) in mathematics; sixth in molecular biology; seventh in space science; and eleventh in clinical medicine. Only in the social sciences, where Israel ranks seventeenth out of twenty, is the situation less satisfactory.[39] In part, this may be the result of the priority that MALAG, and behind it the government, which foots most of the bills, is giving to the natural sciences. Let's not forget that, back in the 1950s and 1960s, Israel's universities were often accused of concentrating on "theoretical" subjects and not being sufficiently practical—meaning commercial—minded. If things have changed, then perhaps this simply proves that some people like nothing better than to criticize.

As if to illustrate the difficulties under which Israeli science, and indeed much of Israeli life in general, must work, there is the case of the space program. In 1988 Israel launched its first satellite, Ofek (Horizon) 1, thus becoming only the sixth member of the exclusive space club. Yet there was an interesting difference. To take advantage of the earth's rotation, countries and corporations routinely launch their satellites from west to east. Israel's neighbors to the east, however, are hostile to it. At least one, Iraq, is formally at war with it. They might very well perceive a missile that appears on their radar screens and heads in their direction as a threat. To avert the danger of accidental war, Ofek 1 and its successors were launched in the opposite direction, i.e., over the Mediterranean. Accordingly, either the booster had to be made about 8 percent more powerful than it would otherwise have been or the payload reduced in proportion.

From this point of view, as well as many others, it might have been better for Israel if it had been established on some island not too far from the equator. Another nice location might have been Western Europe. Not only has that part of the world been well endowed by nature, but it has seen no war for six decades; as a result, defense budgets are in the order of 1–3 percent of its countries' GNPs. Instead, to quote former Prime Minister Benjamin Netanyahu, Israel became a developed country that landed in the Middle East by mistake. There it is its misfortune to be surrounded by neighbors who, apart from being hostile, are technically and scientifically so backward that it is simply no contest. For example, from 1981 to 2005 Israelis published more than thirty-four hundred papers dealing with computer science. During the same period Syrians, who outnumber Israelis three to one, published only two. In 2006, Israelis took out about 1,700 patents. In per capita terms this puts the country in the same league as some highly developed ones such as Switzerland, the Netherlands, and Sweden. The corresponding figure for the leading Arab country, Saudi Arabia, which has three times Israel's population, was forty.[40]

In 1985, the year of the reforms that really enabled Israel to take off, much of this was still in the future. Indeed, the words that form the heading of this section, "The Jewish head invents patents!," were taken from a 1960s-vintage popular saying that poked fun at the backwardness of contemporary Israeli industry. If we divide the years 1981–2005 into subperiods we find that, again with the exception of social science, Israel's relative position in most fields has tended to improve, not deteriorate. Owing to the abnormally large role played by the defense industry, moreover, the above figures probably underestimate Israel's scientific achievements. Much research is done in secret; so much so, in fact, that a rather dubious innovation has developed—the classified dissertation that only a few initiates are allowed to see. Nor is international recognition of those achievements lacking. In 2004, the Nobel Prize in Chemistry went to professors Aaron Ciechanover and Avram

Hershko of the Technion (as well as to U.S. scientist Irwin Rose). A year later, the Nobel Prize in economics was shared by Professor Robert Aumann of the Hebrew University. To lift our gaze a little, the 1966 Nobel Prize in Literature was shared by Shmuel Yosef Agnon. Menahem Begin (with Anwar Sadat) and Shimon Peres and Yitzhak Rabin (with Yasser Arafat) got the prizes for peace in 1978 and 1994 respectively.

At a more popular level, Israelis lead the world in the number of museums per capita. In terms of the number of books they buy, and presumably read, each year, they come in second. The percentage of those who attend the theater is twice as high as those who watch soccer matches; over the last year, one person out of four has gone to a concert.[41] If these data do not prove how successful Israel has been, then I would dearly like to know what could.

"A Brilliant Success"

On December 7, 1987 Shmuel Goren, a former deputy head of Mossad whose official title was "coordinator of activities in the occupied territories," delivered a lecture in front of an audience made up of IDF officers. In it, he claimed that twenty years of occupation had been "a brilliant success."[42] The next day, an Israeli truck drove over and killed a Palestinian boy in the Gaza Strip. The locals quickly decided that the Israeli driver had acted on purpose, though it may have been PLO activists who deliberately spread that rumor in order to stir up the population. In any case the Strip erupted in violence, and the first intifada (the word means "shaking," literally "the orgasm of a female camel") was begun.

To be sure, Goren was unlucky and he soon lost his post. To be sure, too, the Palestinians would have disagreed—to put it mildly—with his conclusion. Still, he did have a point. Late in 1967 Dayan, who as minister of defense ran the territories and treated them almost as if they were his private domain (among other things, he raided them for antiquities), talked to a famous journalist of the time, Joseph Alsop.[43] Asked how long, in his view, it would take the Palestinians to start an Uprising—having gone through the 1936 Arab Revolt, among other things, he never doubted that there would be one—Dayan's answer was, "between two and four years." As it turned out, it took twenty.

How to explain this extreme tardiness? Was it because Israeli counterterrorist measures were effective in rooting out most of the opposition before it could even get under way? Or because the Palestinian leadership, which from 1982 was located in faraway Tunisia, did not know how to stir up the population? Or because that population, however downtrodden and oppressed and economically exploited it might have been, still regarded life under the Zionist boot as tolerable? Or because of some combination of all three? We shall never know. What we *do* know is that at the time this situation finally ended, the IDF was controlling three million or so Palestinians with only three battalions (i.e., fewer than 2,000 men in all): two for the West Bank, one for Gaza. By contrast, policing the 8.25 million residents of New York City takes 36,000 officers.

At the time the intifada started Dayan had been dead for six years. During the last years of his life he had repeatedly warned his countrymen that, if Israel wanted to survive, it was essential that it rid itself—in one way or another—of what he called the Palestinian "hump."[44] Unfortunately those who were in power during those years—Begin, Sharon (until the spring of 1983), Shamir, Arens, and Rabin—were not as prescient as Dayan was. For one thing, none of them spoke Arabic or understood Arab culture nearly as well as he did. With the exception of Rabin, they were also much more committed to holding on to the territories, not just on strategic but on nationalist grounds—he whom the Gods want to destroy they strike blind first, as the proverb goes. During the long periods when those territories were relatively calm, these leaders convinced themselves that there was no need to find a solution and that their plans for building more settlements could go ahead without interruption. During the short ones when things were less calm, they told themselves, and of course the public, that finding a solution was impossible since the Palestinians would surely regard any concessions as a weakness.

This, then, was the conundrum that, for two decades after 1967, blocked any progress toward some kind of political settlement. In the meantime, life did not stand still. Many aspects of Israeli law were extended into the territories. Water and electricity grids were linked, and economic ties of every kind forged. As Benjamin Akzin, a well-known Israeli professor of political science, had written as long ago as 1943 in reference to World War II: "Occupation creates . . . a status quo of its own which, in a great many cases, will tend to perpetuate itself."[45] Above all, Israeli settlements, some filled with real fanatics of the kind that Leibowitz once called Judeo-Nazis[46] but mostly made up of ordinary Israelis looking for a good deal, multiplied. Including Gaza but excluding East Jerusalem, the settlers never even amounted to 5 percent of the population of the territories. Yet in terms of land they took up a much larger share; the longer time went on, the more the territories looked like Swiss cheese.

Since June 1967, the territories had never been completely quiet. Terrorism in the form of stabbings, shootings, and the occasional bomb had been going on for many years (and was to go on for many years after the intifada died down). There were also intermittent riots, especially in places such as Hebron, where Islamic (and Jewish) fundamentalism was strong, but they had always quieted down after a few days and peace of a sort was reestablished. Now first the Gaza Strip and then the West Bank exploded in fury. Thousands of people, including men, women, young people (who, as usual, bore the brunt of the fighting and took the majority of casualties), and even children as young as five participated—an unmistakable sign of the strength of the movement and the determination that fueled it. They wielded every kind of cold weapon such as rocks, bricks, steel bars, bicycle chains, knives, axes, homemade swords, and Molotov cocktails. They demonstrated, rioted, and attacked the few available Israeli troops; to make things worse, most of those troops were scattered in penny packets and could not have mounted an organized response even if they had understood what was going on.

In fact, the Israeli military did *not* understand what was going on. So little perturbed was Rabin personally that, instead of taking charge, he flew to the United States to haggle over the price of some F-16s. Later, asked what effect the uprising would have on the troops under his command, he foolishly said that "looking the enemy in the white of the eyes" was good for their morale; the chief of staff, General Dan Shomron, said that order would be restored "in two or three weeks."[47] Since the few available troops were scattered, it took them weeks to organize a coordinated response. Instead it was every company, platoon, and squad commander out for himself (not herself, since the idea that women should participate in ground combat had not yet been established). Even after it had become clear beyond doubt that this was a serious popular uprising and not simply another riot, the IDF in some ways continued to put its head in the sand. For example, during the entire period from 1988 to 1995 *Maarachot,* its flagship publication, did not carry a single article about this conflict.

Once Rabin issued his notorious order "to break arms and legs"—his intent was to save lives—a dreary routine soon established itself. Every day brought new incidents; during the first three and a half months the IDF counted precisely 6,840 of them. Most were small, but they were punctuated by clashes in which hundreds and even thousands of people took part. Israeli soldiers and civilians in the territories were attacked. Cars and other targets were stoned—pictures of Palestinian youths throwing rocks at Israeli tanks made headlines around the world—tires burned, and prohibited Palestinian flags displayed. Much of the violence took place at random. Other incidents clustered around special occasions such as the funerals of *shahids* ("martyrs"), a variety of Muslim- and PLO-established memorial days, and the visits of foreign dignitaries. Some of them were organized by the PLO's operatives in the field, but many were spontaneous.

In response, Israel's various "security arms" did what others have done, and are still doing, in their situation. They used a mixture of secret service methods, ordinary police methods, and riot police methods. The most visible response were units of army and Frontier Guard troops. Dressed in the same uniform until they became almost indistinguishable, they battled demonstrators with truncheons, tear gas, and rubber bullets. They also set up roadblocks, carried out spot searches, and mounted patrols in the streets of towns, villages, and refugee camps. Other units raided various Palestinian organizations suspected of acting as cover for the PLO leaders and searched the houses of leaders, arresting suspects and taking them for interrogation and, sometimes, torture. Schools and universities were closed, merchants who struck and refused to open their shops fined, and whole districts subjected to repeated curfews that could last for weeks on end.

While these activities soon assumed a somewhat ritualistic character, others were much more sinister. Compared to many other counter-insurgents, the Israelis enjoyed the immense advantage of being intimately familiar with the enemy—the country, the people, the language, and the culture. This often enabled the security service, Shin Bet, as well as special units of so-called Arabists, to go after individual suspects and kill or arrest them. A situation soon developed where Palestinian terrorists tried to dress and act like Israelis, whereas Israeli undercover agents dressed like Palestinians. Some of the more fanatical Jewish settlers played their own game, setting up militias that guarded their homes—they got their weapons from the IDF—and also engaging in independent activities against their Palestinian neighbors. With cases of mistaken identity increasing in number, on both sides any kind of coordinated action became extremely difficult, and chaos and a war of all against all threatened to develop.

For decades on end, first the Jewish community in the Land and then the State of Israel had faced enemies who, on paper at any rate, were much stronger than themselves. In the case of the intifada this was no longer the case—here the "enemy" consisted of men, women, and children without proper organization, proper training, proper weapons, proper anything. The effect on the IDF, which bore the main brunt of the fighting, was similar to the effect similar wars have had on other armed forces around the world. To prevent "innocents" from being hit, stringent "rules of engagement" were established and the troops ordered to obey them. Needless to say, the rules were often violated, either on purpose or inadvertently in the heat of violent clashes when troops, coming under attack of every kind of cold weapon as well as Molotov cocktails, could not always say whether their tormentors were over or under thirteen years old.

If this happened in front of the wrong TV camera an investigation might follow, forcing troops to lie to their commanders and commanders to disown their troops. In case the boot was on the other foot and Palestinians succeeded in killing Israelis—and given how weak the former were—there would also be an investigation. Israelis being a creative people, soon an entire new vocabulary shot out of the ground to describe the new realities. For example, the acronym KASTAH stood for "cover your ass;" ODATZ, for the lawyer who acted as the cover. Officers came to be called *fashlonerim* (from *fashla,* "a blunder"), and it was claimed that the reason why they were often selected to serve on committees of inquiry was because they were used to *fashlot* (plural of *fashla*). Back in September 1973 Rabin, participating in the elections campaign of that time, had held a speech in which he claimed that, in any modern army, the most important thing of all was mutual trust among the troops and between them and the society they served. Now, slowly but unmistakably, that trust started to break down.

To be sure, not all Palestinian terrorist acts were successful—but then they did not have to be. As Begin, following his long and rich experience in making the lives of British troops in the Land unbearable, had written:

> The very existence of an underground, which oppression, hangings, torture and deportations fail to crush or to weaken, must, in the end, undermine the prestige of the colonial regime that lives by the legend of its omnipotence. Every attack which it fails to prevent is a blow to its standing. Even if the attack does not succeed, it makes a dent in that prestige and that dent widens into a crack, which is extended with every succeeding attack.[48]

However, by the time the Palestinian uprising got under way Begin had turned himself into a living mummy. Very few, if any, members of the IDF's General Staff had read his book.

In the summer of 1990, two and a half years after the intifada broke out, there came the crisis that was to lead to the first Gulf War. Partly because it was far away and did not have a common border with Israel, Iraq had long been the most belligerent of Israel's enemies, refusing even to sign a cease-fire. Iraqi forces took part in the wars of 1948, 1967, and 1973. During much of the 1980s those forces were immobilized by the war against Iran. However, in 1988 victory gave dictator Saddam Hussein a free hand. He chose to play that hand, which allegedly consisted of a million troops with no fewer than five thousand tanks, not against Israel but against the Arab sister state of Kuwait, a much smaller, weaker, closer, and above all richer victim.

As the coalition that President George H. W. Bush began to form threatened to liberate Kuwait, Hussein in turn threatened to attack

Israel in the hope of driving a wedge between the Arab members of that coalition and the rest. Since the two countries are separated by several hundred miles, and in view of the superiority of the Israeli Air Force, the only way he could do so was by launching his thousand or so surface-to-surface missiles. At the time Hussein almost certainly had chemical warheads for those missiles. However, Prime Minister Shamir promised "awesome and terrible retaliation" in case any of them hit Israel; probably as a result of that threat, they remained unused.

As the war in the Gulf approached, the atmosphere in Israel grew increasingly weird. Perhaps because they were fascinated by the much greater and more dangerous spectacle about to unfold, the Palestinians calmed down and the intifada was all but suspended. Inside the country it was as if everything slowed. People worked fewer hours and the number of traffic jams declined. Gas masks were distributed, and instructions, some of them foolish and others self-contradictory, as to how behave in an emergency were issued. Tourists disappeared from the streets and foreign airliners gradually ceased to fly to Tel Aviv, until only El Al remained to keep the empty airport going. People bought rolls of sticky paper and plastic sheets to stop their windows from breaking and prevent gas from entering. Others organized "end of the world" parties with wild drinking, dancing, and carousing. When the war did start on January 16–17, 1991, and Iraqi missiles hit Israel, the United States, fearing that the coalition would indeed be torn apart, all but prohibited its ally from joining the fray. As a result, Hussein's aggression did not lead to the military response that, had circumstances been different, it deserved.

Between them, the thirty-nine missiles that landed in Israel carried about ten tons of explosives. The material damage they caused was considerable, but the number of dead was surprisingly small: just three (or ten, if one includes those who later died of their injuries). In part it was a question of luck—a single missile that fell on a barrack in Saudi Arabia killed thirty American service personnel. Another reason why casualties were low was because many residents of Tel Aviv, the city at which Hussein aimed most of his missiles, left their homes. Disregarding their mayor, a former general who called them "deserters," they either spent the nights (the time when the missiles arrived) elsewhere or simply moved altogether. Those who stayed felt as if they were living on a huge dartboard. Missiles were falling more or less at random, but there was nothing they could do. Meanwhile, the Patriot antimissile missiles that the United States had stationed in Israel proved totally useless. Though several dozen were launched, not a single one hit its target.

At the time, in Israel and abroad, much was made of this war. Whole libraries were written about the supposedly terrible experience of sitting in "sealed rooms" and waiting for the missiles to fall; psychologists were mobilized to help, and dignitaries paid visits to those who were suffering from shock. In retrospect, all this appears vastly exaggerated. What the war *did* do was break the military power of Iraq. With it went any threat of an "eastern front," so that Israel's position vis-à-vis the rest of the Middle East was strengthened. The war also helped the IDF acquire new weapons. Feeling guilty about the fact that Hussein's missiles incorporated some German technology, ultimately derived from the V-2s of World War II fame, Germany agreed to present Israel with a number of ultramodern submarines capable of launching cruise missiles—a most welcome addition to the country's deterrent power, as it turned out. On a more minor note, the Americans agreed to leave the remaining Patriots to the IDF, which immediately set about modifying and improving them in anticipation of the next conflict. The war also reinforced Israel in its decision to press ahead and build its own antimissile defense system in the form of the Arrow missile. Since most of the money was provided by Washington, D.C., there really was no good reason why it should not do so.

More interesting than the military consequences of the war were its political ramifications. First the invasion of Kuwait, then the war itself created a rift in the Arab world wide enough to let in half a million American troops. Once things had calmed down President Bush and his secretary of state, James Baker, sought to use the opportunity to push for a settlement between Israel, the Palestinians, and perhaps some Arab states as well. Having put heavy pressure on Shamir in particular, they finally got him to send an Israeli delegation to the Madrid Conference of October 1991. After all the effort spent—Baker calculated that, trying to set things up, he had flown 53,068 miles—the achievements of the conference turned out to be meager indeed. Still, it did mark the first official face-to-face meetings between Israel, a number of Arab countries, and Palestinian representatives from the territories; to that extent, it constituted progress.

In the meantime, the intifada had resumed. Its form, however, had changed. Partly because of the IDF's countermeasures, and perhaps partly because the Palestinians felt they had made their point concerning their determination to liberate themselves, public demonstrations became smaller and farther between. On the other hand, stabbings, shootings, and bombings increased in number. In one incident alone, fifteen Israelis were killed as an Arab passenger in the bus they were riding seized the wheel and steered the vehicle off the road and into an abyss. None of this seemed to impress Shamir. Having recently celebrated his seventy-fifth birthday—getting there had been easy, he said—he remained as obdurate as only he could be. In the end the matter was decided by the Israeli electorate, which in the summer of 1992 voted him out of power. Shamir himself blamed the defeat on "infighting" inside his own party and "the new [Russian] immigrants [who] denied Likud their votes."[49] More likely, by saying no once too often he had tied his own noose; the more so because the United States refused to give Israel $10 billion in loan guarantees so long as it did not budge on the Palestinian question.

The winner of the elections was Yitzhak Rabin. Now seventy years old, with a nose that was turning red as a result of excessive drinking, from late 1987 to mid-1990 he had used his post as minister of defense to do what he could to put down the intifada, but without success. In the process, as he once said, he had made himself "the best-hated man in the world," which blamed him for the daily TV fare of handcuffed Palestinians, beaten Palestinians, injured Palestinians, and dead Palestinians. The total number of Palestinians who died was around 1,200, whereas another 100,000 or so saw the inside of Israeli jails. On the Israeli side, the number of dead was about 140. In using the IDF to suppress the intifada, Rabin did it a lot of harm. To speak with General Amnon Shahak, whom he himself appointed chief of staff in 1995, from the most admired organization in the country the IDF was fast turning into "the national punching bag."[50]

Rabin was something of a slow thinker—flashes of intuition had never been his forte. However, the year he spent in the opposition did him a lot of good. Apparently it made him realize that Dayan had been right all along, that the existing situation was untenable, and that there was no alternative to talking to, and if possible coming to an agreement with, the PLO. That conclusion must have been reinforced in May 1993, when a series of bombing attacks forced him to temporarily shut down all the transfer points leading from the territories into Israel for the first time since 1967. A clearer admission that the "brilliant success" had not been so brilliant after all would be hard to think of.

In Israel as elsewhere, any leader who decides to try the path of peace must first prove how tough he is—as, for example, Richard Nixon did when he ordered the "Christmas bombings" at the end of 1972. To this rule Rabin was no exception. An opportunity came his way in July 1993, when six Israeli soldiers were killed along the Lebanese border. As hostilities escalated, Hezbollah used its standard tactic of firing rockets at Israeli civilian settlements in the region. Rabin's response was different from anything that had been tried so far—instead of simply bombing Hezbollah positions as he and his predecessors had done hundreds if not thousands of times, or launching yet another commando raid, he brought up Israel's powerful artillery. For a full week, dozens of heavy 155 millimeter guns rained down thousands of shells on southern Lebanon. They killed 118, of whom between 8 (according to Hezbollah) and 50 (according to the IDF) were terrorists. Perhaps more important, three hundred thousand residents of the area were forced to flee, putting pressure on those who lived farther north. While the move did far less than break Hezbollah, it did produce sufficient shock and awe to give Israel a breathing space.

By that time, far from the public eye, negotiations with the PLO were already under way. The Madrid meeting had been followed by many others. They appeared very much like a traveling circus; TV cameras were summoned, statements given, hands shaken. However, there was a catch. Considering the PLO a "terrorist" organization, the Israelis insisted that they would only talk to residents of the territories who were not officially its members. Since the PLO considered itself (and was recognized by much of the world) as the sole representative of the Palestinian people, anyone who tried to circumvent it might very well have been murdered. In any event it was Norway's foreign minister, Johan Jørgen Holst, who found a way of breaking the impasse. In September 1992 he suggested to the Israeli deputy foreign minister, Yossi

Beilin, that direct talks between Israeli and PLO representatives should get under way in Oslo.

Located in the left wing of the Labor Party, Beilin was a longtime protégé of Peres, who having lost leadership of the Labor Party to Rabin, was once again serving in his old post as foreign minister. The arrangements on the Palestinian side were similar. Their chief negotiator was Ahmed Qourei, aka Abu Ala. He reported to Mahmoud Abbas, who reported to Yasser Arafat. What really brought the two sides together was not any sudden surge of mutual liking but their common desire to go over the heads of the Palestinians in the territories. In the case of the Israelis, this was because they were forced to recognize the people with whom they had been talking since the 1991 Madrid Conference did not represent anybody. In the case of the PLO it was because, isolated in Tunisia, far from the scene of action, they feared lest they would sink into irrelevance.

At the end of August 1993 an outline of an agreement was becoming sufficiently clear for Shamir, no longer head of Likud but still an MK, to try pulling the brakes. He warned the public about the "almost indecent haste" with which Rabin, in "formerly unthinkable partnership with Yasser Arafat," was putting "Israel's most vital interests" at risk.[51] But early in September the agreement was finalized at the Oslo Accords. Israel and the PLO formally recognized each other. A Palestinian National Authority was set up, and it committed itself to changing the Palestinian National Charter, which had called for the destruction of Israel. The occupied territories were divided into three zones: Areas included in Zone A were to come under the full control of the nascent PA. Those in Zone B were to be shared between the Israelis, who were to look after security, and the Palestinians, who were to take charge of civil affairs. Zone C areas, which included the Israeli settlements, were to remain under full Israeli control, which, however, did not extend to Palestinian civilians. These arrangements were to remain in force for five years, during which an overall settlement would be negotiated. The talks were to start no later than May 1996.

On September 13, 1993, with President Clinton looking on, Rabin, Peres, and Arafat ceremoniously concluded the agreement at the White House. At the last moment there was a hitch. Arafat, it turned out, had planned to come dressed as he always did, complete with *keffiye*, olive green uniform, and gun at the hip; it took the Americans some effort to persuade him to leave the last-mentioned item at home. Then it was time for Clinton to practice some maneuvers designed to make sure that Arafat would not kiss him and Rabin on the cheek, as Arab men often do. Rabin himself, in what was to prove the highlight of a long and honorable career, showed up in one of his usual ill-fitting suits. When the time came for him to add his signature, he pulled out a Pilot pen.

In much of the world, the reaction to the agreement was almost ecstatic. For some two and a half years after it was signed investors flooded Israel in search of real estate. As a result, prices went up by perhaps 60–70 percent and living standards rose to previously unattained heights. Some of the smaller and more extremist Palestinian organizations, such as Hamas (which was then in its infancy), the Islamic Jihad, and the Popular Front for the Liberation of Palestine rejected it in toto. However, the Palestinian man in the street seems to have welcomed it; certainly when Arafat arrived from Tunisia to take over he was given a rousing welcome. In Jerusalem the picture was equally mixed. The right, including Likud under its new leader, Benjamin Netanyahu, did what it could to convince the public that the agreements were the worst thing that had ever happened to Israel. As a result, the Knesset only ratified the agreement sixty-one to fifty, with eight abstentions, a far smaller majority than the one Begin had been able to muster when he made peace with Egypt. Yet one poll suggested that 60 percent of Israelis stood behind Rabin—which was more than he or his party ever got in elections.

Like the peace with Egypt that preceded it, the agreement was a brilliant success; a success for everything that was most rational, most patriotic, most peace loving, least fanatic in Israel. Over the next two years some further progress was made. The Palestinian National Council, a somewhat dubious body with uncertain membership, did in fact meet in Gaza and voted to modify the relevant clauses in the National Charter, albeit that some Israeli Orientalists later claimed that this was a mere charade. Honoring its commitments, Israel stopped building new settlements in the territories. However, since Rabin would not or could not stop the expansion of existing ones, the number of settlers continued to increase. Terrorism, now increasingly taking the form of suicide bombings, continued more or less as before. Yet if the Palestinians were to blame for this, the violence was not all on one side. In February 1994 an American-born religious settler by the name of Baruch Goldstein gunned down twenty-nine Muslims as they were praying in the Cave of the Patriarchs in Hebron. Immediately killing himself, to at least some of his fellow settlers he became a hero and saint.

Later in 1994 a peace treaty with Jordan was concluded. However, it did little to help solve the Palestinian problem. To the contrary, it was rooted partly in the fear both signatories had in common that any violence on either side of the Jordan River might rapidly cross to the other bank, too, and reflected a willingness to cooperate so as to prevent this from occurring. Nevertheless, the treaty did represent an important step on Israel's road to greater acceptance in the region. In particular, some of the Gulf States and Maghreb states now felt free to develop at least some kind of intergovernmental relationship with Jerusalem. In September 1995, following an agreement known as Oslo II, Israel gave the Palestinians self-rule in the towns of Bethlehem, Hebron, Jenin, Nablus, Qalqilya, Ramallah, and Tul Karem, as well as some 450 smaller settlements.

Having failed to stop Rabin, Likud and other right-wing opposition parties took their supporters into the streets. Posters of the prime minister, wearing a *keffiye* and/or dressed in an SS uniform, decorated many walls. During at least one demonstration people screamed "Death to Rabin"; Netanyahu, who was present, claimed he had seen and heard nothing. Rabin himself was unruffled, dismissing his rivals with a characteristic flick of the wrist. Reverting to the Palmach slang of his youth, he promised to "dry up the settlements" as if they were swamps and told the settlers "to revolve like propellers." He refused to take better care of his security, which anybody who ever attended a reception where he was present knew was very bad, or put on a bulletproof vest. Not so Lea, his wife of forty-seven years. Half crazed with worry, she watched over him like a hawk, eyes glaring, and sometimes behaved rather strangely as she did so.

The end came on the evening of November 4, 1995. To counter the

demonstrations in Jerusalem, an assembly was held in the square opposite Tel Aviv's municipal building. Rabin and Peres were invited as
the guests of honor. The prime minister was in an excellent mood. Normally he was shy almost to the point of seeming somewhat autistic, but
that night he lowered his defenses and was caught singing along with a
well-known Israeli songster, Miri Aloni. Under Shamir the song in
question, "A Song for Peace," had been prohibited. This meant that it
could only be broadcast by a privately owned station known as the
Voice of Peace, which was operating from a ship outside Israeli territorial waters. Even Peres, who had spent much of his career trying to
oppose Rabin and take his place, seemed reconciled with his "elder
brother," as he later called him at the funeral. As the assembly ended
and Rabin was returning to his car, he stopped to wait for his wife.
Three shots rang out, hitting him in the spine and causing his death
soon thereafter.

The assassin was twenty-five-year-old Yigal Amir. The totally unknown, skullcap-wearing scion of a right-wing religious family, he
studied law and computer science at Bar-Ilan University, a stronghold
of the NRP. His plan for killing the prime minister was carefully thought
out and well executed. Later the Shin Bet put some of his relatives and
acquaintances on trial, charging them with having known of the plan
and failing to do anything to prevent it from going ahead; given how
bad its own performance had been, the accusations are probably best
understood as an attempt to pass the buck. Having made no attempt to
plan his escape beyond (according to one account) shouting "blanks,
blanks," Amir himself was arrested on the spot. Later he was put on
trial, convicted, and sentenced to life in prison. There, serving his term
under exceptionally harsh and, in the eyes of many, cruel and unusual
conditions, he still remains.

Israeli members of the establishment and representatives of the
media almost always call Amir "the abhorrent murderer" (as if, from
Goldstein down, other murderers were less abhorrent). Much to their
chagrin, he has consistently refused to break down, apologize, express
regret, or beg for mercy. Repeatedly he has explained that he had nothing against Rabin personally—on the contrary, he always claimed to
have liked the man. Rather, he had acted as he did for purely idealistic

reasons. Both personally and politically, he felt, Rabin had what it took to give up part of the Land of Israel. By law of the Torah, as Amir interpreted it, he had to be stopped at all cost. Amir's act, and even more so his subsequent behavior, shows how determined and how brave an individual can be; but also, unfortunately, how misguided.

5

TRAGEDY, TRIUMPH, AND STRUGGLE (1995–PRESENT)

"This is a Different Government"

Rabin's murder was a major tragedy. Most Israelis greeted it, as well they might, with weeping, gnashing of teeth, and the lighting of candles in mournful memory of the dead prime minister. Miracle of miracles, a few on the right may even have engaged in soul searching; not concerning their goals, heaven forbid, but the possibility that their incitement—they had called Rabin a traitor—*might* have some limits after all. The funeral was as splendid as decorum allowed. Numerous world leaders were in attendance, providing living proof of how much store they had set by the man, the peace process he had initiated, and the country he had led. Clinton ended his eulogy with the Hebrew words *"shalom haver"* (good-bye, friend). On that occasion Lea Rabin refused to shake hands with Netanyahu. Served him right, a great many people thought.

The incoming prime minister was Shimon Peres. While few now remember the fact, during a large part of his career he was considered a hawk. Some even accused him of harboring fascist tendencies. It was only during the years after 1977, when he led the Labor opposition to Likud, that a different personality emerged.

Unlike most Israelis, Peres had never served in the IDF, a fact that his enemies, with Rabin at their head, did not allow him to forget. A civilian to the core, he was and remains a highly cultured man. Need-

ing far less sleep than most people, he spends many of his nights reading books. In his later years these qualities helped make him the darling
of foreign public opinion, especially in Europe. However, they turned
off many Israelis who felt that he was not really one of them—the same
kind of feeling that had earlier marked their attitude toward the equally
learned, and even more haughty, Abba Eban. To this, Peres added a
facial expression that sometimes made him look almost like a tired dog.
The gap that separated him from the sweaty, noisy Israeli public was
made glaringly obvious in the summer of 1996, not long after he lost
the elections in which Netanyahu defeated him. In a hall packed with
Labor Party members, he asked, excitedly and somewhat pathetically,
whether he was a loser. "Yes" came a mighty roar from the crowd.
Whereupon they deposed him as party leader; which did not prevent
the "indefatigable intriguer,"[1] as Rabin once called him, from being
elected president later on.

In one sense Peres was unfortunate. One of his first acts probably
turned out to be a bad error. In 1996, Peres ordered the assassination—
the term "targeted killing" had not yet been invented—of Yahya
Ayyash, aka the Engineer. Supposedly he was the technical mastermind
behind recent bombings. Wits claimed that when he and Rabin met
and exchanged views in the afterworld, they both thanked the security
service for their presence there—Ayyash because of what it had done,
Rabin because of what it had left undone. The Palestinian response was
to mount a number of suicide bus bombings in February–March 1996,
killing dozens of people. After that, the real wonder was not that Israelis refused to give their votes to Peres—following a recent change in
the law, this was the first time the prime minister was elected directly—
but that he was only defeated by a margin of less than 1 percent.

Would Rabin, had he lived, have been able to bring the peace process with the Palestinians to a successful conclusion? The best available
answer to this question is maybe. The subject has given rise to a considerable literature, and since no definite conclusions are possible I choose
not to enter upon it here. Yet two points are worth noting. First, the
attempt, even though it did not succeed and perhaps even assuming
that it could not have succeeded, was well worth making—for the
simple reason that talking is always better than shooting. Certainly it did
nothing to harm Israel's security. As long as it lasted it raised the country's

international standing, and its own self-image, to unprecedented heights. Second, if it did fail, then the blame rests not on one side but on both. On one hand the Palestinians, with Arafat at their head, did not do enough to stop terrorism. On the other, the Israelis never ceased settling the territories; when the settlers kept saying that "this tune cannot be halted" they proved all too right. Israel also committed acts such as those associated with the names Goldstein and Ayyash.

Netanyahu, who succeeded Peres in June, was a completely different kettle of fish. Just forty-seven years old, the first Israeli prime minister born after the establishment of the state, he was the son of a Revisionist intellectual who, because of his politics (so he claimed), had failed to get a position at the Hebrew University. Thereupon a disillusioned Benzion Netanyahu took his family to the United States, where the son spent much of his youth. It was in the United States, too, that he studied business administration at MIT. Indeed, in some ways he was as much of an American as he was an Israeli. Returning to Israel, he served in one of the IDF's elite units; his elder brother Jonathan ("Yoni") commanded at Entebbe in 1976 and was killed, a fact that did not prove to be without some benefit for Benjamin's subsequent career. Later he spent time working for a kitchen furniture company before joining the Ministry of Foreign Affairs. As Sharon once said, he was an "excellent propagandist"; it was not meant as a compliment.

In 1988 Netanyahu was elected to the Knesset as a member for Likud. Along with Olmert and Begin's son Benjamin, he was known as one of the party's "princes"; later he served in Shamir's cabinet. In Israel he is known above all for his wife, a former stewardess who is intensely disliked, and for the difficulty he has in separating truth from fiction. On one occasion he reminisced at length about a supposed former member of his cabinet who, in fact, had never held a portfolio in it.[2] An equally infamous characteristic is his luxurious, even ostentatious, lifestyle, so different from that of his two Likud predecessors as well as that of most Labor prime ministers before him.

Once in power, Netanyahu never tired of saying that "this is a different government." Being right wing, it also had a different agenda from its Labor predecessors. To make his point, in September 1996 he ordered some ancient passageways just west of the Temple Mount to be cleaned up and opened to the public. The outcry among the Muslim clergy, who under the terms of an arrangement first instituted by Dayan had stayed in charge of the Mount throughout the Israeli occupation, was immense. The result was widespread and very violent disturbances that ultimately left twelve Israeli soldiers and over eighty Palestinians dead. Later, by way of a half-hearted apology, Netanyahu explained that, having taken up his post as prime minister, it took him "a year and a half to understand where [he] was living," Israeli slang for coming to terms with his surroundings; looking back, one can only wish he had been a little more quick witted.

Though he never explicitly said so, he also all but halted the peace process. During his entire three-year period of office, the only progress made consisted of the Wye River Memorandum of October 1998. On that occasion Netanyahu, having come under heavy pressure by President Clinton and his secretary of state, Madeleine Albright, agreed to hand over another 13 percent of the occupied territories to the Palestinian Authority. In any case, even that modest step was never carried out. The paradox is that it was precisely during this period that terrorism reached its lowest point since the beginning of the intifada in 1987. Perhaps this could be taken as an indication that the peace process was not necessarily foredoomed; supposing a little more goodwill on Israel's side, the Palestinians might have been willing and able to play ball after all.

Feeling more secure than they had for years, tens if not hundreds of thousands of Israelis flocked to Jericho, where, only about half an hour's drive from Jerusalem, some Palestinian businessmen had set up a posh casino. Israelis, who are prevented by law from gambling in their own country, were able to do so here to their heart's content. Judging by the reactions to a popular satirical TV program that sported a puppet modeled after Arafat, many Israelis even started developing a sneaking affection for the Palestinian leader. Whatever he may have told his own people—one reason Netanyahu gave for failing to carry out his part of the Wye River Memorandum was because Palestinian "incitement" was not brought to an end—whenever he addressed Israelis he was all smiles.

As is so often the case when the security situation improves, the Israeli public tended to leave well enough alone. "Eat, drink, and gamble" was the motto. Right-wing nationalists were, of course, happy with the situation. But even most of those in the middle of the political spectrum saw no urgent need to speed up the peace process so as to forestall another intifada. In any case Netanyahu's downfall, when it came, had little to do with foreign policy. In part it was due to his bad relations with the media; as he once quipped, had he walked the water as Jesus did, the papers would have said he couldn't swim. Much more important, the law under which he had been elected, instead of strengthening the position of the prime minister as intended, turned out to weaken it. By separating him from his party, it enabled people to choose the leader of their choice while at the same time casting their votes for all kinds of sectarian interests. The numerous small parties thus created, including the new "Russian" ones, vied with one another in demanding benefits for their followers. When they failed to get their way they saw nothing wrong with bringing down the coalition, leaving the prime minister high and dry.

Netanyahu's own successor was Ehud Barak. Born in 1942, he was a protégé of Rabin who recognized his abilities early on and saw to it that he should enter the fast track. A commando famous, among other things, for his ability to pick locks, he was the most decorated soldier in the entire history of the IDF and rose to serve as its chief of staff. At one stage in his career he commanded the unit in which Netanyahu had served as an officer. During the election campaign he used this fact to claim, repeatedly, that "Netanyahu [was] unsuitable" for the prime minister's slot. In reality they were like Tweedledee and Tweedledum. Barak ran on a platform of "Peace and security"; equally original, Netanyahu's slogan was "Security and peace." In any event, Tweedledee won.

Again, the fact that he won had something to do with sectarian politics. One of Likud's best-known politicians had long been David Levi, a former construction worker from the development town of Beth Shean. A follower of Begin whose rhetorical style he imitated, he rose by the skin of his teeth and was considered the representative of the "Second" (i.e., Oriental) Israel. In trouble with his own party, which he felt did not recognize his true worth, Levi allowed Barak to draw him to Labor's side. How much he really contributed to the electoral victory over Netanyahu is not clear—at the time, some people compared him with a second-hand car, still running but not worth a great deal. Nevertheless, the alliance showed that some Orientals were no longer as resolutely opposed to the Ashkenazi Labor Party as they had been over the last generation or so. Looking beyond politics, perhaps one may see here an early sign that the rift between the different ethnic groups, on which Begin in particular had built much of his career, was no longer as deep as it had been.

Levi's own reward was the foreign affairs portfolio. It was a post he had held twice before, first under Shamir in 1990–1992 and then under Netanyahu. It enabled him to show off—again following Begin, he always wore suits and was forever buttoning and unbuttoning his jacket—without really carrying heavy responsibility; in Israel, the Ministry of Foreign Affairs has rarely been able to compete with the real heavyweights, such as the Ministry of Defense and the Ministry of Finance. The fact that he knew no English (though he did know French) did not help, and was one reason why he became the butt of many jokes. One had him licking a computer; asked what he was doing, he explained that he was IBM-compatible (in Hebrew, the terms "to taste" and "compatible" are similar).

More important, Barak himself also proved a disappointment. He was reputed to be extremely intelligent, but in public he came across as coldhearted, arrogant, and lacking in charisma. He did not have Dayan's knack of expressing himself in what, superficially at least, was simple, straightforward language; instead, engaging in complex intellectual constructs, he seemed to test reality by theory instead of the other way around. His fellow Laborites, with more than half a century of socialism behind them, disliked his total lack of interest in social problems. His collaborators resented his tendency to *tout savoir, tout pouvoir, tout faire.* The phrase used to be applied to Napoléon I, with whom, owing among other things to his small stature, Barak was often compared.

Having entered office Barak was seized by travel mania. He was constantly flying around the world, meeting all sorts of leaders but achieving very little. At home, two important problems demanded his attention. The first was the war in southern Lebanon. It had been dragging on continuously for seventeen years—thirty-one, if one starts counting in 1968, the year when the first terrorist acts got under way—and was claiming about one Israeli life every two weeks on average.

Assisted by Iran, which was said to provide it with $100–150 million worth of aid annually, Hezbollah proved a much tougher nut to crack than any of its predecessors had been. It was well organized, well trained, and well equipped. It had an excellent intelligence service and, above all, very high motivation. In time it also showed that it knew how to use the media, filming its fighters' attacks on Israeli strongholds and broadcasting them around the world.

What didn't the IDF, and behind it Israel, do to deal with Hezbollah? Now it escalated hostilities; now it held its fire in the hope that the enemy would follow suit. Now it attacked; now it remained largely on the defense. Using the world's most advanced fighter-bombers and attack helicopters, it bombed and strafed. Using the world's best commando units, or so many people thought, it conducted raids and mounted ambushes and fought countless skirmishes in the mountainous, vegetation-covered south Lebanese terrain. Brilliant intelligence enabled it to kidnap several key Hezbollah leaders and make them prisoners. It constructed strongholds so well fortified that they could resist anything except, perhaps, a small nuclear bomb, and stocked them with so much ammunition that it could not be evacuated when the time came. It used sixty-ton tanks as well as the world's most powerful armored personnel carriers. Always on call were regiments of heavy artillery and missile boats capable of hitting coastal targets. It raised and organized and equipped and trained local militias that supported it in its battle. All this in trying to cope with a rather small guerrilla organization that probably did not count more than fifteen hundred fighters at any one time; and also one that never deployed anything more powerful than Katyusha rockets, antitank missiles, mines, and every kind of small arm.

To outsiders, approximately 25 dead per year may not seem like an excessive price to pay by a military that, in peacetime, numbers around 150,000 uniformed personnel and that was, after all, defending an important part of the country's population against terrorism. Most Israelis, though, came to think otherwise. As the 1990s drew to an end, a group known as Four Mothers organized opposition to the occupation of southern Lebanon. They derived their mission from the fact that, in Israel, to be the mother of a serving combat soldier means forever looking out for the so-called Job-Patrol (a group made up of an officer, a doctor, and a rabbi whose mission is to inform families that their dearest are no more) to knock on the door; that, too, is part of the price that being "a free people in [one's] own country" entails.

The movement's members gathered signatures and held regular demonstrations. Too often, their reward was to be spat upon and even beaten up; one high-ranking army commander, forgetting who it was who provided him and his ilk with cannon fodder, even called them "the four rags." Later the cause was embraced, not to say hijacked, by Yossi Beilin, now a Knesset member representing the left-wing Meretz (Élan) Party. A year after entering office Barak put an end to the agony, so to speak, by taking the IDF out of Lebanon. As one would expect from so capable a soldier—Barak, incidentally, also held the defense portfolio—militarily the retreat was a minor masterpiece. Not one Israeli soldier was killed, not one usable piece of equipment or stronghold left behind. As the Israelis abandoned their positions, spectacular explosions demolished every bunker. At the time, the move was widely, though not universally, hailed.

Though the border did not calm down completely, from then on there was only one incident every three or four months on the average, far fewer than before. Probably fewer rounds were fired in a year than there used to be in a week. This relative quiet enabled Barak to focus on fulfilling his major promise, namely, resuming the peace process with the Palestinians so as to finally resolve that long-festering conflict. Seven years had passed since the first Oslo Accords, and Arafat and the Palestinians were becoming understandably impatient. On the other hand, the timing appeared favorable. Terrorism had picked up a bit since Netanyahu's departure but was still a fairly minor concern. Barak knew that in President Clinton, who was now entering the last months of his term and would like to leave with a resounding success, Israel had a friend it could count on to help.

It was not to be. In July 2000, at Camp David, the two sides failed to reach an agreement. Again, there is little point in trying to find out who was to blame; in all probability, both parties were. The Israelis considered their own offer very generous. Clinton even praised Barak for his "enormous courage" in putting it on the table.[3] Yet it did not include the Jordan Valley, which was to be leased to Israel for a period of 999 years, no less. It did not give the Palestinians territorial contiguity in the West Bank (since the Jewish neighborhoods in East Jerusalem were to remain in Israeli hands), nor control over water resources, nor even control over the air over the West Bank. The Palestinians, on their part, behaved in such a way as to cast some doubt on their readiness to give Israelis access to the holy places once those were handed back to them. Even more critically, they refused to give up the refugees' "right of return"—a refusal that Israelis, not without reason, saw as a prelude to the destruction of their state.

When Arafat met Clinton for the last time in January 2001, he tried to assuage the outgoing president by telling him what a great man he was. "Mr. Chairman," Clinton replied, "I am not a great man; I am a failure, and you have made me so."[4] By that time, Arafat himself apparently was no longer in full command of his faculties. He had suffered injuries in an air crash a few years earlier, from which he never quite recovered; when he died in 2004, it was claimed that he had had AIDS.

As to Barak, in 2000 he had managed to alienate both the hawks, who felt that he had tried to give away far too much, and the doves, who felt that he had not given enough. Crestfallen, he returned to Israel, where almost the only person waiting at the airport was his wife Nava (Comely). In front of the cameras she welcomed him with a loving hug; her reward, not long thereafter, was to be discarded in favor of an old flame.

By the late summer of that year, Barak's coalition was tottering. He tried to rally his supporters by promising to carry out a "secular revolution"; given that Israel has never succeeded in really ridding itself of what some called "Shas control," meaning not just that of Shas but of the rabbis in general, he might as well have promised the moon. Understandably, after seven years during which nothing happened, the Palestinians got tired of waiting. Perhaps less understandably, Barak, at a dinner party with Sharon, gave his consent to the latter's proposed visit to the Temple Mount. Since 1967 the Mount had been the scene of repeated clashes, many of them very violent, as police battled both extremist Jews, who insisted on their God-given right to pray there, and Muslim worshippers who tried to prevent them from doing so.

Sharon at that time was seventy-two years old. After 1983, when the Kahan Commission officially censured him, he had found himself in a sort of political limbo. Often he occupied important ministerial posts as a Likud member, but he never really succeeded in reentering the inner council. In 1989 he published his autobiography, *Warrior,* a supremely interesting book that, for some reason, he never allowed to be translated into Hebrew. Repeatedly he had sought a way to make a comeback, but just as repeatedly he had failed. He must have felt that it was now or never; time was clearly running out.

The visit, which took place on September 28, lit the fuse for the second intifada, also known as the Al Aqsa Intifada after one of the mosques on the Temple Mount. Sharon himself later claimed that "this has nothing to do with me." Whether he really believed that is, to put it mildly, a little doubtful; it is, however, true that a day before, an Israeli policeman was killed by his Palestinian partner with whom he was on a joint patrol. From Jerusalem the disturbances quickly spread all over the West Bank and the Gaza Strip. Though there were some demonstrations, complete with the usual use of edged weapons and Molotov cocktails, on the whole the character of the uprising differed from the previous one. Much more use was made of firearms, partly because the Israelis, acting under the terms of the Oslo Accords, had given the PA some weapons; this was supposed to help the Palestinians, who maintained no fewer than seventeen different police and "security" forces, control the population and prevent terrorism. Over the next few months both sides fired millions of bullets at each other. However, on both sides the fire was extremely inaccurate. There were casualties, but it would be hard to find another struggle in which so much ammunition was expended to so little effect.

Much worse was to follow. Desperate attempts by Clinton and Barak to reach a cease-fire and renew the Camp David talks led nowhere. Whether this was because Arafat did not want to cooperate or because he was already losing control to a younger generation of activists such as Mahmoud Dahlan and Marwan Barghouti is not clear. Meanwhile, the Palestinians deployed a series of suicide bombers. Of course, suicide bombers were nothing new in the Middle East. Earlier, both Israel and the U.S. Marines that Reagan sent to Lebanon in 1983—to train the Lebanese Army, he said—had gotten a taste of what they could do. It was in terms of the frequency of the attacks that the second intifada differed from the first. Providing additional proof of the Palestinians' determination to liberate themselves, some of the attacks were carried out by women.

As already mentioned, Barak had made his name as a commando, always ready to carry out the Biblical commandment of "By trickery shalt thou make war."[5] This time, though, his response was surprisingly heavy-handed. To cope with the Palestinians firing from the outskirts of Bethlehem at Gilo, a nearby Jerusalem neighborhood, he brought up tanks with their 120 millimeter guns and blasted the homes from which the bullets came to pieces. To destroy Palestinian headquarters, etc., he sent in attack helicopters and fighter-bombers. For the first time since 1967, too, the IDF used armored personnel carriers in the territories— considering all this, one might have thought that, rather than reflecting the "brilliant success" of Israeli rule, they constituted a war zone. Most of the targets that were hit were empty, either because the Israelis had issued advance warnings or because the Palestinians, not requiring much foresight to realize what was going to happen, evacuated them. Among other buildings, the aforementioned casino in Jericho was thoroughly demolished. Needless to say, all this did little to stop the suicide bombings.

In March 2001, following a special election for prime minister in which Sharon beat him, Barak resigned. Since the intifada had started five months earlier he had barely functioned, now taking harsh countermeasures, now talking about a ceasefire. Often he issued orders in the morning only to cancel them that very evening; the impression he gave was that he did not know what he was doing even when he was doing nothing. Of him it might be said what Oliver Cromwell had told the Long Parliament in 1660 and what Leo Amery had told Neville Chamberlain in May 1940. "You have sat too long here for any good you have been doing. Depart, I say, and let us have done with you. In the name of God, go."[6] Yet Sharon had no better idea for how to cope with the uprising than his predecessor, and the only ones who did not know it were those who soon found out. Talking to the new American secretary of state, Colin Powell, who was visiting the region, all he could think to say was that "the Palestinians have to absorb [blows]."[7]

The most powerful blow of all was struck in April 2002. The IDF chief of staff at that time was General Shaul Mofaz (1948–). Like Sharon, he was a tough paratrooper. He did not, however, have Sharon's sense of humor, and indeed few people have ever seen him smile; to the Arabs, he was known as "Rambo." He and Sharon prepared a large-scale operation in the West Bank, reoccupying zones A and B. A particularly important target was the city of Jenin; as so often, the intent was to crush the proverbial head of the snake. Also as so often, the attempt was only a qualified success. Some Palestinian fighters were killed, injured, and captured. Some bomb laboratories were discovered, and a large number of houses demolished so as to open up thoroughfares by which the IDF's vehicles could move into the center of the town. But none of this made much difference to the real problem, namely, the kind of terrorism that is carried out by small groups, in a decentralized manner, and covertly. In retrospect, perhaps the best thing that can be said about the operation is that, according to a subsequent UN investigation, far fewer people were killed in it than the Palestinians, seeking to prove how cruel and inhumane their enemies were, claimed at the time.

While the media around the world fell over each other in denouncing Israel for its operation in Jenin, the suicide bombers kept coming. Some places were not as hard-hit as others; none, though, was completely safe. Settlers inside the West Bank came under attack by Palestinians, hardly ever more than two or three in number, who shot up cars or tried to enter settlements so as to kill as many people as possible by means of small arms and hand grenades. Jewish settlements in the Gaza Strip came under mortar fire and also made the acquaintance of the first small, primitive Qassam rockets. Rural settlements near the pre-1967 border suffered badly from thieves and robbers. Operating at night, they made off with anything they could take with them—cars, agricultural machinery, and the like—and occasionally killed or wounded those who tried to disturb them in their work. Coastal cities such as Tel Aviv, Haifa, Hadera, and Netanya were all repeatedly bombed. Worst of all was the situation in Jerusalem, where some six hundred thousand people, about one-third of them Arabs, lived in close proximity to each other.

To the few people who kept arriving—there were times when Tel Aviv airport had more security guards than passengers, and many foreign aircrews were afraid to spend their nights in Israel—the country presented a strange spectacle. There were few external signs of damage. Following long experience, if there is anything the Israeli authorities and public have become good at, it is in quickly removing all signs of terrorist attacks. First, special teams known as ZAKA (short for "disaster victim identification") and made up of Orthodox men who consider their work a religious commandment appear on the scene, gather the dead, put the injured in ambulances, and often literally scrape up human remains before putting them in plastic bags. Next, municipal crews immediately start repairing the damage or, if it cannot be done on the spot, conceal it behind some kind of awning. Very often it is only a question of hours before life returns to normal, as the saying goes. While burying the dead and, above all, taking care of the wounded, takes longer, it does not attract nearly as many TV crews.

As the situation grew worse, a society noted mainly for the noisy, bustling life that it normally led was enveloped in an eerie calm. Some people took care to avoid buses. They refused to ride them or pass them while driving or even to stand near the stops. Others peered at passersby while trying to figure out whether they might double as bombs. Bars, restaurants, movie houses, even shopping centers and markets where people bought their food, were half deserted; the fact that catering services working for the really well-to-do were able to increase sales by bringing food to their customers' houses was scant consolation. Many businesses were forced to close. Others kept going, more or less, by hiring security guards. While the guards subjected customers to perfunctory searches, quite often they themselves became the first victims of terrorist attacks. Though the number of casualties was never very large—even during the peak year of 2003, far more Israelis died in traffic accidents than by terrorism—the whole of daily life seemed to slow down; it was as if a man accustomed to walking on land was suddenly forced to do so in water. Contributing to the effect were frequent roadblocks set up by the police in their search for terrorists. Each time they did so, the result was monumental traffic jams.

To aggravate the situation, this was when the high-tech bubble of the 1990s burst. Along with the intifada, this event decreased the GDP by 5 percent annually over a period of three years. As unemployment rose to 11–12 percent, per capita income fell even more. Immigration, which during the 1990s had helped create a consumer boom, ceased, and long lines made up of people seeking passports formed in front of foreign consulates. Perhaps worst of all, Israel's international credit rating, critically important for a county that has always relied on loans to cover its foreign currency deficit, suffered badly. At the time, the minister of finance was a small-time, rather conceited Likud politician by the name of Silvan Shalom. His solution to the problem was to travel the world and beg the bankers not to lower the rating further still. As so often, they threatened to remove the umbrella just when it was needed most.

By that time Israelis were ready to do almost anything to end the bombings. By some polls, before the second intifada broke out only about 7 percent fantasized about the right-wing extremist "solution" of "transferring" the Palestinians, i.e., throwing them across the border as had happened during the 1948 War. Now, almost half did. Others demanded that the government construct a wall between Israel and the occupied territories. In fact, it was this author who first proposed this solution, later known as "ingathering," at a Command and Staff College meeting in the spring of 1988—with the result that, during the next two decades, he was not invited again.

During his term as prime minister, Barak did in fact consider the possibility of dealing with terrorism by building a wall, but the idea failed to make it through the cabinet. What he, and after him Sharon, did do was surround the Gaza Strip with a security fence. To the untrained eye the fence looks fragile, almost innocent, no more than some wires strung between poles. Yet so effective are the various means by which it is backed up that, since it has been completed, the only human bomb package that has succeeded in getting through did so because its two members carried British passports. But whereas the Strip is a relatively small piece of land that contains few if any holy or historical sites, the West Bank is a completely different matter. The border is much longer, the topography more difficult. Sites with religious significance abound. Most important of all, whereas the area bordering the Strip is thinly settled, decades of occupation have created a situation where, in many places along the West Bank, Jewish and Arab settlements are so closely entwined that separating them is practically impossible.

By late 2003, nevertheless, there was overwhelming public pressure to bring the suicide bombings to an end. First Sharon's deputy, Ehud

Olmert, and then the prime minister himself started talking about "physically separating" the territories from Israel. As always in Israel, no sooner was the plan put forward than it gave rise to much opposition. Left-wingers, noisily supported by a motley crew of professional international do-gooders with time to spare and other people's money behind them, claimed that the plan was cruel and harsh on the poor Palestinians. Right-wingers, both religious and secular, feared it because they believed it would mean drawing up a border and, eventually, giving up much if not all of the territories. Both sides had in common that they put their own ideology, be it left-wing humanism or right-wing nationalism or religion, ahead of anything else. If that meant that the bloodshed—on both sides, nota bene—should continue, then they were always ready with a supply of crocodile tears.

Since the mid-1990s, when their influence peaked, Israel's left wing had been losing support. Perhaps understandably, the outbreak of the second intifada caused many of their voters to look elsewhere; the way those voters saw it, attempts at negotiating a solution had reached a dead end. The rest of the left constituted a small minority that did their own cause a lot of damage by mixing it with others such as women's rights, gay people's rights, and the like. They fumed and they sputtered, but so far the most they have been able to achieve is to convince the Supreme Court to force the government to move the wall which is now under construction somewhat closer to the pre-1967 border, a most welcome change. But whereas the left was impotent, the fears of the right proved to be well founded. Starting in early 2004, Sharon did in fact come up with a fully fledged plan for "disengaging"—as he called the withdrawal—from the Gaza Strip as well as much of the West Bank. This was the man who, since at least 1974, had been more closely identified with the settlements, as well as a harsh, right-wing policy line, than anyone else. Critics accused him of planning to commit "politicide" on the Palestinians; at some points in his career, the charge may well have contained more than a grain of truth.[8]

Soon after taking over as prime minister, Sharon at one point said he would be no de Gaulle.[9] Just what made him change his mind we do not know, nor, given his subsequent fate, are we ever likely to do so. Most probably it was a mixture of immediate security considerations and long-term demographic concerns; Israelis have long been afraid of what "the Arab womb" (Gaza birthrates in particular are the highest in the world) might do. When he came up with his plan, predictably, the outcome was a storm of opposition not merely among the extreme right but inside his own party. Secular opponents called him a liar and a turncoat. Religious ones held a ceremony known as "a fiery pulse." As one of them described it, "Twenty men, married and over forty years old, went to the grave of the Patriarch Joseph, where they purified themselves in a ritual bath. Next they put on black clothes and begged God's evil angels [literally, "sabotaging angels"] to kill Ariel Sharon ASAP." According to their creed, participating in the ceremony was itself not without danger; still, one of their number said, he was "prepared to risk his life so that Sharon might die."[10] Ten years earlier Rabin had been targeted by a similar ceremony. We need not follow those who believed, as no doubt they still do, that the charm did its work; still, there is no doubt that Sharon's decision took courage uncommon among either politicians or ordinary men.

More important still, the fact that he succeeded in passing his plan through the Knesset speaks volumes for the real inclinations of the Israeli people. It was not the first time they were faced with such a choice. Similar situations had arisen before and may, if the country is very lucky, arise in the future as well. The first time something of the kind happened was in 1937, when the British Peel Commission offered the Jewish community a ministate comprising just 10 percent of the country. The second was in 1947, when the UN voted to give them half of it (but without Jerusalem). The third was in 1979, when it was a question of surrendering the Sinai and, with it, what many thought was a pillar of national security; and the fourth in 1993, when Rabin, supported by a strong if not overwhelming majority, signed the Oslo Accords.[11] Each time, there was bitter opposition on the part of hard-liners who felt that achieving less than all their demands was tantamount to treachery and did whatever they could to put obstacles in the way. Yet each time, the majority gave their approval—as they did on this occasion, too.

As to Sharon, at the time he was felled by a stroke in January 2006 he was more popular than he had ever been in his career. From the brutal bulldozer whom many people feared, he seemed transformed into a smiling, almost avuncular, figure. His bulk, which had long been the target of bitter comments, seemed to help that image. In 2005, as Likud was torn apart by supporters and opponents of the "disengagement" plan, he left it and quickly set up a new party known as Kadima. According to the polls, it was poised to win the scheduled elections by a large margin and would have no trouble setting up a coalition. When the news of his incapacitation came, Israelis familiar with Walt Whitman could only recite his poem:

> O Captain! my Captain! our fearful trip is done;
> The ship has weathered every rack, the prize we sought is won,
> The port is near, the bells I hear, the people all exulting,
> While follow eyes the steady keel, the vessel grim and daring;
>   But O heart! heart! heart!
>   O the bleeding drops of red,
>   Where on the deck my Captain lies,
>   Fallen cold and dead.

Since the summer of 2005, when the settlements in the Gaza Strip were evacuated, not one suicide bomber has succeeded in reaching Israel from that territory. It is true that the surrounding region has become the target of thousands of mortar rounds and rockets. However, these incidents began as long ago as 2002, when the Strip was still under occupation. The volume of fire would probably have continued to grow even if the withdrawal had never been carried out, and casualties among the IDF troops trying to police the area would have been much higher. That these instruments of war, and the members of the various terrorist organizations who fire or launch them, made civilian life in the town of Sderot and the neighboring kibbutzim in the region very unpleasant indeed is undeniable. Still, it should be kept in mind that, during all these years, the total number of Israeli dead that resulted did not equal that which, at the height of the second intifada, fell victim to a single suicide bombing; since early 2009, in any case, the barrage has all but come to an end.

Though the intifada has never been officially ended—in April 2008 the toll stood at 1,053 Israeli and 4,789 Palestinian dead[12]—in the country as a whole, terrorism has declined. Probably Arafat's death in 2004, and his replacement by the relatively moderate Mahmoud Abbas, had something to do with the process. Whatever the new man may be, he is not a crook. Another reason is because the fall of Saddam Hussein led to a sharp cut in the flow of money he used to pay terrorists and their relatives—as much as $25,000 for the family of a suicide bomber. In large part, though, it was because Israeli countermeasures have at long last begun to prove effective.

Specifically, the roadblocks that (assuming people are allowed to pass at all) can turn the fifteen-minute car journey from Ramallah to Jerusalem into a two-hour nightmare have become infamous the world over. Not by accident do they form the focus of Palestinian complaints; not by accident, too, does the IDF seem to set up new ones every time some "goodwill gesture" to the Palestinians leads to a few old ones being pulled down. The advantages of roadblocks, a tactic that goes back at least as far as 1970, when Sharon used them to crush an uprising in Gaza, are simple. When terrorists are prevented from traveling they are forced to communicate by other means, mainly electronic ones. Yet electronic communications can be intercepted and, given the necessary expertise, deciphered. Compared to other Western intelligence services that have tried their hands at this game, those of Israel enjoy the immense advantage of being able to draw on a large community of Arabic speakers. While other factors are also involved, "that is where the dog is buried" (that's the point), as the Hebrew proverb says.

The most important roadblock of all is the wall itself, along with the complex array of security apparatus that supports it. Though it remains incomplete, many of its sections are twice as high as the Berlin Wall used to be. As used to be the case in Berlin, by preventing all communication between people on both sides, it minimizes friction; if an incident does take place, then it is more easily contained than would otherwise be the case. Unfortunately the wall does not run along the old border, as in this author's view it should have (except in Jerusalem). Unfortunately, too, it inflicts considerable suffering on the Palestinian population and, in particular, people who live close to it. Still, it has largely achieved its aim. It has also helped Israel, which as recently as 2003 looked to many people as if it had reached the end of its tether, to make a spectacular recovery from the intifada. It is to that recovery that we must now turn our attention.

"A New Face in the Mirror"

While the intifada, strongly supported by the international high-tech bust, broke the prosperity that had characterized Israel during much of the 1990s, the interruption proved temporary. Much of the credit for this belongs to Netanyahu, whom Sharon appointed minister of finance when he formed his second cabinet early in 2003. Netanyahu's own preference was for the Ministry of Foreign Affairs, where he would have carried less responsibility and had more fun traveling the world; indeed, it is possible that, in all but ordering him to take the treasury, Sharon's intention was to bring down his most important rival within Likud. In any case, Netanyahu rolled up his sleeves and went to work.

The list of measures that were put into effect over the next two years is, indeed, an impressive one. The national airline, El Al; the national shipping company Zim; the telecommunications company Bezek; and one of the three leading banks were all privatized. Ownership over the ports of Haifa and Ashdod was passed from the government to public companies so as to encourage competition between them. Income taxes and social security payments were cut, a move that benefited high-income groups in particular. To stimulate demand, tariffs on imported goods were also reduced. The Histadrut's bankrupt pension funds were consolidated and sold, though not before their members were made to give up some of their benefits in return for having the rest safeguarded.

Whereas these measures represented the carrot, the stick consisted of reduced benefits. The main losers were the unemployed and nonworking married women—some of whom were thus forced to leave the home and take up what paid work they could find. Another group that lost out were single mothers (Israel, like all developed countries, has very few single fathers, and those few do not get nearly as many benefits as their female counterparts do). One of the mothers in question, a woman named Vicky Knafo, started a protest march against the cuts in her "salary," as she called it. For a few weeks she was able to gain much media attention, but later the movement collapsed.

Above all, child allowances were reduced very sharply. First introduced by Rabin in the 1970s in order to alleviate the worst poverty among Orientals in particular, the allowances had been steadily growing until they came to hang like an albatross around the government's, and the taxpayers', necks. The cut in child allowances hit, as indeed it was designed to do, two groups in particular: Israeli Arabs on one hand, Orthodox Jews on the other. In the case of the former the intention, though it was never expressed in so many words, was to bring down the number of children born and reduce "the demographic danger." In the case of the latter it was to force people who had spent their lives praying and studying the Talmud to start working for the first time.

Though Netanyahu had never been an independent businessman, like many Likud activists he had a business background. Accordingly, scant wonder that his measures differed little from those his predecessors had been trying to implement for at least two decades; they were, indeed, broadly similar to those adopted in much of the developed world from the 1980s on. Where he did differ was that he, and of course Sharon, had behind them a very unusual coalition that for once did not depend on the religious Orthodox voice for its majority. In addition to Likud, the coalition consisted of Labor—which, in truth, had long shed most of its socialist trappings—and a smaller party by the name of Shinui (Change). Led by a big-mouthed former journalist by the name of Tommy Lapid, Shinui focused on mobilizing, not to say inciting, the secular vote against the religious Orthodox population. For a time the tactic was highly successful. Unfortunately, owing mainly to squabbles inside the party, it did not last.

While each separate step Netanyahu took was small, together they formed a giant leap for Israel. To use the title of a novel by Dayan's daughter, Yael, looking into the mirror, the country saw a new face.[13] The combination of socialism and paternalism that had characterized Israel since long before it got its independence had all but disappeared. With a few important exceptions, such as subsidies to some basic foodstuffs, health insurance, and higher education, people were increasingly forced to stand on their own feet. Yet even these fields were affected—as is proved, among other things, by the great growth of private medicine on one hand and the creation of at least one fully private university on the other. The battle has by no means been decided. As of late 2009, Shas and Agudat Israel were trying their best to turn back the clock and restore the child allowances in particular. If they get their way, their supporters will once again be able to be "strengthened in their faith" (as the saying goes) at others' expense. Yet by making their children study Torah instead of high tech they perpetuate their own poverty; hence, one can only hope they will not succeed.

Ever since capitalism took over in the early nineteenth century, one of its main characteristics has always been the pattern of boom and bust. In Israel the boom that got under way in 2004–2005 will not last forever; meanwhile, though, its achievements have been extremely impressive. Starting as a desperately poor "developing" country whose main, indeed almost only, saleable product consisted of oranges, Israel during the sixty years of its existence has been able to increase exports eleven thousand (!) times, in nominal terms. As one might expect, a very visible outcome of the change has been the disappearance of the orange groves, because the land on which they stood was sold to developers. The country has a per capita GDP of $26,000 (ppp [purchasing power parity] 28,000).[14] At a time when oil prices are at an all-time high, this figure is well ahead of the corresponding Saudi one. Not merely is Israel among the twenty or so richest countries in the world, but it is poised to join OECD. It is true that the shekel is still not freely traded on the international currency markets. Nevertheless, as *Haaretz* was able to crow in June 2008, it has turned into "the strongest currency on earth."[15] All this and more has been achieved in the face of truly formidable obstacles, including, in spite of the progress made with Egypt and Jordan, the most important obstacle of all: namely, the absence of peace.

As is so often the case, change came at a cost. Israel's welfare state, though comprehensive, had always been rather elementary. It never offered its beneficiaries much more than their elementary needs; "the poor man's bread," to quote the *Hagada,* the book of prayers that is read on Passover eve. Partly because so much of it was taken down, and partly because the ruling capitalist ideology dictated that the state help the strong rather than the weak, the distribution of property and income became much less egalitarian. Israel shed its reputation as a country where, to make a small fortune, one had to have a large one first. Instead it began to produce and attract billionaires. Many billionaires started by founding high-tech companies. Later they sold them to foreign corporations—a good example being Stef Wertheimer, whose company, Iscar—which produces sophisticated blades for jet engines—was taken over by Warren Buffet. Unfortunately they also included the kind who, following the collapse of the Soviet Union and attracted by Israel's lax banking laws, originally instituted to help immigrants bring in their money, made their money by unkosher means.

While money abounds, considerable segments of the population continue to live in poverty. Yet three things need to be said about this. First, as of 2003 the difference in gross income between the highest and lowest 10 percent stood at 22:1. This is hardly a great change since 1966, when a left-wing economist put it at *"twenty to one"* (emphasis in the original);[16] if, at that time, Israel was an egalitarian society, then this was mainly because, by the standards of other developed countries, even the "rich" were in reality quite poor. Second, to the extent that the gap has widened, this is a phenomenon that Israel shares with other developed countries; after all, it was Netanyahu who imitated Thatcher and Reagan, not the other way around. What is more, it is a gap that most economists consider either a cause of growth, or a consequence of it, or both.

Third, and as is also the case in other developed countries, some of the poverty is concentrated among single mothers. About 10 percent of single mothers are widows. The rest are either divorcées, as the above-mentioned Ms. Knafo was, or women who have volunteered to rear their children without male support. To that extent, their poverty is self-inflicted; in Israel as in other developed countries, about two-thirds of all divorces are initiated by women. The same is true of the much larger Orthodox population, both Ashkenazi and Sephardi. As Ovadia Yosef's stated objective—"to restore lost laurels"—indicates, they simply refuse to join the modern world. In doing so, they are encouraged by the rabbis, who are afraid lest their flock will desert them. In fact, the percentage of Orthodox Jews living in poverty is higher than that of either Muslim or Christian Arabs[17]—which makes one wonder whether the constant cry of "discrimination" is really justified. The situation of many Israeli Arabs is similar. Held prisoner by their villages and their clans, they, too, turn their backs on the modern world and everything it entails. They, too, have leaders, in the form of Islamic fundamentalists, who do whatever they can to keep them as backward and as ignorant as they possibly can.

As already indicated, compared to what Israelis had been used to, the new world they were now building was in many ways cold, competitive, and harsh. It was, however, also one in which opportunities abounded as never before and which was prepared to bestow extraordinary rewards on the young, the talented, the hardworking, and the successful. Opening the gates to talent involved many steps, and entailed many possible consequences, only a few of which can be discussed here. One of the most important was to make foreign travel more accessible. Under Rabin the travel tax was abolished for the second and, one hopes, the last time. Though the need for comprehensive security has prevented the opening of the market, which makes the prices of airline tickets remain relatively high, foreign travel underwent a dramatic increase. Tel Aviv airport was rebuilt to cope with the expansion, but just a few years later it was again bursting at the seams. Thanks largely to the peace with Jordan, for the first time the terminal acquired a corridor with the sign PASSENGERS IN TRANSIT. Thus, the old situation whereby Israel was a cul-de-sac was finally coming to an end, albeit very, very slowly.

Israel has never been a totalitarian dictatorship. Still, Ben Gurion's strong paternalist legacy, the extensive powers invested in military censorship, and the fact that the borders were closed and friendly countries far away could not but have had a constraining effect on the public's right to know. In the 1980s, prodded by the courts, military censorship began relaxing its hold; however, it was in 1990 that the really critical step was taken. As cable television arrived, it enabled Israeli viewers to welcome foreign stations such as CNN (now, following a financial dispute, no longer available), FOX News, BBC, ITV, and others into their living rooms. Soon French, German, and Russian stations were added— Israel, after all, has an extremely heterogeneous population—and those who wanted to could watch Arabic stations, too.

Inside Israel a commercial station joined the two existing government-controlled ones. The outcome was to increase diversity. Ferociously competing with one another, the media publish the news regardless of whether it is fit to print and are always ready to cast the first stone. True, most people still do not get the choice American and European viewers expect—instead of hundreds of stations they are likely to receive only a few dozen. To close the gap, many Israelis have taken to surfing the Net. With 7 computers per 100 people, Israel leads the world. The runner-up, Canada, only manages 5.2.[18]

The city that benefited most from these changes was Tel Aviv. Including various satellite cities, which are often so fused with it as to make it impossible to distinguish the borders between them, the region known as Gush Dan numbers approximately three million people, or about 40 percent of the total population. Tel Aviv itself has a small Orthodox minority, whereas the satellite town of Bnei Brak is entirely "black" (as Israelis say, recalling the way members of that minority dress). Thanks to its overwhelmingly secular character and an economy based on trade, it has always been relatively open to the world. Now growing prosperity turned it from what in many ways was a Central European city transplanted to the Mediterranean coast into something much more cosmopolitan. As one resident wrote:

> Someone will tell you: we spent a week in London going to the theater. It's so much better there. Really? . . . excellent plays can also be seen in Tel Aviv. . . . You can listen to all kinds of music from the Philharmonic to Michael Jackson. Evening after evening you can choose from innumerable cultural events. Tel Aviv never sleeps, as the advertisement says. . . . Have a look at the Friday newspapers and your head will spin. Shall I listen to a concert with a world famous conductor, enjoy an opera, go to the theater, see the latest films, hear a lecture on city coins in the second century B.C., or do something else? Shall I eat in a kosher restaurant, kosher or *glatt* kosher, or enjoy a pork chop, lobster or shrimps? There are even kosher Chinese restaurants and kosher shrimps.[19]

He might have added that Tel Aviv's hot, humid climate has resulted in a beach culture. Much of social life takes place outside, in the open-air cafés along the boulevards. For some seven months each year the city sports as many lightly clad, suntanned, often extremely good-looking women as any other on earth. They, too, never sleep.

Whereas Tel Aviv is rich, Jerusalem, two-thirds of whose population is either Jewish Orthodox or Arab, is relatively poor. It is also a place filled with fanatics of every possible religion, creed, and belief.

No doubt this fact turns it into a fascinating city for those who take the trouble to explore it. To stand on Mount Scopus at noon and listen to all the various church bells being rung is quite an experience. So is a visit to the Jewish Orthodox quarter, Meah Shearim. Yet be not misled. The city does have some tall modern buildings and broad, if hardly straight, main streets, many of which would not be out of place in any other city in any other country. Recently it has even received a white, suspension-type Calatrava bridge named Chords Bridge. But in the narrow alleyways; in stone-enclosed courtyards; up and down narrow, often quite rickety, staircases that lead to iron-made, rusty doors, the place teems with tensions and fierce hatreds of every kind.

Specifically, Orthodox Jews detest and sometimes fight secular ones (on the Sabbath they throw rocks at passing cars, and on other days they may set afire garbage cans for any reason or none at all). The members of one Orthodox group will sometimes beat up those of another over such questions as whose rabbi is greater and also over control over the lucrative *kashrut* business. So-called modesty patrols go their way, roughing up men deemed not to be observing Jewish law and women deemed to be immodest. Muslims sometimes stab Jews, and Jews sometimes beat up Muslims. Christian priests of different denominations often engage in fistfights over such questions as whether a window can be opened in the holy sepulchre during Palm Sunday. The infamous black and yellow–garbed supporters of a local soccer club, Betar, will take any opportunity to riot. Things are getting worse—as the number of Orthodox Jews increases, any secular person who wants to escape these tensions will have to leave. As many, in fact, do; young couples in particular vote with their feet, with the result that the population of non-Orthodox schoolchildren is declining year by year and may soon disappear altogether.

Other cities have their own special character. In spite of the presence of the Technion, a university, and the bustling port that also serves as the IDF's main naval base, Haifa remains a somewhat bland industrial town. Its position overlooking the bay is as magnificent as that of any other city on earth. However, its air is badly polluted by the nearby chemical and petrochemical industries, and its social atmosphere is decidedly provincial. Though the city is not without cultural facilities, it has nothing like the museums and media headquarters so abundant in Jerusalem and Tel Aviv. Whereas the latter contains numerous important government offices, Haifa has none. The fact that Israel's only international airport is about sixty miles away does not help, either.

While the site on which Haifa stands has been inhabited since the Bronze Age, the town's greatest advantage is that neither Moses, nor Jesus, nor Mohammed ever set foot in it or so much as knew of its existence. The only religious site of any significance is the golden-domed Bahá'i Temple, world center of that religion, and its magnificent gardens that run down the slopes of Mount Carmel and have recently been designated as a world heritage site. The Bahá'í prophet, Siyyid Alí-Muhammad, is buried not far away; fortunately for the religion he founded, it never acquired enough believers to grow intolerant and try to tell others what to believe. Whether the city's secular character makes its inhabitants more inclined toward sin may be doubted. But it does seem to help Jews and Arabs to live together with less friction than anywhere else.

Until not long ago less important towns such as, to name a few at random, Tiberias on the Sea of Galilee, Afula in the Valley of Esdraelon, Netanya on the Mediterranean shore, Ashdod (with its port) farther south on the same shore, and Beer Sheba in the Negev Desert often made a somewhat neglected, scruffy impression. Prices, incomes, and living standards were much lower than in the main cities. This, however, is changing fast. Afula, an important crossroads that for decades used to be the butt of jokes for not having even a single traffic light, has now grown to the point where scarcely a visitor does not lose his or her way while trying to drive through it. One reason why things are changing is the vast increase in the number of automobiles as well as heavy investment in suburban railway lines linking "the periphery" to Tel Aviv. The country, small to begin with, is becoming smaller by the day. Had it not been for the monumental traffic jams in Gush Dan in particular, it would have become much smaller still.

Elsewhere, Israel probably packs more variety into a smaller space than does any other country of similar size. From the snow-capped peak of Mount Hermon in the north to the desert town of Elat three hundred miles farther south on the shore of the Red Sea, where four countries (Israel, Jordan, Saudi Arabia, and Egypt) meet; from the sweltering Mediterranean coast to the even warmer, but bone dry, Jordan Valley. Where else is God only a local phone call away, where else are the sacred and the profane so closely mixed, and where else can one find a modern (well, fairly modern) street lantern mounted on a Roman milestone erected some nineteen centuries ago by the legionnaires of Emperor Hadrian? In the center of the country one ultramodern skyscraper after another is rising, changing the color of "the city in gray," as Tel Aviv used to be called, to the sky blue reflected in the buildings' windows. But in the Negev Desert, and during the winter season in the Judean one as well, some Bedouin still live in tents.

Rich or poor, over 90 percent of inhabitants now live in the towns. Old or new, many of the towns consist mainly of blocks of flats, some of them prefabricated. Even when they are well maintained, which is often not the case, architecturally they are nothing to boast about. But this is changing. In central Jerusalem and Tel Aviv, in downtown Haifa, people have discovered that the new is not always better than the old. After decades of neglect, quarters made up of turn-of-the-twentieth-century German Templer buildings, 1930s-vintage Bauhaus buildings (thanks to the influx of *yekke* architects, Tel Aviv has more Bauhaus buildings than any other city on earth), and pre-1948 Arab buildings are starting to be restored. Once each job has been completed, it commands astronomical prices—the more so because most of them are located right in the center of town.

Some parts of the country look like Singapore, packed as they are with white-colored high-rise residential buildings (though generally they are not as well maintained as their Far Eastern counterparts). Parts of it, particularly in the north and the southwest, remain open. Much of the open land is extremely fertile, though a chronic shortage of water and not infrequent droughts makes agriculture a risky business. Every time a farmer sows his field, what he really does is gamble, with God acting as the croupier. Though suburbs, mostly consisting not of single-family houses (which, given the scarcity of land, are too expensive) but of town houses, take up much space, here and there one can still find remnants of what is sentimentally known as "old" Israel. It is made up of narrow asphalt roads; tiny one-or two-bedroom, single-story houses; dreamy eucalyptus trees; *sabra* (cactus) fences with large, meaty leaves and sharp thorns; and bougainvilleas with such strong colors that they seem to be shouting the sheer joy of life.

While the northern half of Israel has some of the world's highest population densities, the southern half is desert. It used to be said of Mitzpe Ramon, a dusty township in the center of the Negev, that if you wanted to kill yourself there, you should lie down in the middle of the road and die of starvation. Yet nowadays even the desert is no longer as empty as it used to be. The number of Bedouin who live there has grown from an estimated 10,000 in 1949 to 140,000 in 2004.[20] Another factor is the planned move south of the IDF's Tel Aviv headquarters, known as Hakirya, as well as many training bases. Though the change represents a rather peculiar method of making the desert bloom, it is long overdue. The necessary billions to pay for the move will be raised by the usual method, i.e., selling the land on which Hakirya currently stands to developers to build skyscrapers on.

The people who live in this country are as divided and as quarrelsome as ever. Still, some problems seem to have been solved or, at any rate, to be approaching a solution. The most important one is the gap between "the first" and "the second" Israel. Ben Gurion, in his typical paternalist fashion, deplored it (he once said he could not wait for the first Yemenite chief of staff). Begin, the demagogue, made use of it; and the leaders of the Orthodox parties, Shas above all, do whatever they can to perpetuate it and exploit it. Nevertheless, things have been changing. This is evident, among other things, from the fact that, during the 2003 elections, Shas lost seven out of seventeen Knesset seats. To restore its fortunes, the party has even been thinking of enlisting secular members! One important vehicle for change is the IDF. Taking in people regardless of their ethnic origin, it puts everyone on the bottom rung of a ladder that may lead all the way to the top. In the past this has already resulted in two Oriental chiefs of staff, two Oriental ministers of defense, and any number of Oriental generals. The same is true of politics; with the exception of that of prime minister, hardly a political position remains that Orientals have not occupied at one time or another.

In part, the closing of the gap is due to improved education and the better jobs to which it provides an opening. In part, it is due to the arrival of Russian immigrants during the 1990s. As the latter were relegated to the bottom of the social heap, everybody else was automatically lifted upward. One result, already noted, is that there are now as many Russian maids and prostitutes as Oriental ones. Yet while some "Russians" found life in their new country so hard that they became homeless alcoholics, most have been doing extremely well. They learned the language, entered the education system (like many immigrants at all times and places, they see education as the way ahead), took up increasingly well-paying jobs, and started their own businesses. Much more than any previous group of immigrants, they also succeeded in making their mark in politics. Perhaps the best indication of how successful they have been is a supermarket chain known as Tiv Taam (Good Taste). Originally it specialized in Russian delicatessen, many of them so unkosher as to give the rabbis a fit. By now its well-stocked stores are patronized by all segments of the population except the religious ones.

Back in the 1960s Jacob Talmon used to ask, rhetorically, whether Israel was not a "Western" country. Now that Orientals comprise about half of the population, and about one-third of all marriages are ethnically mixed,[21] this is even less true than it was at that time. The cultural gap between the groups is closing. An early sign of change came in the 1970s, when a wave of what can only be called festivalitis swept the country. Not just highbrow Ashkenazi festivals, as previously, but religious ones, Hassidic ones, rock ones (there does exist an Israeli rock movement, though abroad its significance is underrated), and, most important, Oriental ones. All these, and many more, found both sponsors and eager listeners. It is true that each kind of festival mainly attracts a separate group of people; after all, not everybody who likes Bach also likes the Beatles. Yet all are considered equal, and indeed this has been carried to the point where one popular song, claiming that they were quite indistinguishable, made fun of them all.

To the older generation of *yekkes* in particular, Oriental music (which many of them could barely tell apart from Arab music) sounded like *Katzenjammer,* the wailing of cats. Not so to their offspring, who have learned to accept it and even to like it. They experience it as part of the country in which they live—just as many of them like listening to the Muslim muezzin's call to prayer, so admirably suited to the landscape. One outcome is the fact that Israel has become a haven for anybody who wants to download and sell unauthorized Arab music. Since so many Arab countries refuse to recognize Israel, their citizens cannot sue for copyright, either! Whereas, back in the early 1980s, most Ashkenazis had never heard of the Maimunah, a feast that Moroccan Jews celebrate on the day immediately after Passover, by now it has become a national festival. Along with the feast, new tastes in food and drink have entered the mainstream, transforming it and enriching it. This has been carried to the point where a politician who disdains to eat the Oriental delicacies offered him might just as well give up any thought of being elected. Outside the Ashkenazi Orthodox establishment, which forms the most racist sector of Israeli society and still uses terms such as "*frenks*" and "*shwarze*" (blacks), words like *wuzwuz* and *tshahtshah* have all but disappeared.

In spite of all the cant coming out of the Ministry of Education, which sometimes acts and talks as if the clock had stood still in 1967, the trend toward more and more individualism continues. In part this is because, for all that the "security situation" is always "threatening," Israel is no longer engaged in a daily fight for its existence. Serving soldiers apart, to the younger generation war, as experienced in the summer of 2006, means little more than some slight discomfort in daily life. In part it is because, for decent people to celebrate a society that has been occupying and ruling another for forty years now is not easy. With the exception of the kind that goes into monuments to the fallen, art that revolves around national aspirations, successes, and triumphs has all but disappeared. Often, indeed, it is barely considered art at all. Art focusing on private people is everywhere. This is true even when the setting consists of some "national" event, such as war. As has been said, "Since the establishment of the state every successful Israeli film or book has the figure of a dead soldier, and the part that deals with the dead soldier is always the most touching part of the film or the book."[22]

As of 2008 the most popular playwright was once again Hanoh Levin. Though he had been dead for almost ten years, about a score of his plays—including some that had never been shown before—were being produced or were about to be produced. People flocked to see them, and the productions were awarded one prize after another. As one critic wrote, "He stuck knives into the heart of Israeli culture: militarism, belief, religious ritual, love, life itself";[23] in a play called *The Agonies of Job,* where the hero is impaled, he did so literally. Yet he was by no means the only one. Certainly poets such as Yehuda Amichai (1924–2000) and Daliah Rabikovich (1936–2005) were not unpatriotic. As Simone de Beauvoir wrote, it is not those who criticize their country who love it least. Yet they focused on the human soul; the latter even drew fire by publishing a poem that explored the feelings of a suicide bomber on his way to blow himself up.

Like other countries, Israel has its share of youthful pop stars, male and female. Like comets they appear, cross the firmament, and disappear; only a few last longer, proving that they really have something to say. During the 1990s probably the most important representative of the younger generation was a popular singer named Aviv Geffen (1973–). In a song entitled, outrageously, "We Are a Fucked-up Generation," he described his country as a dangerous area known as "the Land" and his parental home as a pretty disgusting place ruled over by a drunk. Yet reality is completely different. Geffen himself is the son of the above-mentioned Jonathan Geffen, and his home was certainly no worse than most others. While numerous young Israelis like to tour the world after being discharged from military service—the favorite destinations are India, Thailand, and Latin America—most return home after six months to a year. It is true that many ultimately leave the country for good. Yet most of these do not do so because they want to; rather, the problem is that there are limits to the number of bright young people a small country can absorb. Having left, they often spend a lifetime pining for the country of their youth. Taking any opportunity to visit, they also tend to form their own separate communities quite distinct from the local Jewish ones in their new homes.

In 2008, *The New York Times* noted that "a soaring number" of Israeli artists are mounting solo exhibitions in the United States.[24] Israeli writers such as Amos Oz, A. B. Yehoshua, Meir Shalev, David Grossman, and Hanoh Levin (whose plays have now been produced in fifty different countries, no less) are known the world over. Their themes range from the beauty or, in Levin's case, the ugliness of love through the wonders of the Valley of Esdraelon and the harsh charm of the Judean Desert; and from the tensions generated by the communal life on a kibbutz or a moshav to a mother's half-crazed attempt to run away from the dreadful news of her soldier son's death that she fears may be coming for her.

The language these and other writers use, Hebrew, is a miracle in it-self. Until about a hundred years ago it was used almost exclusively for prayer. Even so, many worshippers only barely understood the meaning of the words they uttered. Herzl hardly knew a word of it; today it is spo-ken by only about seven million people, Israeli Arabs included. As has been said, "Every sentence in it reeks of the Old Testament,"[25] reminding Israelis of their roots. But it is not the Old Testament alone. Throughout history, Hebrew never stopped developing and changing. The creation of the state, far from bringing the process to an end, has merely caused it to unfold much faster than before.

As with any other language, one has to distinguish between written and spoken Hebrew, "high" and "low" Hebrew, and the like. Perhaps more in this case than in most other languages, one must also distin-guish between versions of Hebrew as used by members of various eth-nic groups. Many members of those groups are instantly identifiable by their choice of words, grammar, and pronunciation. In spite of the coun-try's small size, there is secular Hebrew, religious Hebrew, Jerusalem Hebrew, and Haifa Hebrew. There is the kind of Hebrew spoken in the kibbutzim and moshavim, and of course IDF Hebrew with its endless, and to outsiders quite incomprehensible, acronyms. The outcome is a mixture no less rich and, if one cares about such things, no less charm-ing, than the one found in any other country. What makes it truly remarkable is its limited starting point—the Old Testament, for all its incomparable literary qualities, only has a vocabulary of less than ten thousand words—as well as the extraordinary speed at which it changes.

To focus on one aspect only, there is the rich and colorful slang people use in day-to-day life. Some of it is unprintable, much of it ex-tremely apt and quite funny. For example, a philistine used to be called a "subaroid," a term dating to the 1980s when, for some inscrutable reason, one out of every three cars sold in Israel was a Subaru. A total idiot is said to have "an IQ as tall as grass." The method of trying to cover one's bald pate with the little hair one has left is called "loans and savings"; a film in which gallons of ketchup are squirted instead of blood is called "an agricultural movie." "To see the world through the hole in the *grush*" reminds people of the time when some coins used to have holes in them and carries the meaning, to be stingy. "Nonsense in tomato juice" means really stupid nonsense. A "schnitzel patrol" consists of parents who anxiously follow their offspring during the latter's military training. "Showing somebody where the fish urinates from" means to show who is boss. "A sausage" is a softie (several decades ago, such a person used to be called "a soap"). "A matchmaker" is a stapler, "white meat" is a euphemism for pork, and "eating gravel" means doing very hard work.

Many of these expressions originate in the IDF, which remains the great melting pot even though the percentage of each age group that serves in it has been declining. Others are adapted from foreign languages. Originally the most influential ones were probably Turkish, Russian, and German. By now, though, English is as dominant in Israel as it is in many other countries. Not just vocabulary but syntax is being imported. For example, there has been a tendency to move the word *gam* (too), to the end of a sentence. At first, the people who did this simply did not know any better. Next the form acquired a subtly ironic connotation, and now it is well on its way to entering mainstream, if not literary, Hebrew. English influence is also evident in the tendency to replace enclitic words, in which Hebrew is very rich and which are partly responsible for its characteristic brevity of expression, with adjectives. For example, an air show (*mifgan-avir*) becomes a *mifgan aviri* (aerial show). Purists at the Academy for the Hebrew Language keep protesting that the adjective "aerial" does not exist in Hebrew. They are right, but life is stronger than they are.

Together, these countless cultural currents, countercurrents, and cross currents create an almighty *balagan* (mess), as Israelis say. In this *balagan,* the borders between the sacred and the profane, the sublime and the earthy, the prohibited and the permissible, are hopelessly vague. Probably in no other country will the roughest *freh* you argue with about a parking space suddenly throw a Biblical phrase at you (probably one picked up from one of the religious radio stations). In no other country will politicians and other public figures resort to such blunt ways of expressing themselves. To foreigners, life in Israel often looks noisy, sweaty, and vulgar. Returning from a year in England, one seven-year-old announced that "here everybody is rough. I want to be rough, too." People eat in the streets and are none too careful in disposing of the remains. Queues, if they exist at all, are merely excuses for people to jostle each other. Everybody gesticulates not merely during face-to-face meetings but as they talk on their cell phones, which Israelis, on a per capita basis, use more often, and for longer periods of time, than any other people. Traveling by bus, one is turned into an involuntary participant in one's neighbor's love life, complete with all the details. In any case the buses never arrive on time, and the trains seldom do. Yet this is just one side of how things are. The other consists of a society that, in many ways, is as varied, friendly to foreigners, open minded, and, above all, creative as any other on earth.

Elvis in Jerusalem[26]

Some seven miles west of Jerusalem is the Arab village of Abu Gosh, the ancient Emmaus where the resurrected Jesus was seen. While today it is mostly Muslim, several churches commemorate the event; we, however, are interested in something completely different. At the entrance to the village is a gas station, and the filling station boasts what the owner claims is the world's largest statue of Elvis Presley.

No doubt partly because the number of immigrants from the United States has always been small, and perhaps also because Israel used to be a poor country, American culture took a long time to settle there. True, as early as the 1920s the owners of citrus groves dreamed of adopting the "Californian irrigation method."[27] However, often they had neither the capital for machinery nor the space needed to plant trees as far apart as that method demanded. In Israel as in much of the world during the 1950s, the term "made in America" meant the best of everything (alas, that is no longer true). Nevertheless, until the June 1967 war transformed the relationship between the two countries, even for the relatively few Israelis who could afford to travel abroad the United States remained far away.

Once American culture arrived, it took over with a vengeance. Over the last quarter century or so, Israel in many ways has become more Americanized than any other country; some have even spoken of it as the fifty-first state. Massive American economic and political support apart, possible explanations are Israel's lack of a solid native culture (as its enemies would say) and the fact that, as in the United States, so many cultures have been thrown into a melting pot. We are not talking just of jazz and rock and sneakers and Levi's jeans and baseball caps. Nor is it merely a question of Hollywood movies and TV series and "reality" shows and Coca-colonization (the phrase many Europeans used during the 1950s) and hamburgers. For good or ill, all of those can be found in any developed country and in quite a number of not-so-developed ones too. My own town of Mevasseret Zion rejoices in the blessings of a kosher McDonald's. Rather, the rest of this section will examine some of the most fundamental ways in which imported U.S. culture has affected, and is affecting, Israeli life.

To start with, there are politics. On the face of things it would be hard to think of two democratic countries whose political systems are so dissimilar. Here we have centralization, there federalism. Here we see a parliamentary system, there a presidential one; here a multiparty system, there one that has rarely allowed more than two parties to co-exist; this is to mention the most obvious differences only. Yet even in this field American influence is evident. All Israeli parties raise much of the money they need in the United States—which not only causes American political ideas and methods to be imported but leads to frequent complaints about the allegedly undue influence of American Jewish billionaires on Israeli politics. More and more, those parties also rely on American political experts to guide them in their campaigns. Yet this is only the beginning of the story. After many decades when each party chose its Knesset candidates in closed meetings where activists intrigued with and betrayed one another, the most important change has been the adoption, in the 1990s, of primaries. Along with primaries came the urgent need, also not exactly unfamiliar to Americans, to raise money, a factor that has caused every prime minister from Shimon Peres on to be placed under police investigation and may yet lead to the incarceration of Ehud Olmert.

American influence is also evident in the changing relationship between the government and the courts. The United States has a constitution that is written, complete in itself, and very finely crafted. Not so Israel, which, owing largely to opposition by the religious and Orthodox parties, only has a patchwork of laws dating to different periods. True, years ago a decision was made to work toward a constitution by adopting "basic" laws. To date, however, only a handful of such laws have been passed; even so, anyone who can cobble together a majority of sixty-one MKs can put them aside. In spite of this, one law in particular, titled "Human Dignity and Freedom," has enabled the Supreme Court, guided by former chief justice Aharon Barak (served 1995–2006), to take the bit between its teeth.

Barak himself has lived in Israel since the age of eleven. Like many Israeli academics, he has close ties to the United States; after all, five-sixths of the world's entire legal literature is published in the United States.[28] Not merely did he spend sabbatical years in that country, but he has received honorary doctorates from Brandeis University and Columbia University. No sooner did he retire than off he went to teach at Yale. Barak's declared aim, exemplified by his statement that "everything is judge-able" (*shafit,* in Hebrew), has been to introduce American-style judicial review into Israel so as to make sure the Knesset does not do some things he personally finds abhorrent. In doing so he has found an extremely powerful tool in the form of that very un-American legal device, Bagatz. Currently about a thousand Bagatzim are served each year—more than four for every working day. A new adjective, Bagitz—meaning Bagatzable—has been born. Partly because people keep turning to it for redress, and partly because of its own activism, the court has extended its influence. In the view of many, it now threatens to usurp the functions of both the executive and the legislative and render them impotent.

Lithuanian born, Barak knows several languages besides English. This is not true of many younger, native-born Israelis whose only second tongue is English and who therefore depend on it for their professional reading and publications. Countless computer experts, engineers, physicians, and natural scientists of every kind, as well as social scientists and academics whose field is the humanities, are tied to the United States as if by umbilical cords. If only because Hebrew-language scholarly publications hardly count in the academic world (one story has it that, had God applied for tenure at an Israeli university, he would have failed to get it because the one book He wrote was published in that language), they regard the country across the Atlantic as the Promised Land. Some of the ideas they pick up in that land are good, others bad. All play a considerable role in shaping Israeli life.

One of the institutions where American influence has been strongest is the IDF. Whereas, until 1967, Israel got most of its military equipment from France, since then the United States has become the most important source by far. The 1973 war in particular contributed to the process of Americanization. It led to the introduction of a flood of American uniforms, flak jackets, and assault rifles, to say nothing of American tanks, cannon, armored personnel carriers, fighter-bombers, attack helicopters, and missiles. Contacts between the armed forces of both countries became very close. Some American defense establishment personnel came to observe the lessons of Israel's wars, even to the point of crawling into and out of damaged tanks to learn what kind of munitions they were hit by. Conversely, a great many Israeli ones spent time training in the United States, studying in the United States, doing R & D in the United States, and supervising the construction of weapons that were being built for Israel in the United States. The IDF in many ways became Americanized—again, with results that were sometimes good, sometimes bad. Judging by its performance in the 2006 Lebanon War, perhaps the bad outweighed the good.

Underlying the process were economic forces. As we saw, until 1967 U.S. financial assistance to Israel was extremely limited. After that year it increased, but the real turning point only came in 1973–1974, following the October War. Since then aid, most of it in the form of grants that did not have to be repaid, may have amounted to well over $100 billion. Even this titanic sum does not include the money raised among American Jews and used to pay for everything from youth centers to ambulances and from hospitals to settlements in the occupied territories. Except for the Palestinians who, on a per capita basis have been receiving even more aid from various international donors,[29] never in history did so few receive so much money for free for so long. Whether this constitutes a sign of the poverty of the Zionist enterprise or of its outstanding success, let others judge.

Almost all of the aid was tied, meaning that it could not be converted from dollars into shekels but could be used only to buy American products in the United States. In this way it represented a hidden subsidy for American defense companies; which, of course, was one reason why Congress has been prepared to extend it as often, and for as long, as it did. In this context one must note that the effect of the aid has not been altogether beneficial. At some times it compelled the IDF to buy equipment it did not really need; at others it enabled U.S. companies to corner the Israeli market without any special effort on their own part. Meanwhile, Israeli firms active in the same field found themselves in a position where they could sell their products in any country except for Israel.

Back in 1985, when Reagan and Shultz agreed to provide Israel with emergency aid, they did so on condition that Peres and Modai enact American-style economic reforms and adopt an economic regime much closer to American-style free enterprise capitalism. The United States-Israel Free Trade Agreement, which was signed that year, worked in the same direction. Its purpose was "to establish bilateral free trade between the two nations through the removal of trade barriers [and] promote cooperation in areas which are of mutual interest."[30] To sell goods to one another both sides had to learn from one another. Given how small Israel is in comparison with its behemoth ally, inevitably much of the learning was one-sided. Why should American executives bother to study Hebrew if their Israeli counterparts can speak English fairly well? Later Rabin and Netanyahu, both of whom had long been pro-American and were all too aware of what American life had to offer, accelerated the process. As the Israeli economy modernized it also became more internationalized. In many ways, this meant that it became more like that of the United States, the largest power of all.

Some of the social changes that the shift to capitalism, as well as Americanization, entailed have already been discussed. One not yet mentioned here, but that is among the most interesting of all, is the change in the status of the 50 percent of the population who are female. With the important exception of the Orthodox, for years before the state was established in 1948 the dominant ideology among the Jewish community in the Land was socialism. As in the Soviet Union during the same period, this meant that the highest term of praise was "worker." Also as in the Soviet Union, women, by helping build the country just as men did, were able to earn that praise, too; decades before anyone heard of political correctness, one popular Israeli song went, *"nihyeh kulanu halutzim vehalutzot"* ("let's all become male and female pioneers").

However, socialism also meant that "exploitation" of one person by another was considered a bad, bad thing. In 1930, one woman—or perhaps it was merely the Mapai ideologue in chief, Berl Katznelson, putting words in her mouth—expressed the resulting dilemma as follows:

> A female worker who desires a life of labor and equality takes on a maid and thereby turns into an employer. The contradiction between exploiter and exploited appears. . . . I come home after a long working day and find that the house has not been properly done. I am irritated, for this is the maid's job. But this maid is also my class comrade; she certainly did not come to the Land in order to dust my furniture. We fight for a shorter working day, but when I come home at six in the evening all I can do is to start a new working day at home, even though the maid has been working in it all day. For us, urban women, there is no way out. Either we stop working and let our husbands support us, or we must turn from a worker into an employer.[31]

Though "worker" has long been replaced by "career," very little has changed. In Israel as in other developed countries, a woman who takes up a career faces a choice. Either she must remain childless (often, single as well), or else she must have several others who will clean for her, cook for her, wash for her, and look after her children for her. Some do so directly as maids; others indirectly as kindergarten mistresses, teachers, etc. Thus, feminism rests on the "exploitation" of some women by other women, which goes far to explain why its achievements have been limited.

In Israel as in other countries, many more men have engaged in paid work outside the home than women; men also tend to stay in the workforce longer than women, who, owing to the requirements of pregnancy, delivery, and child-raising, are always moving out of and into it. Partly as a result, in Israel as in other countries, the vast majority of top positions society has to offer have always been occupied by men. Yet starting as far back as the 1920s, first the Jewish community in the Land of Israel and then the Israeli state also offered women some things that in many other countries at the time were anything but self-evident and had to be fought for. This included the right to vote and to be elected, the right to study and enter the professions, and the right to open an independent bank account. Under socialism, women also benefited from various institutions meant to guarantee the welfare of mothers and their young offspring. Young women even walked the streets in short pants, something found almost nowhere else. When the time for independence arrived in 1948, the declaration that proclaimed it promised "complete equality of social and political rights to all its inhabitants irrespective of . . . sex."[32] That is more than the corresponding American document does.

At the time the War of Independence broke out in December 1947, Palmach was the world's most sexually integrated armed force. Probably about 15 percent of its members were female, and a handful of women even commanded men. During the early months of the war a few women actually fought with weapons in hand, especially in the ferocious battles for controlling the road to Jerusalem and for the conquest of Galilee. Out of 383 Israeli soldiers who were killed in the attempts to capture the fortress of Latrun in May–June 1948, three were female; two were nurses and one a wireless operator. Soon after this episode women were taken out of combat units and confined to service-type jobs only. Nevertheless, by the time the war came to an end, they formed over 10 percent of the IDF, which among regular forces was another record.

In 1949–1950, Israel became the first country in history to conscript women into the military. From that time until the late 1960s it was also the only one to give them weapons training. The training was largely symbolic, and the first thing the IDF did each time a war broke out was to evacuate the women from the battle zones. Still, foreigners, seeing women with Uzi submachine guns, were greatly impressed; Israel also led the pack when it came to allowing women to join the police. To top it all, Meir was one of the first female heads of state in any country. However, seen through subsequent feminist eyes, Israel, by taking it for granted that women's most important task was to have and rear children and allegedly discriminating against them in countless ways, was as much of a male chauvinist hell as any other country at the time. Yet strangely few Israeli women seemed to notice or be particularly interested in feminism. When Simone de Beauvoir visited Israel not long before the 1967 war she received a frosty reception. Yael Dayan, who was later to become a leading feminist, wrote about how much she enjoyed baking for her officer husband when he came home from the fighting on the Suez Canal; in an interview she gave the Italian journalist Oriana Fallaci, Meir herself called feminists "crazy" and "nuts."[33]

All this started changing from the early 1980s on. Very likely one reason for this was that, following the enormous increase in the power of the IDF on one hand and the declaration of peace with Egypt on the other, Israel's "basic" security was no longer in question; as has been said, the rise of feminism is usually an indication that there are no more pressing problems left. The number of Israeli men who were killed while fighting for their country went down very sharply both in absolute terms and relative to the population. The less men died, the louder Israeli feminists demanded that they be given equal treatment both in the military—now that serving in it was no longer nearly as dangerous to life and limb as before—and in every other field. Another reason was the ongoing process of modernization. Modernization meant primarily Americanization. In fact, the "grand dame" of Israeli feminism, Marsha Freedman, was American born and educated. Later, the same applied to several of her followers.

In Israel as in the United States, most feminists were either women who had never had a husband, such as Freedman herself, or who had lost the ones they used to have through divorce, as happened to Orit Kamir, of whom we shall speak presently. In Israel as in the United States, their struggle tried to achieve two things at once. On one hand they demanded equality, which in practice often meant privileges, in respect to such things as pay, working conditions, career opportunities, and the laws regulating divorce, child custody, and medical treatment. On the other they demanded that society act against prostitution (but not against prostitutes), protect women against the evils of pornography, and put an end to violence against women and the (alleged) harassment, abuse, and rape of women. In Israel as in the United States, the outcome was a vast feminist literature written and read almost exclusively by women. Many feminist organizations were created and countless feminist meetings were held. Various government and municipal bureaucracies, as well as the universities, set up special departments charged with looking after women's complaints.

How successful have the feminist endeavors been? In some ways the answer is, very successful indeed. Israeli women, whatever their personal status, are the only ones who have the legal right to be artificially inseminated at the taxpayer's expense, if necessary repeatedly so, until they give birth not to one but two children. In no other nation do women enjoy such a privilege; in 2006, twenty-six thousand procedures were carried out, yielding some five thousand live babies. In 1998 the Knesset, stimulated by the aforementioned Orit Kamir, who herself is a former student of the American feminist Catherine MacKinnon and a Hebrew University faculty member, passed the world's most radical anti–sexual harassment law. Even then, things did not come to a halt. As the law was interpreted by a 2008 labor court decision, *any* sexual contact between a superior, who is automatically assumed to be male, and a subordinate, who is assumed to be female, amounts to rape. *Even if, at the time the act took place, the woman gave her free consent.*[34]

Originally inspired by developments in the United States, much of this went way beyond the American example. Still, whether it really did much to improve the lot of Israeli women is doubtful. Commenting on the right to be artificially inseminated, some feminists have wondered whether it does not amount to yet another kind of male chauvinism. The way they see it, a woman who is left childless is deprived of her rights; but a woman who is assisted in having them is humiliated. Commenting on the above-mentioned court decision, Kamir herself wrote that "assuming that no relationship between a superior and a subordinate can result from her free will [in other words, that a female subordinate is unable to decide whom she may or may not have sex with and should be treated as if she were drunk or mentally deficient] may not be desirable."[35] And rightly so. Furthermore, one may argue, as veteran Israeli feminist and former MK Shulamit Aloni (1928–) has done, that the attempt to defend women against many forms of male attack, real or imaginary, merely emphasizes the "inability of a twenty-year-old to say no."[36] How anyone is expected to take such a ninny seriously, or give her any kind of responsible work to do, remains a mystery.

Take the cause célèbre of a young female IDF officer who was French-kissed—in the midst of a party that took place in the prime minister's office and, as she says, against her will—by then-minister of justice Haim Ramon. She had just been flirting with him, had been photographed hugging him, and had even given him her telephone number in the apparent hope that he would take her on a trip to South America. In any prefeminist era, when women were supposedly weak and dependent and downtrodden, she would have responded with a resounding slap to the assailant's face, turning him into a laughing-stock and making sure he would never repeat his act. Now, claiming she suffers from deep psychological trauma and cannot manage her life without expert help, she requires an entire police department and a public prosecutor to make her case for her.

Not just Aloni but some proclaimed feminists, Freedman herself included, were elected to the Knesset at one time or another. Taking up their seats, they have formed a very active and somewhat aggressive lobby. They helped set up homes for battered women, hotlines for women who feel they have been discriminated against, and the like. However, and as is also true in other countries without exception, no purely feminist movement made up solely or mainly of women and dedicated to advancing women's cause got very far in either local or national politics. Quite often, when an organization appoints this or that woman to look after female employees, the real intention behind the move is to shove her aside to a position where she can do little harm. Among nationally prominent women, such as former ministers of education Limor Livnat and Yuli Tamir, former Knesset chairperson Dalia Itzik, and Kadima leader Tzipi Livni, not one has put feminism anywhere near the top of her agenda. And with very good reason, for doing so would be tantamount to political suicide.

To attract followers and increase their own influence, feminists have a vested interest in exaggerating the sufferings of women. As a result, the statistics they provide on such issues as domestic violence, sexual harass-ment, and rape cannot be regarded as trustworthy. Whether Israeli femi-nists have met with any real success in their efforts to combat pornography and prostitution is, to say the least, uncertain. As they themselves keep pointing out, both kinds of business seem to flourish as much as ever. It is true that the number of women who have volunteered to join men and become wage slaves outside the home has increased—even some Ortho-dox women now look for jobs—and that career women have made some gains. However, there are signs that, in Israel as elsewhere, those gains are to some extent counterbalanced by the declining social prestige and income associated with fields—such as the judiciary, the public prosecution, medicine, and certain university departments—where women are most numerous. Meanwhile, the higher one climbs on the ladder of riches, power, and fame, the fewer, by and large, the women one encounters.

Judging by the number of court cases—one quarter of all male prisoners in Israeli jails have been sentenced either for domestic violence or for sexual offenses against women[37]—relations between men and women have never been as bad as now. Anyone who studies the thousands upon thousands of "talkbackists," slang for people who use the Net to respond to posted newspaper articles, will reach the same conclusion. Israeli women freely vent their hatred for men, those wicked oppressors and discriminators and sexual predators who are always out to exploit women in any way they can. Israeli men vow not to get married and not to hire female employees (in fact, unemployment is somewhat higher among women than among men). They even swear they will not give women a lift; in a few documented cases female hitchhikers have tried to blackmail the men who gave them rides by threatening to accuse them of attempted rape. Does all this represent mere froth? Or does the anonymity that the Net provides bring to light problems that have long been hidden? Or has there been a real shift in attitudes? In case the answer to this question is yes, where is it leading and how long will it last? The answer is that nobody knows.

What *is* clear is that, given the increase in women's education and their growing tendency to take up work outside the home, fertility is falling quite fast. This applies more to secular Jews than to religious ones, more to Jews than to non-Jews, and more to the well-to-do than to the relatively poor. However, the direction in which things are moving is the same for all groups. By rendering children much more precious, this development should have turned the country into a much more friendly place for them. In fact, the opposite may have happened. Some of the problems result from the vast increase in traffic that has made many roads unsafe; the (self-appointed) National Council for the Child now demands that parents not allow children to cross a street on their own before they are nine years old. In many places, gone are the days when children could walk or bike or ride a bus to visit each other after school—and, since mothers were normally at home, be sure of a welcome even if they did not announce themselves first.

Barred from the public sphere, unable to move, children cannot stay at home, either. As has also happened in other Western countries, the fact that most mothers have jobs means that children are often left without parents for most of the day. Family meals, those famous ritual occasions of Jewish life where ties are cemented and problems discussed, have almost become an endangered species. With each passing day communications are becoming more and more limited to cell phone calls. Many parents do not have the slightest idea what their offspring are up to. Worse still, if the media are to be believed, the country is awash with human monsters. Lurking in their lairs, day and night they hatch nefarious schemes aimed at seducing children, abducting them, and abusing them. Thanks to the Internet, they are even able to penetrate right into the family home. One research institute claims that seventy thousand Israeli children, about 6 percent of the total, are abused each year.[38] Whether these figures are more reliable than the ones feminists provide to promote *their* ends is unknown and, probably, unknowable.

In response, parents who can afford help, or who have relatives, especially mothers and mothers-in-law, "solve" the problem by hiring others—which, incidentally, is another excellent example of the way the "liberation" of women usually comes at the expense of other women. The rest manage, or don't manage, as best they can. Hardly a day passes without some new laws being introduced designed to "protect" children by prohibiting them from doing this or watching that. Many parents have grown so anxious about their offspring that the latter barely learn how to move a finger for themselves. Even as serving soldiers, they are still known as "the children," instead of "the sons," as previously. As the Four Mothers movement's success in mobilizing the public and getting the IDF out of Lebanon showed, this fact is not without importance when it comes to Israel's ability to wage war and defend itself. Taking forever to grow up, "the children," instead of seeking independence, obstinately refuse to leave home. The average age at which young people get married has risen so much that many women have difficulty getting pregnant.

The children whose status underwent the most radical change of all were those raised on the kibbutzim. If only because, in them, both men and women worked as a matter of course (though women always did less and lighter work, and worked closer to the home, than men did), the family had to be broken up. Children lived in their own dormitories, which were known as children's "homes." From a very early age they did some work, which grew heavier as they became older, in addition to their studies; democratically running their own affairs under adult supervision, normally they saw their parents only for an hour or two each day as well as during the weekends. Starting in the 1970s, the system came under critical fire. All of a sudden, kibbutz women recalled the horrors allegedly inflicted on them by their unfeeling nurses when they themselves were young. They insisted that their children sleep at home and, as usual, they had their way.

Inevitably, once children started spending their nights at home they also began taking many more meals there. Slowly but surely, the communal dining rooms lost their function. The time was to come when they were used only on special festive occasions. Whereas previously couples lived in "rooms," now larger houses, complete with kitchens and everything that belongs in them, were needed. This in turn caused families to compete with each other over who should get which houses, when, on what terms, and in return for doing what work in the community. Since the financial crash of the early 1980s, the cracks that this issue opened have grown so wide that they have all but swallowed the kibbutz movement itself. The entire carefully constructed complex, consisting of collective ownership, equal pay, and communal living, started breaking down. In today's richer kibbutzim in particular, it has all but disappeared. Step by step they are being privatized, often to the accompaniment of vicious quarrels among the members.

To return to the children, whether individual parenting in separate houses is, in fact, such a great improvement on a well-thought-out, well-organized, caring system of collective living that is responsive to the needs of the individual may be questioned. Though they did not always stress academics as much as their urban counterparts did, the schools the kibbutzim provided were excellent—in many cases, this remains true to the present day. In the words of one world-famous psychoanalyst, Bruno Bettelheim, who was by no means uncritical of the system, the combination of study and work (which, he says, did not amount to exploitation) gave youths "the feeling that [they] understand all the things that count in [their] world [and] enhances beyond measure the feeling of competence, of security and well being."[39] By now, almost all of this has gone with the wind. Still, kibbutz children do grow up in an environment that is generally safe (there is little or no traffic), friendly, and often very beautiful, too. For these privileges, others can only envy them.

With the exception of those associated with kibbutz life, few if any of these problems are unique to Israel. In many ways they were imported from abroad, primarily from the United States, just as Elvis Presley was. Perhaps the one difference is that, since Israel was a semi-developed country for so long, they took a long time before they started making an impact. Yet like Elvis's music, when they did arrive they did so with the full power of the mightiest amplifier money can buy. Whether for objective reasons or for reasons that are self-inflicted, some areas of backwardness persist. On the whole, though, the country is moving into the twenty-first century at dizzying pace. Unless something very dramatic happens, that pace will not be relaxed in our lifetime.

"Scandinavia . . . or Like South America?"

In 1989 a senior economist in Israel's Ministry of Finance, looking back on the inflationary mess that had just been brought under control and that had almost caused the country's social and political fabric to unravel, looked back on that achievement. "The next decade," he wrote, "will show whether, in the future, Israel will be like Scandinavia, as the long term trends suggest, or like South America, as does the recent past."[40]

Twenty years later, Israel had many reasons to look back in satisfaction, even in triumph. Over the entire period since 1900 or so, no other country has confronted greater obstacles or made greater progress in overcoming them. As far as the internal situation goes, moreover, that progress was achieved with very little bloodshed and more or less within the broad framework of liberal/socialist democracy. There have been no attempted coups, military or other; no people who, for opposing the regime, disappeared without a trace; no concentration camps where people are held without trial; no death penalty; and so little attempt at thought control that one show forming part of the officially sponsored Israel Festival organized in honor of the country's sixtieth birthday dealt with "canned cannon fodder." In a way even the numerous and frequently very vicious critiques that Israelis direct against their own state represent a sign of strength, not of weakness. Had figures such as David Ben Gurion (who was always speaking of the need "to build up the country"), Zeev Jabotinsky, Haim Weizmann, and even Theodor Herzl with his utopian vision of *Old-New Land* been able to rise from the dead and look around, no doubt they would have thought they were seeing double.

To demand that a nation of seven million people be perfect—"thy camp shall be holy," as the Old Testament puts it[41]—is a dream; since perfection can only be attained under totalitarian control, probably it is not even a beautiful dream. If only because it has always been about as far from totalitarian as anything can be, the Zionists-Israeli enterprise certainly has its problematic, even seamy, sides. But then what enterprise does not? Besides, given the dynamism by which it is sustained, many of its strands are incomplete. Who knows where they may yet lead! As in any society problems appear, grow, merge with others. They are tackled, or not tackled, and either disappear or stay in place.

At the time of writing, the issue that commands the most attention is that of corruption. If the media are to be believed, the system is corrupt from top to bottom. But is it? Or may some other factors be at work? At the end of 1976, when then–attorney general Aharon Barak was ordering Asher Yadlin to be investigated on that charge,[42] the latter's former wife, Dalia, wrote in *Haaretz:*

> "We are commanded to drive the investigation to the very end" ... said [prime minister] Rabin on television ... but what does "to the very end" mean? To the end of the person under investigation? To the end of the state itself? To the end of its leaders? Only in totalitarian regimes are investigations of this kind driven "to the end"—to the moment when a confession is extracted!
>
> A person refuses to sign on the dotted line. This "compels" the investigating authorities to use more severe means; Yadlin (who, both by law and by his own testimony, is still innocent) is

arrested, incarcerated, humiliated. . . . Is there no way to supervise the process and prevent the river of leaked information
from providing people with bread and circuses? And suppose
errors are discovered in the way the police does its . . . work,
who will pay? Who will be called to account for making mis-
takes that ruin a man's good name, his health, and his family?[43]

In fact, Yadlin was lucky. At the time this article was published he
had been under investigation for just one month. Others have waited
for years, even while under house arrest, before the public attorney finally decided whether to indict. Even then, several more years might
very well pass before the trial opened, let alone before a verdict was
reached. During that period, in the words of a former chairman of the
Knesset, Reuven Rivlin, "the police, the public attorney, and the media
form a symbiosis [in denouncing him]. . . . should he so much as try to
talk back, he will be accused of leaking information."[44]

So far, out of every twenty public figures whom the media have tried
to drown in their slime, perhaps one has been convicted. Certainly this
is not because the judiciary has been intimidated. As we saw, the opposite is the case; under Barak, its independence has grown to the point
where some, including Olmert's minister of justice, Daniel Friedman,
believe that its (unelected) members are putting democracy in danger.
Among the few who *have* been convicted is one of Sharon's sons, Omri,
who helped his father raise some money for the party primaries, as well
as a former Likud MK by the name of Naomi Blumenthal. Her crime
consisted of distributing $3,000 in cash among three or four of her
party council members. This princely sum enabled them to spend a
night or two in a four-star Ramat Gan hotel and made them vote for her
in the primaries. Even the diabolical Ehud Olmert, assuming he is ultimately convicted in court, has only been accused of illegally raising
$150,000 over a period of more than ten years.

Whether Israel is more corrupt than many other countries is unknown. International ratings put it at 30 out of 180 or so,[45] but these
ratings are so much moonshine. What *is* known is that, owing largely to
the ferocious competition in which they engage, Israeli media have become very aggressive indeed. They only publish what they think will
sell; and what will sell is, by and large, not good news about good

people performing good deeds. This, of course, is a problem Israel shares with other developed countries and with many that are a little less developed, too. The better educated the public in any country, the greater apparently its appetite for every kind of scandal; by that standard, the Israeli public seems to be very well educated indeed. The difference is that, in Israel, even the daily that likes to call itself "the paper for people who think" (*Haaretz*) has become about as yellow as yellow can be. If, while giving a telephone interview, one so much as ventures to defend anyone in power, chances are that the journalist one is talking to will hang up without so much as saying good-bye.

Another issue that has often come under the spotlights is the quest for social justice or, to be precise, Israel's alleged failure in achieving it. As President Harry Truman is supposed to have quipped, there are lies, damn lies, and statistics. Given what has already been said on this matter, there can be little question that at least some of the statistics various left-wing groups keep producing on this matter consist, if not of outright lies, then of deliberate distortions. Though some Israelis depend on soup kitchens, nobody starves. A visit to any shopping center will confirm the existence of a solid middle class. Recently, even Arab maids working in Jewish households have begun using cars to go to work. Though living conditions are often not of the best, there are few homeless. Israelis enjoy a longer life expectancy than Americans do (80.6 versus 78.1 years).[46] This applies in spite of all the wars, and in spite also of the fact that the medical establishment consumes only 8 percent of the GDP as opposed to twice as much in the United States.

Furthermore, many of the most common difficulties are self-inflicted. Together, Orthodox Jews and Israeli Arabs comprise approximately 1.7 million people, one quarter of the entire population. Both groups have far larger families than average, which goes far to explain the number of children said to be living in poverty. A little more willingness among them to modernize, study, and work—plus a little more responsibility on the part of women who decide to become single mothers and/or get a divorce at the drop of a hat without giving a thought to their children's future—would do wonders to the statistics as well as the reality they represent.

That said, parts of the problem *are* real. The utopian vision that used to underpin Israeli socialism *has* evaporated (some, however, would claim that it never really existed). The terms on which many people are employed *have* deteriorated. Netanyahu's reforms of 2003 were a great success. They probably saved Israel from economic collapse; but they also caused social gaps to widen somewhat. The bottom line is that many people, children included, *do* live in poverty. But how does one deal with such problems without, at the same time, slaughtering that central pillar of modern life, economic growth? How does one do so without causing investment to dry up, and without taking away people's desire to work? Do Israelis really want to return to the days when almost all of them were equal in poverty? And isn't it true that, even in those supposedly idyllic days, some were much better off than others? Voluntary organizations—of which Israel has a great many—do what they can, but there are clear limits to their activities. Moreover, insofar as they make people dependent on them, some of those activities may well be counterproductive. Even among developed countries, let alone the far more numerous developing ones, Israel is hardly the only one to face such problems. Given the extremely high percentage of resources that it spends—must spend—on defense, to demand that it find quick and complete solutions for them is a little unfair.

Whereas these problems are common to Israel and many, if not most, other developed countries, those surrounding the relationship between state and religion are unique. Right from the beginning of Zionism, its purpose has been to give Jews a country of their own so that they could be like any other people—"a national home, recognized in public law," as Herzl put it. Right from the beginning, perhaps the greatest difficulty was that the only way to define Jews, who for many centuries had been scattered over much of the world and participated in many cultures, was by the religion they professed. There thus was no way in which state and religion could be separated—even if Zionists and Israeli Jews had wanted to do so, which the vast majority did not.

Among the Jewish population, the need for a Jewish state remains all but unquestioned (for non-Jews, see below). Indeed, fully 47 percent of the (Jewish) population define themselves as Jewish first, compared with only 39 percent who identify themselves primarily as Israelis.[47] Even so, there are sharp disagreements as to how Jews should be and just what Jewish-ness should mean. In the eyes of a small ultra-Orthodox minority, the very establishment of the state represented a rebellion against God. Others, including some Orthodox and many "national" religious people, want to give it a much more Jewish character than it actually has; however, when it comes to defining just what that character entails, they cannot agree among themselves. Indeed, the Orthodox are always belaboring the "national" religious for not being religious enough when it comes to such questions as *kashrut,* dress, separation between the sexes, and the like. In response, some of the latter mend their ways, donning black and becoming more strictly Orthodox than before. Many others end up by taking off their knitted yarmulkes, starting to drive on the Sabbath, and merging into the secular majority.

The secular majority, for its part, is always railing against this or that policy that the state imposes in the name of religion or, which amounts to the same thing, the blackmail that religious/Orthodox parties practice. Now it is the fact that Orthodox youths do not serve in the IDF that is highlighted; now, the fact that there is no public transport on the Sabbath; and now, that the rabbinate still maintains too much power over conversions, etc. Yet that majority also recognizes that, but for Judaism, that state's raison d'être would disappear. They themselves might well leave the arid Middle East for greener pastures, and their children would become indistinguishable from any other people among whom they may happen to live. The ideological and political tug-of-war on these issues proceeds on a daily basis. Extreme demands are raised, discussed, forgotten. Pork barrel–type considerations—for example, who should get what post on the rabbinical courts—enter the fray. Now one side, now the other, scores a point. Few people are happy with the status quo, and the result may well be bitterness and even hatred. On the other hand, arguing about these things is part of the fun of being an Israeli.

Looking back on sixty years of statehood, it may be possible to discern several different trends, some of them contradictory. While Israel has a minority of Jews who really detest religion, or at least any attempt it makes to go beyond the consciences of private individuals, the days when left-wing socialist—hence atheist—ideologies played an important part in public life are largely past. Even most kibbutzim, which for decades used to celebrate their own version of Feast of Tabernacles (Sukkot), Passover (Pessah) and the harvest festival Shavuot as if they were some kinds of heathen agricultural festivals, have returned to the fold. While the rabbinate does continue doing what it can to preserve the "Jewish" character of public life, on the whole it has been fighting a rearguard action and not a very successful one at that. Unkosher food is much more widely available than it used to be. Even in Jerusalem, the number of bars and coffeehouses and cinemas and shops that stay open on the Sabbath and feast days has risen dramatically.

Thanks largely to the spread of privately owned cars, the time when Israel's roads were deserted on the days in question are long over. Instead many kibbutzim and other settlements, Arab ones included, make their livings specifically by enacting laws that enable businesses to stay open. In this way they attract customers who do not have the time to do their shopping, or have a family meal in a restaurant, at any other time. Thanks largely to the spread of TV and the Internet, religious and Orthodox people are exposed to a flood of secular ideas concerning dress, comportment, relations between the sexes, and the like. Not for nothing do many rabbis do what they can, up to and including the use of violence, to prevent their flock from owning and using the "extremely unclean apparatus" that causes "such tremendous damage to the soul."[48] In some neighborhoods, the discovery of an antenna that proves one does so may carry consequences ranging from a social boycott to being beaten to within an inch of one's life.

Judging by the placards (*pashquevills,* as they are known) on the walls of Bnei Brak and Jerusalem's Mea Shearim quarter, the world is faced by a tsunami of sin that threatens to drown it at any moment. The only thing standing between it and perdition is a thin dam made up of "true" Judaism and its strict, if often anonymous, adherents. Yet the flood is mighty and its waters are constantly rising. First they start flowing over the top of the dam, then they burst in a hole in it. Pouring down the valley, they may set off mighty mudslides. Women have been observed going around in "immodest" dress, and one or two even dared touch an unrelated man in public. A nearby stand sells secular papers and magazines with pictures of people in various states of undress. To make a profit, X is selling religious artifacts, such as *mezuzot* (small cases containing parchments with passages from the Torah written on them that are fixed to doorposts), that are not quite as they should be (many *pashquevills,* while ostensibly aimed to protect religion, reflect internal struggles among various rabbis and other members of the population).

In response, people are called upon to boycott X's shop. On other occasions they must "tear their clothes, wear sackcloth and raise a bitter cry" to God, or simply mend their sinful ways. Day by day some new danger is discovered. There can be no doubt but that the rabbis are under pressure; in June 2008 some even refrained from mounting demonstrations against the gay love parade held in Jerusalem in the fear that their own children might ask them what the fracas was all about. Many of their followers are deserting the camp. Partly as a result, in spite of the much larger number of offspring that they bring into the world, the percentage in the population of those who put religion at the center of their lives versus those who do not seems to have changed little since 1948.

As will be remembered, one often-discussed issue connected with religion is that of matrimonial law. In Israel there is no civil marriage, so that only religious courts can perform a wedding. Focusing on the Jewish majority, this means one is not free to marry a non-Jew or even certain categories of Jews. For example, a person with the surname of Cohen (Priest) cannot marry a divorced woman; a person born of a married woman who committed adultery cannot marry at all. Of late, many couples have chosen to evade the entire system. They do so either because they cannot marry in Israel, or simply because they hate the rabbinate and everything it stands for. Some go abroad; others resort to a so-called Paraguayan wedding, which is performed by mail. While Israel's population is growing, the rabbis' obstinacy has turned many people against them. The number of weddings they are asked to perform is falling year by year. Not that running away necessarily helps people who choose to use these methods to escape the rabbis' clutches; married couples still depend on the rabbis when it comes to obtaining a divorce, as about 40 percent of them do at some point in their lives.

Israeli feminist publications bristle with bone-chilling accounts of how backward, how obscurantist, how anti-women, and how wicked the rabbinical courts are. Horror stories abound. Here a court took away a woman's children (and the couple's flat) because of her "immodest" dress and because her husband, suddenly discovering his religious faith, allegedly offered them a better education. There one whose husband refused to grant her a divorce—in Jewish law, a woman cannot divorce without her partner's consent—became "anchored" *(aguna)*. She either paid him off or else spent years without being able to remarry. Until recently a female religious lawyer—not that there were such creatures—did not even have the right to represent a client in front of the courts in question. That all the judges are male hardly requires saying.

Some of the claims are true. Others are false, others exaggerated, others still one-sided. However, since the courts, and the men involved in the trials in question, rarely bother to answer the accusations or are given the chance to do so by the media, it is impossible to say which are true and which are false. Though few people realize the fact, as of late 2008 slightly more men than women were being denied a divorce by their partners.[49] It is certainly true that Jewish law has its peculiarities, and that some of these peculiarities work against women who are seeking divorce, child custody, and the like. There is, however, nothing especially Jewish or Israeli about that. The country with a divorce system that will satisfy men *and* women has not yet been created. Sharp as the differences between Orthodox and non-Orthodox people on these and similar issues are, they do not threaten Israel's social fabric any more than, say, the ongoing debates over alimony are about to destroy that of the United States.

Yet there are some signs that real change in the balance between the Orthodox and the secular communities is on the way. Once again it is necessary to mention Netanyahu's reforms; by taking away the child allowances, he forced many Orthodox men to look for work. Forced to look for work, they are even now taking up secular studies, including, not least, computer studies, for which their Talmudic background—based on group study and sharp-witted questioning arguments and counterarguments—provides an ideal preparation. Presumably secular studies and secular jobs will draw them closer to the mainstream, and indeed this may already be happening. In time this may also lead to smaller families and a different lifestyle; even if they do not, the fact that people have jobs will allow them less free time in which to follow the rabbis' call, descend into the streets, and demonstrate against this or that alleged violation of religious law.

Unfortunately, the same cannot be said of the non-Jewish minorities, especially the 90 percent who are Sunni Muslims. As the ongoing debate between the proponents of "a Jewish state"—all of whom are Jewish—and those who demand "a state belonging to all citizens"—almost all of whom are non-Jews—shows, to be an Israeli citizen without sharing in the religion/nationhood of the majority ipso facto means to suffer some forms of discrimination. In practice, if not in law, Israeli Arabs are barred from building their homes in a number of communal settlements erected on land that the Zionist Organization purchased for the benefit of Jews. On a per capita basis Arab municipalities obtain far less government money than Jewish ones do (in its defense, the government says that those municipalities should start by putting their own affairs in order and start levying taxes). As a result, they often provide schools, cultural facilities, leisure facilities, and even sewage systems far inferior to the ones Jewish citizens enjoy.

Coming to the towns, Arab students are hard put to find Jews who will rent them flats or rooms. Having finished their studies, Arab graduates are much less likely to find work in many private and public companies. Wishing to build a home in their own municipalities and villages, Arab men and women will find that many of the lands in question have never been properly parceled out. Sixty-something years after the establishment of the state, no master plans for their use have been drawn up. The outcome is that in Arab settlements such as Abu Gosh or Umm el Fahem, there is a vast amount of "illegal" construction. Partly because the buildings are, strictly speaking, illegal, and partly because the most important social unit still remains the family or the clan and not the individual, disputes over ownership abound. Both places look like rabbit warrens—in many ways they *are* rabbit warrens. High birthrates and insufficient space compel people to build their houses alongside and on top of one another. The municipal council may well find it impossible to build a road, construct a water pipe, or find a lot for erecting a school. As a result, backwardness grows from inside the settlements even when, as is sometimes the case, it is not imposed on them from outside.

One might go on forever listing the grievances—including the fact that Arab persons stopped by the police are much more likely to be harassed and those trying to leave the country much more likely to be searched and questioned. Much of this springs directly from the fact that Israel is still in a state of war with numerous Palestinian organizations as well as several of its Arab neighbors; in other words, it reflects the demands of security and what Machiavelli would have called *necessità*. For example, do the rights of an Arab-Israeli citizen really take precedence over the safety of a jumbo jet (not necessarily one that belongs to an Israeli carrier) taking off from Tel Aviv airport with four hundred passengers aboard? That, however, is not the whole story. When everything is said and done, it is not even the most important part. By the above-mentioned Law of Return, any Jew from anywhere in the world can move to Israel and automatically become a citizen upon arrival. As another law now stands and was confirmed by the Supreme Court, Israeli Arabs cannot even marry their next-door neighbors, residents of the occupied territories, and bring their partners home to live with them. Instead, if they wish to set up a common household, they must move into the territories.

These problems are a very long way from being solved; indeed, given how deeply rooted they are in Israel's very nature, perhaps they are not even capable of being solved. The fact that many Israeli Arabs refrain from voting in the elections—in a democracy, those who do not vote do not count—does nothing to help. At times it can be a question of life and death. From the early days of the state there have been some episodes, though fortunately few and far between, when the Israeli security forces opened fire on Arab citizens. Once, on the eve of the 1956 war, this was because some villagers broke a curfew of which they were unaware; later the trigger was violent demonstrations that caused the police officers to lose their heads. Opening fire, they killed some and injured others. Needless to say, nothing like this has ever happened at times when the demonstrators were Jewish. This even included occasions such as the evacuation of Yamit in 1981, when the demonstrators behaved very violently indeed; or when preparing to evacuate Gaza in 2005, Chief of Staff Dan Halutz promised to proceed "sensitively."

Partly in response to this situation, Israel now has an active and very venomous Islamic Fundamentalist movement. It seems determined to imitate the Taliban as best it can, including a ban on alcohol, strict control over women and the way they dress, and opposition to any kind of secular studies that might make people stray from the straight and narrow. Following the Koran, some of the movement's leaders have publicly called Jews apes and pigs.⁵⁰ They also deny the right of the state, whose citizen they are, to exist.

Still, not everything is dark. On paper, Israel's non-Jewish citizens enjoy the same rights as Jewish ones do. Discrimination is officially prohibited and in many respects equality is real; for example, when it comes to receiving social security benefits, entrance to the universities, etc. Furthermore, the number of Israeli Arabs who have decided to put backwardness behind them is growing. More Israeli Arabs are getting an education and even permitting their women to get one; among Arab students, the ratio of male to female students is almost exactly the same as among Jewish ones. They also read the Israeli press. In fact, *Yediot Aharonot,* Israel's most popular Hebrew-language paper, has more Israeli Arab readers than any Arabic-language one. Israeli Arabs are also limiting the number of children they have, and looking for jobs that will provide them with a proper income and standard of living. While opportunities in the Jewish sector are limited, the number of those jobs found within their own community is growing. Geographically scattered as that community is, it is now large and sophisticated enough to enable even some academics, such as physicians, lawyers, teachers, researchers, writers, and artists, to make a living inside it.

The advantages of being an Israeli Arab are particularly impressive when one compares their situation to that of their brethren across the border. It is true that the life expectancy of Israeli Arabs is about four years lower than that of Israeli Jews; but it is also true that in no Arab country except Kuwait do people live longer (and then not by much). It is true that infant mortality is higher among Israeli Arabs than among Israeli Jews ones; but it is also true that it is lower than in any Arab country.⁵¹ In the entire Middle East, Israel is the only country where Arabs, Arab women included, have the right to cast their votes for the party of their choice and where doing so has any meaning at all. In the entire Middle East, it is the only country where they can publicly pose the question as to where their rulers got their fortunes without being arrested, tortured, imprisoned (either without trial or after one that is only put on for show), and perhaps executed.

Most Israeli Arabs, having lived under Israeli rule for more than sixty years, are acutely aware of the above advantages. With the exception of the citizens of the oil states, economically speaking they are also much better off than most other Arabs. In a sense, Herzl's vision that the Zionist enterprise would only improve the economic situation of Arabs in the "Old-New Land" has come true. The younger ones among them keep saying that they are the "the stand-tall generation," a term taken from a well-known nationalist poem by Samih Al-Qassem.[52] The curious thing about Al-Qassem's terminology is that this and other expressions he uses—"head held high," "I hold an olive branch"—have been taken straight from the Zionist thesaurus in which they also figure and to which the Palestinian National Charter, among other key documents, owes much.

While these people feel alienated from the Jewish state that, they say, denies them their rights, again there is another side to the matter. Each time a Jewish-Israeli politician such as Avigdor Liberman mentions the possibility of transferring land inhabited by Israeli Arabs—not the inhabitants, who, under his plan, will remain just where they are—from Israeli rule to a future Palestinian state, they become almost hysterical. And with very good reason: Visiting the occupied territories, and traveling in the Arab world, they can see firsthand how poor, how backward, how contemptuous of the individual most of that world is. Becoming part of the West Bank would mean joining a society where per capita income is less than 10 percent of the Israeli figure. To make things much worse still, they would be entering a world where "rights" do not exist—indeed, Arabic does not even have a term to describe them. In that world, whatever education a person may acquire can be used for just two purposes, namely, to lick the boots of those in power or to beg their forgiveness. As the late Palestinian poet Mahmoud Darwish, who was anything but a friend of the Jews, once put it, the Zionist wolf was more merciful than his supposed Arab brothers.

Scandinavia or South America? Two decades after the question was asked, the latter alternative at any rate has been practically ruled out. Democracy and social stability have been preserved, and the economy has grown by leaps and bounds. Almost the only thing that could cause things to go seriously wrong is a massive intifada by Israeli Arabs. Barring that, Israel seems ready to become one of the most highly developed societies on earth, complete with a flourishing culture and scientific and technological achievements that are a match for those found anywhere else. But does that mean it may one day turn *into* Scandinavia? If one imagines this in terms of near perfect external peace, very high environmental standards, economic justice, far-reaching social equality, and a stolid, all but corruption-free political establishment that provides citizens with a very good administration indeed, then the answer is almost certainly no.

But then, this is only one side of the coin. In the eyes of many people, much of Scandinavia stands for a pompous bureaucracy that thinks it always knows everything better than anyone else. Supposedly it is characterized by extremely tight social control over the individual, from erection to resurrection, as the saying goes. To this is added occasional inexpressible boredom—everything is so *normal*—coldhearted interpersonal relationships, and a higher-than-average suicide rate. Compare this with hot, messy, noisy, sweaty (but very clean; almost all Israelis, unlike many Europeans, take a shower every day), heterogeneous, undisciplined, warmhearted Israel; the kind of place where almost anybody will lend you his or her cell phone in an emergency and where, sneezing near an open window, one may hear some invisible passerby call out "Bless you." Assuming the stereotype is more or less correct, should Israelis really want to be like Scandinavia?

Epilogue

―――∽∞∽――――

"NO MORE WAR"?

More than a hundred years since Herzl convened the First Zionist Congress in Basel, his self-imposed mission, namely, to create a national home for the Jews, has been accomplished to a very large extent. Whereas a century ago only a minuscule part of all Jews lived in "the Land," now approximately 40 percent do. Whereas, initially, the Jewish community in that land was largely dependent on the Zionist Organization, abroad, long ago the relationship has become much more balanced and the Jewish Agency turned into something very close to a mere arm of the Israeli government. As recently as the 1970s, it looked as though Israel was the only country in the world where the lives of Jews were in physical danger. Since then things have radically changed.

To be sure, one may suffer the bad fortune of being blown up by a terrorist bomb in Jerusalem or Tel Aviv. However, nowadays the same may happen to almost anyone, Jew or gentile, in New York and London, Madrid and Buenos Aires; the events of 9/11 alone took the lives of far more people (a few of them Israelis) than those Israel lost in all the twenty years of the first and second intifadas combined. Judging by the vast boom in Jerusalem real-estate prices that started around 2005 and was brought about by French Jews buying apartments there, some Diaspora Jews already anticipate the day when they and their children may be safer in Israel than in the country where the Dreyfus Affair, which as readers will remember was what first inspired Herzl, took place. But Israel has made a difference in the position even of those

Jews who feel, or claim to feel, perfectly safe in and integrated into the societies where they happen to live. No longer are they like a loan without collateral. Whatever the future may bring, there now is one state on Earth that will always take them in, by force of law and with no questions asked, except some kind of proof that they are, in fact, Jews.

Among Diaspora Jews, one sometimes hears the complaint that Israel, partly by its "irrational" and "illegal" behavior in the occupied territories but partly also by its mere existence, does more to contribute to anti-Semitism than to combat it. This line of thought was especially prevalent in the 1970s, but it is by no means extinct today. The answer is, may those who feel that way enjoy their fears. To ordinary Israelis, who are proud of their country and feel reasonably secure in it, they are of no concern. Indeed, it is perhaps Israel's greatest achievement that it has created a state of affairs where anti-Semitism no longer directly touches its citizens—in other words, where they are in a position to tell the gentiles: "Do you want to be anti-Semitic? That is your problem, not ours."

While Israel has been developing at an astonishing pace, the world around it has not stood still, either. Probably the most important changes were those that transformed the world arena. Israel's birth took place against the background of the Cold War (even though, for a brief moment, it was able to enjoy the support of *both* superpowers). Later, some of its struggles with the Arab states were very much part of that war. However, in 1989–1991 the Cold War came to a sudden end. As the American colossus straddled, or seemed to straddle, the globe, Israel's international position improved out of all recognition. One result of this was a further increase in the already massive flow of U.S. aid. Another is that many countries were eager to resume or improve relations with it, seeing that the road to Washington, D.C., appeared to lead, to some extent, through Jerusalem.

Most probably, the hour of glory will not last. The United States may change its mind; there is no shortage of voices, both on the right and on the left, that are demanding such a policy shift and would love to bring it about just as soon as they can. U.S. power may not remain as it has been, and some believe it is already declining. Yet taking an Israeli point of view, would that be such a bad thing? The alternative to the American hegemony that was created by George H. W. Bush, strengthened by William J. Clinton, and put into question by George W. Bush's adventurism is probably a world divided among five large powers: to wit, the United States, the European Union, Russia, China, and India. All are nuclear armed. All have what it takes to annihilate their rivals, and all balance one another. The days when out of two superpowers one was the Jewish state's bitter enemy, and when China and India refused to so much as acknowledge its existence, are gone. Instead Israel keeps a good relationship with all five. Maintaining normal relations with them, and assuming a minimum of diplomatic skill, it ought to be able to maneuver among them even if, one day, it can no longer rely on the U.S. as its principal protector.

It is true that, in wide parts of the Arab/Islamic world, including some of those who have formally ended the state of belligerence and signed peace treaties with Israel, the latter's existence is still not considered a normal, let alone desirable, part of the Middle East. Some hope for nothing better than that it should disappear; if they regularly vent their spleens against it, then perhaps one reason why they do so is because they cannot see any realistic way to bring that feat about. It is also true that, in terms of size and at least potential wealth, Israel's enemies, declared and undeclared, are far superior to it and will retain their superiority into almost any kind of imaginable future. Yet what are the heads of the states in question to do? Given Israel's nuclear teeth, which are sharp and constantly growing in number, to attack it without acquiring nuclear weapons first would be madness; to attack it after acquiring such weapons, much greater madness still. In fact, there is some reason to believe that one reason Egypt in particular has never brought its nuclear program to fruition is because, to quote one Egyptian academic, such weapons would render a war between it and Israel "unthinkable."[1]

Israel is now formally at peace with two of its former enemies, Egypt and Jordan. With the latter it has long had a common interest: keeping the Palestinians in what both sides see as their proper place; also, in making sure that Syria does not again invade Jordan, as it did in 1970. Since Hamas took over power in the Gaza Strip in 2007, Egypt, too, has discovered it has a common interest with Israel: to limit, and if possible cut back, the power of that organization. To be sure, a revolution that will bring to power an Islamic regime in Cairo cannot be

ruled out. Should it take place, it could have very unpleasant consequences for Israel, for several other countries in the Middle East, and
perhaps for the rest of the world as well. Even so, one must not exaggerate. Any new regime that may arise will still be left with the question of how to deal with Israeli power in general, and Israeli nuclear
power in particular.

Other Arab/Islamic countries pose even less of a problem. Saudi
Arabia has never taken part in any of the Arab-Israeli wars and appears
content to rest on its oil. Lebanon may launch terrorists from its
territory—although, as of early 2010, even that threat seems farther away
than it has been for the last forty years. Iraq, which at one time appeared to present a truly great danger, no longer exists in the same
form and will probably never again rise to that form. Iran's leaders, far
away, will be deterred by Israeli power—or, if they are not, will meet
the Zionists whom they hate so much either in the Muslim hell or in the
Jewish one. Syria, even a Syria that is supported from afar by Iran, does
not have what it takes to really put Israel at risk. True, an exchange of
missiles carrying weapons of mass destruction, including, on the Syrian
side, chemical ones, is theoretically possible; but Damascus would have
to be stark raving mad to engage in one.

To be sure, it would be nice to have peace with all these countries.
If, in the case of Syria, the price of peace is surrendering the Golan
Heights, then—provided issues such as borders, water, and security arrangements in the form of demilitarized zones and early warning stations can be resolved—it is worth paying. Should Assad one day venture
to visit Jerusalem as Sadat did, then there can be very little doubt that
peace will meet the overwhelming approval of the people; in fact, each
time an Israeli prime minister starts behaving as if such a peace were
within reach, the stock market goes up sharply. Still, as long as Israel's
military power holds, such peace is not essential for survival.

Since Sharon took Israel out of the Gaza Strip, thus turning it from
an internal political problem into an external political one, the most
intractable problem of all is represented by the two and a half million
or so Palestinians in the West Bank. Militarily speaking, there is no
question that those Palestinians will ever be able to put Israel at any
real risk. Should the worst really come to the worst, then Israel, the
heroics of the "stand-tall" generation notwithstanding, will always have

what it takes to drive them across the border as it did back in 1948. In the eyes of all but a very small minority, though, that is the most ruthless, least desirable "solution" of all. Heaven forbid that it has to be carried out. Hopefully a better one can be found and implemented, or else Israel will never be able to lead a "normal" life in accordance with its own basic values.

Entire libraries have been written about the issue, and those who want to may consult them. This writer would very much like to see Israel dismantle the settlements, which represent nothing but a thorn in its side, and withdraw to a line as close as possible to the pre-1967 border.[2] This is not out of any concern for the Palestinians, or out of regard to some abstract principle of justice. The former should look after themselves; the latter has no room in the world of strategy. Rather it is because, if Israel wants to have a future, it must rid itself of as many Palestinians as it can. As long as the process is not completed, Israel will continue to resemble the policeman who, while handcuffed to a prisoner, keeps shouting that he himself is free whereas the other man is not.

The change should be carried out by agreement if possible, unilaterally if it is not. If that means building a massive wall between the two peoples—so massive that even the birds cannot fly over it—and postponing the withdrawal until some effective method for defending against rockets is found, then so be it.[3] Judging by history—the Peel Commission in 1937, the UN Partition Plan of 1947, the Camp David Accords of 1979, the Oslo Accords in 1993, and the 2005 withdrawal from Gaza—Israeli public opinion *can* be persuaded to support such a decision not just passively but with some enthusiasm. It is also worth remembering that, out of those five decisions two, those of 1979 and 2005, were made by right wingers who, throughout their lives, were committed to retain as much of the occupied territories as possible; thus even the elections of February 2009, which resulted in a sharp rightward turn, need not necessarily prevent further withdrawals. Indeed it appears that, deep in their hearts, most Israelis know how the struggle will end. This even includes many of the settlers who prefer to bury their dead relatives inside the borders of what is affectionately known as "old" Israel.

Still, it is essential to keep some kind of presence in the parts of East Jerusalem that are most sacred to the Jewish people, such as the

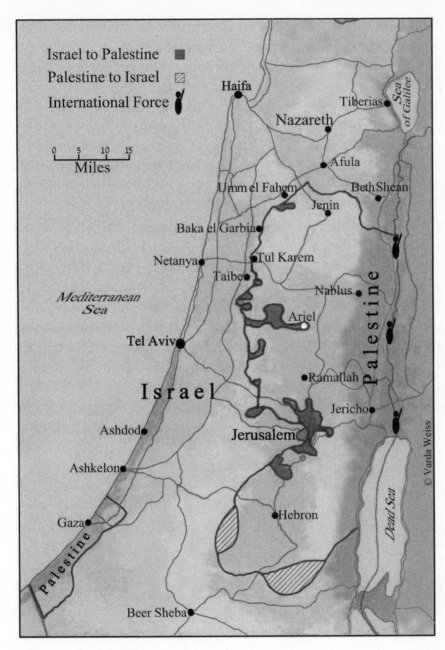

The Israeli-Palestinian Conflict: A Possible Solution?

Wailing Wall. Israel's claim to these places is as strong as that of anybody else; without them, it will be left without its soul.

Perfect peace, the kind that prevails in Scandinavia and Western Europe, is probably out of reach for some time to come. However, to quote President Anwar Sadat during his visit to Jerusalem "no more war"—at any rate, major war that involves major military operations and major casualties—very likely is not. In fact, the last war of that kind is already thirty-six years in the past. For all the excitement that the 2008–2009 offensive in Gaza generated, it only resulted in thirteen Israeli dead, several of them by friendly fire; that is fewer than the number normally killed by traffic in the three-week period it lasted. As bloodshed is brought to an end, the bereaved parents on both sides pass away, the widows remarry or resign themselves to their lot, and the orphans grow up and form families of their own, perhaps the truce will develop into something better. And may the day come when the prayer of all Israeli fathers and mothers whenever a son is born to them and, at the age of eight days, is circumcised—namely that he may not have to wear a uniform and serve in the IDF—is at long last granted.

GLOSSARY OF HEBREW TERMS

Agudat Israel (The Association of Israel) The most important Orthodox party.

aguna (agunot) A woman who has been "anchored" by (1) A husband who refuses to grant her a divorce; (2) a husband who has disappeared; (3) wicked and/or stupid rabbis who refuse to take these facts into account.

Ahdut Haavoda (Unity of Labor) A former left-wing party with an "activist" line in foreign affairs.

askan(im) A party hack.

Bagatz (Beth Din Gavoha Letzedek) (1) The title of the Supreme Court when it sits as a court of first and last resort; (2) a plea served to that court.

balagan A mess.

Betar (1) A now largely defunct youth movement that used to be linked to the Herut Party; (2) a Jerusalem soccer club with notoriously wild fans.

Bnei Akiva (Sons of Akiva) A youth movement linked to the National Religious Party.

Dash A middle-of-the-road party that was set up in 1977, gained thirteen seats in the elections, and promptly broke up.

dunam A measure of land, approximately one-quarter of an acre.

en brera **(no choice)** The term long used by Israelis to sum up their country's strategic situation.

Eretz Israel The Land of Israel.

Eretz Israel Hashlema (The Complete Land of Israel) A term used by those who refuse to give up the occupied territories.

Etzel (Irgun Tzvai Leumi) National Military Organization.

fashla (fashlot) A blunder.

freha **(hen)** Originally a given name; now a loud, cheaply dressed, vulgar woman.

frenk Sephardi Jew.

Gahal (Gush Herut-Liberalim) The National Liberal Block set up by Begin in 1965.

Gashashim (The Trackers) A famous musical troupe that succeeded in capturing Israeli life like no other.

Hagana (Defense) The Jewish community's armed force.

Hakirya (The Town) The Tel Aviv site where the IDF General Staff has its headquarters.

haluka Distribution (of alms).

hared(im) **(anxious one)** An Orthodox Jew.

"Hatikva" (The Hope) Israel's national anthem.

Herut (Freedom) Begin's right-wing nationalist party.

Histadrut (Histadrut Haklalit Haovdim Beeretz Israel) The federation of trade union organizations.

Hovevei Zion (Lovers of Zion) A group of proto-Zionists that arrived in the Land in 1881–82.

Israel Baaliya (Israel in Immigration) A party made up of immigrants From Russia.

Kach (Thus) A right-wing religious movement that used to be active during the 1980s.

Kadima (Forward, or Eastward) The party founded by Sharon in 2005.

kashrut The Jewish system of ritually pure food.

KASTAH (Kissuy Tahat) Cover your ass.

kibbutz(im) A type of communal settlement where all property is held in common and children live separately from their parents.

Lehi (Lohamei Herut Israel) Israel's Freedom Fighters.

Likud (Cohesion) The right-wing party established out of Herut and some smaller groups in 1974.

lira The Israeli pound, which remained in circulation until 1982.

Maccabee A center-of-the-line youth movement that used to be associated with the General Zionist liberal Party.

Maimunah A feast celebrated by Moroccan Jews on the day following Passover, now a semiofficial national holiday.

MALAG (Moetza Lehaskala Gevoha) Council for Higher Education.

Mamram (Merkaz Mahshevim Vemaarahot Meda) Center for Computers and Information Systems, the computer unit that is run by the ministry of defense and the IDF in common.

Mapai (Mifleget Poalei Eretz Israel) The Party of Israel's laborers, ancestor of today's Labor Party.

massorti(yim) A traditionally minded person.

mazkir Secretary, the most important person in any kibbutz.

mehdal Error, oversight, blunder.

Meretz (Energy) A left-wing liberal-socialist party.

Merkaz Harav (Rabbi's Center) A famous right-wing nationalist *yeshiva* in Jerusalem.

mezuzah (mezuzot) Small metal or wooden cases containing passages from the Torah and fixed to doorposts.

mikveh Jewish ritual bath.

mistanen(im) Infiltrators, people who cross the border without authorization.

mitun A recession.

Moledet (Motherland) A right-wing party of the 1980s and 1990s.

moshav(im) A kind of communal settlement with individual lots, and in which the family structure is maintained.

nehentan(im) Hedonists, a term used by right-wing extremists to describe their normal opponents.

Neturei Karta (Guardians of the City) A group of ultra-Orthodox Jews in Jeruslaem.

ODATZ (Oreh Din Tzamud) A lawyer who covers your ass.

Palmach (Pluggot Mahatz, shock companies) Hagana's pre-1948 strike force.

pashquevills Placards that cover the walls of Orthodox neighborhoods.

Pessah Passover.

poel (poalim) Worker, laborer.

Rafael (Rashut Lefituah Emtzaei Lehima) The government-owned agency for weapons development.

Rafi (Reshimat Poalei Israel, List of Israel's Workers) A party set up by Ben Gurion after he left Mapai in 1973.

Shas (Sepharadim Shomrei Torah, Observant Sephardis) An Orthodox party founded by Rabi Ovadia Yosef in the 1980s.

Shavuot A harvest festival celebrated in late spring.

Shinui (Change) A now defunct center-of-the-road, secular party.

shofar A ritual trumpet, made of a ram's horn and blown during the high holidays.

slik(kim) Hidden arms caches.

Sukkot The Feast of Tabernacles.

talkbackist(im) People who use their computers to respond to media reports published on the Net.

Tami (Tenuat Masoret Israel, Movement for the Jewish Tradition) A religious party of the early 1980s.

Tehia (Revival) A right-wing party of the 1980s and early 1990s.

tshah-tshah(im) Moroccan Jew, also meaning rough and vulgar.

tzena The austerity program of the early 1950s.

Tzomet (Crossroads) A right-wing party of the 1980s and early 1990s.

Vaad Leumi National Council, the Jewish Community's supreme organ during the British Mandate.

vuzvuz(im) An Ashkenazi Jew.

Wadi Salib A Haifa neighborhood where riots broke out in 1959 and which has remained as a byword for poverty and backwardness.

yekke(s) Jewish immigrants from Germany.

yeshiva (yeshivot) Talmudic high school, the Jewish equivalent of the Islamic Madrasah.

ZAKA (Zihuy Korbanot Asson) Disaster Victim Identification, an organization made up of Orthodox Jews and dedicated to casualty identification and evacuation.

TIME LINE OF EVENTS

1881–1882 The first proto-Zionist groups arrive in the Land of Israel.

1882 Leo Pinsker publishes *Auto-Emancipation.*

1895 Theodor Herzl publishes *Der Judenstant.*

1897 The First Zionist Congress meets at Basel.

1904 Herzl dies.

1909 Hashomer, the first Jewish self-defense force in the Land of Israel, is founded.

1914 World War I breaks out and the Ottoman Empire enters it.

1915 The Ottomans exile part of the Jewish community in the Land of Israel.

1917 Half of the Land of Israel, including Jerusalem, is captured by the British.
The Balfour Declaration is issued.

1918 The British conquest of the Land and of Israel is completed.

1919–1921 First wave of anti-Jewish riots sweeps over the Land of Israel.

1920 First elections to Histadrut are held.
The Vaad Leumi is established.
Hagana is established.

1922 The British Mandate is formally established.

1929 Second wave of anti-Jewish riots sweeps over the Land.

1935 Zeev Jabotinsky takes his followers out of the Zionist Federation, dividing it.

1936–1939 Arabs revolt against the Mandate.

1937 The Peel Commission recommends that the Land be partitioned between Jews and Arabs and the former be allowed to establish a mini-state.

1939   Britain publishes the White Paper, to a large extent going back on the Balfour Declaration.

1939   The British Empire, and hence Palestine, enters World War II.

1941   Palmach is established.

1942   The leaders of the Stern Gang (Lehi) are liquidated by the British.

1944   Lehi assassinates the British resident minister in Cairo, Lord Moyne.

1944–1945 Hagana cooperates with the British against Ezel (The Season).

1945–1948 The Jewish community revolts against the British.

1947   The UN General Assembly votes for the partition of Palestine and the establishment of the State of Israel.

1947   Israel's War of Independence breaks out.

1948   The State of Israel is proclaimed.

1949   Cease-fire agreements with Israel's neighbors are signed.

1949   The first elections to the Knesset are held.

1952   Agreement for the payment of reparations by Germany is signed.

1953   Prime Minister David Ben Gurion resigns and is replaced by Moshe Sharett.

1954   The Lavon Affair occurs after the failure of Operation Susannah.

1955   Ben Gurion returns to power.

1956   The Suez Campaign is waged from November to December.

1957   Construction of Israel's nuclear reactor begins.

1959   Riots break out in Wadi Salib.
        In the elections, Mapai obtains the greatest number of MKs ever.

1960   Adolf Eichmann is captured and brought to stand trial in Jerusalem.

1961   Work starts on Israel's first skyscraper, Migdal Shalom (The Tower of Peace), in Tel Aviv.

1963   Ben Gurion resigns, and is succeeded by Levi Eshkol.

1966   The military administration that used to govern Israeli Arabs is abolished.

1966–1967 Israel experiences a *mitun* (recession).

1967   The Six-Day War leads to a great victory over the Arab states.

1969   Eshkol dies, is replaced by Golda Meir.

1969–1970 Egypt wages the War of Attrition against Israel.

1973   Israel fights the October (Yom Kippur) War.

1974   Separation-of-forces agreements with Egypt and Syria are signed.
        Meir resigns, is replaced by Yitzhak Rabin.

1976   Entebbe Rescue Operation is successfully carried out.
        The second separation-of-forces agreement with Egypt is signed.

1977	Rabin's government falls. New elections lead to the victory of Menahem Begin and Likud.
	President Anwar Sadat visits Jerusalem.
1979	Camp David Accords between Israel and Egypt is signed.
1981	Israel bombs and destroys Iraq's nuclear reactor.
	Begin wins the elections and sets up his second government.
1982	Israel invades Lebanon.
1983	The stock exchange crashes.
1984	New elections lead to the establishment of a national unity government with Shimon Peres as prime minister.
1985	Israel withdraws from Lebanon, except for a "security zone" in the south.
	An economic stabilization plan is initiated.
1986	Yitzhak Shamir takes over from Shimon Peres as prime minister.
1987	The first intifada breaks out.
	Peres claims to have negotiated the "London Agreement" with King Hussein, but Shamir refuses to sign.
1987–1988	The system of nationwide collective bargaining, and with it much of Israeli socialism, is brought to an end.
1988	Following the elections, Shamir sets up a right-wing government.
1991	Israel comes under Iraqi Scud missile attack during the First Gulf War. Madrid Conference leads to first face-to-face meetings between Israel and some of its enemies, the PLO included.
1992	Elections result in the victory of Labor and lead to the appointment of Yitzhak Rabin as prime minister.
1993	The Oslo Accords with the PLO are signed.
1994	A peace agreement with Jordan is signed.
1995	Rabin is assassinated and replaced by Peres.
1996	A series of suicide bombings undermines Peres's position.
	Elections bring Likud under Benjamin Netanyahu to power.
1998	The Wye River Memorandum with the Palestinian Authority signed (but not carried out).
1999	Elections bring Labor, under Ehud Barak, to power.
2000	After eighteen years, Israel withdraws from Lebanon.
	Talks at Camp David fail to bring about a peace agreement between Israel and the Palestinian Authority.
	The second intifada breaks out.
2001	Elections for the prime minister's office bring Likud, with Ariel Sharon at its head, to power.
2002	In its largest operation during the second intifada, the IDF Israel "conquers" the West Bank town of Jenin.

2003 Parliamentary elections lead to the creation of a national unity government under Ariel Sharon.

2005 Israel evacuates the Gaza Strip.

    Sharon leaves Likud and establishes a new party, Kadima.

2006 Sharon is incapacitated by a stroke. He is replaced by Ehud Olmert. Elections lead to the victory of Kadima and the establishment of a national unity government under Olmert.

    The Second Lebanon War causes Hezbollah to cease its attacks on Israel.

2009 In January, cease-fire with Hamas in the Gaza Strip is signed and holds, more or less.

NOTES

Chapter 1: Forged in Fury (1897–1949)

1. E. W. G. Masterman, "Palestine: Its Resources and Suitability for Colonization," *Geographical Journal*, 1917, p. 15.
2. Masterman, "Palestine," p. 25.
3. According to B. Jaffe, *A Portrait of Eretz Israel* [Hebrew] (Tel Aviv: Dvir, 1983), p. 68.
4. J. Grozowsky in *Hashiloach* (early twentieth-century Jewish newspaper), reprinted in M. Naor, *On the Threshold of a New Century: The Land of Israel in the Years 1897–1902* [Hebrew] (Tel Aviv: Ministry of Defense, 1979), p. 65.
5. Ibid., pp. 67–68.
6. Captain Kuehne to Emperor William II, June 3, 1909, quoted in A. Carmel, *The German Settlement in the Land of Israel at the End of the Ottoman Period* [Hebrew] (Jerusalem: The Hebrew University, 1973), p. 142.
7. M. Lunz, *A Guide to the Land of Israel and to Syria* [Hebrew] (Jerusalem: [private edition], 1891) p. 56.
8. M. Hagiz, *True Words* [Hebrew] (Vilna, 1879), p. 39.
9. A. Mossel, *A Dutch Laborer in the Holy Land, 1913–1914* (Jerusalem: n.p., 2002), p. 4.
10. A. Ruppin, *Syrien als Wirtschaftsgebiet* (Berlin: Harz, 1917), p. 12.
11. *Encyclopedia Britannica*.
12. L. Pinsker, *Auto-Emancipation* [Hebrew] (Jerusalem: Merkaz, 1951), p. 57.
13. M. Lowenthal, ed., *The Diaries of Theodor Herzl* (New York: Grosset & Dunlap, 1962), p. 325; entry for September 3, 1897, p. 224.
14. *Protokoll der ersten Zionistischen Kongress in Basel* (Prague: 1911) p. 131.
15. Lowenthal, ed., *The Diaries of Theodor Herzl*, p. 350.
16. Ibid., p. 224.
17. Quoted in N. Efrati, "The Jewish Community in Eretz-Israel during World War I, 1914–1918" [Hebrew] (Ph.D. dissertation, Jerusalem, the Hebrew University, 1985), p. 9.
18. Quoted in A. Boehm, *Die zionistische Bewegung*, vol. 1 (Berlin: Jüdischer Verlag, 1935), p. 3.
19. Weizmann to Y. L. Magnes, August 8, 1914, quoted in D. Barzilai-Yaeger, *A National Home for the Jewish People* [Hebrew] (Jerusalem: Zionist Library, 2003), p. 5.
20. David Lloyd George, *War Memoirs,* vol. 2 (London: Ivor, Nicholson & Watson, 1933), p. 586.

21. Haim Weizmann, *Trial and Error* (New York: Schocken, 1966) p. 207.

22. Quoted in P. Mendes-Flohr and J. Reinharz, *The Jew in the Modern World: A Documentary History* (Oxford: Oxford University Press, 1995), p. 232.

23. I. Efros, ed., *Selected Poems of Chaim Nachman Bialik* (New York: Bloch, 1965), p. 119.

24. A. Rokeach, "Acte de Folie," *l'Echo Zioniste*, January 15, 1904, p. 2.

25. M. Nordau, "MuskelJudentum," in *Zionistische Schriften* (Berlin: Jüdischer Verlag, 1923), p. 426.

26. The Palestine Mandate, available at http://www.yale.edu/lawweb/avalon/mideast/palmanda .htm#art4.

27. Zionist Organization, *Report of the Executive to the XIIth Zionist Congress* (London, 1921) part 1, p. 30.

28. S. Levitin, "Our Way," *From Our Life* [Hebrew], 1921, p. 15.

29. O. Neumann, *Fahrt nach Osten, Impressionen einer Erez Israel Fahrt* (Mukacevo: Nekuda, 1933), pp. 37–38.

30. Y. Ch. Ravinztky, "About the Crisis," *Haaretz* [Hebrew], July 19, 1923.

31. D. Horowitz, *The Economic Development of the Land of Israel* [Hebrew] (Tel Aviv: Ahdut, 1948), p. 256.

32. David Ben Gurion, *Memoirs* [Hebrew] (Tel Aviv: Am Oved, 1971), p. 7.

33. J. Jabotinsky, *My Life*, in Jabotinsky, ed., *Writings*, vol. 1 (Jerusalem: Amihai, 1961), p. 155.

34. Weizmann to Shertok, October 2, 1936, in Y. Rosenthal, ed., *The Letters and Papers of Haim Weizmann*, vol. 17 (New Brunswick, NJ: Transaction Books, 1979), p. 352.

35. Tz. J. Kalisher, "Greetings from Zion," in G. Kresel, ed., *Rabbi Yehuda Alkelai and Rabbi Zvi Hirsch Kalisher, Selected Writings* [Hebrew] (Tel Aviv: Shreberk, n.d.) p. 138.

36. Quotes from Y. Porath, *The Emergence of the Palestinian Arab National Movement, 1918–1929* (London: Cass, 1974), pp. 49, 59, 60; L. Farago, *Palestine on the Eve* (London: Putman, 1936), p. 63.

37. Farago, *Palestine on the Eve*, p. 115.

38. "We Will Eat the Product of Our Economy" [Hebrew], *Davar Leyladim*, June 4, 1936, p. 16.

39. David Ben Gurion, *Chimes of Independence* [Hebrew] (Tel Aviv: Am Oved, 1993), p. 328.

40. Field Marshall John Dill, chief of the Imperial General Staff, 1941, in L. James, *Imperial Rearguard: Wars of Empire, 1919–1985* (London: Brassey's, 1988), p. 96.

41. *The Daily Telegraph*, September 8, 1947, p. 12; *The News Chronicle*, September 8, 1947, pp. 1 and 7.

42. M. Begin, *The Revolt* (1950, repr., Bnei Brak: Steimatzky, 2003), p. 313.

43. Field Marshal Montgomery to General Dempsey, CIC, British Forces, Middle East, June 27, 1941, in A. Nachmani, "Generals at Bay in Post-War Palestine," *Journal of Strategic Studies* 4, no. 6 (December 1983): p. 68.

44. David Ben Gurion, *War Diary, 1948–49*, vol. 3 (Tel Aviv: Ministry of Defense, 1982), p. 766, entry for October 18, 1948.

45. Israeli Declaration of Independence, May 14, available at http://www.yale.edu/lawweb/ avalon/mideast/israel.htm.

46. See A. Shapira, *Yigal Allon, Native Son* (Philadelphia, PA: University of Pennsylvania Press, 2008), pp. 283–284.

47. Ariel Sharon to author, meeting at Latrun, May 5, 1993.

Chapter 2: Full Steam Ahead (1949–1967)

1. Quoted in Ph. Strum, "The Road Not Taken," in S. Ilan Troen and N. Lucas, eds., *Israel: The First Decade of Independence* (New York, NY: State University of New York Press, 1995), p. 86.

2. Einstein's letter, dated November 18, 1952, is available at http://speakingoffaith.publicradio .org/programs/einsteinsethics/particulars.shtml.

3. M. Margolis, *Strong Pillars* [Hebrew] (Jerusalem: 1962), p. 6; H. E. Shapira, in Y. Adler, ed., *The Last Year*, vol. 5 [Hebrew], (Brooklyn, NY: Munkacs, 1940), p. 80.

4. E.Y. Waldenberg, *State Law*, vol. 3 [Hebrew] (Jerusalem: Harav Kook, 1952), p. 37.

5. Ch. D. Halevi, *Put a Rabbi over You* [Hebrew], vol. 9 (Tel Aviv: The Committee for Publishing the Writings of the Garhad, 1976), p. 175.

6. M. Friedman, "The Structural Foundation of Religio-Political Accommodation," in Ilan Troen and N. Lucas, eds., *Israel*, p. 68.

7. Y. Leibowitz, *I Wanted to Ask You, Leibowitz* [Hebrew] (Jerusalem: Keter, 1999), p. 338.

8. J. Shapira, *In the Politicians' Claws* [Hebrew] (Tel Aviv: Am Oved, 1996), p. 131.

9. A. Dankner, *Dan Ben Amotz* [Hebrew] (Jerusalem: Keter, 1992), p. 195.

10. A. Gelblum, *Haaretz* [Hebrew], April 22, 1949.

11. IDF order quoted in "The First Decade as Formative Years" [Hebrew], in Tz. Tzameret and J. Yablonka, eds., *The Second Decade* (Jerusalem: Yad Ben Zvi, 2000), p. 344.

12. *Haaretz* [Hebrew], July 29, 1959.

13. *Davar* [Hebrew], June 9, 1961.

14. *Lamerchav* [Hebrew], September 10, 1960.

15. Y. Tzur, "The Ethnic Problem" [Hebrew], in Tz. Tzameret and J. Yablonka, eds., *The Second Decade*, p. 120.

16. Y. Bader, *The Knesset and I* [Hebrew] (Jerusalem: Idanim), p. 173.

17. Jeremiah 2:2.

18. Quote from Dvora Dayan (Moshe Dayan's mother), in D. Dvora Dayan, *In Happiness and Sorrow* [Hebrew] (Tel Aviv: Masada, 1958), p. 110.

19. Aaron Apfelfeld, in "The First Decade as Formative Years" [Hebrew], in Tz. Tzameret and J. Yablonka, eds., *The First Decade* (Jerusalem: Yad Ben Zvi, 1997), p. 360.

20. D. Caravan, "The Beer Sheba Palmach Memorial," *Tevai* [Hebrew], 6 (1969): p. 7.

21. D. Horowitz, *The Economic Development of the Land of Israel* [Hebrew] (Tel Aviv: Dvir, 1944), p. 36.

22. This and the Ben Gurion quote from D. Horowitz, *At the Center of Things* [Hebrew] (Ramat Gan: Masada, 1975), pp. 41, 57.

23. D. Ben Gurion, diary [Hebrew], Ben Gurion Archive, Sde Boker, January 26, 1950.

24. "The Craving for a Chicken Leg" [Hebrew], May 9, 2008, at http://www.ynet.co.il/articles/0,7340,L-3539651,00.html.

25. T. Segev, *1949: The First Israelis* (New York: The Free Press, 1986), p. 300.

26. *Knesset Record*, vol. 3 [Hebrew] (Jerusalem: The Knesset), p. 117, November 21, 1949; ibid., vol. 6, p. 2427, August 2, 1950.

27. Quoted in *Y Encyclopaedia* [Hebrew], February 22, 2007, available at http://www.ynet.co.il/articles/0,7340,L-3368115,00.html.

28. Quoted in A. Shillon, *Begin, 1913–1992* (Tel Aviv: Am Oved, 2007), p. 174.

29. Bank of Israel, *The Reparations and Their Impact on the Israeli Economy* (Tel Aviv: Bank of Israel, 1965), p. 181.

30. Ibid., p. 33.

31. Protocol No. 25/2 of the Knesset Labor Committee session, [Hebrew] May 23, 1950.

32. H. Barkai, *The Government Sector, the Histadrut Sector and the Private Sector in the Israeli Economy* [Hebrew] (Jerusalem: Falk Center, 1968), p. 25, table 1; p. 35, table 5; p. 37, table 8.

33. Deuteronomy 25:5.

34. Quoted in D. Giladi, *"Back to Our Ancestors' Fatherland": Z. D. Levontin's Entrepreneurial Alternative to Zionist Policy* [Hebrew] (Jerusalem: Institute for Social and Economic Advancement, 1994) p. 3.

35. M. Etzel, *Personal Diary*, vol. 3 [Hebrew] (Tel Aviv: Maariv, 1978) entry for January 10, 1955, p. 639.

36. IDF order quoted in "The First Decade as Formative Years" [Hebrew], in Tz. Tzameret and J. Yablonka, eds., *The First Decade*, p. 354.

37. Quoted in E. Kafkafi, *Pinhas Lavon—Anti Messiah, a Biography* [Hebrew] (Tel Aviv: Am Oved, 1998), p. 231.

38. M. Heichal, *Cutting the Lion's Tail: Suez Through Egyptian Eyes* (New York: Random House, 1987), pp. 177–178.

39. M. Dayan, *Sinai Diary* (London: Weidenfeld & Nicolson, 1965) p. 117.

40. M. Gur, "The Experience of Sinai Campaign" [Hebrew], *Maarachot*, October 1966, p. 18.

41. S. Peres, *The Next Stage* [Hebrew] (Tel Aviv: Am Hasefer, 1965), p. 125.

42. Golda Meir, *My Life* (London: Weidenfeld & Nicolson, 1975), p. 272.

43. S. Peres, *Battling for Peace* (London: Weidenfeld & Nicolson, 1996), p. 166.

44. General Muhammad Fawzi, chief of staff, quoted in M. B. Oren, *Six Days of War: June 1967 and the Making of the Modern Middle East* (Oxford: Oxford University Press, 2002), p. 64.

45. R. S. Churchill, *The Six Days War* (London: Heinemann, 1967), p. 76.

46. B. Peled, *Days of Reckoning* [Hebrew] (Tel Aviv: Modan, 2008), p. 31.

47. Quoted in *Wikipedia*, s.v. "Abba Eban," http://en.wikipedia.org/wiki/Abba_Eban.

48. E. Weizman, *On Eagle's Wings* (Tel Aviv: Steimatzky's, 1979), p. 216.

49. General I. Tal, quoted in J. Latreguy, *The Walls of Israel* (London: Evans, 1968), p. 145.

50. Peres, *Battling for Peace*, p. 101.

51. H. Bar Tov, *Dado, Forty-Eight Years and Twenty Days* [Hebrew], vol. 1 (Tel Aviv: Maariv, 1978), p. 131.

Chapter 3: The Nightmare Years (1967–1980)

1. Psalms 126:1–2.

2. Printed in Tz. Tzameret and J. Yablonka, eds., *The Second Decade* (Jerusalem: Yad Ben Zvi, 2000), pp. 402, 404.

3. *Wikipedia*, s.v. "Khartoum Resolution," http/en.wikipedia.org/wiki/Khartoum_Resolution #Text_of_the_Resolution.

4. For text, see *Wikipedia*, s.v. "United Nations Security Council Resolution 242," http://en .wikipedia.org/wiki/UN_Security_Council_Resolution_242.

5. *Haaretz*, September 29, 1967, p. 6.

6. Henry Kissinger, in *Yediot Ahronot* [Hebrew] weekend supplement, May 16, 2008.

7. Rabin, quoted in D. Shuftan, *Attrition: Egypt's Post-War Political Strategy* [Hebrew] (Tel Aviv: Ministry of Defense, 1989), p. 247.

8. For more on this, see A. Schwartz and C. Derber, *The Nuclear Seduction* (Berkeley, CA: University of California Press, 1989), p. 96.

9. J. L. Talmon, *The Six Day War in Historical Perspective* (Rehovot: Yad Haim Weizmann, 1970), p. 99.

10. D. Kochav, "The Influence of Defense Expenditure on the Israeli Economy," in M. Sanbar, ed., *Economic and Social Policy in Israel, the First Decade* (New York: University Press of America, 1990), p. 32.

11. A. Zvi, *The Yom Kippur War* (New York: Schocken, 2004), p. 177.

12. Quoted in A. Braun, *Moshe Dayan in the Yom Kippur War* [Hebrew] (Tel Aviv: Idanim, 1992) p. 128.

13. Quoted in Bar Tov, Dado, vol. 2, p. 216.

14. Meir, *My Life*, p. 383.

15. Y. Rabin, *Service Record* [Hebrew], vol. 2 (Tel Aviv: Maariv, 1979), p. 437.

16. Text available at *Wikipedia*, s.v. "United Nations General Assembly Resolution 3379," http:// en.wikipedia.org/wiki/UN_General_Assembly_Resolution_3379.

17. Brown is quoted in *Wikipedia*, s.v. "George S. Brown," http://en.wikipedia.org/wiki/George _S._Brown; for Louis, see Y. Modai, *Eliminating the Zeroes* (Tel Aviv: Idanim, 1988), p. 136.

18. Y. Arnon, *Economy in Tailspin* [Hebrew] (Tel Aviv: Hakibbutz Hameuhad, 1981), p. 11.

19. A. Shillon, *Begin, 1913–1992* [Hebrew] (Tel Aviv: Am Oved, 2007), p. 277.

20. See his *Pourquoi Israel* (1974).

21. M. Bruno, "External Shocks and Domestic Response: Macroeconomic Performance, 1965–1982," in Y. Ben Porath, ed., *The Israeli Economy: Maturing through Crisis* (Cambridge, MA: Harvard University Press, 1986), p. 276.

22. Y. Aharoni, *The Israeli Economy: Dreams and Realities* (London: Routledge, 1991), pp. 87, 255, and table 6.2.

23. D. Brodet, "The Balance of Payments and Economic Growth," in Sanbar and others, eds., *Economic and Social Policy*, p. 83, table 3.1.

24. Arnon, *Economy in Tailspin,* p. 11.

25. N. Halevi, "Perspectives on the Balance of Payments," in Sanbar and others, eds., *Economic and Social Policy,* p. 259, table 12.3.

26. Haim Nahman Bialik, "Bless the Arms," in *Collected Poems* [Hebrew] (Tel Aviv: Dvir, 1997), p. 29.

27. S. Kahn and others, *Saul Tschernichowsky* (Ithaca, NY: Cornell University Press, 1968), p. 95.

28. Quoted in G. Abramson, "Israeli Literature as an Emerging Literature," in S. Ilan Troen and N. Lucas, eds., *Israel: The First Decade of Independence* (New York: State University of New York Press, 1995), p. 248. The year was 1956.

29. The 1924 quote is in Y. Ghanassia, *Abel Pann* (Jerusalem: Mayanot, 1987).

30. Z. Schiff, *October Earthquake* (New York: Schocken, 1974).

31. J. Sobol, *The Joker* [Hebrew] (Haifa: Haifa Municipal Theater, 1975), p. 51.

32. Reuven Yanai, quoted (in Hebrew) in *Wikipedia,* s.v.

33. Asher Yadlin, quoted (in Hebrew) in *Wikipedia,* s.v.

34. B. Gur, *Cohabitation* [Hebrew] (Jerusalem: Keter, 1991), p. 9.

35. M. Goldman, ed., *Israeli Society, 1980, Selected Statistical Data* [Hebrew] (Jerusalem: Central Bureau of Statistics, 1981) p. 163, table H4. "Ashkenazi" was defined as a person whose father was born in Europe or the United States, "Sephardi" as one whose father had come from Asia or Africa.

36. Laqueur, *A History of Zionism*, p. 599.

37. For more on these developments, see A. Cohen, *Israel and the Bomb* (New York: Columbia University Press, 1999); S. M. Hersch, *The Samson Option* (New York: Random House, 1991); *Time* magazine, April 12, 1976, p. 19.

38. Arnon, *An Economy in Tailspin*, p. 43.

39. This and the following figures from Arnon, *An Economy in Tailspin,* p. 24, table 1; p. 157, table 22; p. 162, table 25; also Aharoni, *The Israeli Economy*, p. 82, table 2.2.

40. G. Ofer, "Public Spending on Civilian Services," in Ben Porath, ed., *The Israeli Economy,* pp. 200, 201.

41. Haim Herzog, "Address to the UN on Zionism," 1975, available at http://www.zionism-israel .com/hdoc/Herzog_Zionism_1975.htm.

42. Judges 14:14.

43. Quoted in *Wikipedia,* s.v. "Begin" [Hebrew].

44. Quoted in Shillon, *Begin,* p. 290.

45. Ibid., p. 278.

46. Quoted in Y. Avner, "Bygone Days: The Speech, The Cop and the Psalms," *Jerusalem Post,* April 20, 2008.

47. The full English version is available at http://www.hebrewsongs.com/?song=haleluyah3.

Chapter 4: New Challenges (1981–1995)

1. Rabbi Moshe Levinger, quoted in G. Gorenberg, *The Accidental Empire: Israel and the Birth of the Settlements, 1967–1977* (New York: Times Books, 2006), pp. 106–107.
2. "Niggers" statement of September 7, 2005, available (in Hebrew) at http://oznik.com/beta/?author=91; Supreme Court judges: *Yediot Ahronot*, February 2, 1999.
3. Amos Oz, *In the Land of Israel* (New York, NY: Vintage Books, 1983), p. 356.
4. Quoted in Gorenberg, *The Accidental Empire*, p. 77.
5. U. Benzamin, *Doesn't Stop at the Red Light; A Biography of Ariel Sharon* [Hebrew], (Tel Aviv: Adam, 1985).
6. M. Dayan, *Will the Sword Devour Forever?* [Hebrew] (Jerusalem: Idanim, 1981), pp. 35–36.
7. Quoted in A. Shillon, *Begin, 1913–1992* [Hebrew] (Tel Aviv: Am Oved, 2007), p. 438.
8. Quoted in C. Shindler, *A History of Modern Israel* (Cambridge: Cambridge University Press, 2008), p. 178.
9. Ariel Sharon, *Warrior* (1989; repr., New York: Simon & Schuster, 2001), p. 430.
10. General Yanosh Ben Gal, quoted in Z. Klein and others, *The War on Terrorism and Israel's Security* [Hebrew] (Tel Aviv: Hakibbutz Hameuhad, 1990) p. 93.
11. Quoted in B. Kimmerling, *Politicide: The Real Legacy of Ariel Sharon* (London: Verso, 2003), p. 86.
12. I. Kings 21:19.
13. Shindler, *A History of Modern Israel*, p. 198.
14. Y. Rabin, *Service Record* [Hebrew], vol. 2 (Tel Aviv: Maariv, 1979), p. 417.
15. Quoted in *Maariv* [Hebrew], February 18, 1982.
16. Quoted in *Wikipedia*, s.v. "Meir Kahane," http://en.wikipedia.org/wiki/Meir_Kahane.
17. *Wikipedia*, s.v. "Yitzhak Modai."
18. Y. Aharoni, *The Israeli Economy: Dreams and Realities* (London: Routledge, 1991), p. 86, table 2.3.
19. S. Peres, *Battling for Peace* (London: Weidenfeld & Nicolson, 1996), p. 238.
20. According to S. Fisher and D. Orsmond, "Monetary Policy and the Inflationary Process," in A. Ben Bassat, ed., *From Government Intervention to a Free Market: The Israeli Economy, 1985–1998*, [Hebrew] (Tel Aviv: Am Oved, 2001), p. 167.
21. Quote of September 18, 1985; quoted in Y. Modai, *Eliminating the Zeroes* [Hebrew] (Tel Aviv: Idanim, 1988), p. 192.
22. According to Y. Artstein, "Flexibility in Israel's Labor Market," in Ben Bassat, ed., *From Government Intervention to a Free Market*, p. 511, figure 6; M. Yustman, "Changes in the Structure of the [Israeli] Economy," p. 567; ibid, figure 9.
23. Y. Shamir, *Summing Up* (Boston: Little, Brown & Co., 1994), p. 346.
24. According to Artstein, "Flexibility in Israel's Labor Market," in Bassat, ed., *From Government Intervention to a Free Market*, p. 492, table 2.
25. Quoted (in Hebrew) in *Yediot Aharonot*, June 20, 2004, http://www.ynetco.il/articles/0,7340,L=2934863,00.html.
26. M. Dahan, "The Increase in Economic Equality," in Ben Bassat, ed., *From Government Intervention to a Free Market*, p. 616, table 3.
27. Gale Tzahal (radio news bulletin, Hebrew), March 12, 2008.
28. Joshua 19:45.
29. Aharoni, *The Israeli Economy*, p. 267.
30. *The Marker* [Hebrew], June 7, 2006, http://finance.walla.co.il/?w=/134/1294087/@@/item/printer.
31. According to Shindler, *A History of Modern Israel*, p. 6.
32. U. Naftalovich, "Economic Development of Israel's Industry by Technological Intensity in

1995–2003" [Hebrew] (Working Paper No. 29, Jerusalem, Central Bureau of Statistics, 2007) p. 25 table I.

33. Available at http://www.sciencedirect.com/science?_ob=ArticleURL&_udi=B6V7N-468CBDF -4&_user=626711&_rdoc=1&_fmt=&_orig=search&_sort=d&view=c&_acct=C000032999& _version=1&_urlVersion=0&_userid=626711&md5=389ef4921cas140cdb58f0d7e8a90117.

34. Arnon, *An Economy in Tailspin*, p. 162 and table 26; *Jerusalem Post* [Hebrew], September 8, 2008, p. 6.

35. Y. C. Menschenfreund, "A University—What For?" [Hebrew], in I. Gur Zeev, ed., *The End of Israeli Academia* (Haifa: Haifa University Press, 2005) pp. 126, 127.

36. The actual Latin title is *Omittamus studia.*

37. Deuteronomy 22:24.

38. Report of the Commission of Higher Education [Hebrew] (Jerusalem, 1965), p. 12.

39. Institute of Science Information (Philadelphia, PA) data most kindly provided to me by Professor (emeritus) Gideon Czapski of the Hebrew University.

40. World Intellectual Property Organization, *World Patent Report; a Statistical Review* (2008) at http://www.wipo.int/ipstats/en/statistics/patents/wipo_pub_931.html#a11.

41. *Yediot Ahronot,* weekend supplement, April 25, 2008, p. 15.

42. Quoted in *Yediot Ahronot,* January 14, 1988.

43. *Washington Post*, December 8, 1967

44. Speech of March 6, 1981, quoted in M. Dayan, *On the Peace Process and the Future of Israel* [Hebrew], N. Yanai, ed., (Tel Aviv: Ministry of Defense, 1988), p. 254.

45. Quoted in E. Benvenisti, *Legal Dualism: The Absorption of the Occupied Territories into Israel* (Jerusalem: The Jerusalem Post, 1989), p. 57.

46. See more on him on p. 82.

47. Quoted in *Yediot Ahronot,* special supplement, January 14, 1988; ibid, January 15, 1988.

48. Begin, *The Revolt*, p. 92.

49. Shamir, *Summing Up*, p. 255.

50. Amnon Lipkin-Shahak on Israel TV, channel 1, October 29, 1996.

51. Shamir, *Summing Up,* p. 258.

Chapter 5: Tragedy, Triumph, and Struggle (1995–Present)

1. Rabin, *Service Record* [Hebrew], vol. 2 (Tel Aviv: Maariv, 1979), p. 534.

2. See, for this strange story, *MNS News* [Hebrew], May 25, 2008, quoting Netanyahu speaking on October 17, 2006, available at http://www.nrg.co.il/online/1/ART1/581/185.html.

3. Clinton, *My Life* (New York: Random House, 2004), p. 915.

4. Ibid., p. 944.

5. Proverbs 24:6.

6. Quote from *Wikipedia,* s.v. "Neville Chamberlain," http://en.wikipedia.org/wiki/Neville_ Chamberlain.

7. Quoted (in Hebrew) at Ynet (Web site of *Yediot Aharouot*), March 7, 2002, http://www.ynet .co.il/articles/1,7340,L-1740928,00.html.

8. See B. Kimmerling, *Politicide: The Real Legacy of Ariel Sharon* (London: Verso, 2003).

9. U. Dan, "Not Like De Gaulle," *Hadashot* [Hebrew], 13.1.2005 at http://www.nrg.co.il/ online/1/ART/853/253.html.

10. Hadashot [Hebrew], June 7, 2006, at http://www.nrg.co.il/online/1/ART/963/246.html.

11. There was a 62 percent majority; *Yediot Ahronot* [Hebrew], September 14, 1993.

12. Figures from http://search.yahoo.com/search;_ylt=A0geu74LS0pI1JIAFx1XNyoA?p= %22second+intifada&y=Search&fr=yfp-t-501&ei=UTF-8. See "casualties."

13. Y. Dayan, *A New Face in the Mirror* (Cleveland, OH: The World Publishing Company, 1959).

14. 2007 data from *CIA World Factbook*, at https://www.cia.gov/library/publications/the-world-factbook/geos/is.html. See "Israel."

15. N. Sheva, "Introducing the World's Strongest Currency: The Shekel," *Haaretz*, June 4, 2008, http://www.haaretz.com/hasen/spages/988623.html.

16. 2003 figure available at http://www.cb.gov.il/publications/income_survey/03excel/t03.xls; 1966 figure from M. Bentov, *The Israeli Economy at a Crossroads* [Hebrew] (Tel Aviv: Sifriyat Hapoalim, 1966), p. 115.

17. According to social security figures, in D. Regev, "The Poor in Israel" [Hebrew], *Yediot Ahronot*, September 1, 2008.

18. J. Hoffman, "Study: Israel Leads the World in the Number of Computers per Capita," Haaretz .com, April 10, 2008, available at http://www.haaretz.com/hasen/spages/973717.html.

19. H. Wijsenbeek, *Some Time* (Ranana, Israel: Turbo, 2000), pp. 125–126.

20. Figures from J. Ben David, "Jews and Bedouin in the Negev—Past and Present," in S. Hasson and Kh. Abu-Asbah, *Jews and Arabs in Israel Facing a Changing Reality* [Hebrew] (Jerusalem: Floresheimer Institute, 2004), p. 227.

21. Figure from Tz. Gil, "The Ethnical Problem Is No Longer Relevant to the Elections" [Hebrew], at http://www.faz.co.il/story?id=3350&force_skin=print0.

22. E. Nevo, *World Cup Wishes* [Hebrew] (Tel Aviv: Zmora Bitan, 2007), p. 33.

23. Y. Nuriel and Y. Birenberg, "Solo Performance" [Hebrew], *Yediot* entertainment magazine, August 6, 2008, p. 10.

24. A. Bronner, "Artists Absorb Israel's Six Decades, and Move On," NYT, May 19, 2008, at http://www.iht.com/articles/2008/05/19/arts/19real.php.

25. Nevo, *World Cup Wishes*, p. 277.

26. T. Segev, *Elvis in Jerusalem: Post-Zionism and the Americanization of Israel* (New York: Metropolitan Books, 2001).

27. N. Karlinsky, *California Dreaming: Ideology, Society, and Technology in the Citrus Industry of Palestine, 1890–1933* (New York: State University of New York Press, 2005), p. 131.

28. Figure calculated on the basis of Institute of Science Information (Philadelphia, PA) data, most kindly provided to, and analyzed for, me by Professor Gideon Czapski, the Department of Physical Chemistry, the Hebrew University, Jerusalem.

29. According to *CRS Report for Congress,* U.S. Aid to the Palestinians, 2006, at http://fpc.state .gov/documents/organization/60396.pdf.

30. The text is available at the Trade Compliance Center, http://tcc.export.gov/Trade_Agreements/ All_Trade_Agreements/exp_005439.asp.

31. R. Katznelson, *Female Workers Speak Out* [Hebrew] (Tel Aviv: Histadrut, 1930), p. 137.

32. Israeli Declaration of Independence, May 14, available at http://www.yale.edu/lawweb/ avalon/mideast/israel.htm.

33. *Ms.*, April 1973, pp. 26–27.

34. The court's decision, in Hebrew, is available at http://www.sexualharrasment.info/hblog/ ?p=326.

35. A. Kamir, "Relationships between Superior and [Female] Subordinates—Do They Sexual Harassment Constitute?" [Hebrew], at http://www.notes.co.il/orit/42509.asp.

36. S. Aloni "The Prosecutor Has Already Convicted Haim Ramon," [in Hebrew], October 3, 2006, at http://www.ynet.co.il/articles/0,7340,L-3310255,00.html.

37. Chief warden Jacob Ganot, interview with *Haaretz,* at http://www.haaretz.co.il/hasite/pages/ ShArtPE.jhtml?itemNo=549862&contrassID=2&subContrassID=21&sbSubContrassID=0.

38. Haruv Institute findings, June 12, 2008, available at http://www.ynet.co.il/home/0,7340,L-8,00.html.

39. B. Bettelheim, *The Children of the Dream* (London: MacMillan, 1969), p. 164.

40. M. Sirkin, "Economic Growth and a Changing Structure" [Hebrew], in Y. Ben Porat, ed., *The Israeli Economy: Growing Pains* (Tel Aviv: Am Oved, 1989), p. 73.

41. Deuteronomy 23:14.

42. See above, p. 175.

43. *Haaretz*, November 19, 1976.

44. September 26, 2006, at http://rotter/net/cgi-bin/forum/dcboard/cgi?.az-show-threaed& forum=gil&com=5245=inviewmode.

45. MSN News [Hebrew], June 25, 2008, at http://news.msn.co.il/news/Internal/Internal/200709/20070926124324.htm.

46. *CIA World Factbook* (2008). http://www.bartleby.com/151/. See "Israel" and "United States."

47. Israel Democracy Institute study [Hebrew], May 5, 2008, quoted at http://www.ynet.co.il/Ext/Comp/ArticleLayout/CdaArticlePrintPreview/1,2506,L-3539676.

48. "Galia, Links and Spiritual Messages" [Hebrew], at http://www.k.tora1.com/content/view/823209/.

49. E. Ben Dahan, "To Separate Honorably," Ynet [Hebrew], 28.9.2008, http://www.ynet.co.il/articles/0,7340,L-3603323.00.html.

50. For more on this, see A. Solnick, "Muslim Clerics; the Jews Are the Descendants of Apes, Pigs, and other Animals," November 1, 2002, at http://www.jewishvirtuallibrary.org/jsource/History/memrireport.html.

51. Israeli figures from "Arabs Live Four Years Less" [Hebrew], Ynet, July 9, 2008, at http://www.ynet.co.il/articles/0,7340,L-3566008,00.html; Arab ones from *CIA World Fact Book*.

52. D. Rabinowitz and Kh. Abu Bakr, *The Stand Tall Generation: The Palestinian Citizens of Israel Today* [Hebrew], (Jerusalem: Keter, 2002).

Epilogue: "No More War"?

1. In the words of one Egyptian professor, Adel Safty, an Egyptian nuclear arsenal "would render war between the two countries unthinkable"; "Egypt's Nuclear Challenge," *Gulf News*, September 10, 2006, available at http://archive.gulfnews.com/opinion/columns/region/10073217.html.

2. For more on this see M. van Creveld, *Defending Israel; A Controversial Plan towards Peace* (New York: St. Martin's, 2004).

3. For an in-depth examination of this issue see M. van Creveld, *Defending Israel* (New York: St. Martin's, 2004.)

ACKNOWLEDGMENTS

To me, writing is the loneliest activity in the world—while I have helped edit books, I have never understood how more than one person can work together to produce a single volume. Nevertheless, there are always those who helped and to whom one feels indebted. The most important one is my former student, Doron Arazi; he generously allowed me to use *Land of Blood and Honey,* the title of a book on Israel that he published in German, as if it were my own. Other people to whom I owe thanks are Mr. Mats Berquist, former Swedish ambassador to Israel, and a fine scholar in his own right; Ms. Erika Hughes, the highly educated American lady on whom I tried out this book and who I hope may one day become my daughter-in-law; and my old friend Professor Benjamin Kedar. All three read the manuscript from cover to cover and made suggestions—many of them extremely useful—as well as saved me from quite a number of errors.

My good friend Varda Weiss did the maps, patiently taking them through endless drafts until they were as good as the publisher and I thought they should be. My stepson and stepdaughter, Jonathan Lewy and Adi Mendlin-Dan, looked after my computer as they always do. My grandson Orr, who at the time I wrote was only four years old, did what he could to distract me from writing—fortunately so, or else I would have become even more of a recluse than, living in happy retirement, I already am. My agents, Gabriele Pantucci and Leslie Gardner, deserve my gratitude for putting up with my sometimes impatient queries. Above all, there is Dvora. However, about her I have already said all there is to be said.

INDEX

A

Aaronsohn, Aaron, 29
Aaronsohn, Sarah, 29
Abbas, Mahmoud, 249
Abdul Hamid II, Sultan, 28
Abdullah I, King of Jordan, 36, 119, 120
  occupies West Bank, 65
Abid, Ziab, 94
Abu Ala (Ahmed Qourei), 249
Abu Gosh (Emmaus), 287
Abu Jilda, 138
Academy for the Hebrew Language, 285
Acre, 4, 62, 84
Afula, 4, 279
Agnon, Shmuel Josef, 239
Agranat Commission, 144
agriculture, 100, 106, 107, 280
  as national mission, 108
  relative decline of, 113
Agudat Israel Party, 77, 110, 197, 273
Ahad Haam, 18
Ahdut Haavoda Party, 129, 172, 200
Ahmadinejad, Mahmoud, x
Akzin, Professor Benjamin, 241
Al Ard, 95
Albright, Madeleine, 257
Alexander III, Emperor, 20
Al Hamishmar (newspaper), 172
Alignment, the, 94, 143, 172, 194
Ali-Muhammad, Siyyid, 279
Allenby, General Edmund, 29
Allon, Yigal, 65, 129, 137, 147, 202
  and settlements, 200

Aloni, Miri, 251
Aloni, Shulamit, 295, 296
Al Qassem, Samih, 312
Alsop, Joseph, 239
Altalena, 63, 70, 75, 104
Alterman, Nathan 66, 91, 164
Amdox, 233
Americanization, 287–90
  and Israeli women, 294
Amery, Leo, 264
Amichai, Yhuda, 284
Amir, Yigal, 252
Andres, General Wladyslaw, 74
Andreski, Stanislav, 34
Anglo-Palestinian Company
  (APC), 113
anti-Semitism, 16, 47, 116
  Israel as a refuge from 35, 315
Arabists, 242
Arab League, 65, 127
Arab Legion, 63
Arab Revolt, 57, 239
Arab Salvation Army, 61
Arafat, Yasser, 138, 205, 256, 257,
  261, 270
  and Palestinian Uprising, 262, 263
  Begin's view of, 147
  in Lebanon, 205, 206
  makes peace with Israel, 209, 249, 250
  Nobel Prize recipient, 239
architecture, Israeli 97–9
  change after 1973, 171
  in Tel Aviv, 280
Arendt, Hanna, 91

Arens, Moshe, 190
  as minister of defense, 208, 227, 240
  career, 207
Argov, Shlomo, 205
Aridor, Yoram, 155, 156, 158, 195
Arlosoroff, Haim, 39
Ashdod, 63, 85, 151, 272, 279
Ashkenazis, 90, 92, 96, 181, 195, 198, 259, 282, 283
  and ethnic problems, 176, 198, 208
  culinary habits, 176
  orthodox, 275
  under Ottoman rule, 9–10
Association of Industrialists, 111
Aumann, Professor Robert, 239
austerity program (*tzena*), 102–3, 111
Avigur, Shaul, 52
Avrushimi, Yoha, 211
Ayyash, Yahya, 255, 256

B

Bagatz, 73, 82
  growing role of, 289
Baghdad Pact, 120
Baha`i Temple, 279
Baker, James Cauthen, 245
balance of payments, Israeli, 105–7, 116, 151, 153, 212
Balfour, Arthur, 32
Balfour Declaration, 32
Bank of Israel, 104, 107, 116, 148
  and inflation, 154, 157
Barak, Aharon, 289, 301
Barak, Ehud, 259
  as prime minister, 261, 263, 267
  resigns, 264
  wins 1998 elections, 258
Barak, Nava, 262
Barghouti, Marwan, 263
Bar Ilan University, 235, 252
Bar Kokhba, 35
Bar Lev, General Haim, 84, 139, 143
Baruch, Bernard, 114
basic laws, 288
Bedouin, 4, 50, 100, 107, 183
  attacks on Jewish settlements, 22
  growing numbers of, 281
  women, 166
Beer Salem, 8
Beer Sheba, 5, 84
  conquered by IDF, 97, 108, 279
  University of, 235
Beer Tuvia, 51, 85
Begin, Benjamin, 204

Begin, Menahem, 105, 115, 143, 173, 175, 201, 210, 228, 240, 244, 250, 258
  and German reparations, 104
  and Herut ideology, 125
  and Judaism, 195–96, 281
  and 1977 elections, 147
  as prime minister, 154, 155, 158, 181, 186, 194, 202, 219
  attitude to Sharon, 204
  biography of, 74
  invades Lebanon, 205, 207
  leads Etzel, 64, 75, 95, 96
  negotiates peace with Egypt, 187–89, 190
  popularity of, 159
  receives Nobel Prize, 192, 239
  resigns, 207–8
  settles West Bank, 200
Beilin, Yossi, 248–49, 261
Ben Amotz, Dan, 208
Ben Gurion Airport, 228, 276
Ben Gurion Gruen, David, 24, 32, 37, 42, 59, 67, 70, 71, 77, 78, 82, 84, 85, 88, 95, 100, 104, 108, 109, 118, 121, 125, 128, 138, 154, 168, 173, 181, 186, 195, 196, 204, 215, 220, 275, 281, 301
  and Eichmann Trial, 91
  and Jabotinsky, 45–6, 47
  and Lavon Affair, 74, 75,
  and 1939 White Paper, 53
  and the Revisionists, 56–7,
  background of, 43–4
  orders sinking of the *Altalena*, 63–4
  orients Israel with the West, 120
  prevents conquest of the West Bank, 65
  proclaims the State of Israel, 62
  resigns, 121
Ben Gurion, Paula, 43, 174
Ben Haim, Paul, 164, 167
Ben Yehuda, Eliezer, 27
Ben Zvi, 22, 24, 42, 173
Bernadotte, Count Folke, 64, 208
BESA (Begin-Sadat) Center, 191
Betar (soccer club), 278
Betar (youth movement), 175
Bethlehem, 2, 8, 251
  in Second Palestinian Uprising, 264
Beth Shean, 62, 238
Beth Yaakov Lehu Venelha (Let's Go to the House of Jacob), 21
Bettelheim, Bruno, 299
Bezalel Art Academy, 25–6, 165
Bialik, Haim Nahman, 23, 34, 162, 163
Biltmore Conference, 47
Black Panthers, 176
"Black Saturday," 58

"Black Thursday," 160
Blumenthal, Naomi, 302
Bluwstein, Rahel, 163
Bnei Akiva (youth movement), 175
Bnei Brak, 277, 306
Brezhnev, Leonid Ilich, 181, 228
Brzezinski, Zbigniew, 189
Buffett, Warren, 275
Burg, Yosef, 76
Burke, Edmund, 75
Bush, George Herbert Walker, 244, 245, 315
Bush, George Walker, 316

C

Camp David Accords, 189, 318
capitulations, 3–4, 28
Caravan, Danny, 97
Carter, James Earle, 148, 189, 212
Cave of the Patriarchs, 251
Ceausescu, Nicolae, 187
censorship, 276
Chamberlain, Neville, 264
Check Point, 233
children, 298–99
Christian Arabs, 2, 11, 82, 99, 275
Churchill, Winston, 32, 58, 119
   and the Land of Israel, 35
Ciecanover, Aaron, 238
Circassians, 99
Clausewitz, Carl von, 185
Clinton, William Jefferson, 209, 251, 257, 262, 263, 316
   and Oslo Accords, 249, 250
   talks at Camp David, 261
Cohen, Geula, 196
Cohen, Jacob, 48
Cohen-Orgad, Yigal, 138
Collins, Michael, 208
Communist Party, 194
computer industry, Israeli, 230–31, 232–33, 238
Council for Higher Education (Malag), 235, 237
Cromwell, Oliver, 264
Crusaders, 2, 108
Custodian of Absentee Property, 107
Cyprus camps, 57
Cyprus wedding, 80

D

Dahlan, Mahmoud, 263
Darwish, Mahmoud, 312
Dash Party, 181
Davar (newspaper), 172

Dayan, Moshe, 37, 101, 125, 126, 131, 138, 144, 152, 162, 179, 188, 195, 202, 240, 247, 257
   as chief of staff, 121, 123
   as foreign minister, 185, 186, 187, 189, 190, 194
   as minister of defense, 128–29, 135, 136, 139, 141, 149, 239
   background of, 24
   hunts Etzel members, 57
Dayan, Yael, 273, 294
Dead Sea, 36, 135
Dead Sea Scrolls, 166
de Beauvoir, Simone, 284
   visit to Israel, 293–94
Declaration of Independence, 62, 77, 81, 88
   and equality of women, 89, 95
defensible borders, 137
Degania , 24, 31, 74, 85
de Gaulle, Charles, 124, 148, 268
   places embargo on Israel, 136
desalination plant, 233
Diaspora, the, 13, 46, 48, 85, 314, 315
divorce, 275, 307, 308
Dizengoff, Meir, 30
Dori, General Yaakov, 59
Dreyfus Affair, 18, 314
Druze, 2, 82, 99

E

"eastern front," 145, 192
El Al, 245
Eban, Abba, 128, 202, 255
Eden, Anthony, 119
Egypt, xi, 36, 63, 74, 117, 124, 137, 152, 184, 250
   attitudes towards Israel, 190–91
   "depth bombing" of, 139–40
   makes peace with Israel, 186–90
Ehrlich, Simha, 161, 195, 212
   implements the "Upheaval," 154–55
Eichmann, Adolf, 91
"eight zero five" jobs, 217
Einstein, Albert, 71
Eisenhower, Dwight David, 120, 123, 124
Elat, 65, 105, 119, 191, 279
Elat (destroyer), 138
Elazar, General David, 131, 169
Entebbe Operation, 180, 256
Esdraelon, Valley of, 3, 61, 130, 284
Eshkol (Shkolnik), Levi, 95, 108, 111, 131, 138, 161, 179, 185, 215, 221
   and Rabin, 126
   background and character, 74
   in June 1967 War, 128, 129, 130

Eshkol (Shkolnik), Levi *(continued)*
  lifts military government, 94
  leader of Hagana, 49
Etzel, 56, 70, 75
  during "Season," 57
  massacre at Dir Yassin, 62, 63
Eytan, General Rafael, 192, 207
  prepares invasion of Lebanon, 203

F

Fallaci, Oriana, 294
fedayeen (freedom fighters), 120
fellaheen, 7, 22
feminism, 292, 293, 294–95, 296, 307
"fiery pulse," 269
fertility, 297
Ford, Gerald Rudolph, 144
foreign labor, 223
Four Mothers, 260, 298
Franz Josef, Emperor of Austria, ix
Freedman, Marsha, 294, 296
Friedman, Daniel, 302
Friedman Milton, 161
"Front of the Revolt," 57
fundamentalism, 241, 310

G

Gadot, Kibbutz, 126
Gahal Party, 76
Galilee, 2, 7
  Jewish settlements in, 53
Galilei, Galileo, 83
Gashashim (Trackers), 111–12, 183
Gaza Strip, 85, 119, 188, 195, 200, 240, 241, 250
  controlled by Hamas, 316
  occupied by Egypt, 65
  overrun by Israel, 122
  Jewish settlements in, 270, 310, 318
  Palestinian Uprising in, 202, 239, 241, 263, 265, 267, 271
Gedera, 21
Geffen, Aviv, 284
Geffen, Jonathan 162
Gemayel, Bashir, 36, 203, 206
General Zionists, 75, 104, 114, 154, 211
  merge with Herut, 175
Genghis Khan, 124
Golan Heights, 125, 138, 143, 152, 169, 195, 203, 317
  annexed to Israel, 194
  occupied by Israel, 131, 137

UN peacekeeping force on, 145
  settlements on, 175, 200
Goldstein, Baruch, 251, 252, 256
Golomb, Eliyahu, 49, 52
Goltz, Field Marshal Colmar von der, 29
Gordon, Aaron David, 163
Goren, rabbi Shlomo, 127, 135
Goren, Shmuel, 239
Gouri, Haim, 92
government of national unity, 215
Green Line, 200, 201
Greenzweig, Emil, 21
Grossman, David, 281
Gulf States, 251
Gulf War, xi, 245
Gur, General Mordechai, 145, 187, 192
Gush Dan, 277, 279
Gush Etzion, 63, 135

H

Haaretz, newspaper, 274, 301, 303
Hadassa Hospital, in 1948, 62
Hadera, 3, 265
Hadrian, Emperor, 280
Hagada (book of prayers), 274
Hagana, 49–51, 55, 57, 114, 118, 173, 179
  in War of Independence, 59–62
Hahavazelet (newspaper), 13
Haifa, 8, 14, 25, 27, 36, 37, 38, 41, 50, 70, 84, 111, 164, 181, 231, 265, 272, 280, 285
  Arab nationalism in, 48
  character of, 278–79
  during 1929 riots, 51
  Jewish settlement in, 9
  occupied by Hagana, 62
  university of, 235
Halevanon (newspaper), 13
haluka (distribution), 10, 11, 13
Halutz, General Dan, 310
Hamas Movement, 203, 250, 316
Hammer, Zebulon, 197
Hannibal, 124
Hanuka, 88
Haolam Haze (weekly), 95
Hashomer (The Watchman), 28
Hashomer Hatzair (youth movement), 175
Hassan II, King of Morocco, 187
Hassidics, 9, 282
Hatikva, 75, 164
Hebrew, ix, xi, 26–7, 79, 85–6, 96, 163, 290
  as language of instruction, 92–3
  becomes official language, 70
  books in, 37

in academia, 289
  modern colloquial, 285–86
  spoken in the IDF, 118
"Hebrewism," 79
Hebrew University, 99, 171, 202, 235, 239,
    256, 295
  origins of, 38, 39
Hebron, 4, 63, 84, 241, 251
  Jewish settlement in, 9, 200
Hecht, Josef, 49, 52
Heikal, Mohammed, 122
Hershko, Avram, 238–39
Herut Party, 74, 75, 76, 143, 175, 177, 194
Herut (newspaper), 172
Herzl, Theodor, ix, 28, 31, 35, 43, 220, 301,
    304, 312, 314
  and national symbols, 76
  on Zionist goals, 177
  turns to Zionism, 18–20
Herzliya High School, 26
Herzog, Haim, 184
Hezbollah, x, 209, 211, 248, 260
higher education, 235–37
high-tech industries, 230
Hirsch, Baron Maurice, 114
Histadrut (Labor Federation), 45, 49, 53, 55,
    70, 73, 90, 99, 100, 105, 198, 107–9,
    110–14, 173, 212, 220, 225, 272
  and wage negotiations, 111
  origins and nature of, 42–3
  reformed, 215–19, 220, 221
  relinquishes control of Hagana, 52
Hitler, Adolf, 117, 144, 204
Hoffman, Christoph, 7
Holocaust, 47, 87, 133
  survivors of, 90–1
Holst, Johan Jorgen, 248
Horowitz, David, 102, 107
Hurwitz, Yigal, 155, 159, 195, 220
Hushi, Abba, 164
Hussein, King of Jordan, 120, 140, 201
  joins June 1967 War, 130
  talks to Israeli leaders, 202
Hussein, Saddam, 244, 245, 246, 271
Husseini, Haj Amin, 53

I

immigration, 38–9, 87, 149, 281–82, 267
  first wave, 21
  from the former USSR, 224–25, 281–82
  in the 1960s, 106
  second wave, 23
  third and fourth waves, 38

inequality, 225
infiltrators (*mistanenim*), 118
inflation, 101, 112, 151, 212, 226
  during 1970s and 1980s, 153–57
  peaks, 158
Institute of Tehnology (Technion), 27, 234,
    239, 279
Iraq, 37, 125, 127, 145, 317
  refuses to sign cease-fire, 64
Isaiah, 166
Iscar Corporation, 275
Islamic Jihad, 250
Israel Aircraft Industries (IAI), 105, 181, 225,
    228, 229, 230
  Lavi aircraft cancelled, 227
Israel Baaliya Party, 196
Israel Defense Force (IDF), 55, 59, 64, 114,
    119, 124, 137, 141, 145, 149, 160, 171, 174,
    190, 198, 200, 208, 210, 218, 239, 240,
    279, 281, 290, 298, 320
  after 1973 War, 152–53, 169, 178–80
  and Hebrew language, 285–86
  and Hezbollah, 260
  and high-tech industries, 231
  and infiltrators, 118
  and military government, 94
  and Palestinian Uprising, 242, 244, 264,
    270, 271
  and War of Attrition, 139
  as integrating factor, 92
  created out of Hagana, 63
  during Gulf War, 246
  during Suez Campaign, 122
  in June 1967 War, 126, 128,
    130–31, 133
  invades Lebanon, 205, 206
  in War of Independence, 65, 66
  in Yom Kippur War, 142–43, 144
  military ensembles of, 165, 169
  "national punching bag", 247
  women in, 168, 293–94, 295–96
Israel Electric Corporation, 220, 225
Israel Festival, 301
Israeli Arabs, 273, 275
  discrimination against, 309–10
  dispossessed of land, 107
  poverty among, 303
  progress of, 311–12
  "stand tall generation," 312, 317
Israel Land Administration, 107–8
Israel Museum, 99
Israel Philharmonic Orchestra, 167
Israel Shipyards, 181
Itziq, Dalia, 296

J

Jabotinsky, Zeev, 56, 74, 90, 154, 301
  buried in Jerusalem. 95
  founder of Revisionism, 45–6
Jackson, Michael, 277
Jaffa, 2, 9, 14, 21, 23, 26, 41, 48
  during Arab Revolt, 50, 52–3
Jamal Pasha, 28, 29, 43
Jenin, 251, 265
Jericho, 202, 257
Jericho I missile, 179
Jerusalem, 2, 4, 8, 9, 13, 25, 30, 39, 49, 56, 104,
    165, 166, 189, 193, 208, 218, 241, 262, 269,
    271, 285, 306, 307, 314, 318, 320
  architecture in, 97
  contrasted with Tel Aviv, 41, 277–78
  divided, 63, 68
  during 1929 riots, 51, 56
  Palestinian Uprising in, 263, 265
  planned internationalization of, 58
  post-1973 neighborhoods of, 171
  united during June 1967 War, 130, 133, 135,
    136, 150, 151
Jerusalem Post newspaper, 88
Jesus, 279
Jewish Agency, 35, 36, 43, 58, 88, 101, 224, 314
  negotiates with the Nazis, 38
  and Partition Plan, 59
  takes over Hagana, 52
Jewish Battalions, 45
Jewish Brigade, 55
Jewish Colonial Trust, 19
Jewish Historical Society, 16
Jewish National Home, 35
"Job Patrol," 260
Jordan, Kingdom of, 1, 35, 117, 127, 140, 145
  annexes West Bank, 65
  IDF plans for, 117
  Israeli raid into, 138
Jordan Valley, 200, 289
Judea, 5
Judean Desert, 284
Judean Plain, 23
"Judeo-Nazis," 241
June 1967 (Six Day) War, 129–32, 141, 162, 287

K

Kach Movement, 211
Kahan Commission, 207, 262
Kahane, rabbi Meir, 211
Kadima Party, 75, 76, 270, 296
Kamir, Orit, 294, 295
Kaplan, Eliezer, 101

kashrut, 78, 79, 80, 82, 305
Katz, Shmuel, 147
"Ka-Tzenik," 91
Katzir, Ephraim, 179
Katznelson, Berl, 292
Kedar, Lou, 141
Keynes, John Maynard, 148
Khartoum Meeting, 136
kibbutz movement, 24–5, 74, 88, 96, 195, 197,
    300
  and Palmach, 55
  and religion, 44, 305
  architecture in kibbutzim, 98–9
  decline of, 174–75, 176, 217–18
  women and children in, 299
King David Hotel, 56
Kiryat Gat, 115
Kissinger, Henry, 128, 144, 145, 185
Knafo, Vicky, 272, 275
Knesset, 70, 73, 76, 82, 83, 84, 99, 103–4, 158,
    174, 183, 185, 187, 189, 190, 199, 208, 211,
    261, 269, 281, 288, 298
  annexes Golan Heights, 194
  character of, 71
  feminists in, 296
  first elections for, 73
  1977 presidential elections, 195
  ratifies Oslo Accords, 250
  religious parties in, 78
  Sadat's visit to, 188
Kol Haam (newspaper), 172
Kroy, Moshe, 170

L

labor courts, 220
  and women, 295
labor laws, 215–16
Labor Party, 173, 177, 194, 195, 197, 209, 215,
    222, 249, 254, 255, 258, 273
  and 1984 elections, 208
  and 1973 elections, 143
  and Sephardis, 258–59
Ladino, 9, 14
  supplanted by Hebrew, 25–6
Lamerhav (newspaper), 172
Land of Israel, 28, 30–1, 32, 34, 35, 39, 46, 48,
    50, 55, 62, 63, 65, 66, 68, 74, 85, 114, 163,
    292, 314
  conditions in 1900–1914, 2–6
  under the Mandate, 36–7
land ownership, 107–8
Lanzmann, Claude, 151
Lapid, Tommy, 273
Laqueur, Walter, 177

Laskov, General Haim, 55
Latrun, 64, 65, 293
Lavi aircraft, 227, 230
Lavon Affair, 74, 121
Lavon, Pinhas, 74, 121
Law of Return, 83, 310
Lebanon, 1, 62, 127, 160, 208, 209, 210, 248, 317
  as basis for terrorism, 145–46, 203, 213
  IDF plans for, 119
  invaded by Israel, 205–6, 227
  Israeli withdrawal from, 260–1, 298
Lehi, 56, 58, 70, 208
  assassinates Bernadotte, 64
Leibowitz, Professor Yeshayahu, 82, 241
Lempel, Avraham, 233
Levi, David, 258
Levin, Hanoh, 171–72, 282, 284
Levinger, Moshe, 200
Levontin, Zalman David, 113
Liberman, Avigdor, 312
life expectancy, 303
Likud Party, 155, 174, 196, 199, 211, 215, 218,
    247, 250, 254, 258, 263, 267, 269, 272,
    273, 302
  and 1984 elections, 208
  heir to Herut, 143
  in power, 154, 156, 181, 185, 186, 222
  wins 1977 elections, 147
Livnat, Limor, 296
Livni, Tzippi, 296
Lloyd George, David, 32–3
Lloyd, Selwyn, 122
Lovers of Zion (Hovevei Zion), 21
luftmenschen (air men), 34
Lydda, 8
  conquered by IDF, 64

M

Maalot, massacre at, 145
Maarachot Magazine, 242
Maccabees, 35
Maccabee Hatzair (youth movement), 175
Machiavelli, Nicolo, 310
MacKinnon, Catherine, 295
MacMichael, Harold, 56
Madrid Conference, 246, 248
Magal Ldt., 228
Maimunah, 283
Mamram, 231
Mandate, British, 36, 43, 47, 57, 62, 64, 69, 70,
    72, 97
  economic policy during, 100–1
  ends, 59
  establishment of, 35

manufacturing, 46, 106, 112
  in kibbutzim, 113
Mapai Party, 71, 73, 104, 108, 114, 139, 173,
    174, 194, 217, 292
  created, 45
  transformed into Alignment, 94
Mapam Party, 172, 175
media, Israeli, 302–3
Meir (Meyerson), Golda, 85, 94, 108, 115, 176,
    200, 202, 215, 293
  and Black Panthers, 174
  and feminism, 294
  appointed foreign secretary 125
  as prime minister, 138–39, 141, 142, 143
  "kitchen cabinet" of, 72
Meretz Party, 261
Merkava tank, 227
Merkaz Harav, 197, 200
"Merry Widows of Windsor", 129
Metula, 21
Mevasseret Zion, 288
Migdal, 85
Milson, Menahem, 202
Mitnagdim, 9
Mitzpe Rimon, 281
Modai, Yitzhak, 211, 218, 225, 290
  fights inflation, 212
Mofaz, Shaul, 264–65
Mohammed, 279
Moledet Party, 196
Montgomery, Field Marshal Bernard Law,
    52, 58
Morgenthau, Henry, 114
Mosenzon, Yigal, 163
Moses, 279
moshav movment, 25, 74, 94
Mossad, 40, 239
  role in invasion of Lebanon, 210
Mossel, Avraham, 14, 16
Mount Carmel, 279
Mount Hermon, 279
Mount Scopus, 278
Mount Sinai, 122
Moyne, Lord, 56
Mubarak, Hosni, 192
Murray, General Archibald, 29
"muscle Zionism," 35
Muslim Brotherhood, 191

N

Nablus, 1, 63
Nahalal, 38
Nahariya, 39, 85
Napoleon I, 259

Naqba (Disaster), 59
Nasser, Gamel Abdel, 119, 122, 124, 141, 186,
    191
    and June 1967 War, 126, 127
    and War of Attrition, 139
Nasrallah, Hassan, x
National Council for the Child, 297
national water carrier, 125
National Religious Party (NRP), 76, 129, 175,
    199, 252
    changing character of, 196–98
Navon, Yitzhak, 190
Nazareth, 2, 4, 61, 84
Neeman, Yuval, 119
Negbah, Egyptian Army halted at, 64, 85, 174
Negev, the, 2, 66, 107, 119, 125, 161, 279, 280,
    281
    conquered by Israelis, 65
    Jewish settlements in, 53
    outbreak of hostilities in, 59
Nehemya, 33
Netanya, 279
Netanyahu, Benjamin, 114, 238, 251, 259, 261,
    290
    as minister of finance, 272, 273, 275, 304
    as prime minister, 257, 258
    biography, 256
    opposes Oslo Accords, 250
Netanyahu, Benzion, 256
Netanyahu, Jonathan, 256
Neturei Kara (Guardians of the City), 82
Neumann, Oskar, 40
Nietzsche, Friedrich, 66
Nili (espionage ring), 29
Nissim, Moshe, 218
Nixon, Richard Milhouse, 248
nonprofit organizations, 226
Nordau, Max, 35
nuclear program, Israeli, 179–80, 316

O

Ofek 1 satellite, 237
Ofer, Avraham, 173, 176
Old-New Land, 20
Oliphant, Laurence, 17
Olmert, Ehud, 174, 190, 226, 268, 288
    corruption charges, 302
Or Akiva, 110
Organization for Economic Cooperation and
    Development (OECD), 234, 274
Orientalists, 165–66
Orthodox Jews (*haredim*), 80, 183, 275, 278,
    305, 308
    and labor force, 273, 303
    and women, 296
    oppose the State, 304–5
Oslo Accords, 249, 251, 261, 263, 269, 318
Ostjuden, 20, 22
Ottomans, 3–4, 7, 9, 22, 28, 30, 32, 36, 50, 98
    "the Sick Man of Europe," 17
Owen, Robert, 4
Oz, Amos, 44, 59, 144, 199

P

Pale of Settlement, 41
Palestine Liberation Organization (PLO), 124,
    127, 138, 203, 204, 209
    and Palestinian Uprising, 239, 241, 248
    defeated in Jordan, 201
    in Lebanon, 205
    Israeli attempt to undermine, 202
    recognized by Israel, 249
Palestinian National Authority, 249, 257, 263
Palestinian National Charter, 249, 250, 312
Palestinian National Council, 250
Palestinians, 149, 189, 317, 318
    negotiate with Israel, 262
    uprisings of, 223, 241, 242, 244, 245, 247,
        263, 266, 268, 270
Palmach, 35, 55, 59, 61, 63, 65, 69, 118, 135,
    144, 174, 251
    disbanded, 64
    women in, 293
Palmerston, Lord, 17
Pann, Abel, 165
Partition Plan, 318
Peace Now Movement, 207
Peel Commission, 269, 318
Peqiin, 8
Peres, Shimon, 122, 123, 124, 126, 128, 173,
    181, 215, 218, 223, 252, 255, 256,
    288, 290
    and Olso Accords, 249
    as prime minister, 208, 210, 211, 12, 225
    Nobel Prize recipient, 239
    replaces Rabin, 254
    rivalry with Rabin, 209
"pickle peddlers," 219
Pineau, Christian, 122
Pinsker, Leo, 17, 20
Placards (*pashquevilles*), 306
Popular Front for the Liberation of Palestine,
    250
Post-Zionism, 79
Powell, Colin Luther, 264
Presley, Elvis, 287, 300
primaries, 288
Progressives, 75

Q

Qalqilya, 251
Qawuqji, Fauzi, 61

R

Rabikovich, Daliah, 284
Rabin, Dalia, 223
Rabin, Lea, 223, 251, 254
Rabin, Yitzhak, xi, 63, 84, 86, 139, 141, 164,
    173, 174, 181, 186, 215, 242, 254, 255, 275,
    290
  and Oslo Accords, 249, 250, 269
  as chief of staff, 126, 128, 131, 135
  as prime minister, 144, 145, 147, 153, 154,
    222
  as minister of defense, 209, 210, 215, 227,
    240, 241
  assassinated, 251, 253
  increases transfer payments, 182, 272
  Nobel Prize recipient, 239
  wins 1992 elections, 247
Rabinovich, Yehoshua, 154, 158
Rafael, 225, 228
Rafi Party, 109
Ramallah, 2, 251, 271
Ramat Gan, 93, 112, 235, 302
Ramle, 4
  conquered by IDF, 64
Ramon, Haim, 219, 295
Rand, Ayn, 170
Rathenau, Walter, 34
Ratosh, Jonathan, 79
Reagan, Ronald Wilson, 204, 212, 218, 228,
    285, 290
  sends Marines to Lebanon, 263
recession (mitun), 116
Refaim, 8
refugees, Palestinian, 117, 206
reparations, German, 104–5
Revisonists, 45, 74, 57 256
"right of return," 262
Rishon Lezion (Zion's First), 9–10, 113
ritual bath (mikveh), 10, 80
Rivlin, Reuven, 302
Rogers, William, 139
Rose, Irwin, 239
Rosen, Pinhas, 72
Rothschild, Baron Edmond de, 10,
    22–3, 114
Rothschild, Baron James de, 33
Rubinstein, Elyakim, 188
Ruppin, Arthur, 14
"rural fraternities," 202

S

Sabbath, 77–8, 150, 197, 198, 211, 278 305
  and religious minorities, 82
  pioneers' attitude to, 21, 34
  public observance of, 306
  used to bring down Rabin, 147
Sabra and Shatilla, 206
Sadat, Anwar, 36, 141, 143, 144, 191, 192, 239,
    317, 320
  assassinated, 190
  negotiates peace with Israel, 145, 186–89
  succeeds Nasser, 139
Safed, 9, 62, 84
Said, Edward, 166
Saint Simon, Henri, 24
Samaria, 2, 5
Samuel, Herbert, 36
Sapir, Pinhas, 115, 161, 215
Sarona, 8, 26
Saul, King, 163
Schiff, Jacob, 114
schools and education, 92, 104, 234
  Israeli Arab, 311
  Jewish in the Land of Israel, 11–2
  percent of GDP spent on, 234
  religious instruction, 80
  role in the success of Zionism, 167
Scouts, 93, 175, 176
Sderot, 279
Sea of Galilee, 36, 61, 125
Season, the, 57
Second Lebanon War, 290
Security Service (Shin Beth), 243, 252
separation of forces agreement, 145, 153
Sephardis (Oriental Jews), 9, 11, 88–90, 92,
    104, 195, 208, 224, 272, 275, 281, 283
  and Labor Party, 258–59
  culinary habits of, 177
  discontent among, 176
  political parties of, 198, 199
Seter, Mordechai, 164
Sevres Agreement, 122, 123
Shalev, Meir, 40, 284
Shahak, General Amnon, 247
Shaham, Nathan, 163
Shalom, Silvan, 267
Shamir, Moshe, 163
Shamir, Shulamit, 208
Shamir, (Jazernicki), Yitzhak, 85, 190, 195,
    210, 246, 247, 252, 259
  as prime minister, 208, 209, 215, 219, 240
  threatens Iraq, 245
Shapiro, Avraham, 110
Sharett (Shertok), Moshe, 85, 118, 173

Sharon (Scheinerman), Ariel, 66, 75, 85, 122,
    143, 190, 195, 205, 207, 209, 210
  and Begin, 204
  and Netanyahu, 256, 272
  as minister of defense, 191, 240
  as prime minister, 262–63, 264, 265, 267,
    268, 269, 273
  evacuates Gaza Strip, 317
  invades Lebanon, 205–6
  settles West Bank, 200
  suppresses Gaza uprising, 202, 271
Shas Party, 198, 215, 262, 273
  and 2003 elections, 281
  and women, 199
Shaveh, Yitzhak, 195
Sheinkin, Menahem, 30
Shiites, 2
Shinui Party, 273
Shohat, Avraham, 223
Shomron, General Dan, 241
Shukeiri, Ahmed, 127
Shultz, George Pratt, 213, 290
Siddon, Ephraim, 169
Smilansky, Yizhar, 168
Smuts, Ian, 32
Sobol, Joshua, 169, 172
social security, 115, 183
socialism, Israeli, 18, 73–4, 76, 77, 94, 114–5,
    212, 259
  among the pioneers, 23–4
  and women, 291–92, 293
  demolished, 219–21, 225–26
  in the 1970s, 182–83
  rejected by Revisionists, 45
South Lebanese Army (SLA), 209
Speer, Albert, 99
"stand tall generation," 312, 317
Stalin, Josef Vissarionovich, 144
start up companies, 231
Stern, Avrahanm, 56
Straits of Tiran, 122, 123, 128, 188
  closed by Nasser, 126
Struma, 87
Suez Canal, 120, 126, 130, 137, 138, 143, 171
  opened to Israeli shipping, 188
  nationalized by Nasser, 121
suicide bombings, 251
Sunnis, 2, 308
Supreme Court, 72–3, 81, 198, 268
  and the Sabbath, 82, 98
  growing role of, 289
Syria, 1, 62, 65, 117, 124, 131, 137, 145, 317
  and origins of 1967 War, 125–26, 127
  defeated in Lebanon, 205
  invades Lebanon, 203

T

Taba, 191
Tahal (water supply company), 221
Taliban, 310
"talkbackists," 297
Talmon, Professor Jacob, 70, 282
Tami Party, 198, 199
Tamir, Yuli
tariffs, 221–22
Taylor, Elizabeth, 180
Tehia Party, 196
Tel Aviv, 25, 30, 38, 49, 58, 62, 66, 85, 93, 111,
    112, 115, 145, 152, 154, 171, 207, 218, 220,
    228, 251, 265, 279, 280, 281, 310, 314
  architecture in, 97–8, 280
  Ben Gurion on, 42
  cultural life in, 277
  during the Gulf War, 245
  during 1920 riots, 50
  evacuated during World War I, 29
  foreign labor in, 223
  foundation of, 26
  high-tech industries in, 231
  origins of name, 85
  university of, 235
Tel Aviv University, 170, 235
Tel Hai, 49, 85, 164
Temple Mount, 256, 257, 262, 263
Templers, 7–8, 98, 280
terrorism, 203, 244, 251, 256, 261, 267
Thatcher, Margaret, 218, 295
The Jewish State, ix
Tiberias, 4, 9, 84
  occupied by Hagana, 62
Tolstoy, Leo, 24, 163
traditionalists (massotiyim), 78
Truman, Harry S., 303
Trumpeldor, Josef, 49, 164
Tshernichowsky, Saul, 163
Tuhami, Hassan, 187
Tul Karem, 4, 63
"two-legged beasts," 204
Tzomet Party, 196

U

Ulbricht, Walter, 99
Umm el Fahem, 309
United Nations, 58, 62, 65, 136–37, 144, 147,
    184, 209, 265, 269
  condemns Zionism, 178, 183
United Nations Special Commission on
    Palestine, 58
Upheaval (mahapah), 154–55

V

Vaad Leumi (National Council), 43
Vance, Cyrus, 189
Voice of Peace, radio station, 251

W

Wadi Salib, riots in, 90, 176
Wailing Wall, 51, 133, 195, 320
Waldenberg, rabbi Eliezer, 77
Waldheim, 8
War of Attrition, x, 139, 140, 143
War of Independence, 26, 59–65, 94, 108, 116,
    163, 174, 218
  cost of, 100
Weinberger, Caspar, 201
Weizman, Ezer, 127, 129, 212
  as minister of defense, 185, 186, 190, 194, 227
Weizmann, Haim, 32–3, 35, 89, 161, 301
  overshadowed by Ben Gurion, 47
  President of Israel, 71
Weizmann Institute, 235
Wertheimer, Stef, 274
West Bank, 64, 75, 189, 201, 240, 262, 267, 312
  IDF plans for, 118
  Jewish settlements in, 200
  Palestinian Uprising in, 241, 263, 265
  under occupation, 150, 195
White Paper (1939), 53
Whitman, Walt, 270
Wilhelma, 8
William II, Emperor, 16
Wolf, Lucien, 15
women, Israeli, 89, 141, 199, 225, 297
  and rabbinical courts, 308
  Arab, 311
  before the State, 290–91
  divorce, 275
  hardship suffered by, 110
  in the early kibbutzim, 25, 40
  in the military, 118, 168, 293
  in "Orientalist" art, 166
  in the workforce, 220, 292–93
  of Tel Aviv, 277
  single mothers, 272

World Zionist Organization, 14, 24, 31, 37,
    46–7
Wye River Memorandum, 257

Y

Yadin, General Yigael, 59, 118
Yadlin, Asher, 173, 176, 301, 302
Yadlin, Dalia, 301
Yamit, 191, 310
Yariv, General Aharon, 126
Yediot Aharonot (newspaper), 311
Yehoshua, A. B., 284
Yehud, 228
yekkes, 39, 280, 282
Yiddish, 9, 14, 82, 99
  supplanted by Hebrew, 25–6
Yom Kippur, 80, 170
Yom Kippur War (October 1973 War), x, 141,
    142–43, 153, 184
  economic impact of, 151
Yosef, Dov, 103–4
Yosef, rabbi Ovadia, 198–99, 275
Young Turks, 28
youth movements, 175

Z

Zaim, Hosni, 119
Zaka (disaster victim identification),
    266
Zatulovsky Dvora, 24
Zeevi, Rehabam, 196
Zeira, General Eliyahu, 141
Zim (shipping company), 272
Zionism, 35, 44, 45, 48, 136, 168, 178
  condemned as racism, 183–84
  doubts about, 178
  origins 16–7
  religious attitudes to, 76–8, 116
  seeks to transform Jews, 34
  success of, 304–5
Zionist Congress, First, x, 19, 314
Ziv, Yaacov, 233
Zmora, Moshe, 72
Zweig, Stefan, ix